THE LAUNDRYMEN

OTHER BOOKS BY JEFFREY ROBINSON

FICTION

The Margin of the Bulls

The Plutonium Conspiracy

The Pietrov Game

NONFICTION

Bardot: An Intimate Portrait

The End of the American Century

The Risk Takers: Five Years On

Rainier and Grace

Yamani: The Inside Story

Minus Millionaires

The Risk Takers

Teamwork

Bette Davis: Her Stage and Film Career

THE
LAUNDRYMEN

INSIDE MONEY LAUNDERING,
THE WORLD'S THIRD-LARGEST BUSINESS

JEFFREY ROBINSON

ARCADE PUBLISHING • NEW YORK

FIRST NORTH AMERICAN EDITION

First published in Great Britain by Simon & Schuster Ltd.

Library of Congress Cataloging-in-Publication Data

Robinson, Jeffrey, 1945 –
     The laundrymen / Jeffrey Robinson. — 1st North American ed.
          p.   cm.
     Includes bibliographical references and index.
     ISBN 1-55970-330-X
     1. Money laundering. I. Title.
     HV6768.R63 1996
     364.1'68 — dc20   96 – 8626

Published in the United States by Arcade Publishing, Inc., New York
Distributed by Little, Brown and Company

10 9 8 7 6 5 4 3 2 1

BP

Designed by API

PRINTED IN THE UNITED STATES OF AMERICA

This book is for Uncle Tonton Robby

With love from Joshua Seth and Celine Chelsea

CONTENTS

THE LAUNDRYMEN

PROLOGUE

Robert Torres had it all.

He had money. He had fancy cars. He had status. He had all the women he could ever want.

For a guy who started out in life as a welder, a cook, and a gas station manager and once thought that the big time meant peddling dope on street corners in the Bronx, Torres came as close to living the American dream as anyone he was ever going to meet.

It was a family business.

His cousins were the ones who set him up in 1978. He was 22, a kid from small-town Puerto Rico, a place called Guayama, who'd come north to New York with a chip on his shoulder because life had dealt him a rotten hand. The great melting pot was more like a cauldron in which you could drown. So he told his cousins he needed a job, that he wanted a shot at makin' it, and they supplied him with little plastic bags of product.

For a while Torres thought he had life knocked. He had the cash he earned and what cash he could steal. But the more he watched his cousins getting rich, buying cars and buying property and keeping pretty women in expensive clothes, the more he realized dope was strictly nickel-and-dime stuff. He reminded himself that he had ambition, that he had plans. He persuaded himself that selling "shit" to kids and whores and getting beaten up by pimps was not the ticket. So he hit on his cousins for more of the action and they made him a manager. Now he ran other guys hawking stuff on street corners and had more cash in his pockets.

By 1985 he'd been on the streets for seven years. Closing in on 30, he got it into his head he needed to branch out, to take a better shot at makin' it. That meant going out on his own. And going out on his own meant heroin.

It took time. And because dealing heroin is a business in which one wrong step can mean violent death, it also took *cajones*. But Torres managed to muscle his way in. He was smart enough to do it slowly, step by step. He was also lucky enough to stay alive while he worked his way up.

First he sold product himself. Then he put salesmen on the street to hustle it for him. Then he found ways to import it and learned the tricks of wholesaling. He even had his own brand names — Liberty, Blue Moon, Turbo Powder, Midnight Train, Sunshine, White Eagle, White Tiger, and Pink Diamond.

Within five years Torres had a hundred *amigos* working for him — he called them "Los Brujos," the Warlocks — and commanded twenty distribution centers in Manhattan and the Bronx. To defend his network, he armed Los Brujos to the teeth. He loved guns, and every now and then he'd go on a buying spree, such as the afternoon he bought nineteen semiautomatic pistols, thirteen .38-caliber pistols, and a classic .45 that he wore in a shoulder holster because it made a macho bulge under his armpit.

He owned twenty properties in New York and forty more in Puerto Rico, including a tourist resort near San Juan. He owned a sand and gravel company, two beauty parlors, a restaurant, a garage, three heavy equipment rental companies, seventy pieces of heavy construction equipment, a woodworking shop, a limousine service, a pile of blue-chip securities, a 46-foot boat, a handful of professional race cars, and a semipro basketball team in Puerto Rico that also called themselves Los Brujos.

By the beginning of 1993, Torres was moving close to half a million dollars worth of heroin every day.

That's when the Feds busted him.

They swooped down on him like a heavily armed commando force taking a beachhead, shackled him in chains, rounded up Los Brujos, and started unraveling his financial empire.

Once upon a time, Robert Torres had it all.

He had fancy cars. He had status. He had all the women he could ever want. At the age of 37, he was worth in excess of $60 million.

And all the time, lurking in the background was a man who showed Torres how to grab the American dream by the throat — a former senior officer at the Chase Manhattan Bank. His laundryman.

1

THE MAGIC TRICK

"When the President does it, that means it is not illegal."
— **Richard Nixon**

Money laundering is all about sleight of hand.

It is a magic trick for wealth creation.

The lifeblood of drug dealers, fraudsters, smugglers, kidnappers, arms dealers, terrorists, extortionists, and tax evaders, it is perhaps the closest anyone has ever come to alchemy.

Myth has it that the term was coined by Al Capone, who, like his arch rival George "Bugs" Moran, used a string of coin-operated laundromats scattered around Chicago to disguise his revenue from gambling, prostitution, racketeering, and violation of the prohibition laws. It's a neat story, but not true.

"Laundering" perfectly describes what takes place: illegal, or dirty, money is put through a cycle of transactions and comes out the other end as legal, or clean, money. In other words, all traces of illegality are scrubbed away by a succession of transfers and deals, so that those same funds reappear as legitimate income.

Romance has since been added to myth with the name Meyer Lansky.

Whereas cronies such as Capone, "Lucky" Luciano, and Frank Costello made their way through the world using muscle, Lansky — a 5-foot 3-inch, Polish-born, New York–raised, ninth-grade dropout — used his wits to become the highest-ranking non-Italian in what used to be called "The Syndicate." He was affectionately known in those days as the mob's accountant. He is often affectionately remembered these days as the patron saint of money launderers. It's an epitaph that would have amused him.

Lansky became particularly distressed in October 1931 when Capone's carelessness allowed the Feds to send him to Alcatraz for something so obvious as tax evasion. Determined to avoid a similar fate, Lansky theorized that any money the Internal Revenue Service (IRS) didn't know about was, by default, not taxable. With that as his premise, he embarked on a quest for ways to hide money, and soon discovered the benefits of numbered Swiss bank accounts. Some twenty years later, after helping his long-standing partner in crime Benjamin "Bugsy" Siegel to finance The Flamingo — the first major hotel and casino complex in the desert that would become Las Vegas — Lansky convinced his pals that their nontaxable future lay in offshore expansion. Even if the IRS suspected money was being stashed outside their jurisdiction, they couldn't get their hands on it. So he took the mob to Havana, and with the blessings of strongman Fulgencio Batista almost single-handedly turned the Cuban capital into a boomtown. But his dreams of a world beyond the reach of the IRS ended with a rude awakening. In 1959, Fidel Castro battled his way down from the mountains and with the help of guns provided by American gangsters threw out the Americans.

Some of Lansky's cohorts brooded over such bad luck, but he was typically philosophical. He admitted he'd backed the wrong horse — very few people believed that Castro, his comrade Che Guevara, and their ragtag band of merry men could pull off an entire revolution — took his losses, and learned the lesson that the best guarantee for any offshore investment is a politically stable environment.

In pursuit of somewhere safe, he turned to the Bahamas. Thirty minutes by air from Miami and in the same time zone as the eastern United States, the seven hundred islands and cays that made up the then-British colony were ideal. Communications were good, real estate was cheap, access was easy, the market was ripe, and, best of all, the local politicians were crooked.

The fly in the ointment, where Meyer Lansky's beatification is concerned, is that he was hardly a saint and definitely not a money launderer. His fundamental concern was with evading taxes. He did little more than come up with some basic procedures for capital flight. There's nothing to suggest he ever intended to repatriate any money and spend it legally. Lansky is to money laundering what the Wright Brothers are to the Concorde. He got the business off the ground, but it was left to other people to break the sound barrier.

In fact, it wasn't until 1973 that the term *money laundering* actually appeared in print for the first time. And when it did, it had nothing to do with Meyer Lansky. The earliest sightings were in newspapers covering the Watergate scandal.

At the end of February 1972, Richard Nixon took the first formal steps toward renewing his tenure at the White House. He announced the creation of the Committee to Reelect the President — abbreviated to CRP and, bizarrely, pronounced "creep" — and named a former law partner, Attorney General John Mitchell, to run it. But that was strictly for public consumption. The real campaign drive had begun at least a year before, when Mitchell and Secretary of Commerce Maurice Stans, who later took the chair of CRP's finance committee, secretly built a presidential war chest. Among the earliest contributors was the American dairy industry, which wanted to reward Nixon for having raised federal milk subsidies. Also on the Stans–Mitchell list was the recluse billionaire Howard Hughes, who reportedly handed $100,000 directly to Nixon's closest friend, Florida banker Charles "Bebe" Rebozo.

Then there was the international financier Robert Lee Vesco. Under investigation at the time by Mitchell's Justice Department, Vesco thought enough of Nixon and, evidently, the prospect of some Oval Office sympathy, to arrange for a cash donation of $200,000.

When Mitchell and Stans squeezed American Airlines for $100,000, George Spater, then chairman and chief executive of the airline, was faced with the dilemma of how to divert corporate funds that were otherwise accountable. He arranged to have a Lebanese company called Amarco submit a fraudulent invoice as commission on parts sold to Middle East Airlines. American Airlines paid the invoice and Amarco deposited the money in Switzerland, then wired it to their account in New York. There, Amarco's agent withdrew

$100,000 in cash and handed it to Spater, who turned it over to Mitchell and Stans.

Braniff Airlines, also hit by the duo, laundered their beneficence through Panama. The airline's regional vice president for Latin America collected $40,000 by instructing the company's man in Panama City to raise a false invoice from a local company for "goods and services." To cover the shortfall, they sold blank tickets for cash.

Stans next turned to the oil industry. Ashland Oil's chairman, Orin Atkins, obliged with money funneled from a subsidiary in Gabon. Gulf Oil laundered its $100,000 gift to Nixon through a subsidiary in the Bahamas.

Vesco's donation was eventually returned, but under the statutes then in force, CRP was not technically under any obligation to report these contributions. However, Congress had just passed a law, to come into effect on April 7, specifically prohibiting anonymous campaign donations. Knowing it would severely cramp their style, Mitchell and Stans decided to pull in as much as they could before the deadline. They dusted off an old Mexican connection to guarantee that anonymous donations could not be traced and went back to work, now targeting private citizens who would appreciate discretion in these matters. They also went in search of corporations that might otherwise be banned by the new law from making substantial and undeclared political contributions.

Never known for a subtle approach, CRP bullied potential donors with lectures on the debt of gratitude they and all patriotic Americans owed to Richard Nixon. In the same breath, he reminded them that his Mexican connection was not subject to American audits.

With hindsight, it was a fairly adolescent scheme. Among the contributions were four cashier's checks in sums of $15,000, $18,000, $24,000, and $32,000. Totaling $89,000, they were each drawn on a different bank in the United States and made payable to a Mexico City lawyer named Manuel Ogarrio Daguerre. In mid-April, Ogarrio forwarded checks to Miami, where on April 20 they were deposited into the bank account of a local real estate salesman named Bernard L. Barker. Were anyone ever to question him about the source of the money, Barker was under instructions to say it was his share of a land deal he'd made with an anonymous Chilean businessman. Were anyone ever to ask why he subsequently withdrew the $89,000 in cash, Barker was to answer that the deal had fallen through and he needed to repay the commission.

Had Mitchell and Company then gone on a binge, blowing the money on wine, women, song — even campaign advertising — it's likely no one would ever have found out about it. Instead, they decided to finance a different part of operation.

On the evening of June 17, 1972, five burglars broke into the Democratic National Committee headquarters at the Watergate office building, west of Juarez Circle. They were: Virgilio Gonzalez, a Cuban-born locksmith; Eugenio Martinez, a Cuban-born anti-Castro activist and CIA informant; Frank Sturgis, a Miami soldier of fortune with CIA connections; James W. McCord, Jr., a former employee of both the FBI and the CIA; and one Bernard L. Barker of Miami, Florida. As it turned out, Barker had also worked for the CIA and had been involved in the 1962 Bay of Pigs invasion.

The five men were arrested immediately. At first, the most interesting member of the group appeared to be McCord, because at the time of the break-in he was coordinating security for the CRP. Then came the arrest of G. Gordon Liddy and E. Howard Hunt. The brains behind the break-in, both had direct links to the CIA, the CRP, and, shockingly, the White House.

Yet the thread that would unravel the conspiracy turned out to be Barker.

Too clever for their own good, the CRP folks never reckoned anything could go wrong. Nor had it dawned on them that if anything did go wrong someone might somehow find those four checks and trace them back through the Mexican lawyer to the CRP. Once Bob Woodward and Carl Bernstein of the *Washington Post* broke the story, however, and it gained enough momentum for them to run with it, every other investigative reporter in America tried to get in on the act. Competition for front-page scoops became red-hot. In the end, it was the *New York Times* that headlined the Mexican money connection.

Subpoenas flew and investigators got inside Barker's bank account. A fifth suspicious check was uncovered, this one for $25,000 and dated April 10. Drawn on the First Bank and Trust Company of Boca Raton, Florida, it was made payable to Kenneth H. Dahlberg, a Nixon fund-raiser. When a reporter asked him about the check, Dahlberg admitted he'd long since turned it over to Maurice Stans.

Bathed in Mexico, $89,000 was just the tip of the iceberg. The amount soon jumped to $750,000. That's when it was revealed that Stans was maintaining a slush fund at the CRP, though he was later acquitted of all charges of conspiring to violate campaign finance laws.

The sheer amateurishness of their money laundering scheme linked the CRP to the Watergate break-in. By March 21, 1973, Nixon, already so tangled in his own lies that his fate was sealed, tried to convince his legal adviser John Dean that he might be able to buy his way out of the crisis with more laundered money.

Prophetically, in a private Oval Office conversation, Dean warned Nixon, "People around here are not pros at this sort of thing." He went on, "This is the sort of thing Mafia people can do — washing money, getting clean money and things like that. We just don't know about those things, because we are not criminals and not used to dealing in that business."

It was only a matter of time before the president's meager lines of defense were split open so wide that no one, least of all Richard Nixon playing the laundryman, could have halted the process that brought him down.

Like any great thriller, the story is filled with ironies. One is that Nixon had been so far ahead in the polls, and his opponent, George McGovern, politically so far out in space, that the CRP hadn't needed to solicit illegal funds. He could have stayed in the Oval Office, never made a speech, never kissed a baby, never hit the campaign trail, and still have won in a landslide.

A second is that in the wake of Watergate, Congress took action to prohibit government intrusion into the lives of ordinary citizens. One new law virtually enjoined financial investigators from comparing notes, which has turned out to be a boon for the laundrymen.

A third irony is that money laundering was not yet a crime anywhere in the world.

2

DOING THE WASH

"Money possesses a strange kind of purity."
— **Bernie Cornfeld**

There are four factors common to all money laundering operations.

First, the ownership and source of the money must be concealed. There's no sense in laundering money if everyone knows who it belonged to and where it originated after it comes out the other end.

Next, the form it takes must be changed. No one wants to wash $3 million in $20 bills only to wind up with $3 million in $20 bills. Changing the form also means reducing the bulk. Contrary to popular belief, you cannot stuff $1 million into an attaché case. A million dollars in $100 bills stands five feet high and weighs over twenty-two pounds.

Third, the trail left by the process must be obscured. The whole purpose of money laundering is defeated if someone can follow the money from beginning to end.

Finally, constant control must be maintained over the process. After all, many of the people who come into the picture while the money is being laundered know that it is dirty money, and if they steal it, there's little the original owner can legally do about it.

That said, there are three distinct stages to the washing cycle.

To begin with, there is immersion, which means consolidation and placement. A drug dealer who amasses $5 million in cash is faced with the Herculean task of injecting as many as a quarter of a million pieces of paper into the banking system. Unlike the counterfeiter, who only needs to get his forged notes into circulation, the laundryman is forced to rely on bank accounts, postal orders, traveler's checks, and other negotiable instruments to funnel the cash into the world's financial system.

The second step, known as layering, might also be called heavy soaping. This is where the laundryman disassociates the money from its illicit source. By moving the money between as many accounts as he can — in and out of dummy companies he's set up around the world for just this purpose — and by relying on bank secrecy and attorney-client privilege to hide his own identity, he creates a complex web of financial transactions that frustrates any audit.

The last stage is the spin dry, sometimes described as repatriation and integration. The washed funds are brought back into circulation, now in the form of clean, and often taxable, income.

With small amounts of money, the three-step process can be quick. If all you want to do is wash $20,000, you merely have to walk into ten banks and buy $2,000 worth of traveler's checks at each one. Or stop by the same number of post offices and purchase a handful of international money orders. Negotiable anywhere in the world, traveler's checks and money orders can be deposited in any foreign bank account, or held onto until you want to spend them. As long as you keep the acquisitions down to realistic sizes — and $2,000 in cash isn't going to set off bells the way a single $20,000 cash transaction might — you can manage it with little or no inconvenience.

If, say, you find yourself with $200,000 in cash, you might swagger into a Rolls Royce showroom and turn the money into a brand-new Silver Spirit. As cash is not the usual form of payment in places like that, it's fair to assume the dealer will sit up and take notice when you produce a Bloomingdale's big brown bag stuffed with bank notes. Legally, the dealer's obliged to report such a cash transaction. Except he may not be aware of his obligation to do that. Or, for the sake of a sale, he might not be willing to do that. If he deposits the cash in his bank, the bank will report it. To avoid that, he could keep the cash in his safe. But even if he does deposit it, and even if the bank reports it, by the time the IRS spots the transaction, you'd have had plenty of time to sell the Rolls and deposit your cashier's check, made out to a false name, into your offshore bank account.

To launder ten times that amount, you might opt for any of several traditional cash businesses, such as the antiques trade. You begin by purchasing a $100 shell company — a registered name that is licensed to do business. Agents selling ready-made companies advertise them every day in the financial section of most newspapers. Now, as an employee of your new company, you drive around the country paying cash for Chinese vases, or Louis XV chairs, or George II candelabras, or fine Persian rugs. Gems, stamps, and rare coins are also easily converted into and out of cash.

Say you buy forty Ming vases for $5,000 each. You put everything up for sale, dividing the cache between a dozen auction houses, preferably in a dozen different cities. When one of the vases comes up, either you allow it to be sold to the highest bidder or you send your favorite uncle into the salesroom to buy it back. You are paid by check for every item sold, so when your uncle hands the auction house $5,500 in cash for one of the vases — that's the $5,000 hammer price plus the 10-percent buyer's commission — they give you a check for $4,500, which is the hammer price minus the 10-percent seller's commission. The fees are simply written off as the cost of washing the funds. And, in this case, you also have the vase to sell again.

Retail stores, bars, and restaurants are even more cash-intensive, making them all the more attractive in high-density drug trafficking areas. Perhaps that's why South Florida is filled with restaurants that don't accept credit cards or checks. Take-out goes out the front door, dirty money comes in the back door.

The video rental business provides another ideal sink. You simply feed cash into the system. Done gradually, it is almost impossible to spot an extra $500 coming in daily through the tills of a storefront stocked with fifteen thousand videos. Nor would anyone question the accountant who certified that the owner took a legally declared $182,500 bonus every year. Nor would anyone's suspicions necessarily be raised if that same owner ran a chain of twenty video rental stores and, backed up with the appropriate audits, awarded himself an annual bonus of $3.56 million.

Laundrymen have long understood that, contrary to Gordon Gekko's much-quoted line in the film *Wall Street,* greed is not good. It's possible to build a network of small businesses into a money laundering conglomerate with only a little long-term planning.

Take the actual case of the Italian-American who set his son up in the grocery business. Papa gave Figlio enough cash to open a store, and Figlio paid his carpenters, painters, and delivery people with cash, which they were happy to accept because they saw it as nontaxable. Figlio then stocked his grocery through a wholesaler who happened to be Papa's brother. But when Figlio ordered fifty cases of tagliatelle from Uncle Zio, he only received forty. So Papa gave Figlio cash to make up for the shortfall. The same happened when Figlio ordered milk, cheese, and frozen brownies. Uncle Zio shorted the delivery and Papa made up for the missing 20 percent. At the end of the month, Papa also topped up Figlio's accounts with additional cash. Figlio's bookkeepers were happy, the taxman was happy, and before long the business was making enough of a profit that Figlio could open a second grocery. Two became four, and four became eight.

As his empire expanded, Figlio decided to import olives from the old country. Luckily, Papa had a cousin in Palermo. But Figlio didn't buy them directly from him. Instead, Papa set up a business in the Bahamas called Mio Cugino, Inc. His cousin sold 100 cases of his olives to the Bahamian company for $500, or $5 a case. The Bahamian company billed Figlio for 120 cases at $10 each. At the end of every month, Papa was always there to make up the difference.

Several hundred million dollars got washed that way before anyone noticed.

No one knows for certain how much dirty money circles the globe each year, looking to get scrubbed clean, but reasonably authoritative guesses range anywhere from $200 billion to $500 billion. After foreign exchange and the oil industry, the laundering of dirty money is the world's third-largest business.

For this alternate economy to function, two things are necessary. When coffee is poured from a pot into a cup, there must be enough room in the cup to hold the coffee and enough coffee in the pot to fill the cup. Similarly, there has to be enough money available to create an infrastructure and an infrastructure capable of handling so much money.

The world's parallel, or underground, banking system was apparently invented by the Chinese, who named it *fei ch'ien* — literally, "flying money." Known in other parts of the world as *chop, hundi,* or *hawalah,* the system was born out of political turmoil and a hearty distrust of banks. It is almost always based on family or tribal connections and traditionally reinforced with retributive violence.

In its simplest form, chits or tokens are substituted for cash. Money deposited at a Hong Kong gold shop is exchanged for a small card bearing a picture of a dragon, a $10 bill stamped with a special seal, or a small, innocuous piece of paper, such as a secretly coded laundry ticket. When the object is presented to a money changer in San Francisco's Chinatown, the bearer is given cash.

During the days when certain European countries had exchange controls, a variation on the *fei ch'ien* system was facilitated by the tourist trade. For example, a Parisian businessman would stake American friends to whatever money they needed while visiting France. When the Americans got home, they added up what they owed their host and deposited it into his undeclared U.S. bank account.

Throughout most of the Vietnam War, a thriving black market propelled the underground economy across Southeast Asia. At least until the Tet Offensive in January 1968, Saigon was alive with all sorts of scams and swindles. The official exchange rate in those days was 118 Vietnamese piasters to the dollar, but the black-market rate was closer to 200. A lucrative corner of that trade was controlled by a small group of Indian nationals who'd emigrated to South Vietnam from Madras. They bought dollars at black-market rates and smuggled them out of the country to be deposited in Hong Kong and Singapore. From there the money was wired either to Europe or, more often, to the Middle East, where it was used to purchase gold. The gold was smuggled back into Vietnam and sold for piasters, which were in turn sold to the Americans for more dollars, completing the circle.

By the time the South Vietnamese authorities were wise to the Indian laundrymen and began confiscating dollars leaving the country — in contravention of the currency restriction laws — the Indians were already working an improvised version of the *hawalah* system. They traded GIs' personal checks drawn on American banks for chits. The checks were deposited into New York accounts held by the Indians. When the checks cleared, the chits were exchanged for piasters and the New York banks wired dollars to pay for gold.

These days, a staggeringly large but very straightforward *hawalah* business exists between India, where currency controls are in force, and Great Britain, where there is a sizeable Indian population and therefore a substantial interest in transferring funds from the subcontinent to Europe. Facilities abound for Indians to deposit money with *hawalah* bankers and within hours to collect their money, minus a commission of 5 to 15 percent, from someone in London. The system works because there are enough people in both countries with large cash surpluses — legitimate businessmen as well as criminals — willing to pay for the privilege of using a paperless banking system.

The British are particularly concerned with *hawalah* networks linking London with two Indian regions, the Punjab and Kashmir. Laundered money has been known to finance terrorist violence, specifically by Sikh and Kashmiri secessionists, and to finance drug traffickers working out of Pakistan.

A few years ago, Scotland Yard busted a *hawalah* banker whom they'd had under surveillance for several months. After watching him work twelve-hour shifts, seven nights a week, police officers raided his house and found bags of cash in his living room containing more than $1.5 million. His scribbled notes showed he was moving $12 million a week. They later arrested a consortium of six *hawalah* bankers who admitted to having laundered, annually, $120 million.

Crooks need money washed because they need to avoid the attention that comes with sudden wealth and to place the proceeds of crime beyond the reach of asset forfeiture laws.

In 1986, when the FBI finally arrested him, Dennis Levine was a 33-year-old New York investment banker, a managing director of Drexel, Burnham Lambert's mergers and acquisition department. For over eight years, using inside information to deal in the stocks and bonds of fifty-four companies, he'd amassed illegal profits of $13 million.

Knowing from the outset he'd have to wash his money before he could spend it, Levine bought a pair of Panamanian-registered companies. Both Diamond Holdings SA and International Gold Inc. came complete with nominee directors, so his name never appeared in any company documents. When he opened accounts for the two companies at Bank Leu International in Nassau, the Bahamas, he made equally certain his name was not used on any of the bank's records.

Levine's main contact was the portfolio manager, a Swiss national named Bernhard Meier, who was under strict instructions never to phone or write Levine, under any circumstances. Extremely cautious, Levine would always call Meier, and then only from a pay phone, so that no one could trace calls back to him. When he wanted to see his money, Levine flew to the Bahamas using an assumed name, and never stayed overnight for fear that someone working in a hotel might later identify him.

Unfortunately for Levine, he became a victim of his own success. He got his trades right so often that some people, including Meier, decided to follow his lead. They piggybacked, buying and selling whenever he bought or sold. That, coupled with an abnormally high batting average, eventually attracted too much attention. The Securities and Exchange Commission (SEC), which unashamedly monitors big hitters, moved in for a closer look. Discovering that Levine had accomplices in other brokerage houses, they began to pressure him. Levine elected to save himself by selling everyone else down the river. When the SEC later managed to intimidate a few Bank Leu officials, Levine's friends returned the compliment and sacrificed him, trading information for immunity.

Beno Ghitis-Miller suffered a similar fate. A 32-year-old travel agent from Cali, Colombia, he moved to Florida in early 1980 and set up a currency business called Sonal. He opened a corporate account at the Capital Bank in downtown Miami and during the first seven months of business deposited large amounts of cash, occasionally as much as $1 million.

That spring, a man named Victor Eisenstein, whose business card indicated he ran a company called American Overseas Enterprises, waltzed into the bank and introduced himself as Beno's agent. Eisenstein told bank officials that he too would be making cash deposits for Sonal. Within a month, the Capital Bank notified Eisenstein that they could no longer accept his money. Someone at the bank was apparently beginning to have some doubts about their clients. Eisenstein objected, but the branch manager said the decision was irreversible. And so it was . . . at least until Beno went over the manager's head and met with the bank's president.

Sonal had been paying Capital one-eighth of 1 percent for sorting and counting each deposit. Now, to stay friends, Capital offered to maintain the account, but only if Sonal upped the commission to one-half of 1 percent. Beno agreed.

Over the next several months, as the cash deposits fast approached $2 million each, the local manager again expressed his concern. This time, though, it had nothing to do with the quality of Capital's clients. He was simply wondering whether Beno and Eisenstein would mind moving their account to a better-equipped branch. They happily switched to Capital's North Bay Village office. When Beno was told the bank had commercial space for rent upstairs, he moved Sonal to North Bay Village, too.

Before long, Beno and Eisenstein were depositing several million dollars per visit to the bank, three and four times a week.

Claiming he didn't know the true nature of Beno's business because he was only acting as Sonal's agent, Eisenstein decided it might be prudent to ask where all of this cash was coming from. Beno explained in a friendly and straightforward letter that the money was connected with exchange transactions involving the import and export of agricultural products, and with sales commissions received abroad by Colombian businessmen. He insisted everything was perfectly kosher. He added that although they were handling a lot of cash, none of it was derived from illegal operations.

Apparently no one spotted the humor in Beno's reference to

agricultural products and sales commissions. More to the point, no one at the bank bothered to walk upstairs and look at Sonal's new offices. If they had, they might have asked themselves why a company dealing in cash, especially the sums that Sonal was, had no security. There was no armored door. There were no video cameras. There was hardly any furniture. There wasn't even a safe. But then, the folks at Capital liked Sonal's business. Beno and Eisenstein were reasonably friendly. They dealt in big numbers, amounts that substantially increased the branch's "cash in" figure, making the manager look like an aggressive young banker on the way up. In fact, the folks at Capital liked Sonal's business enough to negotiate a flat fee for sorting and counting Beno's cash — $300,000 per month.

Between January 1 and August 20, 1981, Beno and Eisenstein and Sonal's so-called staff — thirty-seven Spanish-speaking guys who had only nicknames — deposited $240 million at Capital. That included the $7 million they dropped off in the final two days of their operation. Until U.S. authorities said enough was enough and shut them down, Sonal's deposits had averaged $1.5 million a day.

The greedier they are, the cockier they become, and, given enough time, greed and cockiness undo them. The converse is also true. The French father and son team Henri and Charles Borodiansky were slightly less greedy and slightly less cocky than Beno and Eisenstein, and subsequently fared better.

But only just.

Their act was maritime fraud in general, and phantom cargoes in particular. In early 1990, the Borodianskys claimed to have fourteen shipping containers of Hennessy VSOP Scotch whiskey for sale. The price was right, so a department store in Tokyo took the bait. It forwarded a letter of credit for $3.3 million to a shell company called Mozambico Inc. Ltd., whose registered office was a convenience address in central London.

When the cargo failed to arrive, the Japanese store officials asked the police to find out why. An inquiry was conducted by the International Maritime Bureau (IMB) in London, the Interpol of the shipping business. It revealed that Charles Borodiansky, using the alias Manuel Martins Casimiro, had negotiated the letter of credit in June through the Banque Bruxelles Lambert in Brussels. He'd then moved the funds to Liechtenstein's V&P Bank, straight into an account opened by his father under the alias José Costa Da Santos. Over the next few weeks, half a million dollars was wired from Liechtenstein to a bank in Luxembourg. The rest of it, the IMB learned, had been sent to an account at the Commerzbank in Cologne, Germany.

The Borodianskys had been at this for several years. Using names such as Deck, Borod, and Da Silva, in addition to the ones they chose for the Hennessy scam, they'd set up shell companies across Europe. There were at least four in Belgium, one in the Netherlands, one in Spain, five in Britain, two in Luxembourg, one in Hong Kong, and four in Germany. They are known to have sold two thousand tons of nonexistent maize bound for Dakar, $2.6 million worth of nonexistent commercial fertilizer bound for China, six thousand metric tons of nonexistent steel bound for Vietnam, and two thousand metric tons of nonexistent cement bound for Aqaba.

After IMB agents discovered that the Borodianskys had paid cash for at least one vessel, they were able to locate the ship and impound it. But they needed to prove that the men calling themselves Casimiro and Da Santos and Da Silva were in fact the Borodianskys. So they published a photo in a Norwegian shipping trade magazine and asked if anyone knew the whereabouts of these two men. A ship broker in London identified them immediately and provided enough information for the German police to find them.

For some reason, it took the Germans six days to arrest Charles Borodiansky. By then, Henri was gone. And three safe deposit boxes, in which they'd supposedly hidden $3 million in freshly washed cash, were empty.

Crooks aren't the only ones who launder money.

Corporations do it to avoid or evade taxes, to defraud their shareholders, to get around currency control regulations, and to bribe prospective clients. Gulf Oil once moved $4 million through the Bahamas to bribe Korean and Bolivian politicians. The Lockheed Corporation laundered $25.5 million through a Liechtenstein trust to pay off Italian politicians. Lockheed also subscribed to the laundry facilities of Deak-Perera, then an important American foreign-exchange dealer, to bribe Japanese politicians. At Lockheed's behest, Deak put $8.3 million into the washing cycle, then brought it out as fifteen untraceable payments to a Spanish priest in Hong Kong, who hand-carried the cash in flight bags and orange crates to Lockheed's customers in Tokyo.

Individuals do it to hide money from a divorcing spouse, or to halt erosion of their assets, by inventing a business deal that moves those assets through a shell company and into a less taxed jurisdiction. Italian designer Aldo Gucci washed more than $11 million through shell companies, stashing it in Hong Kong to keep it out of the hands of the IRS.

Governments have been known to do it as well, whether to subvert terrorists or to arm "freedom fighters." That's what Iran-Contra was all about.

In November 1986, Ronald Reagan confirmed the much-circulated rumor that the United States had surreptitiously sold arms to Iran. His initial version of the events was that this had been done to improve relations with Iran, not to obtain the release of American citizens held in the Middle East by terrorists. But that soon got changed to an embarrassed admission that indeed this had been an arms-for-hostages swap.

Although some elements of the scandal still remain clouded in mystery, it appears that the United States, with the help of Saudi Arabia's King Fahd, furnished the Iranians with weapons in exchange for payments that were then diverted to the Contra rebels to aid them in their fight against the Marxist regime in Nicaragua.

CIA Director William Casey wanted to find a way to open a dialogue with the Iranians, the direct route having been closed off by the arms embargo that followed the 1979 seizure of American hostages in Tehran. He turned to his old pal King Fahd, who had no trouble securing the services of Saudi arms dealer Adnan Khashoggi. Once touted as the richest man in the world — he never was, but for obvious reasons didn't spend a lot of time correcting that misconception — Khashoggi was a professional middleman, a globe-trotting broker who knew how to get a deal going and cut himself in on the action. Through him, two other players came on stage: Manucher Ghorbanifar, an Iranian middleman who, while having gone into exile at the same time as the shah, still maintained high-level contacts with the Revolutionary Government; and Yaaccov Nimrodi, an Israeli with intelligence experience and considerable contacts in Tehran.

Enter Lieutenant Colonel Oliver North, U.S. Marine Corps, and deputy director of political affairs at the National Security Council. Beginning in late August or early September 1984 — working initially under the president's national security advisor, Robert McFarlane, and later in partnership with McFarlane's successor, Vice Admiral John Poindexter — North formulated, then executed, the plan. Within a year, he'd convinced the Israelis to sell five hundred U.S.-made TOW antitank missiles to Iran.

Because the contracts were guaranteed by Khashoggi, the Iranians paid him. He took his share, then passed the rest along to the Israelis. They paid North, who diverted the funds through Swiss banks, and on to the Contras. North recruited Richard Secord, a retired Air Force general, and Secord's business partner Albert Hakim, an Iranian-American. The three were so successful that by early 1986 they'd managed to buy some two thousand TOW missiles from the CIA for $12 million and, again with the intervention of Khashoggi and Ghorbanifar, to sell them to the Iranians for $30 million.

In Switzerland, that money was washed through a dummy Panamanian company called Lake Resources. The chairman of Lake Resources was a Swiss accountant named Suzanne Hefti, who worked for Auditing and Fiduciary Services in Fribourg. Her firm was directly tied to a California company, Stanford Technology Trading Group International, which was controlled by Albert Hakim. In turn, Stanford Technology's Swiss affiliate was headed up by a man named Jean de Senarclens, who also happened to run an accounting firm, in Geneva, called CSF.

First, North moved money from Lake Resources' Swiss account into a CSF account in the Cayman Islands. Next, a CSF subsidiary in Bermuda wired the money to Alban Values, a Panamanian corporation in which CSF owned an interest. Alban Values then sent it to Amalgamated Commercial Enterprises, a shell company registered in

Panama but owned by a Miami freight carrier called Southern Air Transport. And they were the ones who actually supplied the Contras.

It's believed that in just two years, from 1984 to 1986, as much as $50 million might have gone this route. But the Contras claim they never got anywhere near that amount. Despite 250 hours of testimony before the Senate Select Committee on the Iran-Contra scandal, including sworn statements from twenty-nine witnesses and some 250,000 pages of documents, it is unlikely that anyone will ever know the full extent to which the government joined the laundrymen in making a fortune evaporate.

One prominent variation on the government-as-laundryman theme is political insurance. Despots of all shapes and sizes insure against unexpected retirement by shifting money from their own national banking system into less hostile environments. Most of the more visible political heads of state throughout the Middle East and Africa have set up financial arrangements in Switzerland. Apparently, having them goes with the turf. The Shah of Iran hid a king's ransom in secret bank accounts as an emergency pension fund.

So did Ferdinand and Imelda Marcos of the Philippines. Hardly able to manage on a presidential salary of $4,700, the couple reputedly stashed $5 to $10 billion in various parts of the world, much of it laundered through Hong Kong. According to the Philippine government commission originally assigned with tracking down the Marcos money, Ferdinand and Imelda used at least ten dummy corporations registered in the Philippines, Hong Kong, Panama, and the Dutch Antilles to get half the assets into the United States, a third into Switzerland, and the rest into France, England, Italy, Panama, and Australia. Recently, a stash of Marcos money was uncovered in the Cook Islands, although the bulk of it was lost when the local branch of the Bank of Credit and Commerce International (BCCI) went out of business.

Obsessed with secrecy, Ferdinand Marcos was committed to weaving an impenetrable web of deceit around his looted fortune. For instance, to purchase three buildings in Manhattan, he used three bearer-share companies registered in the Dutch Antilles, each of which was owned by a separate Panamanian bearer-share company.

In other words, whoever physically held the stock certificates owned the dummy company that owned the other dummy company and, ultimately, the property. By making each transaction so complicated that no one could trace anything back to him, Marcos lost track of which name went on which account and which company controlled which property.

The Marcoses have since been accused of using the same dummy corporation formula to help friends finance property deals, among them George Hamilton, who purchased Charlie Chaplin's former home in Beverly Hills. Hamilton denied those allegations when they were lodged in a lawsuit against him and has since sold the house to a company registered in the Cayman Islands, rumored to be controlled by the Khashoggi family.

The Marcos's finances became such an international embarrassment that even the otherwise unblushable Swiss decided to give up on him. They froze nearly $1.5 billion in bank accounts he'd used, many of them ascribed to aliases, including fourteen he'd set up in the names of various foundations.

Needless to say, Ferdinand and Imelda are not the only ones known to have gotten carried away with preparing their nest egg. The Ceausescus of Romania harbored stolen assets in Switzerland, as did most of Latin America's tin-pot dictators. The same goes for literally hundreds of former Communist officials, many of who raked in fortunes from drug trafficking. One of the most flagrant offenders was East Germany's Erich Honecker. It's no coincidence that a company registered in East Berlin, Novum Handelsgesellschaft, and controlled by an Austrian Communist named Rudolfine Steindling, moved $260 million out of East Germany within hours of the fall of the Berlin Wall in 1989. The money was washed through the Z-Laenderbank — known as Bank Austria — and its subsidiary in Zurich, which was then called Bankfinanz. Whereas $150 million was eventually transferred back to Communist party accounts in Vienna, at least $3 million was later withdrawn in cash.

It was standard procedure for Communist leaders to salt something away, hedging their bets, as it were, on the remote possibility that Marx and Lenin were wrong.

3

TAKING CARE OF BUSINESS

"You don't refuse a customer just because his money isn't clean."
— **Nicholas Deak**

It's like a stone tossed into a pond.

You see it hit the water because it makes a splash. As it begins to sink, the water ripples and, for a few moments, you can still see the spot where the stone hit. But as the stone sinks deeper, the ripples fade, and by the time the stone reaches the bottom any traces of it are long gone and the stone itself may be impossible to find.

That's exactly what happens to laundered money.

The immersion stage is when the laundryman is most vulnerable. If he can't get his dirty money into a washing cycle, he can't clean it. However, once his cash is converted into numbers — blips on a computer screen — and those numbers are flashed back and forth across the globe, the ripples have disappeared and the stone is buried in silt.

Realizing that the optimum time to strike is when the laundryman is most exposed, the Bank Secrecy Act of 1970 attempted to force banks, savings and loans, and other financial institutions to report all cash transactions over $1,000 to the IRS. But the ceiling proved to be too low. In spite of a provision exempting certain retail businesses, allowing banks to set higher limits based on a client's specific requirements, the government was still inundated with forms. Because there weren't enough people to process them, most of those forms wound up decomposing in a Detroit warehouse. Anyway, far too many legitimate nonretail businesses deal in large amounts of cash. Compliance became so time consuming and awkward that banks either exempted all of their biggest and best customers or simply gave up.

Over the years, the scope of the law was broadened to include nonbank financial institutions, such as travel agencies, money wire services, credit unions, car dealers, insurance agencies, money changers, brokerage houses, and check-cashing businesses. Even a local convenience store selling money orders was expected to comply. Finally, Congress dictated that "all trades and businesses" dealing in cash fell under the scope of the act and increased the cash limit to a more realistic $10,000.

Although forty-three otherwise upstanding banks, including Chase Manhattan and Bank of America, were penalized for a total of $20 million, the currency-reporting requirement was still widely disregarded until 1985. That's when the government decided to call time. It accused the Bank of Boston of gross and flagrant violations of the Bank Secrecy Act, alleging that the bank had failed to report 1,163 cash transactions amounting to $1.22 billion. Among the companies the Bank of Boston had supposedly exempted from cash reporting was the law firm of F. Lee Bailey. More ominously, the bank had given dispensation to a pair of real estate agencies controlled by a local organized crime boss. In the face of overwhelming evidence, the Bank of Boston pleaded guilty, admitting to an additional $110 million worth of violations, and was fined a then-record $500,000.

The government drove home its point by going after another sixty banks. Chemical Bank admitted to 857 cases of nonreported cash transactions worth $26 million. Irving Trust Company acknowledged 1,659, worth $292 million. Manufacturers Hanover Trust confessed to 1,400, worth $140 million. But the process was still in its teething stage, and justice was arbitrary. When the Bank of New England was found guilty of 31 offenses, it was fined $1.2 million. When Crocker National Bank was found to have committed 7,877 infractions, worth $3.98 billion, it was fined just $2.25 million.

Despite such anomalies, banks across the nation were forced to sit up and take notice. Over the years, the Justice Department has become more adroit at digging deeper into a bank's affairs and rooting out the laundrymen, and more severe about holding the bank responsible for the actions of its employees. At the end of 1994, the government's wrath was directed at the American Express Bank International, after two of its senior officers were indicted in Houston for helping to wash $40 million belonging to Mexican drug trafficker Juan Garcia Abrego.

A Mexican gas station owner named Ricardo Aguirre Villagomez — known by his friends as Kenny Rogers because he looked like the singer — was Abrego's primary laundryman. Under Villagomez's supervision, drug money collected on the streets of Texas was sent through exchange houses and banks along the Mexican border to Switzerland. From there it was wired to a holding company in the Cayman Islands established for Villagomez by Antonio Giraldi and Maria Lourdes Reategui at the Beverly Hills branch of AMEX. Some of his money was invested in a Blockbuster Video franchise, and some in lithographs by the Mexican artist Rufino Tamayo. But the lion's share went into American real estate. Giraldi and Reategui accepted $29 million as collateral for $19 million worth of property loans, reputedly making Villagomez the bank's biggest customer — at least until U.S. Customs identified and froze the funds in the Caymans. Giraldi and Reategui both pleaded not guilty to several charges, including money laundering, but a Brownsville, Texas, jury found otherwise. He was sentenced to 10 years, and she got 3 1/2. The government then went after the bank, fining it $7 million. American Express Bank International also had to forfeit $40 million of Villagomez's laundered money and assets, and was obliged to spend $3 million on employee training.

The fine is the largest assessed to date against a U.S. bank for money laundering. But that's a record that probably won't stand for long.

In the name of responsible banking — but largely at the insistence of the United States, Great Britain, France, and Japan — nations around the world have endorsed the doctrine that financial institutions must do their part to help identify money being laundered at any stage of the washing cycle. The result is "Know Your Customer," a campaign to target clients who maintain accounts that are not in keeping with the type of business they do, clients with accounts fed by deposits from a large number of individuals, or anyone opening a low-interest-bearing account with a sizable sum of money. Cash remains the giveaway, especially when someone makes unusually large deposits, makes multiple deposits at different locations, transfers large deposits quickly to other accounts, or makes an inordinately high number of very small deposits that add up to a very large sum.

For the most part, banks throughout the industrialized world have shown a sportsmanlike willingness to cooperate, despite the fact it means they have to spend their own money to train staff in the skills of financial vigilance. A front-line strategy, akin perhaps to reminding children to drink their milk and brush their teeth, it sometimes works. But not all the time.

Agip [Africa] Ltd., registered in Jersey, Channel Islands, was a company drilling for oil in North Africa. A wholly owned subsidiary of the Italian state oil company, its chief accountant was a crook who over the course of several months used fraudulent invoices to wire $10.5 million from the Banque du Sud in Tunis to the London account of the Baker Oil Corporation, a shell registered on the Isle of Man.

Any bank manager might fairly assume that Baker Oil was in the petroleum business. However, almost as soon as funds were bedded down in that account, instructions arrived directing the bank to transfer everything to the Euro-Arabian Jewelry company. The money was then immediately wired to a company in Paris pretending to be a jewelry store. Suspicious? Perhaps. Illogical? Almost certainly. Yet the bank manager who handled the transfers, and charged Baker Oil a fee for the service, earned his living not by knowing his customers but by catering to them. His job description did not include interfering with an oil company sending all of its money to a jewelry store.

Responsible banking, it must be said, is a terribly vague concept. Admitting as much, some governments do more than merely encourage bankers to know their customers; they force banks and other businesses to engage the enemy by decreeing that ignorance of the laundrymen's methods will not provide an adequate defense where laws have been violated. The onus therefore falls on corporate officers to monitor and report suspicious activities. Any officer of a financial institution in America found guilty of being involved in money laundering risks up to ten years' imprisonment and/or a fine of $500,000. Under certain circumstances, the government can also impound the offending company.

That was the dilemma faced by Banque Leu, a Luxembourg corporation operating in Northern California, after agents from the IRS and the Drug Enforcement Administration (DEA) followed a trail of drug money from Los Angeles to Colombia, then back to a pair of accounts at the bank. Several arrests ensued, including those of two Colombians and a rogue bank officer. Confronted with the threat of a federal grand jury indictment against the corporation that, in theory, might have shut them down, executives at Banque Leu opted for damage control. They accepted legal responsibility for the actions of their account officer, conceding that he "either knew or was willfully blind" to the fact that specific accounts were used to launder drug money. In exchange for the U.S. attorney's waiver of that indictment, the management of Banque Leu pleaded guilty to money laundering, forfeited $2.3 million, paid an additional $60,000 fine, agreed to submit special audit reports to the U.S. government for the next three years, and was obliged to conduct an anti money-laundering education project.

According to a recent federal court ruling, foreign corporations with branches or subsidiaries in the United States can now be prosecuted no matter where they're laundering money. A classic illustration came out of a 1988 Securities and Exchange Commission investigation into insider trading.

Stephen Sui-Kwan Wang was a trainee analyst in the mergers and acquisition department of merchant bankers Morgan Stanley in New York. Lee Chwan-hong, an investor who called himself Fred Lee, was president of two British Virgin Island companies with headquarters in Hong Kong. According to the SEC, over the course of eighteen to twenty-four months Wang provided Lee with nonpublic information, which allowed Lee to take positions in twenty-five companies through thirty different brokerage accounts. Lee came out the other end with a profit of $19.4 million.

In keeping with current procedure, the SEC filed against Lee for $19.4 million, then used the Racketeer Influenced and Corrupt Organizations Act (RICO) to seek a civil penalty of three times that amount, for a grand total of $77.8 million. Knowing that Lee had moved his money out of several company accounts around the country and put the bulk of it in the New York branch of the Standard Chartered Bank, the SEC attempted to freeze his accounts. But Lee was one step ahead. He'd already ordered Standard Chartered New York to wire his money to Standard Chartered Hong Kong. So now the SEC sought an order against the Hong Kong bank to repatriate the assets.

Standard Chartered's lawyers argued that the American courts had no jurisdiction in the matter and could not enforce an action in Hong Kong. But a U.S. district court thought otherwise. It agreed with the SEC, ruling that if Standard Chartered Hong Kong did not return the money to the United States, the New York branch could be held in contempt. Risking daily fines and the possibility that its bank officers in the United States could be arrested, Standard Chartered sent the funds back to New York, to be held there by the courts, awaiting the determination of the SEC's claims against Lee.

Needless to say, Lee was anything but pleased by his bank's decision and demanded that his money remain at his disposal in Hong Kong. He insisted that Standard Chartered had a contractual duty to him. When the bank pointed out that the money was already in the States, two of Lee's companies sued Standard Chartered in Hong Kong on the grounds that it had acted unlawfully.

The case posed the terribly awkward question, Where should a bank's allegiance lie? Must a bank comply with a court order, albeit in another jurisdiction, or are banks bound by contract to their client, no matter what?

The High Court in Hong Kong ruled against Lee, saying that because the money was a result of a crime, the bank had acted correctly in sending it to the United States, subject to a ruling there. The underlying message was a warning by the U.S. Justice Department to all banks: When you deal with the proceeds of crime, we reserve the right to hold you responsible.

At first glance, a ruling like that would appear to be an effective weapon. But it can take forever to locate the proceeds of the crime and work the case through several jurisdictions. The world is no longer a collection of independent financial markets. It's a global bazaar, backed by an electronic infrastructure that permits the instantaneous transfer of funds from anywhere on earth to anywhere else. Pinpointing one or even a series of transmissions is extremely difficult. So Congress now takes the approach that banks and nonbank financial institutions have a watchdog's role to play.

As dangerous as that might be — and there are those who argue that bankers should not be turned into policemen — as of 1996 Wall Street broker-dealers and other nonbank financial institutions are required to determine, as best they can, that wired funds are not crime related. They must also maintain their wire transfer records for five years.

Simply because a client represents himself as being engaged in a lawful business, the government no longer excuses the companies he hires from reporting inconsistencies that might document an illegal source. Because laundrymen prefer financial institutions where they aren't known and where they can't be identified through records of previous transactions, the government insists that companies pay particular attention to clients who don't normally hold accounts or otherwise transact business. That's led one critic of the law to call it "Know Your Noncustomer."

As banks have cracked down, laundrymen have turned to nonbank financial operators. They use money changers — known as *casas de cambio* along the U.S.-Mexican border, which is crawling with them — money transmitters, such as Western Union and American Express, neighborhood check-cashing businesses, and Giro houses, which are wire-transfer businesses. But more often than not, finding dirty money in a sea of wire transfers means putting the dirty money there in the first place.

World Telecom was a storefront business at 373 Broadway, Chelsea, Massachusetts. Owned by a 32-year-old named German (pronounced Herman) Cadavid, the company offered various services, such as faxes, post-office boxes, beeper rentals, and money exchange. Five doors down was the World Travel Service, a money transmitter and licensed franchise agency for Vigo Remittance Corporation of New York. It was also owned by Cadavid. Both were related, through Cadavid, to World Travel Service and World Telecom offices in Rhode Island.

U.S. Customs had reason to believe that from the time he went into business in 1992, and for much of the next two years, Cadavid and his associates were laundering dirty money. His volume of transfers was greater than it ordinarily might have been for a new business, almost all of the transfers went to the Dominican Republic, and the local Dominican population was not affluent enough to account for the sums he was moving. However, without someone on the inside, busting him was next to impossible. So customs set up a sting. An undercover operative convinced Cadavid to handle three transfers totaling more than $100,000. After taking his usual 7-percent commission, Cadavid unsuspectingly wired the money into the Barclays Bank account of a U.S. Customs front company in London.

As a Vigo franchisee, he was under an obligation to observe certain strict rules, such as never accepting an order over $5,000 without demanding proper identification to verify the full name and address of the sender. To get around Vigo's rules, Cadavid simply assigned the transfers to fictitious names, partitioned them into $4,500 parcels, and staggered transmissions.

By isolating specific transfers and following the money trail, Customs was able to arrest him. But more than five hundred thousand wire transfers, representing in excess of $1 trillion, electronically circle the globe daily. Even if there weren't too many to keep tabs on — and there most definitely are — there isn't enough information on any single wire transfer to determine whether the money is clean or dirty. Changing the system would mean implementing a global strategy for accurately identifying the sender, the recipient, and the source of all wired funds. Any hope of doing that, of getting every country in the world to make wired monies ultimately traceable when it is clearly not in every country's interest to do so, exceeds wishful thinking.

American law requires that a cash transaction report (CTR), technically known as IRS Form 8300, be filed with the IRS for any and all cash dealings over $10,000. This applies not only to banks and other financial institutions but to all sorts of businessmen, from antique dealers, builders, and shop owners, to garage owners, restaurateurs, barbers, and dentists. Banks and financial institutions are additionally bound to maintain records of every cash transaction of $3,000 or more for five years.

Although a CTR is also mandatory if the total amount of transactions over a twelve-month period exceeds $10,000, one way laundrymen get around the law is by spreading out their dealings. In a recent case, $29 million in cash nearly vanished on its way to Ecuador because the laundryman was willing to lumber it through 40,000 separate transactions.

Phony bank accounts are another ruse and, believe it or not, the government has investigated cases in which accounts were opened in the names of Marilyn Monroe, Abraham Lincoln, James Bond, Mae West, and Roger Rabbit.

Nevertheless, cash remains legal tender. It even says so on the face of every bill. That means there's nothing to prevent someone from handing their bank $1 million in used $5 bills. But when that happens, the government wants to know who's doing it and where the money comes from. Consequently, more than eight million IRS 8300 forms are now being filed annually. They wind up at a collation center in Detroit, where the information contained on them is fed onto computer tape. From there, the tapes are sent to the headquarters of the Financial Crimes Enforcement Network (FINCEN) in Vienna, Virginia.

Housed in a modern office complex behind a huge ellipse — a hint perhaps that one is about to slip through the eye of a needle — FINCEN consists of several floors' worth of locked doors protected by security cameras and armed guards, of restricted-area open-plan offices in which desks with computer terminals are separated by half-height movable walls, and of over-air-conditioned rooms, access to which is off-limits to just about everyone because that's where they keep their superpowerful computer mainframes.

Information on the tapes from Detroit is fed into those mainframes, melded into FINCEN's already enormous database of cash transactions. Specialists continually prowl through the database, looking for patterns of unusual financial transactions from which to build a detailed diagram of illegal activity. Whether they're working on an investigation for the Treasury Department or answering one of the more than six thousand requests for information that come in annually from diverse law enforcement agencies across the country, the bedrock of FINCEN's research is the set theory of Venn diagrams — overlapping circles to indicate relationships.

Say research begins with the names of five individuals suspected by Customs of money laundering. Checking those names in the database reveals several residential addresses. Cross-checking those addresses matches one with a company under investigation for drug dealing by the San Francisco police department. That company has used several bank accounts, one of which shows up on an IRS Form 8300, having accepted a cash deposit from a gentleman whose home address is the same as a company currently the object of a probe by the Pittsburgh office of the DEA. As the search broadens, FINCEN links the original five individuals to a dozen more, adding fifteen companies and thirty bank accounts to the investigation.

It is an expensive and lengthy process, and all too often, by the time programmers input the paperwork and the analysis section sorts through the data, many trails have gone cold. But when FINCEN does score, the results can be staggering. In June 1995, a pair of law enforcement agencies requested information on two individuals who had no apparent affiliation. By cross-checking patterns of their financial dealings, a FINCEN specialist was able to tie both to two small businesses. Although neither business reported annual sales of more than $1 million, the specialist soon linked those businesses to $120 million in cash deposited at banks across the country at the rate of $50,000 to $80,000 a day. By August, the FBI was on to a huge drug-and-arms-dealing conspiracy.

Further strengthening the government's hand is the 1990 Depository Institution Money Laundering Amendment Act, which reemphasizes that the burden is on banks to report. By turning a blind eye, bank directors are risking everything, including the possibility of the government taking over any financial institution convicted of money laundering offenses.

Along with those laws, RICO statutes permit the government to seize laundered money, regardless of the source, to confiscate all assets derived from the use of those funds, and to levy fines of up to three times that amount against anyone involved with money laundering. RICO has also given renewed vigor to the asset-forfeiture program. Today, thanks entirely to drug traffickers and laundrymen, the government has owned horse farms, yachts, planes, cars, watches, oil wells, cattle, and hotels, and for a while found itself the owner of a house of prostitution. It has seized and sold enough art to fill dozens of museums. Not long ago it grabbed a 1972 Salvador Dali self-portrait. The painting had been bought in Spain with drug money by a known trafficker who'd taken it back to Colombia, then shipped it to Miami, intending to sell it at auction. The government obligingly put the painting on the block, but after the hammer went down at $500,000, Uncle Sam kept the money.

The government has also owned the occasional film set. When Ken Mizuno and an associate sold some fifty thousand memberships to an exclusive Japanese country club that only allowed eighteen hundred members, bilking investors for nearly $800,000, the Feds got Mizuno for fraud and money laundering. They confiscated his mansion in Los Angeles and sold it for $1.8 million, having marketed it as any good real estate agent might — with a glossy brochure emphasizing that the house had been widely featured in Eddie Murphy's 1987 movie *Beverly Hills Cop II*.

Nowhere else in the world is money laundering given the same prestige.

In the United Kingdom, several pieces of legislation are aimed at stopping the laundrymen, yet each falls short of America's get-tough approach. Instead of requiring that cash transactions over a certain amount be reported, the British chose a system called suspicious cash transaction reporting. Which means the front-line battle against the laundrymen gets bogged down in the definition of the word *suspicious*.

If someone deposits £50 in cash and an employee at the bank thinks there's something odd about it, he is obliged by law to file a CTR. If another client deposits £500,000 in cash and no one finds anything odd about it, the deposit goes unreported.

Having opted for suspicious cash transaction reporting because mandatory reporting costs more than they were willing to spend, the British are getting what they paid for. A two-year survey by the British Police Foundation revealed that twenty thousand suspicious cash transaction reports had led to fewer than six investigations, and that out of those six investigations no one could say how many arrests were made, or if any convictions resulted.

The police can confiscate drug-derived assets. However, bankers can defend against this by proving they did not know or did not suspect they were dealing with laundered money. Or, having suspected as much, that they disclosed the facts to the proper authorities.

It is much the same story throughout Europe.

The Dutch have anti money-laundering laws, and have made a conscious effort to force banks to report. But it doesn't always work. A drug cartel from Surinam, working out of a gold and jewelry shop, washed $59 million through two Rotterdam branches of the Dutch bank ABN AMRO between 1989 and 1993. There have since been prosecutions, but when bank officials first reported suspicious transactions, the Central Bank told them to leave the matter alone, that it was of no real interest.

In 1995, the Dutch police decided that at least half of Holland's 110 foreign-exchange bureaus were laundering drug-tainted guilders. The central bank took over direct supervision of those exchanges and many of them, especially those owned by foreign bearer-share companies, quickly folded. But almost as many have since reopened just across the border in Belgium.

Although no one can put an accurate figure on the amount of money being washed through the Netherlands, a former minister of justice said in 1993 that it could be more than twice as much as flower exports, Holland's most profitable crop.

In Germany, money laundering has only recently become a crime. Unification, which soldered an important chunk of the Eastern Bloc to the West, created a massive sink. Helmut Kohl's government had no choice but to fly in the face of a traditionally secretive banking industry and comply with European Community directives. He signed a law that requires banks to record the names of anyone depositing cash in amounts over DM 20,000 ($12,000), and to alert

the police when they suspect that money has come from drug dealing or other criminal activity. But prosecutions haven't followed.

The French, too, have made money laundering a criminal offense, but have weakened the effort by using a suspicious-cash-
transaction reporting system. They created TRACFIN, modeled
after FINCEN, specifically to expose money launderers. But in the
end, TRACFIN is like an NFL expansion club: the players know the
rules of the game (at least most of them think they know how to play
it), they've got the jargon down pat, and they wear nifty multicolored
uniforms, but they just haven't learned how to win. It took the
French over six years to bring their first money laundering prosecution to court. And then, it only happened because the DEA handed
it to them.

It is an offense in Italy to launder money, but only in cases
involving kidnapping, robbery, or blackmail. In 1989, the Italian
Banking Association asked that member banks identify every cash
transaction in excess of 10 million lira, not quite $7,000. They are
also supposed to register all bearer savings passbooks, and to refuse
service to any customer who fails to cooperate. Ignorance, abuse, and
sheer disregard of the law are widespread. Promises of change have
come fast and furious since recent scandals rocked the government
and implicated many politicians of complicity with organized crime.
But before Italy can tackle the laundrymen, it needs a government
with credibility, one that will last long enough to survive the constant
mayhem that has been Italian politics since 1945.

In Luxembourg, banking secrecy is guaranteed by legislation
that prohibits any bank from disclosing information either to local or
foreign tax authorities. Luxembourg has been known in the past to
cooperate with other countries investigating drug-related crimes. But
the Grand Duchy emphatically draws the line there. One result of its
blatantly freewheeling company-registration policy is that banks such
as BCCI could be securely headquartered in Luxembourg while running amok throughout the rest of the world. A 1989 law did make
money laundering a crime. However, it stipulated that the authorities
could only seize assets after the owner of the funds had been convicted of a crime. As a result, the courts found themselves in a very
embarrassing position. $36 million belonging to known drug traf-

ficker Heriberto Castro Mesa had been laundered through thirty-three banks in Luxembourg and eight other European countries. When Mesa was killed in a shootout with police, Luxembourg authorities arrested and convicted his two laundrymen, Franklin Jurado Rodriguez and Edgar Garcia Montilla, and ordered that their assets be frozen. That's when Mesa's widow, Esperanza, and his daughter, Ampara Castro de Santacruz — who was married to José Santacruz Londono, a founding member of the Cali cartel — went to court to get those funds unfrozen. In January 1993, the case reached a court of appeals, which ruled that the money must be released because its owners, Esperanza and Ampara, had broken no laws. Their links to Cali drug trafficking were of no significance. They'd never been convicted of a crime. Nor, for that matter, had Castro Mesa.

In the midst of the ensuing publicity and international criticism, the Grand Duchy decreed that any money confiscated in drug cases would be used to fight trafficking and money laundering. It also promised to close the offending loophole. Credit institutions and professionals in the banking sector would now be required to report any activities that might be construed as money laundering. The immediate response was a bloodcurdling scream from local bankers, who insisted that the decrees would jeopardize the nation's unique financial position by nullifying banking secrecy. Weighing one argument against the other — the social consequences of drug trafficking and money laundering versus the pecuniary benefits of secret banking — the legislators did precisely what you might expect them to do. They voted for their wallets. A compromise bill was passed allowing the authorities to clamp down on money laundering. But the information they would need before they could act would be made available by banks only "on their own initiative." Business in Luxembourg is back to normal.

The European Community set the tone right from the beginning, letting banks off the hook by declaring that it was not their responsibility to detect money laundering. Instead, bankers are politely requested to know their customers so that money launderers will find it more difficult to operate, to comply with existing legislation and law enforcement agencies in the fight against money laundering, to improve their record-keeping systems so that suspicious activities can be detected early, and to train their staffs to recognize and report money laundering activities.

The Japanese have copied the British, obliging banks to report suspicious cash transactions, though they've gone one step further in forcing banks to report all domestic cash transactions in excess of $240,000 and all foreign cash transactions in excess of $40,000. Where drugs are concerned, prosecutors can put banks and financial institutions in the dock for laundering money.

Closer to home, Canadian banks sometimes report suspicious transactions, but only on a strictly voluntary basis, and following procedures instituted by the banks themselves. The government does not demand reporting.

The United Nations climbed on the bandwagon in 1988, proposing that money laundering be an internationally extraditable offense. Some eighty nations agreed in principle to ratify a pact. But eighty is much less than half the UN membership, and in the first five years only four actually signed. Notable among the holdouts were Luxembourg, Liechtenstein, the Netherlands Antilles, the Cayman Islands, Panama, Uruguay, Hungary, Russia, Pakistan, and Bulgaria.

Brian Bruh, the first director of FINCEN, is quite frank when he compares the American system with what's practiced elsewhere in the world: "A suspicious-cash-transaction reporting system is essentially a voluntary system. If someone walks into a bank, a narcotics trafficker or a money launderer, and wants to conduct a financial transaction, and he sees that the bank officer is very alert, he simply says, 'I forgot something' and walks down the street to another bank, until he's able to conduct a transaction where the bank official is not so suspicious. In our country, if someone walks into a bank, conducts a large cash transaction, a report must be filed. If I were a money launderer, I would prefer to do business in a country with suspicious-cash-transaction reporting. Although, suspicious-cash-transaction reporting is still better than no cash transaction reporting."

In the good old days before cash transaction reporting, laundering huge sums of dirty money used to be a fairly easy stunt. All anyone had to do was send runners around the country depositing cash into a lot of bank accounts. Each runner, known in the trade as a "smurf" — the nickname was first used by investigators in Florida because the runners reminded them of the television cartoon characters — would be assigned a daily route, exactly like a mailman or a milkman. Once the runners had collected the day's cash from their contacts, they'd work their territory. If each runner deposited $200 in twenty accounts — hardly enough in any one bank to raise suspicions — ten runners could put $40,000 in dirty cash per day into the banking system. That's $200,000 a week, or $10.4 million a year. One California drug trafficker bragged when arrested that his smurfs had gotten so good at it they could buy up to 2,000 cashier's checks a day and deposit them within a few hours in 513 banks.

The secret of good smurfing is speed. To deposit the most money in the shortest amount of time, areas are targeted in which banks are located close to one another and business isn't too hectic. Small towns are no good because tellers there remember clients. Banks with little business are no good because tellers have too much time to think about a deposit or a familiar face. The best smurfing is done in affluent suburbs, where there are just enough banks with just enough customers. Big cities, it turns out, are as bad as small towns. Lines are usually too long.

Anyway, that's the way the game used to work, before the government got wise to such capers and forced the laundrymen to find new approaches. So the laundrymen turned their attention to non-bank financial institutions, such as casinos.

A cash-intensive industry, casinos routinely perform many banklike services. They cash checks, exchange foreign currency, offer the use of safe deposit boxes, and pay out large sums in cashier's checks. They also frequently extend credit, which means you can leave your money on deposit in one casino and get it back from a casino in another jurisdiction. Not only is a well-established, well-organized gambling den an obvious place to reduce the bulk of a stash, to change $10 and $20 bills into $50s and $100s, it is a believable source of revenue. All you have to do is stroll into a casino, buy $1,000 worth of chips, play for a few hours, cash out, and hand your bank manager $500,000. You might someday have to substantiate your claim of having won it at a casino, but that's no problem for anyone with a friend high up in the casino's management.

Better still, if you owned a casino you wouldn't have to bother pretending to play the roulette wheel. You'd simply shove your cash into the till and make sure your accountant lists it in the profit column when he files your tax returns.

Acknowledging this natural alliance, Congress subjects casinos to the same cash transaction reporting requirement as banks. Furthermore, a 1993 law requires casinos to file suspicious-cash-transaction reports if they witness questionable transactions, to institute programs for training employees, and to improve the procedures they use to identify customers applying for credit accounts. But the law as it was passed and the law as it was proposed turn out to be two different matters. "Pending further study," Congress backed down from forcing casinos to maintain a list of customers who are known by aliases, to keep a chronological record of all transactions at the cashier's window, and to verify the identity of any customer whose cash transactions exceed $3,000. The casino lobby also took a healthy bite out of the suspicious-cash-transaction requirement by getting Congress to exempt smaller casinos from the obligation. Nor did Congress include all of the Indian reservation casinos, of which there are about 130 in sixteen states, doing an estimated $27 billion a year in business.

At the beginning of January 1993, the Treasury Department fined ten casinos in Atlantic City a total of $2.5 million for "willfully failing" to report cash transactions that took place between 1985 and 1988. The gaming industry now insists that it has cleaned up its act and is in full compliance with the 1993 law. But then, it has always said it was in compliance with the 1985 law, which requires any commercial casino with a turnover of at least $1 million a year to keep records of large cash transactions — except if they happen to be located in Nevada.

Racetracks provide laundrymen with much the same opportunity as casinos. The strategy here hangs on the natural reluctance of some winners to let the IRS know just how much they're putting in their pocket. A winning ticket is a negotiable instrument, and some laundrymen are only too happy to help the lucky punter avoid taxes by giving him cash for his ticket. Racetracks across the country are filled with these "flies," who stalk the tracks looking for folk with tickets to sell.

Purchasing lottery tickets is slightly more complicated because the winners aren't in a single place at any given moment. But here again, it's a no-lose situation for all parties involved, even the IRS. The big prizes in most state lotteries are paid out over a twenty-year period, so a $10-million win is worth $50,000 a year for the next two decades. From the laundryman's point of view, a twenty-year annuity is well worth a suitcase filled with cash. The original winner gets his money up front — although the burden of dealing with so much cash now rests on his shoulders — and the laundryman has turned millions of dollars of dirty money into a totally legal, tax-declarable entity.

Such stunts have been going on for the past decade, but the FBI only cracked their first major lottery laundering scheme in 1995, when they stopped a fugitive from collecting $1.9 million from the Massachusetts lottery.

In July 1991, Michael Linskey's ship came in, bringing him a $14.3 million jackpot in the state's Mass Millions game. A few days later he sold half his winnings to a syndicate led by James "Whitey" Bulger. Brother of Massachusetts state senator William Bulger and leader of Boston's so-called Winter Hill Gang, Whitey had apparently joined forces with the Patriarca crime family run by "Cadillac Frank" Salemme, uniting New England's Italian and Irish underworld. Indicted in 1994 on federal racketeering charges, Whitey promptly went on the lam. So did Cadillac Frank, though he was soon arrested in Florida, thanks to tips from viewers who recognized him from the show "America's Most Wanted." To get at Whitey, the FBI went after his lottery winnings. Three days before he would have been eligible to collect his annual installment, they filed a seizure warrant with the Massachusetts Lottery Commission.

Casinos, racetracks, and lotteries offer variations on Meyer Lansky's legacy to the money laundering industry. He instinctively understood, and helped to nurture, the natural coalition between organized crime and licensed gambling. Lansky was, after all, the man who once said, "There is no such thing as a lucky gambler. There are just winners and losers. And the winners are those who control the game."

One man who controlled the game for a very long time was Nicholas Deak, once the uncrowned laundry king of the nonbank financial operators. In 1953, the 48-year-old refugee from Hungary helped his pal Kermit Roosevelt launder money for the CIA when it wanted to finance the overthrow of Iran's Mossadegh regime and reinstate the Shah. The empire he subsequently built, Deak and Company, was for a time America's largest retail foreign-exchange and precious-metals broker. The holding company's subsidiary, Deak-Perera, was America's foremost retail currency and gold trader.

In 1984, President Reagan's Commission on Organized Crime added another feather to Deak's cap, naming the company one of the biggest money laundering sinks of all time. In its report, "The Cash Connection," the commission detailed the extent of Deak's laundry services. For instance, on October 5, 1981, Humberto Orozco and brother Eduardo — professional drug-money launderers — walked into Deak-Perera's office in downtown Manhattan carrying 233 pounds of cash stuffed into cardboard boxes. It took the staff there most of the day to verify the total of $3,405,230. At the brothers' instructions, the money was deposited into Deak account 3552, held in the name of Dual International (Interdual). Over the next two weeks, Orozco made four more cash deposits, putting $3,892,889 into the 3552 account. Before the month was out, he had topped it up with another $3.3 million.

When the brothers were finally arrested, investigators established they'd systematically used eleven banks throughout New York to launder $151 million. Between November 1980 and March 1982, they'd washed nearly two-thirds of their stake, close to $100 million, through 232 unreported deposits at Deak-Perera.

The absence of any serious money laundering laws allowed Deak to construct his sink, and though that is a defect that has since been corrected, there are still enough loopholes in the laws to drive a cash-laden armored car through. And because the bad guys these days tend to have more money than the good guys, exploiting loopholes is a productive business.

Today's nonbank battlegrounds are in the securities and commodities markets. Under the banner of "Operation Eldorado," a joint task force, created in 1992 and consisting of agents from U.S. Customs and the IRS, is probing Wall Street to determine whether brokers have willfully invested drug profits or otherwise engaged in transactions to conceal the source and ownership of dirty money. Word came out in September 1994 that several Wall Street firms were under investigation, and that clients' accounts had been examined at Merrill Lynch, Dean Witter Discover, Bear Sterns, Prudential Securities, and Paine Webber. A specific area of interest appeared to be brokers' business in offshore havens, among them Panama. In March 1993, two Merrill Lynch brokers working out of the company's office there were indicted for money laundering by a federal grand jury in Tampa, Florida.

Federal interest in Wall Street may be new, but the fundamentals of the game have been around for centuries.

4

A TALE OF TWO BANKS

"Because banks is where the money is."
— Legendary bank robber Willie Sutton

Roberto Calvi, a 62-year-old Italian with mournful eyes and a distinctive black mustache, was found hanging under Blackfriars Bridge in London on June 18, 1982. At first glance, his death appeared to be suicide. Today, hardly anyone believes it was.

Known as "God's Banker" because of his close associations with the Vatican, Calvi had been chairman and president of the Milan-headquartered Banco Ambrosiano. Having started work there in a very junior position in 1946, he rose slowly through the ranks until the mid-1960s, when he met Sicilian financier Michele Sindona. Six years later — thanks to Sindona's encouragement, friends, and backing — Calvi was not just running the bank, he was well on his way to owning a good chunk of it.

Banco Ambrosiano soon became Italy's largest private banking group. But for a bank with that sort of prestige, it seemed odd that there were no offices in the City of London or on Wall Street. Instead, there were branches in the Bahamas, Luxembourg, and Nicaragua.

And all sorts of strange dealings were going on.

In June 1979, the Nicaragua branch loaned $9 million to Nordeurop, a Liechtenstein shell company set up by Calvi in the United States. Nordeurop sent the money to another Calvi-created shell, this one in Panama, where it was recorded as a fee. No proper explanations for the movement of this money have ever been located. There was no paperwork to support the original loan, and no paperwork to substantiate the payment of a fee. By May 1982, the newspapers reported that $1.3 billion of the bank's money was unaccounted for. Three weeks later, Calvi was dead.

The mystery surrounding his death unquestionably revolves around that missing money, much of which turns out to have been washed through shell companies registered in Panama and Liechtenstein — shell companies that had affiliations, direct or otherwise, with the Vatican's private bank.

The Istituto per le Opere di Religione, which translates literally as the Institute for the Works of Religion and is usually referred to as the IOR, functioned as an offshore merchant bank in the heart of Rome. The Vatican was its principal client. By design, the bank's directors were never answerable to anyone outside the hierarchy of the Roman Catholic Church. Suitably beyond the reach of Italian banking authorities, the IOR could send currency anywhere in the world without contravening any currency control laws. For Calvi, who needed to fund the web of shell companies he was establishing around the globe, the IOR was a perfect sink.

To cement the relationship, he brought the IOR in as his partner on several offshore deals. One of them was Cisalpine, Banco Ambrosiano's subsidiary in the Bahamas. The chairman of the IOR sat next to Calvi on Cisalpine's board. Together they used that bank to loan each other money, creating an elaborately tangled paper trail. By 1978, the IOR reportedly had $114 million on deposit with Cisalpine, and Cisalpine — in other words, Calvi — had $236 million on deposit with the IOR.

The chairman of the IOR in those days was the athletic, American-born Archbishop Paul Marcinkus. Michele Sindona had been influential in his appointment to the bank. Marcinkus later claimed no knowledge of Calvi's machinations and maintained that the IOR was the real victim, having lost a fortune when it was naively lured into an elaborate fraud, enticed by Calvi's attractively high interest rates. Never admitted, but now known to be true, is that as a result of the Calvi-Marcinkus relationship the IOR skirted the brink of bankruptcy. When the Banco Ambrosiano scandal broke,

Marcinkus sequestered himself in his offices at St. Peter's, protected from questioning and prosecution by the immunity afforded to the Vatican City as a foreign state.

Another key figure was Tuscan businessman Licio Gelli. An admirer of Mussolini and Juan Peron, Gelli was grandmaster of the Masonic-like lodge Propaganda Due (P-2), a secret Italian society, among whose members were cabinet officers, leading parliamentarians, financiers, high-ranking military officers, the heads of all three secret services, and the nation's most influential jurists. Not surprisingly, it functioned very much as a parallel government, wielding real influence and enormous power. It has since been revealed that P-2 received financial support from various factions of organized crime in Italy and that these monies were laundered through Switzerland by Gelli. He knew Swiss banking well, having spent much of his life in the murky world of illicit arms dealing. When the Banco Ambrosiano scandal broke, he fled the country, was arrested in Switzerland, bribed his way out, and spent the next five years hiding in South America, where he had heavyweight contacts, especially in Argentina.

A third player was Calvi's mentor, Sindona. Born in 1920, he was generally considered to be one of the wealthiest, most important businessmen in Italy. Fond of saying, "Money launderers bridge the gap between the underworld and the rest of society," he claimed to be worth $500 million. A devotee of Mussolini and Machiavelli, he advised Pope Paul VI on financial matters — which accounted for his nickname, "The Pope's Banker" — controlled half a dozen banks in four countries, owned the CIGA hotel chain, and controlled nearly five hundred other corporations. One of his companies, Moneyrex, ran a currency brokerage in Milan that was a major conduit for Mafia money laundering. Another, ironically, for a money launderer, owned the Watergate complex in Washington.

Sindona's financial muscle was such that he was the predominant force on the Milan stock exchange and could hold it for ransom. Less visibly, he was Gelli's partner in P-2, and the Mafia's foremost financial *consigliare*. In 1980, Sindona had been convicted by an American court for fraud and perjury and sentenced to twenty-five years for having used $15 million of misappropriated funds to buy shares in two American banks illegally — one of which, Franklin National, had crashed spectacularly in 1974. Coinciding with that bankruptcy, Finabank, a private bank in Geneva, also had gone under. The bank had been a funnel for Mafia and P-2 funds earmarked for the United States, and Sindona had maintained a numbered account in it code-named MANI-1125. His cosignatory was the IOR.

When Banco Ambrosiano erupted, Sindona was in prison in the States. Two years later he was extradited to Italy to face fraud charges and sent to prison there. In 1986, the man who knew where all the skeletons were buried was found dead on the floor of his cell. Someone had laced his coffee with cyanide.

Sindona taught Calvi the ins and outs of laundering money through offshore companies. Quick study that he was, Calvi formed several offshore shells over the years, using many of them in his deals with Marcinkus and the IOR. They supported Banco Ambrosiano's share price, bought companies with questionably exported lire, and, with or without Marcinkus, defrauded Banco Ambrosiano's investors.

When the Italian parliament passed a law in 1976 that made it a criminal offense to export lire illegally — until then, it had only been a civil offense — Calvi faced a massive investigation into the way he'd been using the bank's funds. To cover his tracks, he devised a restructuring scheme that increased Banco Ambrosiano's share capital 50 percent. But to pull it off, and at the same time underpin the bank's precarious share price on the Milan exchange, he'd had to bring funds into Italy from those shell companies. Frantically juggling his assets, he moved money in and out of shells to create the aura of stability. But his timing was off and his creditors were nervous. Worse still, his luck had run out.

In June 1980, one of Banco Ambrosiano's biggest clients, a leading Italian construction company, went bankrupt, putting a huge dent in Calvi's treasury. In January 1981, the government clamped down on all Italian banks owning nonbank foreign holding companies. Three months later, the Milan stock exchange changed the dealing rules for Banco Ambrosiano. Previously, its shares had been traded only weekly, over the counter. The exchange ordered that they now be traded daily, and on the main floor. Calvi could no longer support his own shares. The following month, Calvi was arrested for illegal currency transactions.

Many people expected Banco Ambrosiano to go down with him, yet it somehow managed to stay in business. One very good reason might have been that Marcinkus was handing out letters on IOR stationery confirming that his bank was the beneficial owner of eleven shell companies registered in Panama and Liechtenstein, which were now holding Banco Ambrosiano shares and assets. Suddenly it appeared as if the IOR were covering Calvi's debts.

Calvi hoped to salvage the situation. On bail at the time and awaiting an appeal hearing, he managed to persuade the entrepreneur Carlo de Benedetti into both becoming deputy chairman and purchasing 2 percent of the bank's shares. But de Benedetti, who'd been chairman of the Olivetti office equipment group, resigned after three months because he couldn't get past the bureaucratic brick walls Calvi built to protect his own fraudulent activities. De Benedetti later claimed he received phone calls at home threatening his life if he maintained a presence at the bank.

For the rest of 1981, the pressures on Calvi became intolerable. The Bank of Italy was closing in on him. Utterly desperate by early 1982, Calvi turned to Marcinkus, asking him to confirm that the IOR was indeed responsible for those shell companies and therefore would back Banco Ambrosiano's outstanding loans. Now Marcinkus refused. The Vatican was on his case about money missing from the IOR. Various "guestimates" put the total anywhere from $100 million to $500 million. So Marcinkus gave Calvi until June 30, 1982, to pay it back. When Calvi realized he couldn't meet the deadline, he begged for more time. Marcinkus said no.

That's when it was discovered that Banco Ambrosiano had a gaping $1.3-billion hole right through its middle.

Marcinkus would later conveniently produce a secret letter, claiming it had been signed by Calvi, absolving the IOR from any debts incurred by those eleven shell companies. He used this letter as the basis for his argument that the IOR had no financial obligations whatsoever in the Banco Ambrosiano bankruptcy. The liquidators and the Italian banking authorities weren't as sure, and although

Marcinkus never gave evidence about the affair, the Vatican did eventually agree to pay a relatively minor settlement.

Intriguingly, the authorities soon uncovered evidence that Calvi had paid more than $100 million to Licio Gelli and to one of his henchmen, Umberto Ortolani. Those funds were washed by Banco Ambrosiano through the complex web of Calvi shells, and at least some of it wound up in a secret account controlled by Gelli on the Caribbean island of St. Vincent. This money was sent, according to the Italian authorities, "without any commercial justification."

Yet there might well have been a very good reason: Calvi's health. It's known he'd been paying Gelli and the P-2 — and therefore the Mafia — since 1975 to protect him from the Italian authorities. He apparently laundered as much as $10 million just to hand out as bribes. But he obviously didn't get what he was paying for because some people now viewed him as a liability. And as he grew increasingly desperate, he also became increasingly dangerous. He left Italy on Friday, June 11, 1982, with his briefcase, going first to Austria, then to London. On the following Monday, Banco Ambrosiano's shares crashed. On Wednesday, the bank's board was dissolved. On Friday, Calvi was dead.

Rumor has it that Calvi was murdered for the contents of his briefcase. There is a strong suspicion, shared by some of the people with inside knowledge of the saga, that Calvi came to London to meet with certain bankers in the hopes of blackmailing them into bolstering his bank. To convince them he was serious, he'd brought with him documents showing how those particular bankers had knowingly laundered money for Licio Gelli. Calvi's papers apparently proved the money had been washed through the heart of the British capital and then used by Gelli, who was at the time acting for the Argentineans, to buy Exocet missiles, which were fired at British forces during the Falklands War.

Banco Ambrosiano was the greatest banking collapse in Europe since the end of World War II. It was shortly to be followed by the greatest banking collapse in the history of banking.

In 1988, the Justice Department launched Operation C-Chase, the letter *C* standing for *currency*. Posing as drug dealers, undercover agents put out the bait that they had loads of currency to launder. And BCCI fell for it.

A costly and complicated five-year operation — involving agents from Customs, the IRS, the DEA, and the FBI — C-Chase produced more than twelve hundred conversations and nearly four hundred hours of clandestinely recorded videotape. By assisting drug dealers to wash $34 million, the Justice Department was able to indict, and in 1990 to convict, several BCCI bankers and dozens of other individuals. In one blow, the Americans had unknowingly pulled the bottom out from under a gargantuan house of cards.

The man who built that house was Agha Hasan Abedi. Born in 1922 in Lucknow, India, heart of the former Mughal Empire, Abedi always claimed to be the son of a wealthy landowner. And he might well have been, but most of what Abedi said over the years wasn't true. He was, however, president of Pakistan's United Bank Limited from 1959 to 1972, when Pakistan nationalized its banking industry. Abedi, who had spent those years building up a network of wealthy Arab clients and friends, now appealed directly to them, and with their deep pockets started his own bank, initially capitalized at $2.5 million.

Abedi's main backer was Sheikh Zayed Bin Sultan Al-Nahayan, ruler of Abu Dhabi and president of the United Arab Emirates. Also behind Abedi were various members of the Saudi royal family, as well as officials from the Bank of America, then the largest bank in the world. Bringing the Bank of America on board was an enormous coup because it gave Abedi's venture instant credibility. Needless to say, he shamelessly capitalized on the association. When the Bank of America finally got wise to him and pulled out in 1980, Abedi was coolheaded enough to play it down so that at least some people actually believed he was the one who ended the marriage.

His skill in setting up what he claimed would be the first multi-national bank for the Third World was astounding. To begin with, he deliberately registered the holding company in Luxembourg so that he could hide behind the Grand Duchy's strict banking secrecy codes. A year later, Abedi opened BCCI branches in four Gulf states and in Asian neighborhoods in several British cities. Then, in 1975, he registered the bank in the Cayman Islands, but moved his top management to London, where the Bank of England gave BCCI additional credibility by awarding it a sound bill of health every year for the next fifteen years.

As set out by Parliament, the Bank of England authorizes and oversees all banking activities in the United Kingdom. To make certain that everyone complies with the rules, it sends accountants into banks to spot irregularities. It is therefore the direct responsibility of the Governors of the Bank of England to avoid a crisis by ensuring that all irregularities are properly dealt with. If, on the other hand, a bank operating in the United Kingdom can convince a Bank of England accountant that it is doing business by the book, that's the end of the matter until the next audit.

Until a few years ago there were two types of banks in the United Kingdom. There were full-status banks, which, having complied with a set of very orthodox requirements, were empowered by the Bank of England to offer a complete range of financial services. And there were Licensed Deposit Takers — smaller banks offering a limited range of services. The public often confused them as being much the same thing. In reality, authorized banks were the genuine article and Licensed Deposit Takers were not, because they were not supervised as thoroughly and did not enjoy the full confidence of the Bank of England. BCCI was a Licensed Deposit Taker.

By 1977, Abedi was bragging that BCCI was the world's fastest-growing bank, with 146 branches in thirty-two countries and total assets of $2.2 billion. Although he had forty-five offices in the United Kingdom, the grand prize, as Abedi saw it, was a banking network in America. To help him get that, he had turned to Jimmy Carter's friend, and slightly disgraced former budget director, Bert Lance. Initially, Abedi hired Lance as a BCCI consultant. Shortly thereafter, when Lance needed to sell his shares in a Georgia bank, Abedi came up with a willing buyer named Gaith Pharaon, a Saudi businessman whose father had once been a court physician in Riyadh. Pharaon fancied himself a young Khashoggi and tried to do flashy deals throughout the West. Some of them went right. Many of them didn't. Still, when Abedi needed a front man, Pharaon was always available.

Abedi also helped Lance pay back a $3.4-million loan. Such kindness gave Abedi access to Carter, whom he proudly declared to be one of his closest friends. While Carter has, these days, tried to explain away the relationship in a very different vein, there's no denying that Abedi was generous in his support of Carter's pet charity, Global 2000, and of the Carter Presidential Center in Atlanta.

Three years after his initial foray into the United States, Abedi expanded into Panama, where General Noriega soon became one of his largest clients. A year later, Abu Nidal, the Middle Eastern terrorist, began channeling funds through BCCI. Nidal was soon followed by members of the Medellín cartel. By 1988, Abedi controlled 417 branches in seventy-three countries and reported assets of $20 billion. And, all this time, the Bank of England maintained that everything was just dandy.

Clearly, it had somehow missed a few vital points.

Under the provisions of the act that established Licensed Deposit Takers, BCCI should never have been allowed to use the word *bank* in its name. Next, when BCCI attempted to buy the Chelsea National Bank in New York in 1976, state regulators weren't happy with what they saw and refused to approve the deal. An affidavit lodged in a U.S. court in 1978 showed that Bank of America, then holding a 30-percent share in BCCI, wasn't pleased with the way Abedi's managers were lending money. The Bank of England was aware of all this, but apparently didn't feel that any of it should affect BCCI's status in the United Kingdom. To give the Bank of England some credit in 1980, it did refuse a BCCI petition for full status. In 1985, when banking regulators in Luxembourg tried to get the Bank of England to assume full responsibility for BCCI, the Governors flatly refused. It was about this time the Bank of England received an anonymous letter outlining massive fraud at BCCI, but it took no formal action.

It was also around this time that BCCI's treasury posted such huge losses from its irregular practices that Abedi became desperate to find fresh cash, and turned to Latin America. He'd already opened an outpost in Colombia. Now he added seven branches, five in Medellín alone, and increased his assets there to over $200 million. It's hardly surprising the Medellín offices were awash with cash. One of their major depositors was José Gonzalo Rodriguez Gocha, known even in those days as a cartel kingpin. Establishing an important presence in Colombia was a logical extension of BCCI's corporate culture. Abedi exerted such severe pressure on his employees to bring in deposits, putting their jobs and lifestyles on the line, that no one much cared where those deposits were coming from.

BCCI Miami was another noteworthy base, constantly accepting cash deposits in excess of $10,000 and then not reporting them to the IRS. In some cases, the bank's private jets would fly the cash to branches in Panama or the Caymans, deposit it there, then wire it to BCCI in Luxembourg, where it disappeared. In other cases, to get around reporting regulations, large cash deposits in Miami were receipted as if they'd been deposited at BCCI Bahamas — this at a time when BCCI did not even have a bank in the Bahamas.

On the heels of the Bank of Boston affair in 1985, BCCI shifted a lot of its laundry work to Canada. Abedi also opened extensive networks in the United Arab Emirates (UAE) and in Hong Kong. He explained BCCI's success by saying that he'd found small, lucrative niches that other banks weren't willing to exploit. Many thought he was talking about foreign exchange dealing. But the UAE operation was put in place to serve drug traffickers who dealt in heroin from the Golden Crescent, and the Hong Kong operation catered to the Golden Triangle crowd. BCCI also did remarkably lucrative business in Nigeria, despite the world oil glut that had depressed the local economy, and became the most important sink for the massive heroin trade being developed in black Africa. Knowing his clients, Abedi quickly expanded BCCI's operations throughout the Caribbean — opening branches in marijuana-rich Jamaica, Barbados, Curaçao, and Trinidad, and finally the Bahamas — where he also set up strings of shell companies to facilitate the movement of dirty money.

But the faster he opened banks, the faster leaks started to spring. In 1986, Abedi stole $150 million from a staff pension fund to plug holes in his balance sheet. Now, fearful that the Bank of England was on to him, he decided to take the treasury out of Britain. International banking supervisors in Basle had by this time examined how Abedi was managing his assets, and duly reported their concerns. Yet the Bank of England's auditors still did not cotton to what Abedi was doing and categorically failed to uncover any fraudulent practices at BCCI. And so the Governors approved Abedi's request to move the treasury to the sanctuary of Abu Dhabi.

The following year, auditors Ernst & Young reviewed the books of the holding company and informed Abedi that they were worried about "excessive management power" and serious weaknesses in BCCI's systems and controls. Meanwhile, in Basel, those bank supervisors were so unhappy with BCCI they forced Abedi to appoint one auditor — for the entire international network. Then came the indictments in Florida. BCCI was fined $15.3 million for its money laundering activities. Despite Abedi's insistence that this was an isolated incident, official investigations were launched in Canada, France, Luxembourg, Brazil, Singapore, Bermuda, the Caymans, Cyprus, and even Nigeria. Several of these investigations involved currency control violations, and a number of them uncovered evidence of more sinister endeavors.

At the Bank of England, the Governors were handed two reports — one from the City of London Fraud Squad, the other from a Middle Eastern accountant, both of which indicated fraudulent practices at BCCI. Nothing was done about either report.

It wasn't until 1989, after the Governors were shown a Price Waterhouse audit revealing a series of false and deceitful practices, that they finally took action. Too little, too late. The Governors merely approved a bailout scheme that had been proposed by BCCI investors in Abu Dhabi who claimed they were ready to save the bank from total collapse. And in spite of the incontestable discovery of fraud, no official inquiry was ever requested by the Bank of England.

In the States, one investigation went back ten years, to the time when BCCI was romancing Bert Lance and owned Financial General Bankshares, a financial holding company in Washington, D.C. Under American law, anyone controlling more than 5 percent of the shares in a public company must file a disclosure form with the Securities and Exchange Commission, but Abedi thought he'd found a way around the law. He'd convinced a group of BCCI clients to each buy less than 5 percent. When the SEC ultimately figured out what was happening, it filed suit against eleven people, including Abedi.

Faced with the prospect of going to jail, the defendants worked out a deal, part of which gave them the right to make a tender offer to all of Financial General's shareholders.

The takeover took several years, and when it was finally completed in 1982, Financial General was renamed First American Bankshares, a new entity totally independent of BCCI. The Americans demanded this because the Office of the Comptroller of the Currency didn't trust BCCI, and said as much in a letter to the Federal Reserve Bank. The exact wording was, "BCCI is not subject to regulation and supervision on a consolidated basis by a single bank-supervisory authority." In other words, they weren't about to permit a rogue like BCCI to run a bank in the United States.

Nonetheless, the National Bank of Georgia and the Independence Bank of Encino, California, both supposedly owned by Pharaon, had been surreptitiously funded by Abedi through a $500-million loan from BCCI. As collateral, Pharaon had signed over the shares of the two banks. And although Abedi later arranged for First American Bankshares to buy the National Bank of Georgia, he had effectively, albeit illegally, gained control of three U.S. banks.

Being a staunch believer in the doctrine that "credibility is contagious," Abedi and his cronies installed prominent Americans on First American's board. Clark Clifford, an elder statesman who'd served as an adviser to or was a personal friend of almost every president since Harry Truman, and one of the most respected attorneys in Washington, was named chairman. His law partner and protegé Robert Altman, who was married to TV's "Wonder Woman," Lynda Carter, became the bank's president.

By the time C-Chase indicted BCCI in 1988, the dossier on Abedi had become pretty weighty. Senator John Kerry had already opened subcommittee hearings on BCCI and its relationship with Manuel Noriega. Under oath, a pair of convicted drug dealers claimed they'd laundered funds through BCCI in Panama, and that their introduction to the bank had come from Noriega himself. Further Senate inquiry revealed that Noriega had used BCCI since 1982 to wash millions of dollars.

New York County District Attorney Robert Morgenthau had also taken an interest in BCCI's activities, specifically in Abedi's

manipulation of First American. Already in his seventies, Morgenthau's half-century of legal experience, including more than thirty
years as a prosecutor, had produced sharply honed instincts where financial crime is concerned. An authentic hero and a major political
force in New York since the days when Jack Kennedy asked him to
serve as the U.S. Attorney there, it was Morgenthau who went after
the local Mafia, winning convictions against fifty-two members of
the Luchese, Bonanno, Gambino, and Genovese families. It was
Morgenthau who brought indictments against Roy Cohn, Joseph
McCarthy's partner in the Communist witch hunts of the early
1950s. And it was Morgenthau who attempted to shut the door on
Americans hiding funds in Swiss bank accounts.

Because First American had branches in New York, Morgenthau claimed jurisdiction. On several occasions, attorneys and investigators from his office traveled to London, hoping for assistance from
the Bank of England. And for the most part, they were turned down.

Undaunted by either the Bank of England's obtrusive attitude,
or the lethargy displayed by U.S. federal prosecutors, Morgenthau took
aim with his biggest guns. Knowing that the best way to nab white-
collar bad guys is "to follow the money," he and his brilliant assistant
John Moscow relentlessly went after Abedi and everyone involved
with the takeover of First American, including Clifford and Altman.

By March 1990, the Governors at the Bank of England had
their eyes forced open by the British intelligence services, which had
produced evidence that Abu Nidal was among the many dubious account holders at BCCI, and that he held no fewer than forty-two accounts at branches around London. Eight months later, a report to
the Governors compiled from private files seized from Abedi's right-
hand man, BCCI's chief executive Swaleh Naqvi, detailed extensive
fraud throughout the bank. Among the practices outlined by the
Naqvi files were diverted deposits, phantom loans to Abedi's friends,
and totally fictitious loans laundered through other banks to obliter-
ate the money trail. Two months after that, in January 1991, the Governors were informed that BCCI had amassed some $600 million in
unrecorded deposits. On March 4, 1991, almost as if they had run
out of excuses at last, the Governors ordered an audit of the bank,
using the independent accounting firm of Price Waterhouse. It was

only when that report was finished in July that the Governors shut down BCCI.

Back in New York, Morgenthau and Moscow had indicted several people, among them Clifford, Altman, Abedi, and Naqvi. The first two were ordered to stand trial, although the case against them subsequently petered out. The second two became the subject of extradition warrants. A separate warrant was issued for Gaith Pharaon. Among other things, they wanted him to explain his dealings in the failed Florida savings and loan CenTrust.

It seems that in 1989, when Abedi realized First American was not properly situated to expand his money laundering activities in Miami, he'd conspired with Pharaon to buy CenTrust. So the prosecutors allege. Pharaon secretly acquired 5 percent of CenTrust on behalf of BCCI. By the time federal banking regulators closed down CenTrust, Abedi and/or Pharaon and/or BCCI owned, and never declared, at least 28 percent of it. The government claimed Abedi and Pharaon used CenTrust not only to launder BCCI funds but to funnel various political donations through CenTrust, mainly to Democratic campaign funds, including a $50,000 gift from Pharaon to the Carter Presidential Center.

In May 1994, Abedi's number two man at BCCI, Swaleh Naqvi, was extradited to the United States from Abu Dhabi. A month later, a court in Abu Dhabi convicted twelve BCCI officials in absentia. Naqvi was sentenced to fourteen years in jail. Abedi, who by that time was bedridden in Pakistan, was sentenced to eight years.

With very little left to gain, Naqvi pleaded guilty in America to conspiracy, wire fraud, and racketeering charges. He was sentenced to eleven years in prison and ordered to pay $255 million. Pharaon's assets in the States, valued at more than $37 million, were frozen. Although the Pakistani government never formally replied to the U.S. application for Abedi's extradition, the chief minister of the Sindh province, where Abedi was living, repeatedly told inquiring journalists that he would never consider such a request.

It became a moot point when Agha Hassan Abedi died in Karachi in August 1995. He was 73.

*   *   *

With as much as $9.5 billion believed to be missing worldwide from BCCI's books, seven times more than disappeared into Banco Ambrosiano, it would be unfair to say that there was just one culprit. It took a lot of people a lot of time, and a lot of people to turn a blind eye, for that much money to disappear. It's true the CIA had amassed damning information about Abedi and BCCI that should have been passed along to other federal agencies, and wasn't. It's also true that various U.S. law enforcement agencies made bad decisions, which delayed any direct action against BCCI. But if only one damning finger is to be pointed, it must be at the Bank of England.

A House of Commons Treasury and Civil Service Select Committee felt that as the supervisor of BCCI, the Bank had to accept responsibility for its failure. The committee concluded that the Bank could have prevented the fiasco had it not been party to a tragedy of errors, misunderstandings, and failures of communication. In his 1992 report to Parliament, *Inquiry into the Supervision of the Bank of Credit and Commerce International,* Lord Justice Bingham wrote, "The Bank of England failed to discharge its supervisory duties in respect of BCCI."

By virtue of their mandate from Parliament, the Bank of England could have taken appropriate action to correct inefficient or unsatisfactory practices. Where money laundering is concerned, the Bank of England must meet the same conditions as all other banks. It seems reasonable to conclude, therefore, that if the Governors knew BCCI was laundering dirty money, they were clearly delinquent and in violation of the law. If they didn't know, they were incompetent, because it was their obligation to know.

Yet the Governors have arrogantly maintained that the Bank of England did nothing wrong. Facing a Select Committee of Parliament, the then-Governor of the Bank of England, Robyn Leigh-Pemberton, made the astonishing statement, "If we closed down a bank every time we found an incidence of fraud, we would have rather fewer banks than we do at the moment."

One would have thought that was exactly what he was supposed to do.

In the end, BCCI unraveled not because the Bank of England

was doing its job, or even because Abedi had been so greedy for so long. It fell apart because Robert Morgenthau and John Moscow wouldn't be placated.

Since BCCI's closure on July 5, 1991, banking authorities around the world have tried to jam plastic wood into the holes that permitted such a thing. There are those who believe the full facts will never be known. The most interesting of blanks in the Bingham Report come in Appendix 8, headed "The Intelligence Services."

The role of the intelligence services in the BCCI debacle will not be revealed in Britain for at least thirty years, if ever, although it should eventually come to light in the United States, thanks to the Freedom of Information Act. When it does, both the American and British intelligence services are expected to have a lot of questions to answer.

One of them is, Why did the U.K. security services insist that the Bank of England delay closure of BCCI for perhaps as long as fifteen months?

Another is, Why did the Bank of England comply?

Both answers lie in the fact that BCCI had a working relationship with Saddam Hussein. The National Security Council used BCCI to launder funds for the Iran-Contra affair. The CIA maintained accounts with BCCI in order to wash money destined for Afghan rebels. The Defense Intelligence Agency also kept a slush fund with BCCI. One of Abedi's front men in the United States was Kamal Adham, the former chief of Saudi intelligence, who was allowed to pay a $105-million fine to avoid a jail sentence. Through him, it has been suggested, the British M.I.6 found BCCI to be a convenient channel as well. It is known that BCCI was involved in the transfer of North Korean Scud-B missiles to Syria. It is known that BCCI helped to broker and then to finance the sale of Chinese Silkworm missiles to Saudi Arabia. And it is known that BCCI acted as middleman when the Saudis needed Israeli guidance systems for those missiles.

Whether or not the Bank of England was doing the bidding of the intelligence services a) to protect an ongoing intelligence operation, b) to allow the intelligence services time to cover themselves, or

c) both, people living in a democracy have an inalienable right to know what is being done in their name and why.

Appendix 8 is guaranteed to make interesting reading. But because the red faces that would result are certainly not confined to the Board of Governors at the Bank of England, the public may not be permitted to see it for a very long time. What's more, there's no reason to believe that the lessons of BCCI have been learned by any of the banking regulatory bodies around the world. Although there's little doubt that the lessons of BCCI have been learned by those bankers who are running more modest versions of BCCI.

5

FUNNY MONEY

"'Funny money' is a highly sophisticated, logically alternative economic system used by a long list of international criminals, tax evaders, drug traffickers, arms dealers, terrorists, and governments. The difficulty is often to decide which is which."
— **Former British Fraud Squad detective Rowan Bosworth-Davies**

When he raped Kuwait, Saddam Hussein ordered his soldiers to commandeer whatever automobiles they could drive away. A few of the more expensive cars — Rolls Royces, Mercedes, Lamborghinis, Porsches, BMWs, and Ferraris — were given to Ba'ath Party officials as a gift from Saddam, or appropriated for use by the government. When he visited Baghdad during the Gulf Crisis, former British prime minister Edward Heath was chauffeured about in a stolen Kuwaiti Mercedes. However, fifty of the choicest cars, including an armor-plated Mercedes and an armor-plated BMW, were driven from Baghdad to Amman, then flown to Geneva by Royal Jordanian Airline cargo planes under the protection accorded diplomatic shipments. Once in Switzerland, they were put on the market and, within hours of their arrival, turned into cash.

Months after their country was liberated, the Kuwaitis discovered what they'd always suspected — that the Iraqis had stormed across the border with shopping lists. Not only had they come looking for cars, but had pillaged following a very elaborate, predetermined agenda. They were under orders to plunder machinery, the contents of entire factories, computers, construction cranes, plus parts and supplies from ports and airports. They were told to steal two hundred thousand books from the Central Library in Kuwait City, as well as books, furniture, and even blackboards from schools. They had instructions to take hospital fixtures and furnishings and every piece of medical equipment they could find. They were directed to drive away with thirty-five hundred school buses and most of the nation's public transport system.

One obvious Iraqi target was Kuwait's central bank, whose gold and currency Saddam looted. After the war, however, he was forced to repatriate all of that money because the exact amount of the bank's reserves was known. But the invading army also raided private homes and offices — tens of thousands of them — pilfering a fortune in cash and jewels, and none of that was ever returned. Some of the ransacked gold was melted down and sold by Saddam in the amenable markets of Yemen, the Sudan, and Mauritania. Most of the jewels were broken up and sold in the *souks*. The cash is still being used to pay the hordes of smugglers from Iran and Turkey who have successfully broken the embargo ever since it was imposed.

Although incidental shipments of Iraqi oil continued to turn up in Turkey and Jordan, in direct violation of the boycott, the country's primary source of revenue was cut off. It is believed that without his oil income, Saddam fed his people with those Kuwaiti assets, managing to launder enough money to keep the country alive. It has been established, for instance, that to soak up whatever precious metals or stones appeared in Baghdad after the Gulf War, Saddam merely printed more bank notes. The inflationary effect on the economy was of little significance as far as he was concerned because he needed those Kuwaiti assets to survive the coalition embargo. Still, the money he stole from Kuwait is small potatoes compared with the money he's systematically stolen, and successfully laundered, from his own country.

In June 1972, Iraq nationalized its petroleum interests. Saddam, who was then deputy president, convinced the ruling Revolutionary Council that the commissions they'd been paying to Westerners under long-standing agreements should instead go to the Ba'ath Party. So he took a page out of the life of Calouste Sarkis Gulbenkian.

A Turk of Armenian descent, Gulbenkian was the power be-

hind the founding of what came to be known as the Iraqi Petroleum
Company. For his efforts, he laid claim to a royalty on every drop of
its oil. His fee gave birth to his nickname, Mr. Five-Percent. When he
died in Lisbon in 1955, the royalty was passed on to his son Nubar.
Some seventeen years later, Saddam confiscated Nubar's 5 percent in
the name of the Ba'ath Party. Saddam personally assumed joint custody of the funds, sharing signature authority with Defense Minister
Adnan Khairallah and Petroleum Minister Adnan Hamdani.

According to a document some claim represents a true accounting of those funds, $51 million was deposited in a major Swiss bank
in Geneva in 1972. With interest, the balance in the account climbed
to $92 million the following year and, as the price of oil quadrupled
during the Yom Kippur War, to $327 million in 1974. By the time
the Iran-Iraq war broke out, with Saddam firmly in control of the
country, the account held in excess of $1.69 billion. Today, it is reliably
believed that Saddam controls funds worth in excess of $32 billion.

As his power base has always been his grip on the nation's only
political organization — he and the Ba'ath Party are for all intents
and purposes one and the same — Saddam has used some of this
money to buy continued reverence. He pays handsomely for loyalty.
And on those occasions when devotion has proved less than unqual-
ified, he's stopped writing checks and started having people killed. In
1979, he ordered the execution of his old friend and cosignatory Adnan Hamdani. Ten years later, his pal Adnan Khairallah died in a mysterious helicopter crash. The full extent of Saddam's early interests in
Swiss banking went with them to their graves.

Some of the money has also been spent on whims and fancies.
When the Empress Faradiba, wife of the late Shah of Iran, sold a few
of her jewels, Saddam pulled $352 million out of Switzerland to buy
them for his wife. Faradiba denies it, for obvious reasons. But two
sources, both reliable and both independent of the other, confirm
the story.

For the most part, though, Saddam has converted the 5 percent
into a giant safety net for himself, his family, and his closest Ba'ath
Party associates. To protect his nest egg, he's moved a lot of the
money out of Geneva, washing it through a network of companies
he's set up around the world. One of them, Montana Management,

a holding company registered in Panama, is controlled by Midco Financial, a Geneva shell. In 1981, Midco, through Montana, began buying into the French broadcasting and publishing conglomerate Hachette SA. At one point Saddam is said to have owned as much as 8.4 percent of Hachette's shares.

Another Saddam company is Al-Arabi Trading, headquartered in Baghdad, which purchased a large stake in the British-based Technology and Development Group. In 1987, TDG bought a precision engineering firm called Matrix-Churchill. A few years later, U.K. Customs and Excise became aware of the connection, took a closer look at Matrix-Churchill, moved in on them, and wound up confiscating parts of an alleged supergun destined for Iraq.

The Americans also took a closer look at Saddam's dealings, and by April 1991, the U.S. Treasury's Office of Foreign Asset Control had identified fifty-two businesses and thirty-seven individuals with direct financial links to him and/or his Ba'ath Party. Of those fifty-two companies, twenty-four were in the United Kingdom, a number of them using the same address — 3 Mandeville Place in London's West End. Of the thirty-seven named individuals, a dozen also had addresses in Britain.

American sources quickly determined that "Saddam International Inc." was run by his half-brother Barazan al-Takriti. Officially Iraq's special ambassador-at-large, he lived for years in Switzerland, always protected by diplomatic status, where he is known regularly to have received currency, gold, and jewels by diplomatic pouch that he easily washed through Swiss banks. But his main contribution to Saddam's retirement fund was to have sought the best Western legal advice money could buy, and to have used that counsel to design a fabulously intricate laundromat. This is not about fifty-two companies and thirty-seven people supplying Iraq with superguns; this is about five hundred shell companies staffed by people paid handsomely to wash Saddam's money.

Intelligently and with enormous patience, Barazan spent the better part of two decades setting up a worldwide network of friendly businessmen, taking most of what had accumulated from the 5-percent royalty and bedding it down with them for safekeeping. Some are Iraqis, but most are Jordanians and Palestinians. The money is put in their name, and washed by Barazan via bank loans and investments. It then shows up on the books of legitimate businesses in Spain, France, Brazil, Indonesia, Hong Kong, Britain, and the United States.

Ultimately, the funds are administered by Barazan and so skillfully disguised that none of it can possibly be traced back to Saddam Hussein or the Ba'ath Party. Those friendly businessmen know whose money it is and are constantly reminded what the penalty would be should they ever claim it's theirs. When the Western allies seized Iraqi assets to punish Saddam for his foray into Kuwait, the lion's share of his money had long since been scrubbed clean, thanks entirely to Barazan and this network of docile custodians.

Perhaps Manuel Antonio Noriega should have taken lessons from Saddam Hussein.

In the early 1970s, as chief of Panama's military intelligence, Noriega discovered how to play both ends against the middle by turning himself into a CIA spy, a DEA informant, a staunch American ally, a Panamanian diplomat, and an international drug trafficker. He also dabbled in gun running, supplying arms to leftist guerrillas in El Salvador and right-wing guerrillas in Nicaragua. In his spare time, he became commander of the Panamanian Defense Forces, which made him de facto ruler of the country.

Unlike Saddam, he wasn't clever enough to become a major-league laundryman.

The heart of Panama's money laundering industry is the Colón Free Zone, a 500-acre site on the Atlantic end of the Panama Canal. Established in the 1950s, it is today the second-largest duty-free trading center in the world, after Hong Kong. Unhampered by government regulation, hundreds of ships carrying tens of thousands of containers move in and out of the Free Zone daily, carrying everything imaginable, from Japanese electronic goods, Scotch whiskey, and French perfumes to German precision widgets, American running shoes, and Colombian cocaine. Nearly $10 billion worth of duty-free goods are traded annually in the Free Zone. That's not counting narcotics — the 19 tons of cocaine stuffed inside containers of Brazilian tiles destined for Maryland, or the 5.2 tons of cocaine shipped to Miami, after being packaged in the Free Zone into 318 cases of coffee.

For years, Celeste International operated in the Free Zone without anyone knowing it was owned by the Cali cartel. In fact, the authorities only got wise to Celeste when they stumbled across a multiton shipment of cocaine sitting in a warehouse. Until then, Celeste had been issuing false invoices for consumer goods, against which it deposited tens of millions of drug dollars in Panamanian banks. Unfortunately, for every front the authorities discover, there may be ten or twenty or fifty they haven't yet heard about.

Under the terms of a 1904 treaty with the United States, the dollar is legal tender in Panama. In compliance with that treaty, whenever there is a shortfall in the supply, the U.S. Treasury ships dollars to the Panamanian National Bank, which acts exactly like a federal reserve for the local banking system. But it seems that cash transactions over the past few years in the Free Zone have been so enormous that the U.S. Treasury Department has demanded a formal investigation.

In one instance, twelve thousand U.S. money orders were shipped in a container from New York to Panama, where they were cashed by thirteen companies — mainly jewelry stores set up for the sole purpose of laundering these money orders — then deposited in accounts held at the Hongkong Bank of Panama. Mostly in the $500 to $700 range (staying well under the U.S. reporting limit), each canceled money order was stamped on the back with a tiny seal used by the Colombian cocaine cartels to help compliant banks identify the correct account to which the deposit should be credited. Once deposited, the money was wired back to the States to an account at the Marine Midland Bank of New York that had been opened by the drug traffickers who originally bought the money orders.

Although the Justice Department seized $7.7 million in New York, the amount probably only represented about 10 percent of the money these particular traffickers had laundered over a two-year period. And when U.S. agents handed their Panamanian counterparts detailed information on those thirteen local money laundering enterprises, the Panamanians said thank you, but did nothing.

Panama was the perfect stage for Noriega.

Born in 1934, he seized the reins of the government at the age of 39 and held on to them for five years. One of the traditional perks of high office in Panama is a cut of the various rackets that go on just beneath the surface of local officialdom, including regular handouts from all sorts of traffickers. Noriega was personally in touch with the Colombian cartels for several years. In the mid-1970s, he met and helped to protect Ramón Millan, a Miami accountant who shuffled money out of the States to Panama for drug baron Carlos Lehder Rivas. In 1979, along with Pablo Escobar and Jorge Ochoa, Lehder asked Millan to set up a deal with Torrijos. Noriega, who was then Torrijos's henchman, negotiated a standard protection racket contract, whereby the Panamanian government would safeguard Lehder's drug trafficking and money laundering in exchange for a slice of the action.

When Torrijos was killed in a July 1981 plane crash, command of the Guardia, the real power in Panama, passed to Florencio Florez. Florez was betrayed by Ruben Paredes. After unseating Paredes, Noriega renamed the Guardia the Panamanian Defense Forces (PDF), reassured his old pals at the CIA — who were reportedly paying him $200,000 a year — that he was still America's man, and picked up where Torrijos left off, banking Lehder's protection money. Then Noriega did Torrijos one better. He set up a series of well-hidden airstrips and allowed Lehder to transport cocaine bound for the United States. Noriega reportedly charged the cartel $500,000 per flight, representing 1 percent of the cargo's wholesale value. By the end of 1983, he was said to be pulling down $10 million a month.

The DEA came to Noriega concerned about drug trafficking and money laundering that might be coming through Panama. Noriega handed them Ramón Millan. Thanks to evidence provided by Noriega, Millan was convicted by a U.S. court and sentenced in 1983 to forty-three years. The DEA decided Noriega was their best friend. He reinforced the notion two years later when he ordered the closure of the First Interamericas Bank. A few of his Colombian chums had been a little too obvious this time. They weren't just using the bank to wash dirty money, they owned it outright. The majority shareholder was Gilberto Rodriguez Orejuela, head of the Cali cartel.

Also on the board were Rodriguez's brother, Miguel Angel Rodriguez Orejuela, and Edgar Alberto Garcia Montilla, the cartel's main financial adviser and the brains behind their international money laundering activities.

Shutting down First Interamericas might have endeared Noriega to the DEA, but it didn't do much for his relationship with the cartels. Insult was added to injury when Noriega ordered a raid on a drug lab he'd personally allowed the cartel to set up in Panama. The Colombians felt that for $10 million a month he might be a little more sensitive to their business needs. Their response was to put out a contract on Noriega's life. One source says they asked Basque separatists to kill Noriega the next time he came to Europe. The claim is supported by the fact that Noriega never accepted Spanish asylum when it was offered, preferring to take his chances with the American courts. The story goes that Mossad agents got wind of the contract. The Israeli secret service maintains an active interest in all terrorist groups around the world, and they alerted Noriega. Knowing firsthand that Colombian drug dealers have no sense of humor, the Panamanian turned to the one man who might still have some influence over them, Fidel Castro. Noriega begged for help and the Cuban dictator intervened, negotiating a truce with the cartels.

There was no love lost between the two men, but Noriega and Castro were doing business together and Castro felt it made good economic sense to keep his partner alive. With the United States still enforcing an embargo on Cuban goods, Castro had been sending shrimp and lobster to the Colón Free Zone, where Noriega's people repackaged it as Panamanian export and shipped it to the States. In return, Noriega paid Castro with embargoed American-made high-tech merchandise that Castro sold to the Russians.

In the beginning, Noriega used Panamanian banks to hide his money. When he hit the big time, he branched out and began laundering his money around the world. He used a large network of banks, among them BCCI, Banque National de Paris, First American, and the Algemene Bank Nederland. In some cases, he kept accounts in his own name, but he put a number of his larger accounts in the name of the PDF, his signature being the only one that could authorize the use of funds. Records confiscated from BCCI show that at one time Noriega had as much as $50 million on deposit, much of it in a PDF account in London. BCCI hired Noriega's daughter to work in its Miami branch, and issued him and his family Visa cards, against a PDF account, with which the Noriegas ran up monthly bills in excess of $25,000, shopping at Gucci in Paris, Bloomingdales in New York, and K-Mart in Miami.

With his share of the cartels' money, Noriega bought houses all over Panama, an apartment in Paris, a château outside Paris, a home in Spain, two houses in Israel, and one in Japan. He also had residences in the Dominican Republic and Venezuela. He invested in local cable TV companies, a newspaper, an explosives manufacturer, and four retail stores in Panama City. He owned commercial real estate in Panama, Florida, and New Orleans. And all this time the DEA thought of their pal "Tony" — which is how he signed hundreds of photos of himself that wound up hanging proudly on office walls across Washington — as a swell guy.

Noriega's troubles began in the mid-1980s. They stemmed from a routine investigation into a money laundering operation working out of a warehouse on the perimeter of Miami International Airport. DEA agents infiltrated the place and identified one of the men as Floyd Carlton Caceres, who turned out to be Noriega's personal pilot. When they arrested him, Caceres immediately asked if there was any way to make a deal.

Indicted by a pair of U.S. grand juries in 1988 — a lot of those autographed pictures were suddenly taken down — Noriega was charged with drug trafficking, including conspiracy to smuggle cocaine and marijuana into the United States, racketeering, and money laundering. As quickly as they could, prosecutors froze $26 million of his assets, which was all they could find at the time, though they were required eventually to turn $2 million of that back to him so that he could pay for attorneys.

The evidence presented to the grand juries was largely circumstantial: fuel receipts from private airplane rides, records from visits to hotels, sales slips from whatever he bought, and phone logs. None of it actually proved that Noriega was drug trafficking and money laundering. But it did substantiate the government's claim that he was double-dealing. It also backed up the testimony of a slew of less-than-respectable witnesses, convicted smugglers, drug dealers, laundrymen, and other Noriega associates, who were willing to testify in exchange for lighter sentences.

Obviously, Noriega wasn't in much of a hurry to respond to those accusations, so in December 1989 George Bush sent an expeditionary force to Panama to kidnap him. When Noriega sought refuge in the Vatican Embassy, the marines smoked him out with their secret weapon — nonstop, overamplified rock 'n roll! The Army delivered him to Florida and into the hands of the Justice Department, which held him without bail in a suite of cells. When federal prisoner #41586's legal appeals ran out, he was put on trial. Convicted in 1992 on eight of the eleven counts lodged against him, Noriega was sentenced to forty years in prison.

As one of Noriega's supporters said at the time, "This is no way to treat a friend."

That's when it was revealed that DEA administrator Peter Bensinger had written Noriega on December 14, 1978, to thank him for his "excellent efforts which have contributed substantially to the ongoing battle against drugs." Such praise had been repeated six years later by DEA administrator Francis Mullen, Jr., who'd assured Noriega, "Your long-standing support of the Drug Enforcement Administration is greatly appreciated."

Two years after that, in May 1986, DEA administrator John Lawn had echoed those sentiments. "I would like to take this opportunity to reiterate my deep appreciation for the vigorous anti drug-trafficking policy that you have adopted, which is reflected in the numerous expulsions from Panama of accused traffickers, the large seizures of cocaine and precursor chemicals that have occurred in Panama and the eradication of marijuana cultivations in Panamanian territory." Ironically, Lawn had added, "I look forward to the day when all governments develop the means to systematically identify and seize those illegal profits and drug trafficking starts becoming a self-defeating enterprise."

The following year Lawn had heaped even more praise on Noriega, this time for his assistance with a multinational drug bust called Operation Pisces: "Many millions of dollars and many thousands of pounds of drugs have been taken from the drug traffickers and international money launderers. Your personal commitment to Operation Pisces and the competent, professional, and tireless efforts of other officials in the Republic of Panama were essential to the final positive outcome of this investigation. Drug traffickers around the world are now on notice that the proceeds and profits of their illegal ventures are not welcome in Panama."

No one at the DEA realized Noriega was simply using them to eliminate the competition.

Besides taking out Noriega, the American invasion of Panama unearthed a huge cache of bank records, tapes, and documents that helped the DEA make money laundering cases against a group of major players, plus a hundred pounds of cocaine and $6 million in cash. However, this did not end the problem. Panama is still struggling to clean up its reputation as a major international cocaine market and sink. In early 1992, two containers were confiscated in the Colón Free Zone when they were found to be holding $7 million in cash. No one ever claimed the money, and some of it has since disappeared. At the end of that year, Panama's attorney general Rogelio Cruz was charged with illegally releasing $37 million from previously frozen bank accounts that were believed to belong to the Colombian cartels. His deputy attorney general for drug prosecution, Ariel Alvarado, was also arrested. It's hardly a coincidence that Cruz once served on the board of First Interamericas Bank.

Very little seems to have changed since Noriega's ouster. The Colón Free Zone is alive and well, and despite rhetoric aimed at pacifying Washington, every indication is that it's going to stay that way. The secret banks are wide open. Cash is the commodity of the day. Everyone agrees that asking too many questions is bad for business. It's a pipe dream to think that any Panamanian leader is going to risk thirteen thousand jobs and $10 billion worth of business by cooking up regulations that might make the place less attractive than it already is.

When Harry Truman signed the 1947 National Security Act, creating the Central Intelligence Agency, he seriously believed its mission would be nothing more sinister than the collection and collation of foreign intelligence information. He seriously believed that it was strictly an "overt" operation. His mistake was to staff it with highly motivated men, such as Allen Dulles, who'd learned the old-fashioned spying trade from the famous General William "Wild Bill" Donovan during the Second World War, in the Office of Special Operations. To a man, they believed "overt" was not the way this game should be played.

Right from the beginning, the agency's more consequential role in foreign affairs would be "covert." Officially included in that category have always been subsidies to individuals; financial support and "technical assistance" to political parties; support of private organizations, which includes labor unions, business firms, cooperatives, and so forth; economic operations; and paramilitary or political actions designed either to overthrow or to support a regime. Obviously, the CIA could never finance any of these things publicly. It was out of the question for the nation's primary espionage service to go to Congress and beg for funds to kick the Mossadegh regime out of Iran. So they operated their own laundry.

Even today, the director of Central Intelligence maintains a top-secret slush fund — a huge pile of invisible money for which he is accountable directly to the president, and the president alone. What's more, Dwight Eisenhower created a top-secret group to advise the CIA on the best use of those funds and, when necessary, to procure additional monies for specific covert operations. Every president since has followed suit. In Ike's day, the group was called the 5412 Committee, named for the National Security Council paper that authorized it. It remains the most secret organization in the United States. A subcabinet-level organization, 5412 is charged with reviewing and approving all of the nation's clandestine operations in order to protect the president from the consequences of any clandestine operation gone wrong. Those few men who know about it refer to it simply as "The Special Group." Not even the National Security Council is kept informed of its activities.

For whatever reasons, various administrations have changed the name from 5412 to such obscurely derived numbers as "The 303" and "The 40 Committee." But the concept behind it remains the same: it is the Special Group, and not the president, that must officially approve certain plans, such as illegal interventions into the internal affairs of another sovereign state. Traditionally, the cabal consists of a chairman, most often the president's national security advisor, the secretaries of state and defense, and the CIA chief. For obvious reasons, the president is not a member. There's no denying that the buck stops at the Oval Office and that ultimately the president must authorize a Special Group proposal, but his approval is only given verbally. The members of the group work out the details among themselves, then brief the president. Nothing is written down with his name on it. Nothing is ever signed by him.

It was the 5412 Committee that approved the CIA's use of the U-2 spy plane, which Allen Dulles and his assistant Richard Bissell financed entirely out of the director's slush fund. If, as has been alleged, the CIA assassinated Salvador Allende in 1973, it would have been a topic of discussion among Richard Nixon's Special Group. And if, as has often been suggested, Ronald Reagan knew anything at all about the Iran-Contra affair, the matter would have been decided by his administration's equivalent of the 5412 Committee.

Iran-Contra is, in fact, a perfect example of what the Committee is supposed to do. If Director William Casey committed the CIA to engage in the illegal activities for which Oliver North was tried, he almost certainly would have brought the issue up in a Special Group meeting. The secretaries of state and defense would have known about the plan, agreed to it, and presented it for final approval to the president. But because nothing is written down and therefore nothing can ever be traced back to a president, Reagan's denial that he had any prior knowledge of the affair is an impenetrable defense.

During those years, Reagan's Special Group empowered the CIA to funnel money to right-wing forces trying to overthrow the leftist government of Mauritius, to spend millions trying to destabilize Colonel Qadhafi's regime in Libya, and to bankroll the Afghan rebels with hundreds of millions of dollars. White House and CIA records now suggest that in the first six years of his administration, Reagan knew of and/or approved of at least sixty money laundering plots to finance CIA covert activities.

One of the most infamous CIA-financed covert operations came out of John Kennedy's Special Group. Called Operation Mongoose, it was a White House–sanctioned plot to assassinate Fidel Castro.

After the Bay of Pigs invasion failed, Bobby Kennedy, who was then attorney general, convinced his brother that getting rid of Castro had to be a priority of the administration. The president turned to the CIA, which was already staffing a huge command post on the campus of the University of Miami. Using the code name JM/WAVE, operatives there directed the activities of three thousand Cuban agents they'd set up in false businesses, known in the vernacular as "cutouts." The CIA not only paid the bills for these businesses, but washed money through them to pay for all sorts of covert activities. They poisoned the cargo of a Russian ship that had docked in Puerto Rico, counterfeited Cuban money, broadcast propaganda to the island, and regularly financed anti-Castro guerrilla warfare. They paid for planes, speedboats, and arms.

One CIA operator found he could make more money running an agency cutout than he could by staying on the payroll. According to regulations, he was required to turn the extra money over to the government. So he simply resigned from the CIA, kept the business, and kept the profits. CIA officials never said a word because they couldn't admit they'd owned the business in the first place.

They have, however, admitted to eight separate plots to murder Castro. In an early attempt, they smuggled poison pills to an operative in Havana, but he failed to get anywhere near his target. In another, they sent a box of toys to a Cuban dissident in Havana who was believed to have access to Castro. Included in this box were a poison pen, pills, bacterial powders, an exploding cigar, and a cigar deeply impregnated with botulinum toxin, a poison so potent it would have killed Castro the moment he put the cigar to his lips. This too failed. In a third plot, they recruited and dispatched professional hitmen.

The roots of that one go back to the summer of 1960, during the Eisenhower administration, when ex-FBI agent Robert Maheu was instructed by Richard Bissell to enlist some men willing to do the CIA's bidding. First to sign up was Johnny Rosselli, a Las Vegas gangster who'd previously been connected to gambling interests in Havana. Next was the man who ran the mob in Chicago, a fellow who called himself Sam Gold but whose real name was Momo Salvatore Giancana. Then there was an exiled Cuban Mafia don living in Miami, known as Joe to his friends and Santos Trafficante to everyone else. Together they located a Cuban working at a restaurant frequented by Castro and convinced him to poison Castro's food. They even supplied him with the pills. But by early spring 1961, when the attempt was scheduled to take place, Castro had changed restaurants.

A year later, following the Bay of Pigs fiasco, the poison pill plan was resurrected. This time the gangsters retained a Cuban willing to carry out the murder. He was to be paid with a small cache of weapons and communications equipment. The Mafia trio turned to Bissell. The CIA agreed to fund the operation through their cutouts in Miami. The assassin failed, though not before the CIA's front companies had financed the purchase of explosives, boat radar, radios, and handguns, and shipped them off to Cuba. Years later it would be revealed that some of the people who dealt with the CIA at JM/WAVE, or who were involved with washing funds through cutouts for Operation Mongoose, also had links, circumstantial or otherwise, to the assassination of John Kennedy in Dallas in 1963. They included Lee Harvey Oswald, Jack Ruby, Earle Cabell — brother of the deputy director of the CIA general Charles Cabell and at the time the mayor of Dallas, who mysteriously changed the route of Kennedy's motorcade at the very last minute so that it would pass directly in front of the Texas School Book Depository — Sam Giancana, and Santos Trafficante. The five guys who broke into the Watergate building in 1972 also had direct links to Operation Mongoose. No conclusions here, just food for thought!

The point is that with the tacit approval of the White House the CIA became one of the greatest launderers of all time. In the name of national security, it continues to run more businesses than most Fortune 500 conglomerates. None of these cutouts are associated in any obvious way with the U.S. government. Often staffed by retired military officers and former CIA operatives, they tend to employ Cuban exiles, Vietnam veterans, Israeli agents, soldiers of fortune, Middle Eastern businessmen, and on several occasions, international drug traffickers. Services offered range from air cargo to money laundering. At least thirty cutouts were created just to back up Iran-Contra.

During George Bush's presidency, the CIA went into the coke-smuggling business. Using a cutout in Venezuela, in 1990, the agency adroitly smuggled a ton of pure cocaine into the United States. The idea was to use it to snare traffickers. Instead, it wound up being sold on the streets, a fact that came to light only three years later, thanks to the investigative skills of the CBS television program "60 Minutes." Later, CBS revealed that when that CIA cutout had tried to enlist the support of the DEA, it refused to take part, arguing that the plan was unworkable. The CIA eventually admitted that the entire affair was "most regrettable."

The classic CIA cutout was Air America. Based in Southeast Asia throughout the Vietnam War, the airline was hardly an effective masquerade, in that every peasant in every rice paddy from Saigon to Hanoi knew that Air America was the CIA. However, despite a natural tendency toward clumsiness, it was capable now and then of showing a touch of subtlety.

In 1973, two young men decided to go into the banking business. One was Michael Hand, a 31-year-old former CIA operative from the Bronx. The other was Frank Nugan, 30-year-old Australian playboy, and heir to a fruit-processing fortune built on Mafia connections. The Nugan Hand Bank was headquartered in Sydney and survived seven years. It collapsed when Frank Nugan was found sitting in his Mercedes with a rifle in one hand, a Bible in the other, and a hole through his head. Stuck among the pages of the Bible was a list of names that included Bob Wilson, then the ranking Republican on the House Armed Services Committee, and William E. Colby, former director of the CIA. Also on the list were the names of known international drug dealers, as well as personalities from politics, business, sports, film, and television. Next to each name were five- and six-figure dollar amounts. Shortly after Nugan's body was found, Michael Hand made a hasty exit from Australia and supposedly hasn't been seen since.

A precursor of BCCI, Nugan Hand was running a con game — bilking investors, cutting itself in on arms dealing, handling drug deals, and laundering cash. The bank's president was retired U.S. rear admiral Earl Yates, who'd once been in charge of the Navy's strategic planning; Colby was its legal counsel; Walter McDonald, a former deputy director of the CIA, was a consultant; Richard Secord, of Iran-Contra fame, had a business connection with the bank; and one of the bank's in-house commodity traders was also one of Australia's major heroin importers. In February 1977, Nugan Hand opened a branch in the unlikely location of Chiang Mai, Thailand. Unlikely, that is, until you know that that's where most of the opium produced in the Golden Triangle gets turned into money. The bank's office was adjacent, apparently with connecting doors, to offices used by the DEA.

The Senate investigated the Nugan Hand bank and its connections with the CIA, heard sworn testimony from the agency behind closed doors, and promptly locked that testimony away.

It's a typical pattern. In 1980, a company called Associated Traders Corporation set up shop in Baltimore, Maryland. At first sight, ATC appeared to be involved with import or export or general trading, something as vague as that. They must have had at least some international connections because from 1980 to 1985 they deposited millions of dollars into an account at the First National Bank of Maryland, then wired the money on to other companies in the Cayman Islands and Panama. Compounding the vagaries of their business dealings, ATC asked their Maryland bankers every now and then if they wouldn't mind making certain that the name ATC was removed from, and could therefore never be associated with, these transfers.

Over those five years, ATC laundered at least $20 million through First National. In one particular deal, $5.2 million was wired to Associated Traders Grand Cayman, moved from there to a dummy company account in Panama, and then transferred on to Switzerland. In another, $2.25 million followed the usual route through Grand Cayman and Panama before making its way to India, where it financed the purchase of sixty thousand Enfield rifles for the Mujahideen in Afghanistan.

By 1986, ATC had folded its tent and gone out of business. It is no coincidence that ATC's demise coincided with the unraveling of Iran-Contra.

None of this would have come to light had a young banker at First National not discovered who his client was. Stressed out by the thought that he might be breaking the law, he suffered a nervous breakdown, and then sued both the bank and the CIA for endangering his health.

But then, this is nothing new.

In the late 1970s, the junta ruling Argentina decided to help General Luis Garcia Meza Tejada, a known cohort of South American drug traffickers, to launch a coup in Bolivia. To help finance it, the Argentine intelligence service planned to open a laundromat in Florida. To help them do that, they approached their contacts in the CIA. In fact, two businesses were opened in Miami. One was called Argenshow, which was supposed to be a booking agency to bring music groups to Argentina. The second was a pawnshop called the Silver Dollar. Deliberately opened next to a gun shop, with the idea of picking up some business in illegal weapons, it was to be the operations center for Argentine intelligence activities throughout Latin America.

The CIA believed it was safer to have Argentine military advisers in El Salvador, Costa Rica, and Honduras than Americans stationed there. So Argenshow and the Silver Dollar arranged weapons shipments to Central America, laundering the necessary funds from Switzerland, the Bahamas, the Cayman Islands, and Liechtenstein, through Panama, and sending them to wherever they were needed. In just eighteen months, one shell company in the Bahamas facilitated the transfer of $30 million for the pawnshop.

Argenshow and the Silver Dollar handled a multi million–dollar deal between the junta generals and Roberto Suarez Levy, a prominent Bolivian drug dealer. Levy's funds were washed through Florida. In exchange, Argentina shipped ambulances to Bolivia, every one of them loaded with weapons intended to overthrow a center-left coalition and restore the military to power. It came to be known as "the cocaine coup." Later that same year, Argenshow recruited the Nicaraguan Contras to attack a shortwave radio station in Costa Rica. It's not clear whether that contact was made through an already established CIA channel, or whether it was itself the original CIA channel, but it turned out to be at the heart of Iran-Contra. A few months later, Argenshow was dissolved, the Silver Dollar was sold, and the CIA moved on to the next gig.

6

THE PROFESSIONALS

*"There's no such thing as good money or bad money.
There's just money."*
— Charlie "Lucky" Luciano

Increased compliance with reporting requirements has not solved the problem. Instead, it has made the laundryman's cost of washing money that much higher, and that, in turn, has displaced the problem.

More and more, laundrymen have been forced to seek "user-friendly" nations where there are no currency controls, where banking secrecy is assured, where no one cares who deposits what. It's true that there are international agreements that are supposed to enhance collaboration among law enforcement agencies and thwart this kind of cross-border ablution. But compared with the extent of smuggling that goes on, the degree of cooperation is negligible. Where crime is concerned, especially money laundering, jurisdiction all too often ends at the airport.

Most borders are so porous that even when they are heavily patrolled the amount of contraband getting stopped represents only a tiny percentage of the contraband coming through. What's more, many borders are single-sided, meaning goods are checked at the point of entry but not at the point of departure. Theoretically, it is easier to get cash out of the United States than to get drugs in, and literally billions of dollars leave the country every year, according to the Senate Permanent Subcommittee on Investigations. However, $1 million in $20 bills weighs fifteen times as much as the cocaine it buys, so the laundryman has a bulk problem the drug trafficker doesn't.

The U.S. Post Office used to be the courier of choice for send-ing dirty money out of the country, mainly because it's so secure. Commercial services such as FedEx and DHL have, unknowingly, taken some of the business away from Uncle Sam. But as inspectors have learned what to watch for, seizures have risen. In response, the laundrymen have diversified, hiding cash inside cars, furniture, tires, and television sets, which they ship out of the country labeled as gifts or as legal commercial exports. One group working in Los Angeles had a thriving venture in exporting refrigerators to Colombia until the Feds got wise to them. Another in New York was in the sealed metal container trade, until U.S. Customs at Kennedy Airport opened some of their products and discovered $6.5 million.

Lifting another page out of the drug traffickers' book, many laundrymen have reverted to basics and smuggle money out of the country with mules — people they hire to stuff cash in their under-wear, suitcases, socks, and pockets, or to tape it around their bodies. Increasingly, condoms are filled with cash and then ingested. A rela-tively new phenomenon, the first reported case of "cash swallowing" occurred in 1991. Working on a tip-off, customs agents at Kennedy stopped a woman from Ghana boarding a flight to Europe. They asked how much money she was carrying. She told them $9,000. A search of her luggage revealed $24,000 stuffed in clothes, and several bottles of shampoo packed with wads of $100 bills. A medical search then revealed that she'd hidden six more wads vaginally and had swal-lowed a dozen condoms with money rolled inside. The total haul was $55,000.

As the authorities shut one door, the laundrymen open two more.

The so-called "South African method" is a brazen approach concocted by a Johannesburg businessman who beat currency export controls by faking a badly sprained ankle. Booked on a flight to Lon-don, he asked the airline to supply a wheelchair to help him get to the gate because he had a cast on his leg. Departure scrutiny in those days was very strict, and on the day of his flight an anonymous call came into South African customs warning them that a man with a cast on his leg was using it to smuggle a large sum of money out of the country. When he wheeled up to the Customs and Immigration checkpoint, he was stopped. Officers opened his luggage, went through it, found nothing, then announced they wanted to search him. He refused. They insisted. He demanded he be permitted to call his attorney. Senior officials were summoned and the argument continued. By the time his lawyer arrived, the man's flight had taken off without him. The man threatened to sue. His lawyer managed to calm him down and explain that the officers were acting well within their rights. Protesting to the very end, the fellow had no choice but to sit there while his cast was sawn off.

It was empty.

Now the man raised hell. He started calling everyone he knew in government. Red-faced apologies, though plentiful, were inadequate. He ordered his lawyer to file law suits against the government and the airline for allowing this to happen. He said he not only wanted retribution, he wanted blood. He caused such a rumpus that when the man returned for a flight the following day, with a new cast plastered over his ankle — and cash packed firmly inside — Customs and Immigration officials personally helped him onto the plane.

A less nerve-racking method is the identical suitcases trick. More difficult to do these days than it used to be — for security reasons, airlines demand that every suitcase be accountable to a passenger on board — it can nevertheless be done. A laundryman packs two suitcases, one with clothes, the other with money. The trick is getting the second suitcase onto the plane without it being linked in any way to him. At his destination, he then retrieves the suitcase with the money and takes that one through customs. If he's stopped and the suitcase is opened, he says with appropriate shock it isn't his. He returns to the baggage claim to show the officers the identical suitcase, properly registered to him, with his clothes and identification inside. The money is abandoned, written off as the cost of doing business.

Professional smugglers who service the laundry trade may be a rare breed, but they are hardly an endangered species. Their numbers are growing because the work is so handsomely rewarded.

Call him Pancho. A medium-size man with delicate features and thick glasses, giving him an innocuous look, his biggest single coup to date was making $18 million in small bills disappear for a New York drug dealer. Working on a fee of 10 percent plus expenses,

Pancho began by getting the cash out of the United States and into Canada. That proved no more difficult than driving it to Montreal himself, with a woman and two kids in the car, making the border crossing look like an ordinary family outing.

In Montreal he sent runners posing as tourists to airports, railroad stations, post offices, and crowded banks, converting $10, $20, and $50 American bills into $100 Canadian bills and U.S.-dollar traveler's checks. Because of the sum involved, reducing the bulk of the cash took nearly one month.

From there, Pancho dispatched his mules to London. Well-dressed people traveling alone or in couples carried cash in attaché cases and stuffed the overflow into their pockets. They walked innocuously through the "Nothing to Declare" channel at Heathrow along with thousands of other ordinary businessmen and tourists.

Most airport customs rely on "profiling," an agent's ability to spot certain characteristics common to smugglers. Profiling was introduced many years ago by U.S. Customs, when someone high up in the bureaucratic hierarchy wondered what would happen if he fed into a computer all sorts of seemingly unrelated data about people who'd been apprehended bringing illicit goods into the country. The result was a list of several dozen shared traits, the profile of a smuggler, which remains deeply embedded in the psyche of customs inspectors around the world. It's mostly based on common sense.

For example, an extremely well-dressed elderly woman traveling alone with nothing to declare will almost always get stopped and searched, because profiling indicates she's the sort of person who has bought something expensive. An equally well-dressed couple in their mid-thirties who hand the inspector a written declaration will almost always be waved through, because profiling says they're probably too scared to cheat. A man obviously traveling on business, using a business class ticket paid for by his company, wearing a rumpled suit with only carry-on luggage and an especially jet-lagged expression, will have less trouble strolling through customs than a neatly dressed, first-class-flying, one-eyed Pakistani man weighing three hundred pounds, bearing an Italian passport, getting off a flight from Colombia, and carrying a blond-haired, blue-eyed, two-year-old baby girl.

Pancho understood that unless he made a serious error of judgment in the couriers he used, or unless customs was tipped off, or unless an officer somehow recognized the same courier coming through every third day, the odds were weighted in his favor. As long as he never gave customs a reason to suspect something, it was unlikely they would ever get their hands on this money.

From Britain the cash was sent to the Channel Islands, where it was deposited, by prearrangement with a friendly banker, into fourteen accounts. No sooner was it bedded down there than it was wired out. Some of it is known to have headed for Luxembourg. The rest evaporated into thin air.

To increase their gain, some professionals are willing to increase their risk by combining money laundering with drug smuggling.

John is in his late twenties. Tall and athletic, he has a very particular philosophy of life: if you're going somewhere to do something illegal, do it once but do it right, and make enough doing it to absolutely change your life, so that you never have to do it again; then get out and stay out.

He decided to change his life in Gibraltar. Because "The Rock" is overpopulated with company-formation agents who never ask questions, John had no trouble establishing himself there with a £100 import-export company. Using cash he'd collected from smuggling tobacco to the Spanish mainland, John bought stereos, VCRs, CD players, televisions, portable telephones, answering machines, fax machines, and camcorders. He obtained the necessary export licenses and shipped the inventory across the Strait of Gibraltar to Tangiers. After declaring everything at Moroccan customs and paying import duties, he sold it all and used the money to buy cannabis, which he smuggled by speed boat into Spain. Selling his dope there, he deposited the cash back in Gibraltar, authenticating the source of it with his export license and Moroccan import receipts. Then he closed his business, took his money, moved away, and, at least so far, has never been back.

The trickiest part of John's equation was dealing drugs. Still, triangular trade has gone on in the region for centuries, making the Strait of Gibraltar one of the most congested smuggling routes on the planet. Little has changed since the days of the Barbary Coast pirates, except the value of the cargoes and the sophistication of the smugglers. In early 1993, for example, two rings working out of the Spanish North African enclave of Cueta were known to have ferried one hundred tons of Moroccan hashish across the Strait hidden in trucks carrying fresh flowers. They'd washed their profits, $220 million worth, through seven banks in Cueta, Morocco, Spain, and Gibraltar. So John knew what he was doing when he put all his chips on this roll of the dice. After all, Morocco is Europe's principal exporter of marijuana and hashish; because of its historical, cultural, and linguistic ties to Central and South America, Spain is Europe's premier port of entry for the Latin drug trade, and has a highly developed trafficking infrastructure; and Gibraltar is the region's most suitable sink.

Despite Spain's occasionally draconian border checks and British threats to impose direct rule in Gibraltar if sufficient action is not taken by the Gibraltarians themselves, the Rock remains fertile territory for laundrymen. Reacting to London's caveat in June 1995, Gibraltar's customs police did intercept forty-two smuggling crews and confiscate sixty-three vessels. Spanish officials say that at least a hundred new Gibraltar-registered speed launches have taken up the slack. And Gibraltar has had laws against money laundering on its books since 1988. But it wasn't until late 1995 that anyone was ever prosecuted for it.

Admittedly, Pancho and John are the exceptions. The difference between them and the amateur is that they approached smuggling and money laundering like professionals, having worked out ways to minimize risk and maximize gain. Amateurs learn on the job and hope to get lucky, which can make for a very expensive education.

A fellow with a pilot's license in Ft. Lauderdale, Florida, decided there was no trick to moonlighting as a flying laundryman. He found some people who were looking to get cash out of the country, stuffed his plane with their money, and flew south. Before long, he had more clients than he could handle and upgraded to a Learjet. Obviously, there are plenty of people in the States who fly private jets, but when you regularly file a flight plan in Ft. Lauderdale that indicates that you're going to the Bahamas, and air traffic control regularly tracks you to Panama, it shouldn't come as a surprise when someone starts wondering what you're up to.

The usual ruse is to file point-to-point. You fly from Ft. Lauderdale to Nassau. In Nassau you file to Caracas. When you land in Venezuela, you file to Costa Rica. From there, if you want to go to Panama, it's a good bet American authorities have long since lost track of you. But the fellow from Ft. Lauderdale hadn't worked that out, and one morning, just before he left on a run, the DEA came to call. Inside his plane they found $5.5 million in cash. At his home, they discovered nearly $20 million worth of drugs and a small cache of weapons, including a submachine gun. They not only arrested him, they confiscated his new toy.

It's well known that the airlines frequently cooperate with law enforcement agencies. Air crews arriving in Miami on flights from countries where there are drug-related activities, such as Colombia, Peru, Ecuador, and Venezuela, are offered cash rewards by U.S. Customs for pointing out passengers who did not eat or drink anything during the flight. It all gets back to profiling. Most people eat something on a four-hour flight, unless there's a particular reason not to, such as a stomach laden with drug-filled condoms. Less publicized is that the airlines are actively encouraged to look out for and report frequent flyers making unusual journeys. Someone departing from Chicago, going first to the Bahamas, then on to the Caymans, then to Cali, back to the Bahamas, and into Miami every week is bound to attract attention.

To get around ambitious airline employees, some laundrymen have friendly travel agents ticket them on circuitous routes. Smarter laundrymen own their own travel agencies, pay for tickets with cash, and write their own tickets to suit their own circumstances. There's never any need to arrive in Miami on a flight from Cali. They can issue themselves a ticket in one name from Bogotá to Rio, in another name from Rio to Paris, in a third name from Paris to London, and in their own name from London to New York. That way, they are not only impossible to track but also avoid entry into the United States from someplace suspect.

Travel agencies come with the added benefit of providing an ideal sink. Cash can simply be funneled into the agency. Cash can be substituted for legitimate payments, meaning that the client's check can be deposited offshore. And cash can pay for blank tickets, which are negotiable outside the country. The Orozco brothers, of Deak-Perera fame, proved the point by purchasing the Calypso Travel Agency in New York. They opened an account at Chase Manhattan after the bank agreed to put the agency on its exemption list for reporting. At least three cash deposits were made before Chase withdrew the exemption, not because the Orozcos were money launderers, but simply because the bank had changed its own administrative procedures.

A professional group operating out of Marseilles found it could wash funds through plastic surgery clinics where wealthy French and Italians paid to have their bodies adjusted. The laundrymen had no problem finding physicians happy to up their turnover with cash from drug sales.

Another gang, this one working in Paris, laundered money through the European thoroughbred market. Gang members bought registered racehorses with the various jockey clubs and then hired professionals to help them put their horses up for sale. Other gang members bought the horses back. The horses' names were changed after each transaction and fed through the system again. When suspicious authorities asked to inspect the thoroughbreds, they were told the poor things had tragically died.

Indeed, the racing industry is a favorite with professional laundrymen. They hang out at small tracks — where it's easy to make contacts with jockeys, drivers, and trainers — and pay cash for tips. This is known as "The Sydney Method," having been made infamous by an Australian drug dealer who legitimized hundreds of thousands of dollars that way. He'd bribe an insider with up to $5,000, bet his cash on the winning horse, and use the betting receipt to corroborate his cash deposits.

Over the past ten years, as legislation aimed at stopping the laundrymen has become more sophisticated, a new breed of laundrymen has come into the business. Respectable white-collar professionals who have the training to manipulate complex laundering schemes have been enticed with commissions ranging from 4 to 10 percent. Where drugs are involved, the guys moving the narcotics no longer have to worry about moving the money, and the guys moving the money never have to touch the drugs.

For many, it turns out to be a hugely lucrative sideline. A politician from Georgia found money laundering an easy way to finance an $850,000 mortgage; a California businessman got involved because washing $1.1 million through his company's account required very little effort, and the $77,000 he was paid for the use of the account was too much to pass up. Richard Silberman, a fund-raiser for Jerry Brown's 1980 presidential bid, admitted to an undercover FBI agent he'd been making fast money as a laundryman for twenty years. In New York, Eddie Antar, owner of the now-bankrupt Crazy Eddie discount electronics chain, got into money laundering because it was a expeditious way of boosting his share price. Over a period of several years, he siphoned cash from his business, carted it away in shopping bags, and deposited it in a secret account in Israel. From there, the money was washed through a Panamanian bank before coming back to the Crazy Eddie stores in the form of checks payable to the company. Increased sales artificially inflated the company's profits. When his share prices peaked, he sold and pocketed $74 million.

Fast money was also undoubtedly the motivation for car salesmen in the Washington, D.C. area, willing to take cash from drug traffickers. And sending out a message to car salesmen across the country was what the government had in mind when Larry Best and Tyrone Evans, a pair of D.C. cops, went undercover.

Cars are a favorite with laundrymen because they're easily resold in South America. The streets of Bogotá, for example, are flooded with newly imported BMWs, Mercedeses, and Toyota Land Cruisers. There is also a gigantic market in Harley-Davidson motorcycles. So in the spring of 1991, Best and Evans walked into Rosenthal Nissan-Mazda in Vienna, Virginia — a suburb of Washington — and paid cash for a Nissan Maxima. A CTR was filed for $23,560, listing the buyer under the fictitious name Jerry Johnson. A few weeks later, they were back with $46,600 in cash, this time to buy an Infiniti Q45. The CTR listed the buyer under the fictitious name Raymond Steven Smith. Next came $42,190 for a Nissan 300ZX sold to a fictitious William Thomas Jones, and then $53,000 for a Jaguar Sovereign sold again to Jerry Johnson.

Over the course of two years, Best and Evans went to several dealerships. During that time, the undercover cops later testified, they regularly explained to the dealers that the source of their cash was drug money and made it perfectly clear that they could never be associated with any of these cash payments — that false names had to be used. In all, they bought or contracted to buy eighty-five cars for cash. Their efforts led to five convictions for money laundering offenses. The government then saw to it that the case was publicized in the trade press, so that auto dealers would now have to suspect that any customer coming in with cash might be an undercover cop.

A few million dollars might have been enough to tempt some car dealers, but the amount pales by comparison with the sums that actually went through the books of a gold and coin trader in Cranston, Rhode Island.

Stephen Saccoccia opened a shop after leaving high school in 1973, building his business by fencing gold and coins for his teenage friends, who were stealing it from their parents. In 1985, he pleaded guilty to a federal charge of tax evasion. Following his release from prison in 1988, he began laundering money for a local Mafia family. But it wasn't until a few years later that he opened a sink to service the rival Medellín and Cali cartels, apparently becoming the first and only laundryman ever to do business with both of them at the same time.

Drug money was collected at dummy jewelry shops in New York and Los Angeles, packaged as gold shipments, and shipped to Saccoccia's offices in Rhode Island, New York, and California. He converted the cash to cashier's checks, which he deposited in various company accounts. Using falsified invoices and sales receipts to explain the sudden increase in turnover, Saccoccia then wired the funds through phantom companies to Colombia.

Saccoccia charged a flat 10-percent commission. And whereas one report noted that in under fifteen months he and his employees

washed $200 million for the cartels, federal authorities claim the total was closer to $750 million. In May 1993, he was convicted on
fifty-four counts of money laundering and conspiracy, fined $15.8
million, subjected to a confiscation order for $136.3 million, and
sentenced to serve 660 years in prison.

It is now claimed that Robert Maxwell also did his share of
money laundering. Not that this would necessarily come as a surprise
to anyone who knew the flamboyant Czech-born British businessman. It seems he did his money laundering in the States, which many
Brits find highly amusing.

Maxwell bought the *New York Daily News* in March 1991, nine
months before he fell or was pushed off the stern of his yacht. Within
a few days of his death, the paper filed for bankruptcy. Accountants
trying to figure out Maxwell's bookkeeping discovered he'd siphoned
company money and pension funds from Maxwell Group Newspapers PLC in London and sent it to the *Daily News,* depositing as
much as $238 million in accounts controlled by the parent company,
Maxwell Newspapers. The money didn't stay in New York very
long. It was wired to any of several hundred other Maxwell-
controlled companies, most of them designed to be inaccessible to
anyone except Maxwell himself. In one case, the money was used to
secure a $78-million loan to the *Daily News* from Bankers Trust,
though only $8.45 million ever showed up on the newspaper's books.
In another, he borrowed $86 million from Bankers Trust for Maxwell
Group Newspapers — money that made its way through several different accounts before coming out of the *Daily News* to repay a different loan from Bankers Trust.

When the *Daily News* teetered on the verge of bankruptcy in
October 1991, and one of his newsprint suppliers refused to deliver
unless he was paid cash, Maxwell spun $113 million through the
Maxwell Newspapers account, left it there for four days so that he
could borrow enough against it to pay the supplier, then wired the
money out, leaving the newspaper with $376,000 less than when he
brought the laundered money in.

Undoubtedly, Maxwell ran an audacious scam. But the prize for
moxie must go irrefutably to the money laundering rabbi.

Abraham Low, an ultraorthodox Los Angeles clergyman, was

arrested by the FBI in early 1993 when they uncovered a $2-million laundry operation soon dubbed "the holy network." Taken into custody with him were a Hollywood physician named Alan Weston and Bernadette Chandler, a woman known to the FBI simply as Charlie. Low had realized that the synagogue was having financial difficulties and that his congregation stood to lose $18 million in bad investments. He later claimed that all he was trying to do was keep the synagogue solvent. The FBI had already stumbled onto Low during an investigation into a stolen check racket. In September 1991, his wife went into a bank and turned a $500,000 cashier's check into four smaller checks. When bank officials discovered that the original check was stolen and forged, they called the police. Agents learned that Low had been combining cashier's checks pilfered from a bank in West Los Angeles with phony loan papers establishing a legitimate source for the funds. Using bank accounts held by various charitable organizations — hence the "holy network" tag — he was laundering large cash deposits.

Chandler came into the picture when Low purchased a stolen $500,000 check and two diamond rings from her for $30,000. After Chandler told Low and Weston she had set up a $1.5-million money laundering deal, they bragged that they could provide the same service. An FBI informant introduced them to a special agent pretending to be a loan-sharking drug dealer named Ronnie. Low and Weston offered Ronnie use of their sink, assuring him they were prepared to handle substantial amounts on a weekly basis. Low even outlined the system, explaining that money delivered to trusted members of his congregation, in this case diamond dealers, could be washed through those charitable accounts and then wired anywhere in the world. Ronnie agreed to a test transaction and provided $10,000 in cash. The moment the deal was done, the FBI moved in.

If nothing else, a money laundering rabbi must be proof positive that these days laundrymen don't fit any of the usual hoodlum stereotypes. They are not machine-gun-toting men in black shirts with white ties. Nor are they generally street-level drug dealers, who are predominately black. For the most part they don't have previous criminal records. In many cases they are people who might not otherwise have considered crime but were keenly attracted to a quick-buck, clean-hands hustle. Working on their own account, or on behalf of their drug-dealing, fraudster, smuggling, kidnapping, arms-dealing, terrorist, extortionist, and tax-evading friends, these people have turned money laundering into the most sophisticated element of organized criminal activity.

White, affluent members of the professional classes have turned money laundering into the world's leading financial growth industry.

The Money Laundering Control Act of 1986 upped the stakes for professionals by making money laundering a criminal offense when associated with any crime. The theory is, because nine out of ten crimes are profit-motivated, to do something about crime society must go after the profit. If someone merely wants to move their own money through a series of jurisdictions, in and out of shell companies, to see what happens when it comes out the other end, that's his business. But if someone does it in conjunction with insider trading, fraud, drug trafficking, income tax evasion, theft, whatever, then money laundering can be tagged onto the charge sheet. It is very much the law enforcement flavor of the month, the in-vogue catchall offense, taking over from such old favorites as income tax evasion and conspiracy to defraud.

The government used the act to nab Michael Monus, the former president of the Phar-Mor discount drugstore chain. Indicted for defrauding investors of $1.1 billion and embezzling a further $1.1 million, he was also charged with 118 counts of money laundering. It also used the act to get at William Aramony, the man who'd made The United Way of America into the nation's biggest charity. Over much of the twenty-two years he served as president, Aramony defrauded the charity of more than a million dollars in order to support his lavish lifestyle. His seven-year sentence was based on convictions for fraud, tax evasion, and money laundering.

Not to be oudone by a laundryman rabbi, there was the Reverend Martin Greenlaw, a Roman Catholic priest in San Francisco. When parishioners noticed he was buying property, which was hardly in keeping with his vow of poverty, they contacted the archdiocese. The DA was called and the result was an indictment against the priest for embezzlement, grand theft, tax evasion, and ten counts of money laundering.

They also got "Chuckie the Meat Man" Cugliari for money laundering. A Trenton, New Jersey, meat broker, he'd engineered a pyramid scheme that cost his investors as much as $80 million. Selling single shares in his company for $25,000, Chuckie promised an annual return of 40 percent on contracts for the delivery of meat and seafood. But instead of investing the money, Chuckie ran a Ponzi scheme, using money from new investors to pay dividends to old investors. That's fraud. And these days, it's also money laundering.

When Marcus Arthur Rodriguez, deputy director of the Los Angeles County Museum of Natural History, was arrested for embezzling more than $2 million, he was charged with five counts of grand theft, two counts of misuse of public money, one count of forgery, two counts of conspiracy, and twelve counts of money laundering. And Richard Hersch, president of the tax preparation service Quick Tax Dollars, was convicted of filing 431 falsified tax returns and claiming more than $1 million in refunds. The jury agreed with the prosecution that he'd laundered the proceeds through several bank accounts, and sent him to jail for five years.

But most of all, they got Heidi Fleiss for money laundering.

A 28-year-old high-school dropout, Fleiss was arrested in June 1993 after a sting operation in Beverly Hills had rounded up some call girls who claimed they were working for her. She was charged with pandering and a drug violation. She pleaded not guilty. It's likely that none of this would have mattered to anyone had she been living in Eufala, Alabama, but the "Hollywood Madam" was a tabloid's dream come true. As the story of her life unfolded — told in vivid detail by just about everyone who'd ever met her and lots of people who hadn't — it was revealed she had a reputation for being into anything and everything as far as sex was concerned, had gorgeous girls working for her, and had famous clients. Among them were actor Charlie Sheen; Sidney Shlenker, former owner of the Denver Nuggets and part owner of the Houston Rockets; Mexican businessman Manuel Santos; Australian tycoon Kerry Packer; and real estate magnate Bob Crow. Capitalizing on her fifteen minutes of fame, she

encouraged more headlines by posing for magazines, selling interviews, and opening Heidi Wear, a Pasadena lingerie boutique.

But the fun was short-lived. In July 1994, when a federal grand
jury was considering her case, they were told that her call girls, some
of whom charged up to $10,000, kicked back to her a 40-percent
commission. The money was put through family accounts to hide
its source. Fleiss hadn't filed income tax returns in either 1991 or
1993, and in 1992 declared only $33,000. It then came out that
her father, Dr. Paul Fleiss, a 60-year-old Beverly Hills pediatrician,
had deceived a bank into thinking he was the purchaser of a $1.6-
million home that had once belonged to actor Michael Douglas
when Heidi was the one actually buying the house with her laundered money. So a grand jury indicted daughter and father for money
laundering.

The state case against her brought convictions for pandering,
and a three-year sentence. Meanwhile, federal prosecutors quickly
backed her into a corner by working out a deal with her father, who,
convicted of the original charges, faced a maximum sentence of
more than a hundred years. On the promise that he would not have
to testify against Heidi, Paul Fleiss pleaded guilty to one charge of
conspiring with her to launder money and two charges of making
false statements to banks. He also agreed to surrender $375,187, the
proceeds from the sale of the house. In return, he was sentenced to
serve one day in prison, fined $50,000, put on three years probation,
and ordered to perform 625 hours of community service.

Heidi refused to plea bargain and mounted a defense. Part of it
was based on her claim that ex-boyfriend Bernie Cornfeld had regularly been sending her gifts and that she therefore didn't need money
from prostitution. Cornfeld, of IOS fame, had "discovered" Fleiss
when she was still a teenager. Over the course of several years, while
living in Beverly Hills, he jet-setted her around the world. But Cornfeld's attention span for ladies was famously short. And tax problems
with the IRS drove him into European exile. He stayed friends with
her, however, and even though he was the object of an IRS probe
right up until the time of his death, he did send her some money. But
not $1.6 million. Cornfeld hadn't seen that much in years. And what

little he sent her was intended mainly intended to help pay legal bills after she'd been arrested.

The jury convicted her.

Alex Daoud, the former three-term mayor of Miami Beach, was indicted by a grand jury for racketeering, extortion, and money laundering. California state senator Paul Carpenter and lobbyist Clayton Jackson were arrested on political corruption charges. Because they'd tried to make bribe money disappear, prosecutors threw in money laundering. But there have been occasions when politicians have constructed a scam specifically to launder money and the statutes have been shoved conveniently aside. This is not to insinuate that any particular politician has taken part or is otherwise indictable. Still, somewhere along the way, a politician or two may have benefited.

During a routine audit of San Francisco's 1991 mayoral race, election officials uncovered several suspicious contributions. Much to their surprise, the source of the funds appeared to be the San Francisco 49ers. The team had, in fact, made thirty contributions they clearly knew were questionable, because it had washed the funds through thirty different individuals in order to circumvent the city's campaign contribution limit of $500 per person. The thirty individuals were later reimbursed by the 49ers. The club and its chief financial officer got off with a $60,000 fine.

The company that stages the Los Angeles Marathon did much the same thing, although they fared less well. After admitting in 1994 to laundering $73,000 in order to make illegal campaign contributions to members of the city council and former mayor Tom Bradley, Los Angeles Marathon Inc. was fined $436,250.

However, money laundering has cachet if you happen to be a congressman. U.S. Senator Rick Santorum, a Republican from Pennsylvania, decided he could help his party's cause in the 1996 elections by setting up a "leadership fund." Usually formed as the prerogative of more senior legislators, the fund is essentially a discretionary account through which contributions are funneled. The law stipulates that no individual can give more than $2,000 to a Senate candidate every six years. As Santorum is not up for reelection until the year 2000, contributions to his leadership fund are not covered by those federal contribution limits.

So that no one should think he is trying to hide anything, it's only fair to point out that Santorum publicly announced the creation of the fund, explaining that he was using it to support GOP campaigns and to pay for his travel expenses.

It is, arguably, money laundering. Although in this form it seems to be perfectly legal, and apparently there are fifty leadership funds alive and well and living on Capitol Hill.

7

THE MARLBORO MURDER

"The crooks keep so far ahead of us,
we'll never completely close the net."
— **A Department of Justice spokesperson**

Colonel Hector Moretta Portillo, with his nifty, multibraided, starched white uniform, held a privileged place in the Mexican army. As a relative of a former president, he was an accredited member of his country's delegation to the United Nations. In his spare time he sold gold and whiskey.

Stocky, 5 feet 6 inches tall, with black hair and a mustache, Portillo at one point in his career — while on holiday at the home of the minister of interior on the island of Cozumel — was murdered. Press reports noted that his bullet-ridden body was found floating face down in the swimming pool, and that his killer was still at large.

A few years after his assassination, he turned up in Santo Domingo as Colonel Gomez, an officer in the army of the Dominican Republic and a relative of a former Dominican president. Sporting a brand-new, nifty, multibraided, starched white uniform, he sold sugar in his spare time.

But in 1988, when a few of his clients complained to the authorities that the colonel's sugar was nonexistent — just as his gold and whiskey had been — he was arrested. Under questioning, he told Dominican authorities that his real name was Michael Austin Smith. That might have been the closest he's ever come to telling the truth, because that is his name, except it wasn't the name he was born with.

Although it was only later revealed that he'd used as many as thirty aliases, when he came into this world, in Brooklyn, New York, in 1955, he was Michael Sporn. He'd changed his name to Austin somewhere along the line, adding Smith to the end of it whenever it suited him, much the way he changed — almost effortlessly — back and forth from fluent Spanish to the broken English you'd expect from your average well-connected Latin American colonel.

By the time the 1990s came along, he was Hector Portillo again, and living in New York. Now his angle was cigarettes.

Knowing the world is awash with commodities in the parallel markets — you can buy and sell just about everything, from oil, pork bellies, precious metals, and timber, to grain, steel, precious stones, sugar, gold, whiskey, and cardboard boxes — he was taking aim at the lucrative, well-established traffic in Marlboros. An ideal commodity for a con, not only is the brand name instantly recognized, it is traded globally, outside the manufacturer's normal distribution routes. For all sorts of reasons, gargantuan quantities of legitimate Marlboros are forever spinning around the world through diverse wholesale channels: a state tobacco monopoly buys too many and needs to sell the surplus; a cargo gets stolen and needs to be fenced; a middle man buys a shipment at an advantageous price and wants to unload it for a fast profit; someone defaults on a payment and needs to sell the cargo to recoup costs.

In many Third World countries — notably in the former Communist bloc — Marlboros have become a kind of currency. Cases of cartons are often the icing on the cake, the bribe that caps a deal. In Russia, for example, where no one wants rubles, you barter first with dollars, then throw in some Marlboros. In fact, for years the best way to get a taxi on the streets of Moscow has been to wave the familiar red-and-white box — a signal you've got something to offer that even nonsmoking taxi drivers can use.

It's the old joke about the soldier who sells his only pack of Marlboros to another soldier for a dollar. The second soldier sells it to a third for two bucks. The third sells it to the fourth for $3, and so on until the price reaches $10. The soldier who pays that for the pack rips it open and starts smoking. The other soldiers are aghast. What's wrong? puffs the soldier with the cigarettes. Pointing to the

Marlboros, the first soldier explains that they're not for smoking, they're for buying and selling.

So Austin cooked up a scheme to sell a hundred containers — 4.8 million cartons — of nonexistent Marlboros. Enough to supply the entire Russian Confederation for four months, the bait was more than handsome enough to attract the attention of the literally thousands of middlemen who prowl the parallel markets, hungry to deal. But flogging something in this game is not like finding some tourist and selling him the Brooklyn Bridge or the *Mona Lisa*. To make the scam work, he had to create what is known as "evidence of reality." He had to convince some relatively sophisticated buyers both that the product was available and that he had access to it.

In order to cover those bases, Austin — in the guise of Portillo — scripted several variations of the same story. One went: factories in Mexico that Philip Morris had closed were back in operation, producing fraudulent Marlboros. Another version claimed: factories that had never had anything to do with Philip Morris were banging out counterfeit Marlboros. A third account was: through his connections with the Mexican government, he'd acquired the cigarettes illegally and wanted to move them as quickly as he could. He supported all three with official-looking documents proving that the cigarettes were in fact waiting for him in Mexico.

Next, he needed to make the punters believe they were getting a bargain. But that was the easy part, because P. T. Barnum was undoubtedly right: there's a sucker born every minute. Austin knew from experience that you snare them by playing to their greed. That when you dangle fat and easy profits in front of guys who live for fat and easy profits, half their brain shuts off — the half that should warn them that when something seems too good to be true it generally is. So he padded the deal to let everyone think they would make a killing, that the jackpot was theirs simply for the price of admission. He put out the word that he was looking to wholesale each container for a nominal $160,000, which was about $3.33 a carton, or roughly fifteen cents on the retail dollar.

Now, commodities of any type — whether they're on clandestine offer in parallel markets or moved openly in any market — are bought and sold on letters of credit. One bank guarantees payment to another bank without money ever changing hands before the cargo does. The buyer pays his bank and the bank holds on to the money until the seller delivers the cargo, which the seller does as soon as the buyer's bank promises to transfer the money to the seller's bank. The system is predicated on mutual trust between banks, guaranteeing that payment has been arranged and will be made. This makes sense because when high-priced cargoes are at stake, there is little reason for either the buyer or the seller to trust each other.

Understandably, before a bank will make any such guarantee, specific documents are required. Austin needed to provide bills of lading that adequately defined the cargo; a certificate of inspection affirming that the cargo, as described by the bills of lading, was on board a ship going to the buyer; a certificate of freshness, so that the buyer knows his assets have not passed their sell-by date; and a certificate of insurance to protect the cargo.

Forged papers were never a problem for Austin, who had access to people who could forge anything, including passports. But maritime transport documents had to list the name of the ship carrying the containers, the whereabouts of the ship, and the cargo on board — all things that anyone with a little know-how could readily verify.

So to get his scam going, Austin decided he needed a ship.

David Wilson was a fool.

At times too gullible, at other times too susceptible to avarice, he was the sort of man always just within arm's reach of the next get-rich-quick scheme. Having long ago convinced himself that he was more savvy and more talented than he really was, he was the sort of man only too willing to gamble with his family's future by staking his own money for pie in the sky.

Born in England in 1944, Wilson studied to be an accountant, but he never qualified as a CPA and wound up calling himself a "financial adviser." He did tax returns for small firms and dabbled in whatever business ventures came his way. Basically, he was an honest man. The people who hired him to handle their bookkeeping spoke well of him. The police never found any evidence that Wilson had previously been involved in any criminal activities. However, because he wasn't above the odd minor-league fiddle — he toyed with dubious offshore shelters and loved to show clients how to pay their personal taxes out of company funds — it wasn't long before he became involved with some intelligent, well-connected, company-owning criminals. They were the ones who told him about the untold wealth on offer in Marlboro cigarettes. They were the ones who told him that a well-connected Mexican colonel was looking for an accountant in Europe — preferably in England because of the language — to set up a company to buy a ship.

It was a perfect match: in Portillo, Wilson saw someone offering him the biggest get-rich-quick scheme of his life; in Wilson, Austin had a stooge.

They promptly struck a deal, and on Portillo's behalf Wilson bought an Isle of Man company called Alamosa Ltd., housed it at his office in Lancashire, then went in search of someone to finance a ship. He found the backing they needed in Norway, where a fellow with shipping interests agreed to put up $2.8 million to purchase a 3,400-ton bulk carrier built in 1970 called the *Gregory*.

On paper, the business was sweet for everybody. The vessel would be purchased by Alamosa, then transferred to Wilson Overseas Ltd., a holding company registered in the Bahamas. For his money, the Norwegian would be the principal shareholder of Wilson Overseas, which meant that he would retain title to the ship. As a bonus, for every ten containers of cigarettes the Norwegian subsequently purchased, Portillo was willing to throw in one container for free. It worked out that if the Norwegian took the entire cargo, he'd be paid back in full for the ship, and therefore wind up owning it for nothing. Once the papers were signed, Wilson changed the name of the ship to the *Lisa Marie*, after his youngest daughter.

With Wilson now running interference for him on the high seas, Austin put up a shield to protect himself from the land-based punters. He stipulated that none of them could deal with him directly. If they wanted to buy cigarettes, they had to go through his agents, whom he seduced by offering jumbo commissions on each container. When an agent asked why Portillo wasn't selling the cigarettes himself, he replied that because of his position with the government of Mexico, he couldn't be seen as taking part. It was plausible enough. The truth was that there was no reason for Austin to take any unnecessary risks that might expose his true identity. The world is filled with agents — middlemen who earn their living like pilot fish, hanging off the backs of people trading in the parallel markets — and if one balked, another could be found to replace him. His agents were each given his private number in New York and sworn to secrecy that they would never reveal it. But when they called, all they ever got was someone on the other end telling them that Colonel Portillo wasn't in and asking if they wanted to leave a message. The New York number was nothing more than an answering service.

Even from the little Portillo told him, Wilson soon realized the really big money was going to the middlemen. So he convinced Portillo to let him sell some containers. His first client was a Scotsman living in Houston named James McMillan, who paid his share in cash. Alamosa then used that cash to refit the *Lisa Marie*.

Had anyone bothered to check — and, clearly, no one did — he might have noticed that the *Lisa Marie* was not a container ship and that even after the refit, there was no way she could handle a hundred containers. But details like that didn't seem to concern Portillo's agents — least of all, Wilson — who together sold several times the ship's maximum cargo.

Whether or not any of them suspected what was actually going on once they learned that suddenly there were too many people selling too many Marlboros in the parallel market is a matter of conjecture. If they had suspected something, they could always rationalize going along by remembering that they were acting only as agents. Minor details, such as whether or not the cigarettes really existed, were Hector Portillo's problem.

Now that he had a ship, Austin's next step was paperwork.

For forged insurance documents, he called on an ex public-school boy who'd been thrown out of Lloyd's of London and was available for dubious projects. Bills of lading were no problem, either, as they were also easily faked. But to obtain the certificates of freshness, Portillo needed the services of a maritime survey company. The most convenient way to arrange that was to invent one himself, which he did, calling it Sealand Maritime Surveyors. And as long as the *Lisa Marie* was getting overhauled in Miami, Portillo figured he might as well put Sealand Maritime Surveyors there, too.

On its letterhead, Sealand's phone number noted the appropriate 305 area code. However, thanks to call forwarding, anyone who dialed the number in Miami got an Englishman in Spain. Except for on those odd occasions when someone asked how the weather was and the Englishman mistakenly replied that it was sunny when in fact Miami was deluged with rain, no one ever suspected that they weren't speaking to a company of surveyors in south Florida.

Originally, Portillo claimed the hundred containers were waiting for the *Lisa Marie* in Vera Cruz, Mexico. Yet the first batch of paperwork that arrived on David Wilson's desk indicated that fifty of the containers had been loaded in Miami on November 12, 1991, and that when she sailed on November 23, the *Lisa Marie* was bound for Hamburg instead of Mexico. That didn't necessarily bother Wilson, because he knew that ships were always being rerouted. But a couple of weeks later, he received documents dated December 3, indicating that the *Lisa Marie* had loaded only three containers of Marlboros and was destined for Naples, Italy. To protect his own clients, he'd agreed with Portillo that letters of credit could not be exchanged until a full inspection of the cargo was carried out at the port of delivery. So he felt confident that everyone's money was safe. However, the conflicting paperwork bothered him. The more he looked at it, the more he began to think something didn't ring true.

He wasn't the only one asking questions.

After paying cash for two containers, James McMillan also signed on as a Portillo agent. Hoping to interest a group of punters in buying some or all of the fifty containers supposedly en route to Hamburg, he'd set up a December 2 meeting at the Rotterdam Hilton. His idea was to bring all of his prospective clients together and make a great pitch. To entice them to the meeting, he'd furnished them with copies of the November 12 documents.

One of McMillan's prospective clients read the documents, saw it as one of those too-good-to-be-true deals, and had enough com-

mon sense to seek professional advice. He forwarded copies of the
paperwork to the International Maritime Bureau. They landed on
the desk of the IMB's director, Eric Ellen. A former chief constable
for the Port of London Police and an acknowledged world-class expert in maritime fraud, Ellen instantly spotted the fly in the ointment. The bill of lading showed that the containers on board the *Lisa
Marie* were numbered 440001 through 440050. Every container
bears its own serial number, because it is constantly on the move
around the world, each one carrying different cargoes to different
ports. But finding fifty consecutive numbers like that on one ship is
as much a virtual impossibility as finding fifty cars in a traffic jam
with consecutively numbered license plates.

Ellen notified the Dutch police, and the Dutch police raided
McMillan's meeting.

The Scotsman's defense was that he was merely acting as an
agent. He swore that he firmly believed the cargo existed and reminded the police that he'd even put his own cash on the line. He
said if you don't believe me, ask David Wilson.

When Wilson heard of McMillan's arrest, he demanded to know
where the ship was. So did Wilson's Norwegian backer. By phone —
supposedly from New York — Portillo reassured them, explaining
that at the last minute he'd diverted the ship to Hong Kong to deliver
a cargo of cigarettes there. It seemed plausible enough. Then Portillo
added that instead of sailing through the Panama Canal and into the
Pacific, the *Lisa Marie* was taking the long way, via South Africa and
the Cape of Good Hope. As bizarre as that sounded, because Wilson
wanted to believe, he did believe. That is, until January, when he received a phone call from the *Lisa Marie's* distraught captain. Having
failed to reach Portillo in New York, the captain wanted Wilson to
know that the ship had taken water into the engine's cooling system
and that he'd been forced to limp into his scheduled port of call,
Puerto Cabello, Venezuela, where he was stuck, awaiting repairs.

Puerto Cabello? Venezuela?

In a panic, Wilson and the Norwegian jumped on a plane and
flew to South America. They found the *Lisa Marie* there, sure
enough, with fifty containers securely strapped down onto her decks.
But when they ordered the crew to open the containers, they

discovered that all fifty were empty. Wilson immediately took steps to stop the ship from leaving Puerto Cabello. Then he began notifying his clients that the whole thing was a scam.

On the night of March 5, two men forced their way into Wilson's house. Their faces concealed by ski masks, they tied his hands behind his back, marched him into his garage, and, at point-blank range, shot him twice in the head.

There were a lot of things David Wilson didn't know when he arrived in Venezuela looking for the *Lisa Marie.* He didn't know that Puerto Cabello is one of the main drug transit ports for Colombian cocaine. He didn't know that police authorities around the world had begun collecting evidence that suggested Austin, still as Portillo, had Colombian drug contacts. He didn't know that to hedge his bets, Austin had secretly purchased a second ship — the *Wei River* — and was working the same swindle without him.

He didn't know that Austin had already written him off.

Among Portillo's new clients was a man in Greece who'd agreed to take five containers for just under $1 million. Austin forwarded him the necessary paperwork to show that the cargo had been loaded in Houston and that the *Wei River* was expected to sail to Holland on February 24. In fact, the *Wei River* was still in dry dock. With the Greek's money, he bought a third ship, the *Infanta,* and now supplied new agents, who in turn supplied new clients, with identical paperwork for identical cargoes on the *Wei River* and the *Infanta.*

Before long, drunk with success, he'd boldly invented ownership of six other ships — six ships he knew nothing about, having picked names out of a hat — and had documents forged to prove the cargoes were loaded and on the way. With tens of millions of dollars at stake, and Wilson, his major liability, now eliminated, Austin convinced himself he was under no further threat. He especially didn't fear the police, firmly believing that international cooperation among the law enforcement agencies was as nonexistent as his cigarettes.

In that assumption he was fundamentally correct. It would take months before the FBI, Customs, and the numerous authorities throughout Europe — all of whom had, at some point, been alerted to Austin's scam — started comparing notes. Not every agency was willing to share whatever it knew about Austin with others. In fact the only thing that worried Austin was that this game, like genuine Marlboros, also had a sell-by date. He knew he could fend off disappointed customers and much-hassled agents for only so long. He understood that unless he moved on, soon his excuses, and invariably his luck, would run out. But not just yet. It was still going too well.

An agent in California sold $1.6 million worth of Portillo's phantom cargo to a businessman in Hong Kong. A month later, when the cigarettes still hadn't arrived, the man in Hong Kong refused to be placated any further and changed the tone of his complaints from mild to very angry. Yet the California middleman managed to turn the man's anger around, and sold him another $800,000 worth.

A second punter took the documents an agent had given him to his bank to secure a letter of credit. The bank studied the papers and pointed out a whopping forty errors, leading them to conclude that the deal was a hoax. But the client didn't want to know. The bank's officers spoke to him until they were blue in the face. The client insisted they pay out. They did.

To postpone his day of reckoning, Portillo planned to use the perfect excuse — a sinking ship. And there is every reason to believe he planned to sacrifice the *Lisa Marie*. The fifty empty containers he'd taken to Puerto Cabello were to be filled with drugs, or arms, or both, and sent to South Africa. As soon as the containers were offloaded, he was going to scuttle the ship. Because Hector Portillo didn't really exist, the Mexican colonel would also sink without a trace. Then, with his profits from the cigarette fraud, the money he'd raised on the drugs and the arms, plus whatever he could collect on the ship's insurance, he intended to spend the rest of his life in the lap of luxury.

He might well have gotten away with it had he not put out a contract on David Wilson.

In an earlier guise — this time as Michael Austin Smith — he claimed to have had dealings with the Pentagon. According to sources usually referred to as "well informed," Austin once tried to arrange a defense contract, posing as a supplier in the aerospace industry. Later, as Portillo-unmasked, Austin made claims to the FBI that he had, and still maintained, connections with the CIA. Not surprisingly, neither the Pentagon nor the CIA publicly admit to knowing him.

However, as Austin tells the story, the markers he holds with the CIA were a result of the minor role he played — this time under the banner of Colonel Rodriguez, a Nicaraguan army officer — in the Iran-Contra affair. There was indeed a Nicaraguan Colonel Rodriguez involved with Iran-Contra, a fact made public by the Senate hearings. And sure enough, during a television program about Iran-Contra, a man claiming to be Rodriguez was dredged up for the cameras. He didn't look anything like Austin, but that doesn't necessarily mean anything. He may or may not have been the real Colonel Rodriguez.

When Austin was arrested in the Dominican Republic, as Colonel Gomez, he confessed to several crimes, among them fraud and dealing in forged passports. It seemed reasonable to expect that he would have been charged, and brought to trial, and having pleaded guilty, that he would have been sentenced to prison in the Dominican Republic. Except, at the very last minute, the Dominicans set him free. Officially, he'd been released "by instructions of the judiciary," but no one is quite sure what that means. The judiciary never offered any explanations.

Austin initially said he'd bribed someone $1 million to get out of Santo Domingo. Then he changed his story, claiming that friends in high places — unnamed American authorities — arranged his release as a thank-you for his help in Iran-Contra. If he did in fact have some connection with the CIA — and the more you know about them the more you realize that anything is possible, especially the most unlikely affiliations — it didn't seem to help him this time.

On July 15, some seventeen weeks after David Wilson was assassinated, Austin was arrested in New York on his way to pay $3.2 million in cash for an apartment in Trump Towers. He was charged with murder and extradited to Britain. His trial took seven weeks, but the jury only needed two hours. In February 1995, it convicted him of first-degree murder and sent him to jail, without the possibility of parole, for the rest of his life.

The hired gunmen have never been found.

There is some suggestion that during the *Lisa Marie* stage of the scam alone, each of the hundred containers Portillo claimed to have had on offer were sold as many as five times. There were customers in Bulgaria, Poland, Italy, Denmark, the United States, Hong Kong, Austria, Sweden, Greece, Russia — including a man purporting to represent the Russian Army — the United Arab Emirates, China, Holland, the United Kingdom, Germany, Belgium, France, Australia, Singapore, Jamaica, and Bermuda.

No one is sure how many times he sold the cigarettes he claimed to have on the *Wei River* and the *Infanta*. Even less certain is the amount of money he generated with the six ships that didn't exist. Records show, however, that in the name of Alamosa Ltd. David Wilson opened bank accounts in several countries, and moved money through Switzerland, Belgium, Holland, Luxembourg, Germany, and Britain. The largest account was at the Bank of Greece in Rotterdam. But the most active account of all was held in the name of a holding company registered in St. Kitts, by Credit Suisse in Zurich.

Three weeks before the murder, Portillo set into motion some very specific measures to get money out of Switzerland. In particular, he contacted, negotiated with, and then engaged a professional money laundering service operating out of the United Kingdom. For a fee, this bunch will move any amount of money in any direction for anyone who employs them. They run a reliable full-service underground banking facility dealing in all aspects of money laundering, in addition to providing a host of affiliated functions, notably forged documentation, smuggling, drug trafficking, and arms dealing.

Their track record is impressive. For example, some years ago, members of this group sold $6 million worth of illegal arms to the government of Sierra Leone, which almost simultaneously fell to a coup. The shipment was therefore never delivered. The money for the guns, minus expenses, was returned to an official whose death was reported in the papers — reminiscent of Hector Portillo's liquidation in a Mexican swimming pool. That same official has since turned up in Europe, living on the arms money. There is good reason to believe that Portillo had also secured this group's help in his Puerto Cabello deal and engaged them to sink his ships.

The police uncovered evidence that within a day or two of Wilson's hurried flight to Venezuela, Portillo had arranged overnight accommodation in Zurich for seven to nine people. There is also evidence to show that a day after those same people arrived in Switzerland, they traveled from Zurich to New York, and that at least three of them arrived on the same flight. Walking into the cavernous International Arrivals Hall at JFK, the three deliberately got onto three different customs lines. As they were legally required to do by American law, all three affirmed they were bringing cash into the country. The proper forms were filled out, and because the only restriction on anyone bringing in more than $10,000 is that the money be declared, once that was done, all three were permitted to go about their business. Together the three declared a total of $700,000. Unfortunately, no one at customs noticed that three large cash declarations had been made by people arriving on the same flight. In fact, it was only when the British asked customs for certain records that they became aware of this delivery.

Still, it is not the cash from Zurich to New York that makes this a money laundering story. There is a neat twist in the tale.

Only a relatively small amount of Portillo's money has ever turned up. If he did make tens of millions of dollars, no one has been able to find it. According to the FBI, Portillo — or Austin or Sporn — didn't live like a man with tens of millions of dollars. At his trial, he denied that any of these millions existed. The amounts officially claimed as lost — by those few punters and agents willing to come forward — put the total at $20 million. Yet four unrelated sources have confirmed that at one point the main Credit Suisse account contained $80 to $90 million. And a few people close to the case are convinced there was more. A lot more.

So the question is, how much was there and what happened to it?

Consider the fact that the discrepancy between the amount admittedly lost and the amount that went through that single Credit Suisse account stems entirely from one simple premise: that many of the people involved with this matter can't come forward because they have no way of legally accounting for the money they put into the deal. That is a common phenomenon in con games. It is also a factor in money laundering.

The suggestion is, then, that Portillo was working both. That he was conning some people while offering certain others a way to wash substantial amounts of dirty money. That this wasn't merely a sting turned sour because of a murder; it was a gigantic and adroitly managed money laundering operation. A major sink purposely built to accommodate major players.

Portillo stole what he could from the punters and washed what he could for his heavyweight clients, bringing their money out the other end of the cycle as genuine cigarettes purchased in the parallel market, or as a phony insurance payment on the nonexistent cargo, or as money moved from one numbered account to another.

Money laundering explains why no one has ever found the missing $20 to $90 million.

Money laundering explains why no one is ever likely to.

8

THE LAWYERS

"I'm gonna get rich patenting a better mousetrap."
"Not me, I'm gonna get rich finding a bigger loophole."
— **Conversation between two law school students**

Harold Ackerman was a 51-year-old south Florida vegetable importer arrested in 1992 for smuggling cocaine. At first he staunchly maintained his innocence, a position that was highly questionable, especially when Gilberto Rodriguez Orejuela, the titular head of the Cali cartel, and his brother Miguel went public with a passionate plea for Ackerman's release.

It was a very curious thing for them to do. And a bunch of people at the Justice Department started asking questions.

Described at the time by the DEA as the highest-ranking Cali trafficker to be arrested in the United States, Ackerman first came to the agency's attention in late 1991, after a raid on a Miami warehouse uncovered fifteen tons of cocaine in hollowed-out concrete fence posts. In the spring of 1992, after Ackerman's arrest, agents found six more tons of coke in a shipment of broccoli and okra in Ft. Lauderdale. The discovery led to the arrest of several Colombians operating in south Florida, as well as Jaime Garcia-Garcia, a 43-year-old Cali laundryman in Bogotá. The good guys impounded $600,000 in cash, four planes, a cache of weapons, a network of computers, and ninety-four bank accounts in Latin America and seven more in the States.

Ackerman then changed his tune, contending he'd been forced

to sell drugs by left-wing paramilitary groups in Colombia who'd threatened to kidnap his family if he didn't cooperate. The jury didn't buy his explanation and convicted him. In a show of support, the Rodriguez boys published an open letter to the DEA, pleading Ackerman's innocence and accusing the agency of "unfounded, permanent aggression." The DEA responded by inviting the brothers to come to Florida to make their case in person. Understandably, they refused.

But as a result of the Rodriguezes' attempts at intervention, prosecutors now looked beyond Ackerman and at some of the seemingly legitimate acquaintances he had in common with Gilberto and especially with Miguel. A closer appraisal of Ackerman's financial documents and computer files turned up what appeared to be a group of lawyer criminals. One of the men who caught the DEA's attention was Michael Abbell, a partner in a Washington, D.C., law firm with an office in Florida. In 1981, when he was an attorney with the Justice Department, Abbell had worked on a case the government was making against one of the Cali cartel leaders, José Santacruz Londono. Part of his job had been to seek information from the Swiss about bank accounts held by Santacruz.

When he left the Justice Department in 1984, Abbell joined Kaplan, Russin & Vecchi, where within six months he was assigned to help Gilberto Rodriguez fight an extradition charge. Rodriguez had been arrested in Spain, and American officials wanted him to face charges in New York. After obtaining a conflict-of-interest clearance from the Justice Department, Abbell testified as an expert witness against the very people he'd worked with at Justice, the very people who'd prepared the extradition request.

Instead of extraditing Rodriguez to New York, the Spanish returned him to Colombia, where he was tried. Abbell was in the courtroom. Apparently because of his extensive knowledge of the evidence, he'd been hired to brief Rodriguez's lawyers. And Rodriguez was acquitted.

In 1987, Abbell was again working for Rodriguez, this time to write a legal brief about Colombia's ban on extraditing its citizens to the United States. The next year, he submitted statements to the Senate Foreign Relations Committee during their review of evidence-gathering provisions in legal assistance treaties with various countries. Abbell's position was consistent with that often taken by lawyers defending Colombian drug traffickers: that defendants should have greater access to foreign evidence that might prevent extradition. In 1989, he showed up in Miami for the drug trafficking trial of Luis Echeverri Santacruz, José Santacruz Londono's half-brother. He had been retained by Rodriguez and Santacruz to assist on legal and factual issues, though he was not participating in the proceedings. Throughout the trial he and Joel Rosenthal, an attorney in Miami who had also been retained to help the defense, sat together in the back of the courtroom.

Around this time, Abbell left Kaplan, Russin & Vecchi, citing incompatible interests. He went into practice with Bruno Ristau, who'd directed the Justice Department's Office of Foreign Litigation for eighteen years. They opened an office in Washington and another in Florida, which they eventually staffed with Francisco Laguna, a Bogotá-born attorney.

Next, Abbell found himself representing Santacruz's wife.

The DEA had uncovered a significant laundry cycle with a money trail leading to Luxembourg, and $60 million they said belonged to Santacruz. They located another $12 million in New York. Abbell, accompanied by Laguna, attended court hearings in both places, then filed a claim for the money in New York on behalf of Ampara Castro de Santacruz. He asserted her right to it as her inheritance from her father. But the jury said no.

The U.S. District Court judge who heard the case quickly labeled Santacruz as a well-organized, multinational drug-trafficking fugitive. Abbell responded with a letter, criticizing him for misrepresenting his client's husband. Ironically, this was just nine years after Abbell, representing the Justice Department, had pursued Santacruz's money because it had belonged to a well-organized, multinational drug dealer.

Five years later, in part through evidence uncovered in Ackerman's files, Abbell stood accused of knowingly securing false sworn statements from arrested members of the Rodriguez-Orejuela faction of the Cali cartel; submitting fraudulent documents to courts in New York and Luxembourg on behalf of the cartel; arranging, receiving, and transmitting cartel drug money; racketeering; conspiracy; drug trafficking; and money laundering.

By this time, Laguna was also attracting attention. During a 1992 DEA sting operation, undercover agents picked up cash for Santacruz in various cities around the country. When $1.2 million was seized in Chicago, the undercover agents were contacted by a cartel representative who'd come to the States to investigate the bust. He ordered them to speak with Laguna. Questioning the undercover agents, whom he believed to be laundrymen, Laguna allegedly demanded, "Why don't you tell me what you know? We're trying to find out what is happening here." Some months later, a federal indictment charged twenty-one people with money laundering, and Laguna with being a coconspirator.

Also under investigation were Joel Rosenthal and three other Florida attorneys linked to Ackerman and Rodriguez. William Moran, a former federal prosecutor in Miami, was a partner in Moran and Gold, and first dealt with Rodriguez in 1985. He was hired to represent members of the gang who'd been arrested in Florida. Ackerman was introduced to him in 1990 by a mutual friend who supposedly had identified Ackerman as the person to call if and when any gang member got arrested. Donald Ferguson had also been an assistant U.S. Attorney in Miami and now worked for himself. He'd been recruited by Abbell in 1990 to help with the civil forfeiture suit in New York and since then had represented arrested members of the Rodriguez gang. Robert Moore was the attorney hired by the cartel to defend Ackerman.

Moran was indicted on multiple charges, including arranging bail for gang members who he knew would jump bail; aiding and abetting the flight of gang members whom he knew to be criminals; preparing, presenting, and arranging knowingly false affidavits; and arranging for and forwarding monthly payments from Rodriguez to the families of arrested gang members to ensure they would not cooperate with the government. Ferguson was similarly indicted on multiple charges, including the delivery of drug money to be used for legal fees, bail, and living expenses.

The 163-page indictment that named Abbell, Ferguson, and Moran also charged fifty-six other people from every level of the cartel, among them the Rodriguez brothers and Santacruz. Laguna, Rosenthal, and Moore were not named, as they had already pleaded guilty to reduced charges. In fact, Ferguson had cut a deal with the government, pleading guilty to conspiracy to obstruct justice and money laundering and agreeing to testify against the remaining two in exchange for a minimum sentence.

That left Abbell and Moran to tough it out, facing possible life imprisonment for their part in a massive drug trafficking and money laundering scheme.

To make their case against the lawyers, the government needed to get inside their offices. But where an attorney's involvement in a crime is suspected, the normal rules don't apply. Very specific steps must be taken — not to protect the lawyers, but to protect their clients. Before the FBI can get a search warrant that allows access to an attorney's computers and other files, they need to obtain the approval of senior officials at the Justice Department, who must conclude that there is sufficient evidence to justify what is seen as a drastic step. Once the Justice Department gives its approval, corroborating approval must come from a federal judge who independently reaches the same conclusion. The reason everyone treads so lightly is that information exchanged between an attorney and his client is considered confidential. The government cannot get at it except under the rarest of circumstances. Attorney-client privilege is one of the foundations on which we've built our legal system. Attorney-client privilege is also why lawyers make the perfect laundrymen.

Confess a crime to your clergyman and in certain jurisdictions he can be called to testify against you. On the off chance that a court were to subpoena him, it's almost certain a clergyman would refuse to violate the sanctity of your confession. But clerical privilege is not ironclad.

Nor is medical privilege. Certain states oblige a physician treating someone with a bullet wound to report the name of his patient to the police. Certain states oblige a psychiatrist to report to the authorities a patient under his care for child molestation who admits he is going to commit the crime again. Rare as it might be to find a doctor willing to testify against his patient, there are times when a court can demand testimony or hold the doctor in contempt.

Journalistic privilege is even less sure. Some states acknowledge the importance of maintaining confidential news sources, others don't. Serious journalists will almost always automatically invoke their right to keep their sources secret, even where that right doesn't exist in law. But they do so knowing they can be shipped off to jail.

Attorney-client privilege is, however, set in stone. Lawyers are not supposed to lie on your behalf or countenance your own perjury. But if you are charged with a crime and tell your lawyer that you committed it and still want to plead not guilty, he is bound by professional ethics to enter that plea on your behalf and never to betray the trust you've placed in him. In other words, your conversations with your attorney are private. So is whatever business he conducts on your behalf.

When an attorney holds money in trust for someone else, it is customary for that money to be put into the attorney's client account, a segregated trust protected by law. Because the money is often a direct reflection of the business an attorney does for his client, the money trail is as confidential as any conversation. If a banker wants to know the source of those funds, the lawyer can tell him that that is privileged information. If the banker calls the cops, the lawyer can tell them the same thing.

Banking with your lawyer is therefore as close to secret banking as anyone can get in a country where banking secrecy doesn't exist. The charges against those six attorneys indicted in Miami involved some fifty-nine transactions totaling $6,911,497, many of them in cash. Most of them had passed through one client account or another. Given enough time and determination, the courts can get inside an attorney's client account. And in this case, they did. But the road there is long and difficult, and one that legislators seem reluctant to make any easier. But then, most legislators are by profession lawyers.

Although attorney-client privilege is generally thought to derive from the Sixth Amendment to the Constitution, it is not specifically spelled out there. All the amendment says about attorneys is that anyone accused of a crime has the right to "the assistance of

Counsel for his defense." Privilege actually evolved from the courts having decided that a just defense is only possible when the accused is free to speak to counsel without fear that the counsel is an agent for the prosecution.

In 1989, the IRS took aim at lawyers, their client's accounts, and cash-paying clients — notably drug traffickers, who are known to pay for most things, including legal services, with cash — stipulating they must fill out CTRs for any cash received in excess of $10,000. It was, the IRS said, exactly the same regulation imposed on banks and other trades. And, as with banks and other trades, an attorney's failure to file reports is a felony. Significantly, the first lawyers to protest the IRS ruling were the criminal defense attorneys. They objected on the grounds that it unquestionably violated attorney-client privilege.

It happens to be against the law for anyone, including lawyers, knowingly to accept dirty money in payment of a fee. A lawyer who knowingly accepts drug money in payment of a fee can be subjected to various penalties, including fee forfeiture. But because the key word is *knowingly,* many lawyers who defend cash-rich criminals either don't ask where their fees are coming from and make certain their clients don't offer explanations, or allow their clients to supply just enough information to lead someone reasonably to believe the fee was being paid out of legally obtained funds. That way, no one's virtue is compromised, at least in public. In private, there is plenty of cash running around, and it's not only on offer to lawyers who defend dope dealers.

A well-known and highly respected international law firm was approached by a client, on whose behalf they'd acted in the past, to purchase an oceangoing yacht. To the senior partners of the firm it sounded like a terrific way to make some easy money. The gentleman instructed them to find something that would meet his requirements in the $10- to $15-million range. With a handsome fee in the offing, the lawyers contacted ships' agents in several pleasure ports, including some in the Mediterranean. It was only a matter of days before an agent in France faxed them with the particulars of a $14-million yacht that sounded perfect. The lawyers forwarded the details to their client and he decided, almost on the spot, that it was exactly what he was looking for. He told them to buy it.

Negotiations were swiftly concluded, the conveyancing went smoothly, and the appropriate agreements were drawn up. Just before the time came to sign the final papers, the attorneys asked their client how he'd be paying for the purchase. Under normal circumstances, money would be transferred from the gentleman's bank, somewhere in the world, to the law firm's client account. Once all the documents were exchanged, the law firm would wire the money from their client account to the client account of the attorneys acting for the seller. But these weren't normal circumstances. The gentleman buying the yacht told his attorneys he intended to pay for it with cash.

The lawyers were bewildered. It's not every day they do $14-million cash deals. Obviously there are people in the world who traditionally pay cash for everything. It's common practice, for instance, in many Gulf states. But that wasn't the case here. Although the lawyers knew enough to worry, they were apprehensive for the wrong reason. Their concern was that they might somehow be risking unforeseen tax liabilities. So they called for their in-house tax specialist, who inspected every inch of the deal. As the deadline for closing drew near, he reported that while a cash deal might be highly irregular, it posed no material tax risks to the law firm. His only recommendation was that arrangements be made for guards to protect the money en route to the bank. That money laundering might be involved apparently never dawned on any of the lawyers.

Once they were reassured about their tax position, the senior partners set a date for the signing. Only one minor detail remained — how the cash was to be transferred. The client explained that his money was in a bank's safe-deposit box and that he wanted the attorneys to rent their own safe-deposit box next to his. They would then all go into the bank vault together, he would open his safe-deposit box, count out $14 million, and hand it to them. They would put it in their safe-deposit box and give him a receipt for it. At that point he'd walk away with the title and keys to his boat. Once he was gone, he told the lawyers, they were free to do anything they wanted with the money.

The senior partners were instinctively nervous about exchanging so much money in such a bizarre manner, but the handsome fee quieted their anxieties. However, one of the partners was actually amused by such a cloak and dagger payoff and casually mentioned it to one of the junior partners. He looked at the senior partner and screamed, "Have you ever heard of money laundering?" And the deal was immediately killed.

In the United States today, the three groups reporting the largest amounts of cash income are car dealers, real estate agents, and lawyers.

Many lawyers argue that by grouping attorneys with other businessmen and requiring them to put the name of a cash-paying client on IRS Form 8300, the government has found a way around attorney-client privilege.

John Zwerling, a partner in the Richmond, Virginia, firm of Moffitt, Zwerling, Kemler, happens to be one of them: "Our system is founded on an individual's right to seek counsel. So putting a client's name on the IRS Form 8300 is perhaps not a problem for a person who's willing to have the government know that he's gone to see a lawyer. But, for someone who decides that he doesn't want every IRS agent, every assistant U.S. attorney, every bureaucratic cop in the federal system to know his business, in the end, he may choose not to seek counsel. By threatening attorney-client privilege you strike at the heart of the right to seek counsel."

An obvious counterargument is that in a criminal defense practice, people who seek counsel bearing cash are probably criminals who have obtained that money through criminal procedures. But Zwerling does not quite see it that way. "There are a lot of people who have cash. Retailers have cash. Restaurateurs have cash. There are a lot of people in this country who don't use banks. Or, if they do, they only use banks minimally, so they can write checks to pay the rent. They keep the rest of their money under the mattress. It may be not very bright, but they do it because they're afraid of losing their savings in a bank. Why shouldn't they be able to pay in cash without inferring that they're criminals?"

A criminal defense lawyer's first responsibility is, quite plainly, to provide competent legal counsel: to stand up on his client's behalf; to make sure that any evidence presented against his client has been lawfully obtained; to make certain the government's proof is adequate; to ensure his client's side of the story is presented in a meaningful way; and, if his client is convicted, to see that the sentence is no greater than is required under the law. Zwerling argues that the government's use of IRS Form 8300, as it pertains to lawyers, puts the entire system in jeopardy because it becomes a means by which the government can turn a lawyer against his client.

In May 1990, the FBI busted a 35-year-old northern Virginia auto mechanic named William Paul Covington for drug trafficking. In the course of the investigation, they obtained seizure warrants for a safe deposit box, several vehicles, and Covington's residence. To defend himself, Covington hired a local law firm. But in July 1991, the FBI hit Covington with another series of search-and-seizure warrants, which got them into several of his bank accounts. At that point, Covington decided to seek new counsel. Claiming the government had scared his lawyers off the case, he approached Moffitt, Zwerling, Kemler.

When William Moffitt and John Zwerling met with Covington, he explained that as the target of a federal cocaine investigation, many of his assets had already been seized by the government based on probable cause. He admitted to them he'd dealt cocaine since 1985, but insisted it was always small quantities. He maintained the government's allegations against him were drastically overstated.

During that initial meeting, which took place on Wednesday, August 21, 1991, and lasted nearly five hours, Moffitt and Zwerling asked extensive questions about Covington's background. He told them that since 1970 he had been steadily employed as a mechanic and had earned substantial sums of legitimate money. He said his father had always advised him to keep a nest egg of cash, something for a rainy day, so he'd hoarded cash all of his life. He referred often to times predating any drug trafficking, when he had as much as $100,000 in his safe-deposit box, all of it legitimately earned. That's when Covington asked if he could pay Moffitt and Zwerling in cash.

The lawyers responded that cash would only be acceptable under three conditions. First, that the cash be deposited in a bank so there would be a record of it. Second, that they comply with the law and file an IRS Form 8300 reporting the transaction. While they would not name Covington as the source of the cash, claiming attorney-client privilege, his identity might have to be disclosed if the government petitioned the court to know it. Third, that they would not accept drug money.

The next day, Thursday, Moffitt and Zwerling informed Covington that their fee to defend him would be $100,000. He handed them a down payment of $17,000 in cash, and returned Friday with a further $86,800 in cash. Myth has it that Covington delivered the cash stuffed in a Ritz cracker box. Zwerling recalls that it was a shoe box. In any case, the lawyers deposited it in their bank on Monday, August 26, and filed the required 8300 form a week or so later. Keeping their word, they did not name the source of the cash.

Meeting with the prosecutors, Moffitt and Zwerling were able to establish several critical points: that Covington did indeed have access to large amounts of legitimate cash through his business, that he had always hoarded cash, that he'd been a nickel-and-dime dealer, and that the assets already seized from him more than covered the amount he most probably earned from drug dealing. They then set about trying to get their client a deal. But the government insisted that Covington admit to distributing fifteen to fifty kilos of cocaine, which he refused to do, maintaining his position that the actual quantity was significantly lower. When the negotiations failed, a grand jury indicted him.

Two weeks into October, the government monitored a conversation between Covington and his girlfriend in which he discussed the cash payment to Moffitt and Zwerling. The prosecutors then dipped into an IRS database and found the law firm's CTR. With just six weeks to go before the trial was scheduled to begin, the government served a subpoena on Moffitt and Zwerling, demanding to see the firm's fee records relating to its representation of Covington. They threatened to prosecute the lawyers for having withheld client-identifying information from the IRS Form 8300 and, unbeknownst to the lawyers, executed a search warrant for the firm's bank records.

Immediately, Moffitt and Zwerling retained separate counsel for Covington, for the law firm, and for all three principals of the firm.

They then filed motions to quash the subpoena and moved to order withdrawal of the threatening letter. In response, the prosecutors sought approval from the Department of Justice Asset Forfeiture Office to confiscate the $103,800 fee Covington had paid Moffitt and Zwerling, claiming it was drug money. The office granted the prosecutor's request, which is merely a formality, so they filed against the firm. Moffitt and Zwerling quickly filed a defense.

In the meantime, the subpoena was quashed and the threatening letter withdrawn. But the damage had been done. The government had successfully set up a series of smoke screens, which not only prevented Moffitt and Zwerling from properly defending their client, but created a situation in which Moffitt and Zwerling could be called as witnesses against the very person who'd come to them for help. On July 16, 1992, the government asked the court to disqualify the law firm. Four weeks later, Moffitt and Zwerling were officially removed from the matter. Shortly thereafter, Covington pleaded guilty and was sentenced to twenty-one years.

Moffitt and Zwerling were now in an even more dangerous situation. Once a person is convicted under the sentencing guidelines, there's only one avenue for him to take to get the sentence reduced. It's called "substantial assistance to the government." That person is invited to sit down with the prosecutors and say, "I will help you make a case against another human being, and in turn you will reduce my sentence." In other words, to go after their friends, their family, and sometimes, their attorney. And if cash has been involved in a criminal defense — which the government can determine through Form 8300 — especially drug-related crimes, the convicted person's lawyer has to worry that he's going to be the next defendant when his former client tries to get his sentence reduced.

Which is exactly what the government did in this case. They offered Covington a chance to reduce his sentence by helping them in their fee-forfeiture case against Moffitt and Zwerling. The courts have proven reluctant to order the entire fee forfeited, but the government has scored points in every round. Moffitt and Zwerling continue to appeal and promise to do so up to the U.S. Supreme Court.

Several questions lie at the heart of the matter. Can a drug dealer use illicitly obtained funds to pay for the counsel of his choice?

Apparently not. Is it a breach of attorney-client privilege if the attorney is forced to divulge the nature and/or source of his fees? There are those who argue it is. Would the government have been able to split Covington and his lawyers had he paid for their services with a check? Clearly not. Has the government violated any of Covington's rights by using Form 8300 to get around attorney-client privilege? The American Civil Liberties Union seems to think that even if they didn't, at the very least they've taken a very dangerous step in that direction. In a brief submitted as a friend of the court, the ACLU held, "If the government can unilaterally inject fee forfeiture into a criminal case in a manner that leads to defense attorney disqualification, the government can improperly deny an accused the constitutional right to counsel of choice in cases the government selects."

Adds Zwerling, "We don't believe that the Department of Justice has the ability, in and of itself, to void the language that's on every dollar bill in the United States where it says, this is legal tender for all debts, public and private."

The case against Moffitt and Zwerling is not an isolated one. New York criminal defense attorney Gerald Lefcourt has been placed in a similar situation.

The DEA, FBI, and New York City Police Department knew they'd scored points against the Cali drug cartel in November 1994 when they arrested two lawyers, a Bulgarian diplomat, an assistant manager at Citibank, a cop, a stockbroker, a fireman, and a pair of rabbis for washing more than $100 million of drug proceeds. After a ten-month investigation, twenty-three people were charged with participating in a ring whose operations stretched from New York to Los Angeles, Miami to Canada, Germany to Colombia.

Believed to have been in operation for at least two years, one of the group's leaders — fireman-turned-businessman Richard Spence, or law partners Harvey Weinig and Robert Hirsch — would be contacted by traffickers who had money that needed to be picked up. A courier would be dispatched to fetch the money and deliver it to one of the three leaders. After being counted, it would be taken to the Bronx, where a low-level employee at a Citibank branch would accept it. The money would then be wired to Europe, where, under the watchful eye of the Cali cartel's representative, Juan Guillermo Ocampo, it would wind up in Zurich. There the husband and wife team of Leon and Rachel Weinmann would move it through their Swiss bank before sending it on its way to a senior cartel trafficker, Miguel Omar Garrabito Botero in Cali.

The group managed to wash from $70 to $100 million before it was taken down. The major players were all arrested, and some of them quickly pleaded guilty as part of a deal with the prosecution.

One of the people charged with money laundering in the Federal Court in New York — but not one of the principal gang members — came to Lefcourt seeking counsel. He paid part of Lefcourt's fee by check, and the rest with cash. The amount of cash exceeded $10,000, so Lefcourt duly filed an IRS Form 8300. Like Moffitt and Zwerling, he too refused to name his client, having made the determination that disclosure of his client's identity in connection with the cash payment could and almost certainly would be used against him by the government.

"Being an officer of the court is not the same as being an undercover agent for the prosecution," Lefcourt insists. "It's obvious that the prosecutor would view the fact that my client had cash, whether he was guilty or not, as something that he would like to put before the jury. And how would the prosecutor do that? He would call me as a witness to say that I received this money from this person. So instead of providing effective counsel, which is what the Constitution says my client is entitled to, I've become a witness for the government. This is unacceptable. That's not the way the right to counsel should work."

The prosecution didn't go after Lefcourt, but the IRS did. They promptly slapped him with a $25,000 fine for failure to comply. Being a pay-now/appeal-later situation, Lefcourt had no choice but to pay the fine and then begin the lengthy appeal process. His suit against the IRS claims he was wrongfully assessed, in that he did not intentionally disregard the filing requirement. Instead, he says, he acted in the good-faith belief that he had ethical obligations toward his client and that he was obliged, at a minimum, to let a court decide whether or not there were special circumstances that might have exempted him from naming his cash-carrying client.

In fact, it turns out that in "special circumstances" the law does exempt lawyers from naming a cash-paying client on Form 8300. But the law does not spell out what those special circumstances should be.

Lefcourt continues: "There are all sorts of people who prefer to do business with cash, and none of them should be suspected of being drug dealers, simply because they use cash. The Latino community doesn't necessarily use banks, for cultural reasons, which began with language barriers. That's also true of the Hasidic Jewish community. I've represented members of both groups, and they often come in with cash. In addition, there are all kinds of people who hoard cash, for any variety of reasons. Some of them may be tax cheats. But then some of them may not want his or her spouse to know that they have this extra money. All kinds of people pay cash, including those who are guilty of crimes that generate cash. Simply because they have cash, it doesn't mean they're guilty."

He agrees that if someone goes to a Cadillac dealer and buys a car for cash the car dealer must fully comply and report that cash transaction. But, he claims, the IRS doesn't see the difference between a constitutional right to counsel and a Cadillac dealer. "To them, they're exactly the same. You have no constitutionally protected right to buy a Cadillac. But the right to come to an attorney to discuss your needs in private is based on a constitutional right. A free society should not in any way interfere with a citizen's opportunity to defend himself by consulting an attorney. That is of paramount importance in a free society. The Sixth Amendment allows and requires counsel in criminal cases, and the effective assistance of counsel is interfered with if the first thing the attorney does is to violate the ethics of confidentiality by becoming an investigator against the person who walked in for help. Citizens accused of crime mustn't have their government interfering with attorney-client privilege."

Although there have been some dissenting opinions among attorneys, the profession as a whole continues to voice concern over the matter. The American Bar Association, along with the National Association of Criminal Defense Lawyers, has met on several occasions with the Department of Justice and the IRS, asking them to stop this. So far, the government has refused to budge. Some lawyers hope that eventually the law requiring a cash-paying client's name will be struck down as unconstitutional. So far, however, the Supreme Court has declined to hear an IRS Form 8300 case.

At the end of 1995, the government brought out a revised IRS Form 8300, making it shorter, and slightly easier for banks to use. It did not make any sort of gesture toward attorneys.

And therein lies another contradiction. Generally, it is the honest lawyer who fills out the form and then refuses to disclose the identity of his client. He's the one reporting the information, telling the IRS about it, and trying to live up to the responsibility of keeping attorney-client privilege. It's the unethical lawyer who tells the government what he knows about the client, in direct conflict with attorney-client confidentiality, or the lawyer criminal who doesn't even fill out the form.

Case in point: How many IRS 8300 forms were filed by the six indicted Miami lawyers on behalf of the Cali cartel? None.

9

BRINKS-MAT MELTDOWN

"Gold has no conscience."
— **Detective Chief Superintendent Brian Boyce, Scotland Yard**

Shortly before dawn on Saturday morning, November 26, 1983, armed hoodlums broke into the heavily fortressed Brinks-Mat warehouse at Unit 7 of the International Trading Estate, less than a mile from the main runway at London's Heathrow Airport.

With great expertise, they neutralized the guards — handcuffing them, hooding them, and binding their feet with masking tape. Then, with gruesome brutality, they terrorized the guards — pistol whipping them, pouring gasoline over them, and holding lit matches close enough to make them believe they were going to be torched.

The gang threatened carnage unless the guards barked out the combinations for the locks that would open the underground vaults.

One hour and forty-five minutes later, the gang was gone. With them went sixty-four hundred gold bars. Three and a half tons worth.

The price of gold on the London market had closed the night before at about $357 an ounce, valuing the booty at just under $40 million. The following morning, when word of the size of the haul got out, gold prices jumped $18, giving the thieves an additional paper profit of $2 million.

Although Scotland Yard never established whether there were six men in the gang or eight, it arrested four of them within two weeks.

A year later, three of those four were in jail. One was Mickey

McAvoy, a 38-year-old professional thug known in the business as "The Bully." Another was 41-year-old Brian Robinson, a professional criminal whose organizational abilities had earned him the nickname "The Colonel." As the reputed masterminds, and for the depth of their barbarity, they were both sent away for twenty-five years.

The only thing they had to look forward to was the gold.

A year after the largest heist in British history, the police still hadn't found a single ounce.

Brian Perry ran a minicab agency in east London. Although he'd associated with villains for most of his adult life, he'd never run seriously afoul of the law. John Lloyd also dwelt on the periphery of the crime world, but lived with an archetypal gangster's moll — a woman named Jeannie Savage, whose first husband had been sent down for twenty-two years for armed robbery. They were the ones McAvoy trusted to make sure his share would be waiting for him when he got out.

To help, Perry and Lloyd brought in a crony of theirs called Kenneth Noye. Stocky, 36 years old, with a boxer's build and a broken nose, Noye pretended to be a self-made success with interests in trucking and construction. But most of the time he dealt in watches and jewelry, and, unlike Perry and Lloyd, did have a record — for receiving stolen goods, shoplifting, assaulting a police officer, and gun licensing violations.

One of his pals was John Palmer, a 34-year-old jeweler who some years before set up a gold bullion dealership in Bristol called Scadlynn Ltd. Noye brought Palmer in to use Scadlynn. However, before Noye could safely ship any stolen gold to Bristol, he needed to distance it from the robbery by making the serial numbers disappear. As Palmer had a tiny smelter at home, Noye convinced him to melt and recast each bar. The gold would then be melted again at Scadlynn, mixed with copper and silver coins, and made to look like scrap. From there, it would be forwarded to the Assay Office, where each bar would be weighed, taxed, and legitimized. Scadlynn would then be free to sell it to licensed bullion dealers who would melt the impurities out and market it.

As an extra precaution, on Tuesday, May 22, 1984, Noye flew to Jersey, in the Channel Islands, to purchase eleven one-kilo gold bars from the Charterhouse Japhet Bank on Bath Street in St. Helier. He did not explain to anyone there that he'd settled on eleven kilos — just over twenty-four pounds — because that was as much he could comfortably carry in an attaché case. However, he did say he would not accept any gold with certificates that included serial numbers. Once the bankers assured him that serial numbers were not recorded on the certificates, he left a $75,000 cash down payment and promised to forward the difference from London. Eight days later, with the balance paid, Noye returned to St. Helier, picked up his gold, walked five minutes down the block to the New Street branch of the Trustee Savings Bank, rented a safe deposit box, and stored all eleven bars there. He came home to England that afternoon with the non-serial-numbered certificates.

Now he began transporting McAvoy's gold to Scadlynn — taking exactly eleven resmelted bars per journey — bringing the Jersey paperwork along as insurance, in case the police ever stopped him and asked where he got this gold.

Without realizing it, though, he'd been clumsy in his caution. His preoccupation with serial numbers had aroused suspicions at Charterhouse Japhet, and a banker there notified the local police. During his second visit, Noye was followed to the Trustees Savings Bank by the police agents who learned he had rented a safe-deposit box. And the Jersey police told their British counterparts about the gold in the safe-deposit box.

Scadlynn, meanwhile, sold the resmelted gold at the going scrap rate, plus a value-added tax (VAT), which stood at 15 percent. For its trouble, it would keep the undeclared VAT. The money from the scrap was deposited at a local branch of Barclays Bank, then withdrawn as cash, stuffed into black garbage bags, and trucked to London. Over the next five months, Scadlynn paid Noye, Perry, and Lloyd in excess of $15 million.

Using a false passport bearing the name Sydney Harris, Noye deposited his share at a Bank of Ireland office in south London, where it was wired immediately to a Dublin branch. McAvoy's girlfriend, Kathy Meacock, did the same thing on alternate days. So did

Jeannie Savage. If anyone at Barclays or the Bank of Ireland was in the least suspicious, they apparently weren't troubled enough to tell the police about it.

Brian Perry also had a buddy named Gordon John Parry, a thick-set ex-convict who was trying to make a living in real estate. So Perry brought in Parry, and Parry in turn brought in Michael Relton, a crooked lawyer who'd defended him on a drug trafficking charge. Parry wound up doing three years. With Relton's help, Parry deposited $1,190,250 from Scadlynn into a Bank of Ireland branch in southwest London. The money was then wired offshore to the bank's office in Douglas, on the Isle of Man. Next, Parry convinced his wife's cousin to help, and she used the bank to send $750,000 to the Isle of Man. Other deposits followed, bringing the total washed through that branch to $2.25 million. To confuse anyone who might attempt to follow the paper trail, Parry brought some of the money back from the Isle of Man, redeposited it, and sent it offshore to yet another bank. And all this time, Noye continued to deliver gold to Scadlynn — eleven bars per journey — while Scadlynn kept melting it down, selling it as scrap, and sending the cash to London.

In early August 1984, Relton helped Parry open an account at the Hong Kong and Shanghai Bank in Zurich, where they deposited $1.26 million. A week later, an unidentified man showed up at that bank's headquarters in the City of London with $750,000 jammed into a sports bag and instructed the bank to forward it to Zurich. Two weeks after that — and over a three-day period from Wednesday, August 29, through Friday, August 31 — Perry, Parry, Relton, a jeweler named John Elcombe, a friend of Parry's, and Elcombe's wife Ann all found themselves in Zurich. Although they later claimed it was nothing more than coincidence, each of them opened accounts at the same branch of the Hong Kong and Shanghai Bank. Between them, they deposited a total of $735,000, bringing their Zurich holdings to just under $1.5 million.

And the coincidences continued.

On Thursday, August 30, Perry and Parry went to nearby Vaduz, Liechtenstein, where they each opened an account with

$67,500 cash at a bank simply called The Bank. What's more, they cosigned for each other's account. Instead of numbers, the accounts were given names. Parry called his "Glad," supposedly after his mother, Gladys. Perry called his "Como," in homage to his favorite singer.

And on it went. Parry now purchased an off-the-shelf company in Jersey called Selective Estates, and opened a company account at Barclays in Guernsey, wire transferring money there from the Isle of Man. Selective Estates sent it on to the Hong Kong and Shanghai Bank in Zurich, where Parry opened a second account, this one called "Burton," in tribute to Richard Burton, who'd just passed away. The following month, Elcombe deposited $97,500 in a Zurich account, for which Parry was a cosignatory. The same day, Parry walked into The Bank with a case he believed to contain $600,000. When it was counted, he seemed surprised to discover the amount was $750,000. On September 24, Elcombe put $652,500 into his account, topping it up on December 4 with an additional $960,000.

Scadlynn was proving to be a cash cow beyond anyone's wildest imagination. It got to the point where they were moving so much money that Barclays had to bring in extra tellers just to deal with Scadlynn's business. If this was Mickey McAvoy's money, you wouldn't have known it by the way everyone else was living on it.

Tipped off by the Jersey police, Scotland Yard put Noye under surveillance. After observing him in the frequent company of Brian Reader — a wanted criminal whom they'd believed had been hiding in Spain — they brought in C-11, a specialist unit used exclusively for top-secret, close-target reconnaissance.

On a cold and dark Saturday evening in January 1985, two officers scaled the perimeter wall of Noye's house and positioned themselves to spend the night on the grounds. One of those officers was John Fordham, a nine-year veteran of C-11. One of Noye's rottweilers discovered Fordham. Two more dogs joined the commotion. That's when Noye arrived, possibly with Reader, carrying a four-inch knife.

Fordham's body was recovered with eleven stab wounds, mostly in his back. Noye was immediately arrested, Reader was picked up a few miles away, and the two were charged with murder. Noye pleaded self-defense. Reader claimed he wasn't involved at all. To the utter astonishment of the police, ten months later a jury acquitted both of them.

However, a small cache of gold bars was found at Noye's house — enough to link them with the Brinks-Mat gold. Noye and Reader were charged with conspiracy to handle stolen goods. Within three days, the police also arrested Palmer and moved in on Scadlynn.

John Elcombe knew nothing about Fordham's killing.

He and his wife left London for Switzerland that Saturday, driving Parry's Mercedes, with $1,065,000 hidden in the trunk. They'd already made one trip to Zurich that year to deposit $679,500. Crossing into Germany from Holland, a guard on the Aachen side stopped them and asked if they had anything to declare. The Elcombes admitted to carrying $67,500 in cash, claiming it was their life's savings and that they were taking it to Switzerland. The guard studied their passports, lingered over the vehicle registration papers, then announced he wanted to search the car. He opened the trunk, pulled up the carpeting on the floor, and found the cash. The Elcombes were officially detained for questioning.

The money was piled on top of a desk inside the shack at the border crossing and counted. For some reason, the guard took it upon himself to write down the serial numbers of random bank notes. Then he notified his headquarters in Wiesbaden, asking what they wanted him to do. Wiesbaden notified the German Interpol office, and they telexed a few queries to British Interpol. Are you looking for either John or Ann Elcombe? Have large amounts of currency recently been stolen? Is the Mercedes being held at the Aachen border on the stolen car register?

British Interpol passed the questions to the duty officer at Scotland Yard. He made a fast check, and the answer to all three questions came back no. So Scotland Yard duly informed British Interpol, who duly informed German Interpol, who passed the information along to German Customs, who finally called the border guard near

Aachen. The money was loaded back into the Mercedes and the El-combes were allowed to drive away.

That might have been the end of that had an officer on the Scotland Yard duty desk not noticed that the car Elcombe was driving was registered to Gordon John Parry. The name rang a bell. Later that evening he realized the name was associated with the Brinks-Mat inquiry. He phoned the Brinks-Mat situation room, and when the officers there heard what had happened, they begged British Interpol to ask German Interpol to arrest the Elcombes. But by this point, the couple was long gone.

Clearly shaken by the close call at the border, the Elcombes took their time getting to Zurich. It wasn't until the following Friday, February 1, that John Elcombe deposited $150,000 into his old account and $912,000 into a new account, this one known by the number 720.3. The $3,000 difference between what they took out of England and what they deposited in Switzerland was written off to expenses, including one night to settle their nerves in the royal suite of the Dolder Grand Hotel.

Three days later, someone deposited $740,955 into Parry's "Glad" account. One week after that, Elcombe transferred $2.4 million from his account into 720.3. Then, Parry closed his "Glad" account and moved that money into 720.3, bringing the total there to $3.9 million.

Michael Relton was just as busy as everyone else. On Friday, April 26, he arrived in Liechtenstein to create what is known as a "Red Cross" account.

Nestled between Switzerland and Austria — and the model for the country in the Peter Sellers film *The Mouse That Roared* — Liechtenstein is sixty-two square miles of lush valleys, skiable mountains, and high-tech factories that produce precision instruments, false teeth, and postage stamps. On National Day, the ruling prince invites the entire population to his castle for drinks. The capital, Vaduz, is a cluster of hotels and souvenir shops. Any tourist who wants to have his passport stamped, as a souvenir of his visit, has to have it done at the post office because there's no one to do it at the border. There is no railroad station, only one supermarket, and a single traffic light. There are, however, dozens of banks.

In fact, banks — and the resident company-formation agents who introduce clients to those banks — generate enough revenue to ensure that taxes stay low, that the national budget remains balanced, and that all thirty thousand natives enjoy one of the highest living standards in Europe. The reason is simple: banks in Liechtenstein are just as secret as they are in Switzerland. In some cases, even more so.

The local specialty, formally referred to as a "foundation account," appears to be controlled by an organization, often with the name of a charity — hence the "Red Cross" reference — as if to suggest that the money on deposit is destined for some good cause. Administered by a local attorney — ensuring a double level of secrecy — a charity may be the named beneficiary, but the beneficiary is not necessarily the beneficial owner of the account. Such is the ironclad nature of a Red Cross account: anyone lying about who actually benefits from the account will get away with it every time because it is impossible to prove otherwise.

Relton, as a lawyer, knew the ins and outs of Red Cross accounts and named his the Moet Foundation, referring to his favorite champagne. However, someone must have misunderstood because the bank spelled it "Moyet." In any case, Relton and Parry put $4,751,113 into it. Unfortunately for them, Parry had just bought a farm outside London, paying with monies drawn on the 720.3 account. In his haste to move funds to Moyet, he hadn't bothered to find out if the check for the farm had already cleared, which it hadn't. But because a manager at The Bank knew where the money was, he took it upon himself to transfer the necessary funds back from the Moyet.

Had Parry not bounced that check, the police would never have been able to penetrate the secrecy of a Liechtenstein Red Cross account and associate it with the Brinks-Mat hoodlums.

In the fifteen months that separated the robbery and the killing of John Fordham, the gang now controlling the gold had gotten through almost $32 million. What none of the gang members knew was that the Metropolitan Police had assigned two hundred officers to the

Brinks-Mat inquiry. The largest heist in British criminal history was being investigated by one of the largest manhunts in British police history.

Unaware of just how close the police were getting to them, Parry and Relton began thinking about their old age, and embarked on a series of hefty real estate investments. They formed a subsidiary of Selective Estates called Blackheath Ltd. and bought a residential development in Gloucestershire for $525,000. To finance it, Relton ordered the Hong Kong and Shanghai Bank in Zurich to send $300,000 to the Southeast Bank in Sarasota, Florida, where he maintained an account. Southeast then wired $200,000 to his personal account at Midland Bank in London. From there, he sent $156,000 to the British Bank of the Middle East — a subsidiary of the Hong Kong and Shanghai — which in turn wired the money to the lawyers acting for the sellers. Finally, Blackheath "borrowed" $375,000 from the British Bank of the Middle East, the loan being guaranteed with money in the "Burton" account. Because that deal worked so smoothly, Parry and Relton kept doing it — investing another $3.3 million in residential property — now adding Jersey, Guernsey, and the Isle of Man to the washing cycle.

Spinning money around six countries, Relton believed that even if the police somehow stumbled onto them, they'd need to identify a dozen secret bank accounts and would spend years trying to obtain court orders in six different jurisdictions to open them. And even if the cops got their cases heard, there was no guarantee their requests would be granted. Relton was so utterly convinced they were beyond the reach of the law that he and Parry now took aim at London's Docklands, at the time one of the hottest commercial developments in Europe. They bought New Caledonian Wharf, Upper Globe Wharf, Globe Wharf, Cyclops Wharf, Lower Kings Wharf, and Queens Wharf, and in each case their laundry cycle was basically the same. They borrowed money from one bank, secured their loans with money from other accounts, then moved that money through several banks, until eventually it looked like a legitimate loan secured by the property they were buying. In all, they spent just over $7.9 million in Docklands. By selling most of it at the height of the property boom, they more than doubled their money.

Skillful at playing such lucrative games, Relton and Parry now formed a Panamanian company, Melchester Holdings, and sold Parry a nightclub he already owned. They took $450,000 out of the "Burton" account and gave it to a lawyer acting for Melchester, who put it in his client account. When the paperwork was ready, the lawyer sent the money to Relton for his client account. When the papers were signed, Relton passed the money along to Parry to complete the sale. Finally, Melchester sold the club to a friend of Parry's for $150,000, which wound up back in the "Burton" account.

On February 7, 1984, a man whose identity is still unknown to the police walked into a small merchant bank in the City of London with $456,000. His instructions were to send the money to the Mercantile Overseas Bank in Douglas, Isle of Man. Confirmation of the transfer went onto Mercantile's books the following day. But according to the bank, because no one there knew anything about the money, it was stored in a settlement account — temporary home for monies waiting to be claimed. In this case, Mercantile Overseas named it Mangrove Settlement Account 691,343.

On March 2, a man calling himself Patrick Clarke purchased a $450,000 draft for cash at a Bank of Ireland branch in east London and made it out to John Lloyd. That same day, a Mercantile Overseas Bank officer in London received a phone call from an unidentified man, asking him to pick up the check at a hotel near the Tower of London. The bank officer later told police he walked into the lobby, where a stranger handed him an envelope, told him it was to be forwarded to Douglas, then walked away.

Though it was now more than three weeks after the first anonymous deposit, and though there was apparently nothing to suggest the two deposits were in any way related, and though other monies totally unrelated to the Brinks–Mat laundering operation had come into Mercantile, and though they'd assigned new numbers to those unrelated deposits, bank officials put John Lloyd's $450,000 into Mangrove 691,343-B.

Twelve days later, on March 14, Kenneth Noye sent $450,000 to Mercantile, where it was called Belleplaine Settlement Account

690,227. On April 30 — forty-seven days after his first deposit — Noye sent another $450,000. By coincidence, it went into Belleplaine 690,227-B. A further $300,000 from Noye wound up as Belleplaine 690,227-C. The bank later maintained it didn't know whom any of this money belonged to.

On July 4, an even more curious thing happened. Apparently at the bank's own initiative, $156,549 was moved out of Belleplaine and into Mangrove 691,343-C. Two days later, the bank took $300,000 more from Belleplaine and put it into Mangrove 691,343-D. Seventeen days later, an interbank transfer for $157,500 found its way into Mangrove 691,343-C2.

On July 24, Noye handed $300,000 in cash to the Royal Bank of Canada in London, which was acting as agent for Mercantile Overseas, though not otherwise involved with this matter. He wanted it sent to Douglas. Mercantile automatically stored those funds in Belleplaine 690,227. And on August 10, a man put another $300,000 through the Royal Bank of Canada and it wound up in Mangrove 691,343-E. The last transfer, made by a man unknown to the police, was for $168,334 and became Mangrove 691,343-F.

When the police finally managed to unravel all of these transfers at the end of 1986 and got their hands on the money, they concluded it belonged to Noye. But $1,462,500 was still missing. The bank's explanation was that one day in November of 1986 a man calling himself Captain Schultz walked into the Douglas branch and demanded his money. Bank officials insisted they didn't know what he was talking about, until he detailed the dates of his supposed deposits, the sums involved, and the bank transfers he'd arranged. Because he was able to satisfy the bank that the money sitting in the various Mangrove Settlement Accounts was his, they followed his instructions and wired the money to Germany.

By that time, the police had arrested Relton, Parry, and Noye; had frozen accounts in four countries, in addition to the Channel Islands and the Isle of Man; and had found $2.75 million stashed in Noye's Dublin account, though they had somehow missed the $3.75 million Jeannie Savage had also hidden there. Her money lay dormant until 1991 — five years' interest turning it into $6.15 million —

when the police found it. They also seized accounts for Brian Perry, Gordon John Parry, the Elcombes, and John Lloyd, among others.

Assets totaling more than $33 million were recovered.

Everything changed the night John Fordham was killed.

A cop was killed. That was when the Brinks-Mat investigation clicked into a higher gear.

One of the men suspected of having taken part in the burglary that started it all in 1983 was a professional criminal named John Fleming, who went on the lam in Spain. He'd been kept under surveillance and his phone was tapped, but in those days there was no extradition treaty between Spain and the United Kingdom, so Fleming could have stayed right where he was, safe in the knowledge that he was untouchable. That is, had his passport not expired.

Because an arrest warrant was waiting for him in London, Fleming couldn't get his passport renewed at his local British consulate. And without a valid passport, Fleming couldn't stay in Spain. So he headed for the Caribbean — with British detectives following — but found no country willing to take him. He next tried Latin America. When that failed, he made a big mistake and went to the United States. Arrested on his arrival, Fleming sat in a Florida jail for the next several months, fighting extradition. Within hours of the judgment against him, he was handcuffed and bundled onto a plane for London.

But this time, at least, luck was on Fleming's side. His expired passport had forced Scotland Yard to play what few cards they held. Had Fleming stayed in Spain, they might have had time to build a solid case against him. Unfortunately, they had to take him when the Americans deported him, and at that point they didn't have enough to convince a jury he'd been part of the Brinks-Mat robbery. So the jury let John Fleming walk.

However, while eavesdropping on his phone calls in Spain, the police learned that Fleming had established a business relationship with Patrick Bernard Arthur Diamond, who ran an Isle of Man company-formation service called Comprehensive Company Management (Manx). On several occasions, the police had heard Fleming ask Diamond to wire money to Spain. So Scotland Yard turned their attention to Diamond and, with the cooperation of the Manx police, tapped his phone.

None of the other people involved in the inquiry appeared to have ties with Diamond, although the police did discover Diamond's sense of humor. He'd recently formed companies that were ulti-mately tied to the Brinks-Mat money, with names such as "G. Reedy Holdings" and "Inventive Inventories, Inc." They also discovered that he was a man who liked to party and came to London almost every weekend. So now, when he landed in London, officers tracked him. Most evenings, they followed him to nightclubs frequented by the underworld. Each of his contacts was carefully noted.

On one particular Friday night, Diamond checked into the Westbury Hotel on Conduit Street in London's West End, and met with a young American who'd registered there under the name of Stephen Marzovilla. When a check with the FBI failed to turn up any information about anyone called Marzovilla, officers moved into the hotel and tapped his phone, too.

The next night, when Diamond and Marzovilla left for the evening, one surveillance team followed them while another gained access to Marzovilla's room. Two interesting items were found: a fam-ily tree, showing Marzovilla's occupation as a plumber and listing in-formation about his wife and children, including their dates of birth, and, hidden inside a secret compartment of his toilet kit, a pair of switchblade knives. A family tree is a dead giveaway a suspect is learn-ing a new identity. The police could therefore reasonably assume Marzovilla wasn't his real name. As for the switchblade knives, the police decided they might come in handy later.

That Monday, just before Diamond left for home, the police recorded a call he made to Fleming in which he spoke about a visit later in the week from "The Pizza Man" — a clear reference to Mar-zovilla.

Over the next five days, shadowing Marzovilla, the police lo-cated an apartment he kept in Chelsea and several safe-deposit boxes he'd spread around London. When it became obvious he was about to leave for Spain, the decision was made to arrest him, but with extreme caution. They didn't want to alert him to their interest in Diamond, Fleming, or the safe-deposit boxes. Nor did they want him to suspect they knew Marzovilla was not his real name. So they settled on a scenario as unusual as their interest in him.

Marzovilla left the hotel on Friday and took a taxi to Heathrow. He was allowed to check in for his flight to Spain and proceed to security. The police waited until his carry-on luggage went through the X-ray machine before pulling him aside. They explained something had shown up on the screen that didn't look quite right. He said he didn't know what they were talking about. They hand-searched his carry-on. He waited. When they got to his toilet bag, they uncovered the switchblades.

While he was detained at the airport for attempting to carry dangerous weapons on board a plane, the police got a warrant to open his safe-deposit boxes. They found $100,000 in cash, plus a U.S. passport and driver's license in the name of Craig Jacobs. That name was wired to the FBI. The response came back that Craig Jacobs was a known alias of Scott Nicholas Errico, a man who'd been convicted on two counts of drug smuggling but had jumped bail while awaiting sentencing. A federal warrant was outstanding. Errico was also wanted by the FBI on three counts of murder.

Still not tipping their hand, the police charged him with possessing offensive weapons at an airport, strapped him in chains, and used a huge armed escort to move their prisoner from Heathrow to Central London. Even Marzovilla couldn't help remarking that there were an awful lot of armed guards around just for one guy with two small knives.

By the time they got him to Cannon Row police station, he suspected they were on to him. When they took him to be fingerprinted, he refused to cooperate. Over the next two days, he resolutely stuck to his story — "I'm a plumber named Marzovilla." This put the police in a minor quandary. They needed to prove what they already knew — that Marzovilla was Errico — and the best way to make their case was through fingerprints, but they couldn't force him to cooperate. That's when one officer suggested a stunt so simple-minded the others thought he was joking. It's a stunt cops pull in bad movies, and it doesn't usually work. Yet the officer insisted he wanted to give it a try.

After a particularly long interrogation session, the officer asked Marzovilla if he wanted a cup of coffee. Marzovilla said he did. A few seconds later, the officer reappeared to apologize that the kettle wasn't working. He asked, "How about a glass of water instead?" Marzovilla said thanks, took the glass, drank from it, and put it down on the table.

The instant he did, the officer grabbed it.

Just as quickly, Marzovilla knew he'd been had.

Forensics lifted a perfect set of prints from the glass, and the FBI confirmed Stephen Marzovilla, alias Craig Jacobs, was a fugitive contract killer named Scott Nicholas Errico.

Although Errico fought extradition for more than eighteen months, claiming that the murders he'd been accused of had taken place on a boat outside U.S. territorial waters, the courts didn't see it Errico's way and he was shipped back to the States. There, he was found guilty of murder and sentenced to life in prison.

By unraveling Errico's business dealings with Diamond — they owned a company called Castlewood Investments — the police were able to open all of Diamond's books. That uncovered Diamond's dealings with a Miami attorney named Michael Levine. Evidence that Levine was tied to Colombian traffickers was quickly passed on to the DEA. And once the DEA was able to get inside Levine's bank accounts, they found records proving that Diamond was Levine's laundryman.

Diamond's method was classically simple. He would fly to Miami carrying a bearer check, drawn on one of his many companies, for the sum of $250,000. As U.S. Customs requires anyone coming into the country with cash or bearer instruments worth more than $10,000 to report it, he would fill in the proper forms to declare the check. With a stamped copy of the form to prove he'd brought money into the country, he'd destroy the check. Levine would then give him $250,000 in cash to carry out of the country. On the off chance customs might stop him, Diamond had the proper paperwork to back it up.

Over the course of several years, Diamond had washed Levine's cash through ninety companies. He also spent some of it for Levine, purchasing Strangers Key, a small Bahamian island. When Levine discovered it wasn't large enough for an airstrip — therefore too small to be used for smuggling drugs — he sold it.

Diamond was arrested in March 1986 and admitted his involvement with Fleming. He also admitted to laundering $19 million for Levine. Facing life in prison, Diamond testified against his former pals. For his role in the Brinks-Mat affair, Diamond was sued by the U.S. government under RICO statutes, which allow for tripled damages. Because the Brinks-Mat gold was worth $40 million, the judgment against him came in at $120 million.

A dozen separate cases fell under the auspices of the Brinks-Mat investigation, which resulted in twenty-nine arrests. The trials, however, were marred by jury tampering and death threats. In one case, four separate juries needed to be convened, and each time, the jury had to be protected. Most of the gang went to jail: Noye got fourteen years, Parry ten, Perry nine, Relton twelve, and Savage five. A few are already out. The two who will stay where they are for a long time are Mickey McAvoy and Brian Robinson. The best they can hope for is the possibility of parole in 2004.

In the meantime, their money is gone.

So the two guys who pulled off the greatest robbery in the history of British crime have had to sit tight while a whole bunch of minor crooks laundered their money. It's a safe bet they are both viciously bitter. It's an equally safe bet that when they do finally get out they're going be looking for $40 million worth of flesh from the laundrymen who did them wrong.

There is a very odd postscript to this story.

During the American offshoot of the Brinks-Mat investigation, the DEA seized $380 million. To say thank you to the Metropolitan Police, the American government made out a check for half of that. It's called asset sharing, and it's done to encourage international cooperation. However, there's a string attached. Although the recipient is welcome to spend the money on anything — equipment, weapons, training, ongoing operations — it must in some way be used in the war against drugs. The idea is to use drug traffickers' assets to beat drug traffickers. But the British balked. As one senior official put it, "The Metropolitan Police mustn't be seen to be bounty hunters." A ruling came down from somewhere in Whitehall that instead of going to the police the money had to be given to the Treasury. "No," the Americans said, "that's not the way the deal works. It goes to the police and they have to spend it on the war against drugs." Frantic meetings were held at the Home Office. "Come on," the Americans urged, "you're free to interpret the criteria we've set down in a lot of different ways. You can do whatever you want with the money, as long as it satisfies the single objective of the asset-sharing program — to put the criminals' own assets to use against them."

After months of bandying about, the British decided they could not accept the gift unless it was given unconditionally. So the Americans said "Sorry," and went home with their $190 million.

10

THE ADVENTURERS

"Laundering methods keep changing to stay ahead of the authorities and the good guys are overwhelmed by the size of the problem."
— **U.S. News and World Report**

The poor bastard used to have a real name, but in November 1986, after he'd showed up at the DEA office in Seattle, Washington, with a story to tell, they christened him CI-1. And once the DEA awards you Confidential Informant status, you are forever known by your number.

CI-1's story began: Over a three-day period — from Monday, August 25, 1986, through Wednesday, August 27 — two brothers from Los Angeles ran a gang that smuggled twenty-three tons of high-quality Thai marijuana into the United States.

CI-1 said: Two local fishing vessels, escorted by a surveillance plane loaded with radar equipment to protect them from intervention by U.S. Customs, rendezvoused with the mother ship several hundred miles off southwestern Alaska, and brought the product ashore in Anacortes, a commercial salmon port sixty miles north of Seattle. The shipment was so large it filled two tractor-trailers. The same brothers were now planning a much bigger haul for the summer of 1987.

CI-1's story ended: I didn't get paid what they promised me, and I'm looking to get even.

So Special Agent Gary Annunziata gave him his chance. He wired CI-1 for sound, and sent him back into the smuggling business.

Bill and Chris Shaffer were in search of adventure.

As kids, they'd lived in London because their old man had been stationed there by the U.S. Navy, but after leaving high school in 1963, Bill went back to America, and got a degree from Penn State and a job teaching school in New Jersey. Chris stayed in Europe for a while, running around with a girlfriend. When they were able to put some money together, they bought a sail boat and headed for Australia, where they worked charters. Before long they were able to buy an 80-foot sloop. Slowly but surely, their charter business turned into amateur smuggling. They made a few runs, brought in some dope, and picked up some fast money. It worked well the first few times, so they kept doing it, fetching bigger loads each time. In the meantime, Bill gave up his teaching job, dealt a little cocaine in Florida, and wound up in Los Angeles. He continued dealing drugs because it was fast money with very little risk, an easy way to get through life while trying to maneuver his way past the periphery of the film world. By the time Chris came back to the States in 1983 and joined up with big brother in Los Angeles, they both knew a lot about the drug business.

The Shaffers told people they were treasure hunters, marine salvage experts who went in search of sunken galleons. Chris even set up a company in Britain, China Pacific Films, to fund their salvage work. In reality, all it did was finance a ship for smuggling. By January 1985, the Shaffers had raised enough money to pay $1 million for a fishing vessel out of Hawaii called the *Six Pac*. Along with the boat came its captain, a former British merchant mariner named Terry Restall.

It was a fortuitous encounter. Restall had been smuggling hashish for years and was savvy to the ways of the drug world.

Within two months, the Shaffers sent Restall into the Gulf of Thailand, where he was met by two Vietnamese fishing boats, and took on board seven tons of marijuana. Restall brought the product to a rendezvous point six hundred miles off the coast of San Diego, California, where it was transferred to a fishing vessel called the *Pacific*

Rose and eventually brought ashore near Santa Cruz. On his next trip, Restall returned with eight tons.

Early in 1986, the Shaffers invested in a shipment they weren't transporting themselves — five tons of product — which was seized by U.S. Customs near Hawaii. It shook the brothers into realizing just how vulnerable they were. Suddenly worried that the authorities might be watching them, Bill and Chris went looking for a vessel unlike any ever before used in an American smuggling operation. They found the *Niki Maru,* a 110-foot oil-supply ship, sitting in Japan. They bought it, and then spent $300,000 converting it to look like a Japanese fishing boat.

It was the *Niki Maru* that brought in the 23-ton shipment.

In February 1987, thanks to CI-1, Annunziata learned that the Shaffers had purchased a big fishing boat in Seward, Alaska, the *Stormbird,* and brought it to Seattle to be converted for smuggling. For the next seven months, the DEA patiently gathered evidence on the Shaffers. In September, when the refitted *Stormbird* slipped out of port heading for Alaska, the DEA decided it was time to arrest the entire gang.

But Bill Shaffer had developed a sixth sense — acute paranoia — and something told him he was being watched. He hastily acquired a new boat, the *Blue Fin,* then put out the word it was carrying a load coming ashore in Mexico. Gullibly, CI-1 relayed that story to Annunziata.

Instead, a Shaffer boat called the *Manuia* delivered the product to the *Six Pac* south of Hawaii, the *Six Pac* brought it to the *Stormbird* in the northern Pacific, and the *Blue Fin* met the *Stormbird* south of Alaska. By the time the *Stormbird* arrived back in Anacortes on September 21, empty, the *Blue Fin* had already docked at Bellingham, twenty-five miles north, and had unloaded forty-two tons of marijuana.

And all the time, the DEA were looking toward Mexico.

Because the drug business functions as a subculture, successful dealers find the people they need to know by moving through the underworld. People with access to product. People with access to boats. People with access to distributors. And specialists. People with expertise in buying, off-loading, and money laundering.

The Shaffers worked their way inside this subculture. While Bill was clearly the man in charge, giving the orders and managing the financial side, Chris was the one who dealt with logistics and transportation. But they couldn't do everything themselves, and over the years an organization grew up around them. It started out with friends and soon included friends of friends. The problem was, the larger the group, the more vulnerable they became.

Buying product in Southeast Asia put them in business with two of the world's largest dealers. One was Brian Peter Daniels, an ex-pat American from whom the Shaffers purchased their 1987 shipment. The same age as Bill, with the same taste for adventure and the same appetite for flashy women, Daniels lived in Thailand, and for a time was a serious contender for the title of the world's most important marijuana supplier. Between 1984 and 1988, Daniels is known to have smuggled several hundred tons of marijuana into the United States.

Each bale of Daniels's product was tightly wrapped in heavy, dark-blue nylon canvas, and bore the Eagle Brand sticker — a white tag with a crudely drawn blue eagle and the bold red words "Passed Inspection." Whether he was warning rivals or just being pompous, the Justice Department isn't sure. There is some evidence to suggest that the Eagle Brand was never exclusive to him. What the Justice Department does know for certain is that Daniels couldn't possibly have operated on the scale he did without a lot of help.

The man whose title he was challenging was known in the States as Tony the Thai, but referred to at home as "The Duck." Then in his mid-thirties, although he looked older, he spoke good English and fronted his illicit trade with a small but successful empire in real estate, hotels, and night clubs mainly in the northeastern province of Nakhon Phanom. He was heavyweight champ, the man to know if you wanted to buy high-grade Thai marijuana.

He was also secretly indicted by a federal grand jury in San Francisco in November 1991 on charges of smuggling forty-five tons of marijuana into the United States, conspiracy, and operating a criminal enterprise over a fourteen-year period, between 1973 and 1987. That indictment remained sealed for three years, without his true identity being revealed, while the Feds looked for ways to lure him to the States, where they could arrest him. When he failed to take the bait, they ripped a page out of the textbook 1989 kidnapping of Manuel Noriega. Several plots were bandied about. The basic idea was to lure Tony out of Thailand and into a friendly place, such as Hong Kong, where U.S. agents could bang him on the head and bundle him onto a waiting plane. But three years after the indictment, a newspaper in Bangkok broke the story that Thanong Siriprechapong, a member of Parliament, had been formally incriminated in the States. So the decision was made to unseal the order, publicly acknowledge that Tony was Thanong, and seize whatever assets he had in the States. Those holdings included a $1 million Beverly Hills home and a 1987 Mercedes-Benz.

Of course, Thanong protested his innocence. But the evidence against him was so overwhelming that Washington demanded his extradition. In December 1995, the appeals court of Thailand took the unprecedented step of upholding the American request. A few days later, he was bundled onto a plane and flown to the United States, making Tony the first Thai to face criminal charges abroad since the two countries signed an extradition treaty in 1929.

It now appears that Thanong was not the only Thai politician moonlighting in drugs. The deputy leader of the Chart Thai party and the deputy finance minister have both been named as suspects in drug cases by Washington. Like Tony, they also deny the charges.

The charges against Thanong were minutely detailed by members of the Shaffer gang. According to Restall, Thanong invited him to meet in Bangkok so that he could show the Shaffers what they were buying. When Restall arrived, Thanong personally took him into the jungle, north toward Chiang Mai. When they arrived at the Laotian border, no one asked who they were or what they were doing there. In Laos they were met by a senior, uniformed police officer who escorted them to a heavily guarded warehouse, where Tony had stashed two hundred tons of high-quality dope.

The story came as no surprise to the agents who interviewed Restall, even though marijuana is not the main cash crop in this region, otherwise known as the Golden Triangle. This is heroin country. About half of the heroin sold on American streets originates in the opium fields of Laos, Burma (Myanmar), and Thailand. The triangle extends south through Bangkok and to the Malaysian border, with the Andaman and South China seas used as the gateways to regional markets. What's more, because Thailand has a traditional cash economy, billions of dollars are easily laundered through banks, stocks, and property.

There is sufficient evidence to argue that authorities in Thailand, Laos, and most recently Vietnam regularly turn a blind eye to the traffickers because they're paid handsome amounts of much-needed hard currency for the service. In some instances, men such as Daniels — and in this case, certainly, Tony the Thai — have gotten into bed with those government officials. They have made them partners, having apportioned them shares in the action to command their allegiance. They have done the same to gain the loyalty of local warlords, police chiefs, and provincial governors. Marijuana coming out of Thailand and Laos, crossing Vietnam, and shipped from Da Nang gets waved through every checkpoint as long as it bears the right label. The military is in on it, too. One shipment to the Shaffers was guarded by a uniformed Vietnamese Army detail during the off-loading in the Gulf of Tonkin.

At the U.S. Department of Justice, they read "Passed Inspection" to mean "everyone will get a slice."

As the money rolled in, the brothers set themselves up in Malibu and rented houses all over Los Angeles. Two of Bill's pals from his New Jersey days were Ed and Eileen Brown. She produced porn films and called herself Summer. At Bill's request, the Browns rented a big house in the North Helena section of fashionable Brentwood so that the Shaffers had a place to count their money. The Browns rented a second house in the Hollywood hills, far away from the counting house, so that the Shaffers had a place to hide their money.

Bill and Chris limited their dealings to two distribution groups, one in California, the other in New York. The Los Angeles distributors were an odd couple who came to be known as Greater and

Lesser. Greater was a husky ex-football player named Kenneth Tarlow. Lesser was his more diminutive pal, named Dennis Specht. In
New York, their client was known simply as Sonny. At the time, no
one knew anything more about him than that.

The way Bill Shaffer saw it, doing business with Greater, Lesser,
and Sonny was no reason to trust them. So whenever a payment was
due, he sent his own people to pick it up, and mapped out deliberately complicated routes for their trip back to Brentwood with the
money. Counted and boxed there, it was driven on another tortuous
itinerary to the safe house in the hills. When enough boxes were
piled high, the Shaffers would ask friends like the Browns to take the
money to Switzerland.

Characteristically, Bill planned everything down to the most
minute detail. People who worked for him knew only what they had
to know to get their job done.

On October 20, 1986, he personally packed a motor home with
forty cartons containing $20 million in cash and drove it to Salt Lake
City, where he was met by a small group of friends, including the
Browns, in a chartered Gulfstream II jet. He'd already gone to the
trouble of forming a shell company called Bi-Continental Computers and printing business cards, complete with official titles, for each
of those friends. He also handed out tiny lapel pins, which looked
like company logos, so that no one could show up at the last minute
and claim they'd been invited along.

Each of the forty cartons was labeled "Computer-Related
Equipment," and the pilot's manifest reflected that. The next morning, when Shaffer's friends landed in Zurich, the pilot passed his
manifest along to Swiss Customs. The boxes were taken off the plane
and one of them was randomly opened. To the utter horror of the
Swiss authorities, instead of computer-related equipment, they
found neatly tied stacks of $20 and $50 bills. The officer in charge
summoned the pilot. "You've declared computer equipment," he
screamed, "and we find that your cargo is bank notes. Why did you
make a false declaration?"

The pilot had no answer, so the officer in charge turned to the
passengers and accused them of filing a false declaration. There was
little the Browns could do but admit they'd lied. At this point, the

customs officer explained, "We don't have any problem with bank notes, but we do have a problem with computer equipment. Never, ever, ever file a false declaration again."

In a state of shock, the Browns and the others promised never to do it again.

Satisfied that they wouldn't, the officer in charge allowed them to pile the cartons into a van and leave with it, as planned, for Liechtenstein.

The DEA was looking the wrong way. When the Shaffers didn't land their dope in Mexico, the case against them ground to a halt. It was two years later, during his investigation of Brian Daniels, when Annunziata discovered that the Shaffers had beaten the DEA with an end run, and that forty-two tons of marijuana had been off-loaded in Bellingham. In spite of the fact that the dope had long since left the Bellingham area, and so had most of the suspects, an incensed Annunziata went to Assistant U.S. Attorney Mark Bartlett, determined to reopen the case.

Then in his early thirties, the 5-foot 10-inch, dark-haired, weight-lifting Bartlett was not what cops call "an ivory tower lawyer." He didn't hide in his plush office. He went on busts. He got his hands dirty. When Annunziata told him how much he wanted the Shaffers, Bartlett said okay and assigned it OCDEF status, creating an Organized Crime Drug Enforcement task force. To run it, Bartlett brought in Fran Dyer.

At 48, Dyer had already been in law enforcement twenty-five years. Boston-born, blond haired, about the same height as Bartlett but slimmer, Dyer had served with the Air Force in counterintelligence during Vietnam. He had then spent five years as a Seattle detective before joining the IRS's Criminal Investigation Division.

Because they didn't have any of the smuggled goods to use as evidence, Bartlett and Dyer — and Gary Annunziata, until he was transferred to Malaysia — needed to put together what the textbooks call a "no-dope conspiracy" case. To secure convictions, they'd have to build everything on testimony and support it with documents.

In textbooks, it's easy.

In the real world, it took more than three years.

For the Shaffers, this adventure was turning out to be a very good one. Their 1987 operation netted them in excess of $35 million. In all, they'd earned somewhere around $60 million. And they'd managed to get most of it out of the country.

After the Zurich episode in October 1986, Bill arranged the flights to Switzerland in a different manner. The one constant was that neither Bill nor Chris ever flew with the money. He'd met a fellow named Alex Major, who ran a small chartered jet operation, and used Major to make the runs to Europe. On November 9, 1987, Major took one of his own planes with $11 million to Zurich. On December 8, he flew another of his own planes to Switzerland, this time with $8 million. Changing the routine, on January 24, 1988, Major leased a Canadair 600 jet to ferry $6 million to Zurich on a seven-day charter. Five friends accepted Bill's offer to eat, drink, and be merry on the $130,000 jaunt. Just their in-flight food bill for caviar, smoked salmon, and champagne came to $18,000. Major's fourth trip to Switzerland, on February 27, was to transport $6 million more.

The Shaffers had used brokers to set up shell companies in Liechtenstein and Switzerland, so whenever money arrived it was delivered to those brokers. The brokers made the actual deposits because Bill had decreed that neither he nor Chris should ever go to the banks themselves. Through those brokers, the brothers operated seventeen shell companies in Liechtenstein alone, with accounts in seven banks. Other accounts were eventually located in England, France, Germany, Switzerland, Ireland, and Austria.

Once the money was bedded down inside those companies, the brokers took instructions from the Shaffers to pay for stocks and shares and a mansion that Bill bought in Santa Barbara, California. The brokers paid for their art and jewelry, and the sports cars they started racing around Europe. The brokers paid for the property the Shaffers owned in England, and to cover the walls inside those homes with Picassos and Warhols. Bill also bought himself an oceangoing yacht for $1.2 million through a shell company set up in the Isle of Man.

Spending the money was the greatest adventure of all.

The boat was named the *Henry Morgan,* for the pirate.

With the Shaffers living high on the hog in Europe, Dyer, Annunziata, and Bartlett got together for the first time, eight thousand miles away, in Seattle, in November 1989. After sorting through the mound of information the DEA had already compiled, Dyer and Annunziata decided to begin at the bottom. They started rolling over the little guys, the boat crews, slowly but surely working their way up the ladder. It took six months before they felt they had enough on the Shaffers that Bartlett could take the fledgling case to a grand jury.

In April 1990, an indictment came back, charging Bill and Chris Shaffer, plus twenty-seven others, including Terry Restall and the Browns, with conspiracy to import marijuana, the importation of marijuana, and conspiracy to distribute marijuana. Bartlett also resurrected an earlier indictment in northern California that implicated Chris in a 1983 marijuana shipment. The Shaffers were now officially fugitives from justice. Within a couple of months, Bartlett returned to the grand jury, adding more names to the list. By the end of 1990, he'd indicted a total of forty-seven people.

At that point, Bartlett received a phone call from lawyers in Boston indicating that they were under instructions from two Shaffer associates, one of them being Restall, to strike a deal. Dyer and Bartlett were convinced they already had a highly prosecutable case against the Shaffers, but getting Restall to testify would be a major victory. So the negotiations began. Restall surrendered to Fran Dyer in January 1991, and on the strength of the testimony he was willing to provide, Bartlett agreed to ask the courts for a minimum sentence of five years, and not more than ten. Restall took the deal, knowing that without it he was facing twenty-five years.

Dyer and Bartlett now closed in on the others. Luck seemed to be shifting their way.

Passionate about cars, Dennis "Lesser" Specht drove a very special turbo-charged Ferrari Testarosa, one of only three ever made.

When it appeared on the cover of *Road and Track Magazine,* a source recognized it and Dyer was able to trace him through the magazine. Once he'd found Specht, it was easy to get Kenneth "Greater" Tarlow. Dyer then learned that Sonny, a man in his mid-to-late fifties, once confessed to a Shaffer messenger that he'd always wanted to be in the movies. He felt he could never make it in Hollywood, but had come close because a girlfriend who worked for an ad agency had gotten him a part in a television commercial. Dyer found out what the product was, contacted the company, and discovered that Sonny's real name was Irwin Kletter. A warrant for his arrest was issued immediately.

The Shaffers didn't know it yet, but their days were numbered.

When CBS News went to Geneva in April 1987 to cover Sotheby's sale of the Duchess of Windsor's jewels, they interviewed some of those present. At one point they turned their cameras on a blond guy in an expensive suit, drinking champagne with a gorgeous woman. When they asked his name, he seemed startled, and replied, "Bill Ryan." When they asked him if he was going to buy something, he told them, "There are times when you just have to go for it."

Bill Ryan, of course, was Bill Shaffer.

And both Bill and Chris were going for it in London. They were now carrying several different passports. One was British, and in the name of someone who'd died. Another was stolen. A third, this one German, Bill had purchased in broad daylight for $50,000 cash from a self-proclaimed CIA operative, over lunch at the Serpentine Restaurant in the middle of Hyde Park.

The instant he had reason to believe there might be a U.K. connection, Fran Dyer turned for help to Scotland Yard.

Working through the Justice Department attaché at the American Embassy in Grosvenor Square, Dyer was put in touch with the Metropolitan Police International and Organized Crimes Branch in April of 1990. Within a matter of hours, Detective Sergeants Rick Reynolds and Graham Saltmarsh were on the case. For the next three years, a London-Seattle phone connection was in use several hours every day.

It was Reynolds and Saltmarsh who tracked down and seized Terry Restall's assets, among them an English country estate in Hampshire. It was Reynolds and Saltmarsh who went to see Bill Shaffer at his house in Alexander Square in South Kensington, only to find it empty. It was Reynolds and Saltmarsh who came within hours of arresting Shaffer less than half a mile from Scotland Yard.

In March 1991, Shaffer checked into a suite at Dukes Hotel in the heart of Mayfair, using the name Alan Abill. Still playing the big spender, he was foolishly flashing a lot of money, and his money was attracting attention. One afternoon, he asked the concierge to put $800 worth of roses in his suite. The concierge accommodated him. That night, Shaffer returned to the hotel with a well-known British actress on his arm. Suspicious that their client might not be who he said he was, someone in hotel security decided to make a discreet phone call to a friend at Scotland Yard. But the officer was on a stakeout and didn't return the call for two days, by which point Shaffer had checked out.

Reynolds and Saltmarsh had proof that Shaffer was using false passports. To help identify the names in those false passports, they turned to a BBC television program called "Crimewatch." Until then, the show had concentrated almost exclusively on British bad guys. But on September 12, 1991, the "Crimewatch" presenters asked a huge viewing public for help in locating a pair of American bad guys and showed photos of the Shaffers. More than seventy people called with information. Two of the calls came from the Continent. One of those two placed Bill Shaffer in Germany.

Although Bill now claims that life as a fugitive was a terrible experience, the search for him went on for another four months. It ended on January 15, 1992, in the bar of the Sheraton Hotel near Frankfurt Airport, where he was arrested by the Bavarian state police. When they grabbed him, he shrugged. "Congratulations. Today is your lucky day. You've won the big one."

Dyer and Bartlett hoped they could bring him back to Seattle within a week. Except that Shaffer had other plans. He hired a local lawyer to fight his extradition, or at least to delay it long enough to strike a deal. However, neither Bartlett nor Dyer were in the mood to haggle. Shaffer held out as long as he could and wound up spending the next nine months under maximum security in a filthy, outmoded German prison. He was confined to his cell twenty-three hours a day. The single hour out was for recreation in a garbage-strewn courtyard. The window to his cell was barred and there was no glass, which allowed in both the weather and odors from the courtyard. A single 25-watt light bulb burned continuously day and night. When his appeals ran out, the Germans bundled Bill onto a plane. On the evening of September 16, 1992, Dyer met him at Seattle's Sea-Tac International Airport and tucked him safely away at the Kent Corrections Facility, near Seattle.

Having indicted more than forty-five people and already obtained more than forty convictions, most of them on guilty pleas, Dyer and Bartlett now went after Chris.

Scotland Yard had tracked him to Ireland. The Garda were asked to arrest him, but by the time they got to the house where he was believed to be staying, he'd fled to France. That's about the time Dyer learned the Browns were in Paris, living just off the Luxembourg Gardens. Convinced they were in touch with Chris, he asked the French police to arrest them.

At nine o'clock one morning, a police officer dressed as a workman knocked on the Brown's front door. Summer couldn't figure out what the man wanted, so she turned to her husband. At that very moment, Ed was on the phone with Chris. Ed said to Summer, "Let me get it," told Chris, "I'll call you right back," hung up, and went to the door. As soon as he opened it, the workman stepped in, followed by several armed officers. The Browns were handcuffed and the police began a thorough search of the apartment.

Hiding in a small hotel five blocks away, Chris grew impatient waiting for Ed to call him back, so he phoned their apartment. Aware that Bill was in custody, Chris later admitted he lived in a constant state of panic, changing his address every few days, and constantly looking over his shoulder. For whatever reason, the police chose not to answer the phone, which totally unnerved Chris. Immediately, he checked out of his hotel. Stressed beyond the breaking point, Chris got in touch with an attorney in the States and asked him to negotiate a surrender. Dyer and Bartlett agreed in principle to work out a plea bargain with him. And on December 16, 1992, almost three months to the day after his older brother was taken into custody, Chris made his way to Amsterdam, and then on to Seattle, where he too surrendered to Dyer.

Under the agreement, both brothers pleaded guilty to all charges. They also agreed to make a full and honest accounting of all the currency and assets they possessed or controlled, which would then be forfeited. In exchange, Bartlett promised to ask for a sentence of no more than fifteen years for Bill and no more than thirteen years for Chris.

But there were still matters that needed to be cleared up. To everyone's enormous chagrin, despite four years of work, 550 interviews, fifteen thousand man hours, and the cooperation of law enforcement agencies in eight countries, the task force confiscated only about $12 million of the Shaffers' assets. The Shaffers have insisted all along that there is no more. Dyer has warned them that if there is, he will find it. And Bartlett has warned them that if more is ever found, the deal is off, even if it happens after they get out. That could mean they wind up serving twenty-five to thirty years.

Philosophical to the end, Bill and Chris both claim they'll still be young enough when they get out to lead fruitful lives. If that means there is money hidden away, if they've washed it so clean that no one can find it, and if the money is still there in ten to twelve years, they might well reckon the adventure is not over, just unavoidably postponed.

11

SORTING OUT THE SINKS

"It's not our business to inquire into our client's morals."
— **Banker in Hong Kong**

Ready-made companies, registered in places that most people have never heard of, can be bought from formation agents, who sell them the same way the A&P sells baked beans.

A stock is always available for purchase "off the shelf." Ownership can be shifted in the time it takes to fill out a form. And for the convenience of their customers, most company-formation agents, like the A&P, happily accept credit cards.

Legally speaking, a company is an entity, recognized by statute, established for the purpose of carrying out certain objectives that often, though not always, include the operation of a business. Other objectives might be purchasing assets, entering into contracts, and incurring liabilities. A limited company is one whose liabilities are assumed by the company and not passed along to the management, shareholders, or beneficial owners. Although every company must have a registered office, the location of that office is not necessarily the same as where the company trades. Instead, it acts as the legal address for the service of writs, notices, and other communications.

By law, every company must also list the names of its directors. But directors do not have to be shareholders. In many cases they are merely residents of the offshore jurisdiction paid a fee for putting a brass plaque with the company name on their door and for filing the company's annual report. Directors do not necessarily know who actually owns the company. As shares in companies can at times be issued in "bearer" form, whoever holds the share certificates therefore owns the company.

When a company is formed, authorized capital must be declared. That represents the nominal value of the shares multiplied by the number of the shares the company is permitted to issue, in keeping with its own Memorandum of Association. In other words, a company can authorize itself to issue one million shares at a nominal value of $10 each, and thereby claim that the authorized share capital of the company is $10 million. It looks impressive on the company letterhead but otherwise is meaningless. A company boasting $10 million of authorized capital might have issued only a couple of shares for a total amount of $2.

Off-the-shelf companies sometimes use innocuous names such as Acme Trading and Ajax Holdings. Or names that might have a familiar ring to them: T-Warner Trading is not necessarily associated in anyway with Time-Warner; Belltelecom does not necessarily have anything to do with Bell Telephone; Hilton Properties is not necessarily associated with the hotel chain. The New York–London Financial Exchange SA, registered in the British Virgin Islands, may not necessarily have anything to do with a financial market operating between New York and London, nor Palm Beach Properties Ltd. (Panama) with real estate in Florida. A "trading company" need not trade, a "finance company" need not be in finance, and a "holding company" need not be holding anything. The letters RE on the end of an offshore company name do not automatically mean it is in the reinsurance business; the words *fund management* do not automatically mean the company is a fund manager; nor do the words *trust company* mean the company is a bank.

Ready-mades are inexorably linked to tax havens. Scattered around the world, there are about fifty firmly established jurisdictions where, to varying degrees, you can successfully hide your business activities and the money those activities generate — from Liechtenstein, Luxembourg, and Monaco in Europe, through the Caribbean, which is teeming with them, to half-way around the globe to Nauru and Vanuatu, lost in the middle of the Pacific Ocean.

For many Europeans, offshore havens are as easily accessible as the Channel Islands of Jersey and Guernsey, and the Isle of Man in the Irish Sea. Dependencies of the Crown, these territories are locally governed according to their own constitutions. The authorities boast that they have tightened money laundering laws over the past few years and that even if they were once famous for providing laundrymen with sinks, no washing gets done there anymore. What they really mean is that anyone arriving with a suitcase filled with $20 bills will have to satisfy his banker that the money isn't of suspicious origins.

In other words, not much has changed: banks are domestically regulated, off-the-shelf companies are cheap, and nominee directors are readily available. Buying a Channel Islands company is no more difficult than dialing a 1-800 number to place the order through a company-formation agent who takes credit cards. Because a nominee director doesn't necessarily know the source of any money controlled by the company he represents, it might be fair to suggest that when he wires funds in and out of offshore banks, deliberately layering them on the instructions of someone he has never met, he could be aiding and abetting a laundryman. Legally, it matters only whether or not someone does it wittingly. But there is sufficient evidence to say that plenty of laundered money goes through these jurisdictions.

Once upon a time, some of it belonged to Jean-Claude "Baby Doc" Duvalier.

In September 1986, eight months after Haiti's President for Life was forced into exile on the French Riviera, attorneys acting for him put $41.8 million in Canadian treasury bills in their client account at a Toronto branch of the Royal Bank of Montreal. Within a matter of days, the T-bills were moved to a Jersey account held at the Hong Kong and Shanghai Bank in Montreal. Duvalier's representatives then separated the ownership records from the money, a common ruse to complicate the paper trail, sending the records for safekeeping to a bank in London and taking the T-bills to yet another bank in Montreal.

Two months later, those T-bills were moved to an account of the Royal Trust Bank of Jersey, which is a subsidiary of Canada's Royal Trust Company. Complicating matters even further, that particular account was part of a larger one held by Manufacturers

Hanover Bank of Canada at an office in Toronto used by the Royal Bank of Montreal. Shortly thereafter, the money was wired into a pair of accounts at the Royal Trust Bank in Jersey owned by a locally registered shell company called Boncardo Ltd. As the virtually invisible owner of Boncardo Ltd., Duvalier was issued with bearer checks on Boncardo's accounts.

The scheme worked for more than a year, until February 1988, when French police, acting on embezzlement charges lodged by the Haitian government, raided Duvalier's villa and confiscated private papers. That led to the discovery of the two Jersey company accounts.

Duvalier's agents promptly hustled the money out of Jersey, nesting it in the Swiss accounts of two Panamanian shell companies, Minoka Investments and Modinest Investments. A week later, $30.8 million was wired from Credit Suisse in Geneva to the Royal Bank of Montreal. Canadian treasury bills were purchased and a Duvalier agent took possession of them. For anyone hoping to trace the funds, the trail ended there. The T-bills were left at two nearby banks, but not for long. As the case in France intensified against Duvalier, it was felt his money would be safer elsewhere and was subsequently wired to Luxembourg. That's when fate stepped in to save Duvalier's bacon. The government that succeeded him had located assets and frozen them, but that government was overthrown in a September 1988 coup by General Prosper Avril, a Duvalier compatriot. Avril allowed the case against Baby Doc to disintegrate, along with all traces of what remains of that original $41.8 million.

Back in Jersey, the island's authorities shrug, and wonder if anyone has actually broken any laws. Money laundering statutes at the time applied only to drug or terrorist money. Besides, there are no current laws they're aware of that prohibit the movement of money from one jurisdiction to another, even if the sole motive for moving that money is to keep it out of the hands of a third party. They're keen to emphasize they don't want laundrymen as clients, but in the end, they admit, there's no sure way of telling who's laundering what for whom.

You get a similar response from officials in next-door Guernsey. They even wince at the term *offshore* since they're trying to spruce up their image with the shinier designation "finance centre." Yet over fourteen thousand companies are registered there, which is more than ten times the per capita equivalent in Britain. The only information Guernsey will supply about a company is the names of directors and shareholders. They do not furnish annual accounts. Nor do they release the names of the beneficial owners. Clearly they must be doing something right, as banks on an island once famous for a breed of cows currently sit on assets of £27 billion. But then, one man's sink is another man's full-service financial institution.

Toward the end of February 1993, police in Colombia announced they'd seized $5.9 million and arrested 250 people during a fifteen-month crackdown on drug trafficking and money laundering. The money was a drop in the bucket and the arrests, though perhaps significant in number, didn't touch any of the major players in either of the major cartels. However, by getting inside nine hundred accounts at the nation's five largest banks, the authorities were able to trace drug money through fictitious import-export companies and exchange houses in sixteen countries — among them, significantly, Yugoslavia, Pakistan, Russia, Czechoslovakia, Hungary, and Bulgaria.

Private banking still operates in what used to be Yugoslavia, offering incredibly high interest rates. During the height of the war, for example, it reached 10 to 15 percent per month, amounts way out of line with the rest of Europe. One of those banks, Jugoskandic, was estimated to be holding $2 billion in hard currency. Paying that kind of interest on that kind of money is an expensive proposition. While this is not to suggest that Jugoskandic was involved with anything illegal, private banks in the region were known to be using hard currency deposits to finance drug deals — half of Bosnia is said to be covered with fields of cannabis, and ethnic Albanians have established a firm hold over the heroin market — which in turn financed weapons.

It all worked by means of a typically triangular trade route. An Austrian shell company, whose beneficial owners are unknown, bought arms from Bulgaria and delivered them to Albanians arming the underground in the anti-Serb revolt. The Bulgarians used the money to pay for raw opium in the Middle East, which it sold to the Albanians. In turn, the Albanians refined the opium into heroin and spent their profits buying arms from the Austrian shell. Disguised as a legal business deal and protected by strict banking secrecy, no one caught them breaking UN sanctions.

Nor were the proprietors of the Austrian shell company the only ones who saw opportunity in that part of the world. Arms traffickers operating out of the Czech Republic tried to furnish the Bosnians with $21 million worth of weapons, including 26,800 machine guns, 128,000 magazines, 5,000 pistols, and 17 million bullets. They used Panama as the third side of their triangle. In this case, the weapons never got shipped, but the route through which the money was being washed carbon copied a series of deals the same Czech group is known to have successfully concluded.

In Pakistan, banks happily accept large cash deposits. When foreign-exchange controls were removed in 1991, permitting banks to offer accounts in foreign currencies, a presidential decree guaranteed banking secrecy to an unprecedented degree. The central bank actually instructed Pakistan's bankers not to ask any questions about the origin of foreign cash deposits. Since then, literally billions of dollars have flooded into that country.

It happens that Pakistan is the most fecund part of the Golden Crescent, the opium poppy region that stretches from Pakistan, through Afghanistan, and into Iran. Nearly 70 percent of the world's highest-grade heroin moves into Europe from Pakistan. Opium poppy has been the main crop of the Mahaban Mountains along the Northwest Frontier Province since the nineteenth century, when British colonials planted it because they could legally export the drug. An ideally suited location, with thin soil, steep slopes, and optimum rainfall, the village of Pushton places great value on land ownership, especially since there are very few opportunities for nonagricultural incomes. Drug traffickers in the nearby village of Gandaf, Pakistan's version of Cali, have little trouble encouraging the peasants to devote their tiny plots to opium poppy, as it nets those farmers more than ten times per acre what they could otherwise expect with tobacco or fruit. By growing the raw materials, providing the laboratories to refine them, and offering banking facilities for the traffickers, Pakistan is on the verge of becoming the most dangerous power in an already unstable part of the world.

But it has been the breakdown of draconian control, coupled with food shortages, hyperinflation, and the resulting general despair, that has led to a massive increase in all types of law breaking in the former Communist Bloc. Hard currency is seen by people in this region as the only antidote. It's not simply a passport to the black markets, it's the key to the world's free markets. And here is one instance when Gresham's Law proves wrong. In this case, good money has driven out bad. Throughout the former Communist world, local currencies are almost worthless. No one wants rubles, korunas, forints, lev, or zlotys when they can have dollars. So Eastern Europe has turned itself into one giant sink.

Publicly, the Poles are trying to turn themselves into the Spain of Eastern Europe, offering Western manufacturers a large, inexpensive work force and an economic infrastructure relying on manufacturing and farming. Privately, the Poles are desperate for hard currency. The economy's thriving "gray sector," those sums earned under the table, produces a mountain of cash that needs to be laundered. And as state-owned companies are privatized, opportunities abound for laundrymen representing international crime syndicates. For the past few years, Poland's central bank has been encouraging the financial industry to report suspicious transactions, and money laundering is now a punishable crime. However, the law only applies to funds derived from a small range of criminal activity. Businessmen walk around carrying suitcases filled with cash. Credit cards and checks are still rare. Although Poland enjoys a relatively stable political environment, the national currency is convertible, an infrastructure exists for transferring money abroad, and it remains a nation shackled by an obsolete financial system. It is estimated that as much as one-third of all business is conducted through the alternate economy. Bankers are inexperienced and naive, and financial law enforcement is impotent.

In short, Poland today is a laundryman's dream come true.

Many of Poland's most important financial institutions happily open their doors to laundrymen because they lack capital, or are unable to collect on bad debts. They see the laundrymen as the surest route to solvency. The banks have welcomed the Colombian drug cartels, reportedly to the tune of $3 billion. They've welcomed the Turkish drug barons. And they've welcomed the Palestine Liberation Organization. A few years ago, $75 million of PLO funds were deposited in the Bank of Warsaw and have not been seen since. Under Lech Walesa, the government tried to put a stop to it, and in 1992 passed a law requiring banks to register the identity of all customers depositing more than $12,500. Chides one Warsaw banker, "They might as well have asked the entire population to whistle Paderewski."

Hungary is just as bad, if not worse, because it has been at it longer. Bank secrecy is ironclad. There is no way for anyone to obtain any information under any condition whatsoever.

There are laws against money laundering in the Czech Republic, but there are fifty *cambios* within a five-minute walk of Wenceslaus Square, and not all of their employees, many of whom are not Czech, bother to remind customers about the law. Organized crime is also a thriving sector of the local economy, thanks almost entirely to Russians who were stationed there as an occupying power in the good old days of Communism and stayed on because capitalism turned out to be even more fun.

Just across the border, in the other half of what used to be Czechoslovakia and is now Slovakia, capitalism hasn't yielded the same fruits and they're even more desperate for hard currency. One attraction is that from the capital, Bratislava, there's a good road across a lax border and a forty-minute drive to secret banking in Austria.

And then there is Bulgaria.

The UN embargo in the former Yugoslavia turned Bulgaria's organized gangs into the nation's most successful entrepreneurs. Sanction busting was rife, and with it came money laundering. According to the Ministry of the Interior, Bulgaria is today in the throes of its worst crime epidemic this century.

When the government in Sofia announced it would sell off sixteen hundred previously state-owned industries, it explained that unlike similar sales in other former Communist countries, it would not accept either scrip or vouchers; everything would be sold for cash. Warned by European and American advisers that such a sell-off would be a field day for money launderers, the Bulgarians said they would ask all investors to declare the origin of their funds. As if a Colombian drug dealer would admit he was buying Balkan Airlines with $50 million worth of crack receipts!

For the record, the Bulgarians were among the first from Eastern Bloc countries to comprehend the advantages of money laundering. Under the 35-year regime of Todor Zhivkov, lasting from 1954 to 1989, the government dealt drugs, washed the profits through shell companies that had access to Swiss banks, and then used that money to finance a major international illicit arms business.

Zhivkov's trading outlet was the state-owned import-export company Kintex. Set up in 1968, it was operated exclusively by the KDS, the Bulgarian Security Service, and sold heroin and morphine base to Turkish drug traffickers. With the money, it was able to build up its gun-running business. Kintex became so adept at converting drugs into weapons that it furnished the Nigerians with guns to put down the Biafra civil war in the 1960s; it furnished various Christian militias with guns to escalate the civil war in Lebanon in 1975; it furnished South Africa with guns, in direct violation of various embargoes; and for more than twenty years it was the primary outfitter of guns to the PLO. For their efforts, the Bulgarians reputedly earned up to $2 billion a year in much-needed hard currency.

The extent of Kintex's connections with organized crime in the West only came to light in the early 1980s. Italian police raided a Mafia drug refinery in Trapani Province, on the western tip of Sicily, and uncovered a laboratory that to their surprise was stocked with Bulgarian machinery and Bulgarian-supplied morphine base. This one lab alone was capable of producing a staggering 4.5 tons of refined heroin per year. At wholesale prices, in those days, that represented $1.125 billion. Over the next few years, no fewer than fifteen refineries were uncovered in Sicily and on the Italian mainland, most of them equipped with Bulgarian supplies.

By this time, the CIA had plenty of evidence to prove Kintex's role in international drug trafficking. When the Reagan administration formally protested, Zhivkov cracked down on every amateur drug dealer in the country. Largely to placate Washington, tons of marijuana were seized and assurances were given that the business had been ended. But Kintex continued to trade. Five years later, as a result of continued American protests, Kintex finally became too much of an embarrassment. So, for all intents and purposes, Zhivkov put Kintex out of business. In its place he installed son-of-Kintex, a state-owned import-export company called Globus. But the KDS was still in charge, and its primary mission was still drug trafficking, arms dealing, and money laundering. In effect, the only change was in the company stationery.

The Principality of Monaco came under a great deal of criticism for allowing money launderers to use the local banking system. A French parliamentary report concluded that the Mafia's presence in France was steadily growing, and singled out Monaco as a major European sink. The report noted that its proximity to Italy — only twenty minutes from the border, which, since January 1993, is wide open — together with its secret banking system and casino gambling had combined to give the Mafia a unique opportunity to launder funds through real estate, golf courses, and gambling. A French newspaper then accused the casino at Monte Carlo of being a prime laundrette for Italian crime gangs. The Societé des Bains de Mer, the company that runs the casino, instantly denied the charges. But Prince Rainier III announced that an inquiry into SBM was already underway.

Having very little patience for such charges, the prince, who has always taken a strict no-nonsense approach to crime in his country, insisted that measures be taken to crack down on money laundering. He moved to tighten legislation that obliged banks, insurance companies, and stockbrokers to report suspicious transactions, and to disclose the identity of anyone involved. In line with French law, he required the casino's management to report payments for chips that were suspected to come from drug trafficking or organized crime, and set stiff prison sentences for anyone using illegal gains to buy property. He also agreed that the principality would cooperate with the French police where drug money laundering was involved, but drew the line at establishing how much information could be passed along, explicitly forbidding that any financial information be handed on to French tax authorities. It gets back to not killing the goose. There are reportedly in excess of $13 billion on deposit in forty banks in Monaco, a country with a population of just thirty thousand.

While Monaco tightened its rules, real estate began to boom in the tiny Republic of San Marino — hidden inside Italy — where banking is completely secret, almost exactly the way Switzerland was years ago.

In 1989, the State Department went public with its wrath, singling out three of the world's banking centers for having sold out. Under the heading of the "International Narcotics Control Strategy Report," the Bush administration named the Bahamas as the major transit country for cocaine and marijuana entering the United States, and condemned it for having allowed itself to become such an important money laundering center. It named Hong Kong as the money laundering heart of the Pacific Rim, and condemned it for having become the major transit center of Southeast Asian heroin. And it named Panama as continuing to be the principal money laundering haven for the South American cocaine trade.

That report made the papers.

A more revealing document, which didn't make the papers, was circulated around the DEA. Specifically not intended for public release, it greatly widened the picture, listing eighteen "major conduits and repositories" for illicit drug funds. The world's greatest sinks consisted of Hong Kong, Liechtenstein, Luxembourg, the Channel Islands, Andorra, Switzerland, Singapore, the United Arab Emirates, the Cayman Islands, Mexico, and Panama. Four American cities were also named: New York, Los Angeles, Miami, and Houston. The DEA also pointed an accusing finger north to Montreal, Toronto, and Vancouver.

Hong Kong is an obvious nominee. Ever since the mainland territory and its offshore islands were ceded to Britain by China as retribution after the Opium War of 1842, the Crown Colony has been one of the world's major trading and smuggling ports. Today, it is a designer money center, born out of jet travel, electronic communications, and the mystique of the East. It has a gold market and a diamond market, and a stock market that looks more like Las Vegas than Wall Street. It's a Miracle Mile for shell companies, a formation agents' paradise. Arms smugglers, black marketeers, and organized gangs have always used Hong Kong to wash their funds. So have the Chinese, since Mao's Great March. But Hong Kong had never seen anything like the kind of action the heroin traffickers brought to town. Just as banking secrecy laws tightened and Hong Kong's regulatory infrastructure loosened, the drug trade exploded, creating an unprecedented level of prosperity. From 1978 to 1981, real estate prices quadrupled. Banks were awash in liquidity.

It was Disneyland with dim sum!

The bubble might easily have burst the day the British agreed to return Hong Kong to the Chinese. And some people contend it did. The money men in Hong Kong took fright. No one knew what the world would look like fifteen years down the line. 1997 seemed uncomfortably close. Capital headed west, in haste, most of it finding its way into U.S. and Canadian real estate. Over the next few years the situation worsened. People with money bought their way out. People without money tried selling what they had to raise a ransom. Prices hit rock bottom. That's when the law of supply and demand changed gears. Having moved into the Colony to cater to people wishing to get their money out, Western banks inadvertently established the infrastructure that would now be a Second Coming. With prices way down and black money still readily available, business opportunities reappeared. Beijing made enough of the right noises to lull Western bankers into believing that business under the Communists would be as glorious as it was under the capitalists. So Western bankers revised their view of 1997. They suddenly decided they were in the right place at the right time, and that it was indeed time to gamble on a prosperous future. As native money poured out, foreign money poured in. Especially drug money.

When Law Kin-man, one of the world's most successful laundrymen, pleaded guilty in a U.S. court in 1994 to a host of federal charges, he confessed to using 362 bogus bank accounts in Hong Kong to wash an estimated $93 million of Golden Triangle drug money through the Crown Colony. Another eight in the States were private brokerage accounts so that he could wash funds through the Hong Kong stock market.

The phoenix that rose from the ashes of the 1982 crash is today the world's third financial center, after New York and London. Shell companies generally cost less in Hong Kong than they do in Europe or the Caribbean. Bankers are supposed to ask questions, but tend not to bother. Why should they? The Colony is crammed with more than four hundred banks. It's clear that this is a buyer's market, so much so that the volume of small-denomination American bank notes circulating around Hong Kong today far exceeds the total volume of all currency transactions within any single European country.

Just across the Pearl River delta is Hong Kong's little bad brother, the Portuguese colony of Macao. This is what Las Vegas would have looked like had Genghis Khan beaten Christopher Columbus to the New World.

Nearly 80 percent of Macao's annual revenue comes from the billion-dollar-a-year, Hong Kong–controlled gambling monopoly, through which hundreds of millions of dollars are washed every year. Not only do the Chinese gangs have a marked presence in Macao, the government of North Korea maintains a consular office there, brazenly taking advantage of the colony's easy, and highly secretive, Westernized banking system.

Even with Chinese rule set to return to Macao in 1999, nothing seems to be cooling down. The Portuguese have stipulated that banks in Macao must identify people involved with "significant transactions," and that "involuntary involvement with money laundering or with any criminal activity must be carefully avoided." But that's as far as they go. They don't want to upset the Chinese.

No one appears overly anxious to rock the Hong Kong–Macao boat, least of all the Chinese. They draw nearly half their foreign currency earnings through Hong Kong. Perhaps the idea is to hand the Chinese a pair of diamonds as big as the Ritz so that there won't be any question in their minds about what they should do with them. Most of the money laundered through Hong Kong and Macao is foreign, and it's clearly in everyone's interest to keep the coffers full because that reinforces the case for maintaining the status quo. With so much money riding on the future, it's easy to see why the laundrymen are concerned with political stability, why they want to ensure that the Chinese won't do to them what Fidel Castro did to Meyer Lansky and his comrades in 1959.

12

ISLANDS IN THE SUN

"We have no natural resources and we have to survive."
— Aruba's prime minister, Nelson Oduber

The fact that there is no Meyer Lansky Street running through the middle of downtown Nassau, or for that matter through the heart of any capital on any other island in the Caribbean, has got to be one of the most arrogant oversights in history.

Lansky not only designed the financial framework for postwar organized crime, he opened Caribbean eyes, wallets, safe deposit boxes, and secret bank accounts to the delights of tax havens. He helped show the island nations how to become the world's biggest collection of sinks. Whether or not they'd ever openly admit to it, a huge debt of gratitude is outstanding.

The Caribbean is home to 31 million people, nearly two-thirds of whom speak Spanish. Another 20 percent are French or Creole speaking. Separated from each other by water, culture, history, and politics, the islands in the region are anything but homogeneous. It is easier to reach Barbados from New York than it is from Curaçao. The most convenient route from Kingston, Jamaica, to Santo Domingo in the Dominican Republic is through Miami. What the islands share is the perception that they are America's backyard. At the end of World War II, sugar was the region's main crop and the United States the region's primary market. Since then, sugar exports to the United States have steadily declined, as have the Caribbean's earnings from oil and bauxite. But the islands are still America's backyard. The United

States remains the primary market. Except now the main product is narcotics.

It's no coincidence that a powerful Sicilian family, the Caruana-Cuntrera clan, who control organized crime in Venezuela, bought sizable tracts of real estate in the Caribbean. When Pasquale, Paolo, and Gaspare Cuntrera were arrested in Caracas in September 1992 on heroin trafficking charges that dated back ten years, they were deported home to Italy. Known to have operated a major international money laundering ring and believed to have been behind the 1992 assassinations of a Sicilian judge and prosecutor, they left behind an organization said to own two-thirds of all the land and two-thirds of all the businesses on Aruba.

A resort island forty-five miles west of Curaçao, just off the coast of Venezuela, Aruba is also home to the La Costa cocaine cartel, which came to prominence when sixteen of their ilk were charged in Miami with racketeering, drug trafficking, and money laundering. They had reputedly brought eighty tons of cocaine and 250,000 pounds of marijuana into the United States since 1980, generating an estimated $800 million in profits, until the indictment against their chieftain, Randolph Habibe, in 1993. Habibe has also been charged in a failed attempt to free fellow cartel member Jose Rafael "El Mono" Abello, currently serving a thirty-year sentence in Oklahoma for drug smuggling. To emphasize the amount of money available to these groups, Habibe's rescue plot was budgeted at $20 million.

One reason places like Aruba are vulnerable to organized gangs such as Caruana-Cuntrera and La Costa is because small governments are ill equipped for the fight. Their tourist-based economies are largely cash intensive, as if consciously designed for people wanting to hide money. The Caruana-Cuntrera family had no trouble taking over a large chunk of the island through their control of casinos and hotels. And what the Caruana-Cuntrera and La Costa clans have done in Aruba, others have managed in Bonaire, Curaçao, and St. Maarten.

The larger, more important islands, which include Haiti, the Dominican Republic, and Jamaica, have been turned into "aircraft carriers," staging points for U.S.-bound cocaine. Although coca doesn't grow in the Caribbean, the ships and planes that bring it from Central America pass through there. So does the money generated by those drugs. Haiti, in particular, was singled out in a confidential 1993 U.S. Senate report that accused Port-au-Prince police chief Lieutenant Colonel Michel François, the second most powerful military man in the country, of personally handling in excess of $100 million in annual drug trafficking bribes. The three-page document, compiled from CIA files and witness accounts, notes that more than a thousand Colombians are "stationed" in Haiti, many of them under the direct authority of Fernando Burgos Martinez, a Colombian trafficker who's lived there openly since 1984. Martinez is described as the resident manager and bag man who oversees transshipment of a ton or more of Colombian cartel cocaine each month. One estimate puts his annual turnover at $200 million. Another puts it as high as $500 million. His payments to government officials guarantee access to the Port-au-Prince airport. And the report quotes a man who once worked for Burgos Martinez as saying, "Haiti was our parking lot."

In more touristed nations, such as Jamaica, the authorities strongly object to being tarred with the same brush. Fearing the effect that drug trafficking accusations could have on tourism, they insist that anyone saying the Caribbean is awash with drug money is wrong. Ironically, Jamaica is the only island with a substantial marijuana crop.

Until Castro came along, the Cubans were the entrepreneurs of the Caribbean. In many ways they still are, although now they run business in the Dominican Republic, Puerto Rico, and Miami, a city that is 40 percent Cuban. Having lost a huge chunk of his foreign income to ideology, Castro has tried to make up for it by operating a free port for drug shipments coming through the Gulf of Mexico on their way to the United States.

Reports of Cuban involvement in drug trafficking first came to America's attention in 1960. But those reports were largely unsubstantiated. Ten years later, as tales of conspiracies grew, there was still no solid evidence to substantiate the claims. But in 1982, a U.S. district court indicted four Cuban officials on charges of conspiring to smuggle drugs into the United States, providing documentation that Castro had sold safe haven to the Colombian cartels for hard currency. The *Wall Street Journal* reported in 1984 that the Colombians were paying Castro as much as half a million dollars per shipment for the privilege of using Cuban territorial waters to avoid interdiction by the U.S. Coast Guard and U.S. Customs.

To contend with Cuban transshipment, the United States put the burden on the shipping companies, which are often the innocent victims of drug traffickers. When the Americans found marijuana on board an Evergreen Line freighter, they fined the German company $29 million. As a result, Evergreen stopped bringing goods from Jamaica to the States.

The possibility that Castro might be linked to cocaine trafficking hit the headlines again over the summer of 1989, when Cuban General Arnaldo Ochoa Sanchez, the third-ranking military man in the country after Fidel and his brother Raoul, was convicted on drug charges. Ochoa was put into the dock in a televised show trial, together with thirteen other senior officers and civil servants accused of drug dealing. They'd all made money in Angola dealing in gold, diamonds, and ivory while serving with Cuba's African Expeditionary Force — money the prosecution claimed had then been invested in narcotics. Never stated was the fact that six of them, led by Ochoa, had invested some of their money in a failed plot to overthrow the Castro brothers. Those six were sentenced to death and summarily executed by a firing squad at the end of the trial.

Now American agents renewed their undercover contacts in Cuba.

It took the better part of two years before they hit pay dirt.

The man they eventually coerced into providing them with proof positive was Cuban army major Luis Galeana. In October 1991, while his plane bound for Moscow was making a refueling stop in Madrid, Galeana defected into the arms of DEA agents waiting for him just outside the Barajas Airport transit lounge. Within two days he was under heavy guard in a Washington, D.C.–area safe house.

Assigned to Cuba's Interior Ministry, Galeana brought with him information, supported by half a dozen reels of microfilm, that documented two years' worth of Castro-sponsored cocaine shipments from Cuba to Texas and Louisiana. Those were the same cargoes Castro tried to pin on Ochoa. With his regime no longer getting Russian subsidies, Castro needed foreign trade to keep the Cuban economy from completely disintegrating. But his options were severely limited. So he turned to drug trafficking, an obvious choice given the high markup, his Central and South American contacts, and Cuba's proximity to the United States. At the same time, he'd been bartering with what few nuclear secrets his Russian allies allowed him to know. Castro not only backed Saddam Hussein in the Gulf War but offered to aid Iran in its development of nuclear technology. He's also approached the Chinese and the North Koreans, proposing to help them develop their nuclear capacity in exchange for oil.

Advising Castro has been the fugitive Robert Vesco.

Indicted for fraud in 1972, Vesco had absconded from the United States with whatever remained of the $224 million he'd stolen from investors in Bernie Cornfeld's International Overseas Services. He went first to Costa Rica, protected by presidents José Figueres and Daniel Oduber, living the good life in San José while he invested $13 million in radio and television stations, a newspaper, and a hotel. In 1976, a federal grand jury in New York indicted him for the theft of that $224 million. Two years later, when Rodrigo Carazo was elected president of Costa Rica, the welcome mat was withdrawn, so Vesco moved to the Bahamas, where he followed Meyer Lansky's lead and supported Lynden Pindling. His most noteworthy contribution to mankind there was to negotiate shipments of cocaine from Colombia to the United States. When that contact turned sour, he returned briefly to Costa Rica, then headed for Nicaragua. In 1983, Castro took him in as a favor to Figueres.

Following a DEA investigation into the Colombian drug trafficker Carlos Lehder, combined with allegations levied against him by U.S. Customs, Vesco was charged in 1989 by a federal grand jury in Jacksonville, Florida, with conspiring to smuggle cocaine into the United States. Myth has it that Vesco paid Castro $1 billion to avoid extradition to the United States. But people who know say the figure is greatly exaggerated, as Vesco never had that kind of money. Still, he was given a villa in La Coronela, the most exclusive district of Havana, and permitted to stock it with champagne and lobster. This at a time when ordinary Cubans had little more than beans and rice. He was also given a detachment of security guards, as much to protect him as to keep him on a leash. He was allowed to mingle with the diplomatic set at the country's most fashionable golf club, to send his children to the International School, to throw lavish parties, to invest in sugar and tobacco, to build a series of beachfront homes, to deal in coffee futures, and to run a huge money laundering operation out of Cayo Largo in southern Cuba.

Much to the surprise of the U.S. Justice Department, and probably of Vesco himself, he was arrested on June 1, 1995, and charged by Castro with being an agent provocateur for unnamed foreign governments. American diplomats in Havana were put on notice that Cuba might turn him over. Around Washington, where it was rumored that Vesco's fortune had finally evaporated, the hope was that Castro had come to understand that by giving sanctuary to criminals he was hindering any chance for reconciliation with the United States.

Since 1993, Cuba has cooperated to some extent with the DEA, leading some people to think Castro was finally trying to shed Cuba's image as a refuge for drug traffickers. Yet according to FBI records, Cuba continues to shelter at least ninety-one fugitives from American justice.

Bernie Cornfeld once predicted the day would come when Vesco would simply outlive his usefulness. The day that happened, he anticipated, Castro would quite unceremoniously turn his back on him. Now it appeared as if Vesco had become a liability, as if Cornfeld would have a posthumous last laugh. But then all went quiet. Nothing happened. After thirteen years of allowing the man to sing for his supper by teaching him how to get around the American embargo and how to run an international drug trafficking conglomerate, it was as if Fidel had a sudden attack of uncharacteristic loyalty. Or perhaps he saw how badly the Americans want Vesco and realized that Vesco remained one of his last aces.

No one doubts that Vesco is expendable. Nor is it likely a question of "when." This is all about "how much."

According to Galeana's debriefings in the United States, Castro was petrified by the indictment the Americans levied against Noriega. Furthermore, he was furious that Carlos Lehder Rivas had been willing to testify against his former chums. Until Galeana's defection,

Castro could fall back on General Ochoa's confession that he and the others had masterminded drug runs into the United States "for [their] own personal gain and without the knowledge or approval of [their] superiors in the Cuban government." If anyone believed Ochoa's confessions at the time — and there couldn't have been many who did — Galeana's evidence has since changed their minds. He detailed the extensive use of Cuba's territorial limits — at sea and in the air — as well as its military refueling and repair facilities, military radar cover, and military communications networks. He also outlined how the Cuban navy and air force played substantial roles.

All of this would be categorically unthinkable without the express consent of either Fidel or brother Raoul, or both.

Based on what Galeana revealed to his American handlers, a plan had already been drawn up inside Cuba to hasten Fidel's overthrow. Several high-ranking officers in Castro's army, living in fear for their lives since the Ochoa gang's execution, had concluded they had little to lose by trying to force Castro into exile. It was then suggested at high levels of the Bush administration that Washington might help them by indicting Castro on drug trafficking and money laundering charges, exactly as it had done against Noriega. The indictment would then be broadcast to Cuba to spark a coup. Furthermore, Spain had already secretly agreed to take Castro, and he'd been made aware of that. But for reasons never stated publicly, the plan was rejected by the White House.

Throughout the Caribbean, it is customary to hear politicians say that the drug problem is not one of supply, it is one of demand. And the biggest demand comes from the United States. Their concern is, therefore, that Caribbean economies are being destabilized by drug dependency in America, over which they have no control. In other words, their largest, most important neighbor, which has always been seen as the patron of Caribbean security, has now become its greatest threat.

But their argument falls flat when those same politicians show they are not willing to risk total isolation by dropping back to a safer position. They've replaced sugar with off-the-shelf bearer-share companies. They provide an abundant supply of nominee directors, banking and commercial secrecy, a free flow of currency, a modicum of political stability, and easy access to modern telephone systems, fax machines, and airports with regular services to North America and Europe.

From their point of view, survival is at stake.

A few years ago, the Ministry of Finance in the Bahamas set up the Financial Services Secretariat "to identify and to encourage all types of investment and financial service opportunities." Put another way, the Bahamians were willing, for a fee, to provide the types of financial services required by people who want to hide money. Supporting those objectives in 1990, the legislature passed the International Business Companies Act, which soon became known as "the instant registration package." In under twenty-four hours, and for only $100, you can own a Bahamian company — one with a legitimate-sounding name, such as Chicago Mercantile Financial Asset Management Holdings — whose assets might be nothing more than the bearer shares of some other off-the-shelf company, which in turn can control bank accounts anywhere in the world through which money can pass like water down a funnel.

To prove the point, a phone call to a company agent in the Bahamas went, word for word, like this:

"I need to buy a company and would be grateful if this could be arranged as quickly and as discreetly as possible."

"That is no problem, sir."

"I've seen your list of names, you know, of available companies, but none of them suit my purposes."

"These things are easily arranged. Once you buy a company, we can file to change the name of it to anything you want, as long as there is nothing currently registered with that name."

"I was thinking of something along the lines of a commercial banking corporation."

"That is not a problem."

"Perhaps something like Manhattan County First Fiduciary Trust?"

"We will be delighted to look into that name, or any other you choose, and secure one for you that will suit your purposes."

"Will you also be able to provide an introduction to a friendly banker who will accommodate whatever needs I have, including cash transactions?"

"Yes, of course."

The response is hardly surprising, considering how the Caribbean is famously overpopulated with bankers who do not ask questions when large sums of cash are deposited. Of course, they're supposed to. But what people are supposed to do and what they are willing to do to make a living are often two very different things.

That has never been more evident than a few years ago, when a branch office of an international bank opened its doors at the end of a runway on the island of Anguilla. It has since been closed, but only because this was a little too blatant, even for the Caribbean. However, the shack, with the bank's name painted boldly on the front, did unabated business for several years, servicing private pilots who arrived on the island to make cash deposits before flying off again.

It was drive-in banking Caribbean style.

No one even had to shut down his engines.

The bad guys no longer rob banks, they buy them.

St. Kitts and Nevis are a pair of tiny English-speaking islands in the Leewards, about twelve hundred miles southeast of Miami. A popular stop on the cruise line circuit, the local economy has always thrived on tourism, sugar cane, cotton, and pineapple. But the 44,000 residents of the two islands have in recent years discovered that there is big money to be made by selling banks.

One of these ready-made financial institutions, as advertised by a Canadian firm in British Columbia, is an entity called the Keystone Bank Ltd. According to the prospectus, it is chartered in the "Tax-free Ecclesiastical Sovereignty of the Dominion of Melchizedek." Precisely where that is, the brochure doesn't say. Frankly, you'd think someone could have come up with a less suspect-sounding name. However, along with ownership of Keystone Bank Ltd. comes the Keystone Trust Company, which seems to be the main asset.

For just $15,000, paid to the Canadian company, you can

become the proud owner of a stack of official documents, suitable for framing, plus one brass plaque on the wall of a company-formation agent somewhere in St. Kitts. As the bank is chartered in Nevis, it need not file annual financial returns. Directors, shareholders, and principals may be of any nationality and live anywhere. The value of the stock may be quoted in any company, and bearer shares are permitted. A corporation may serve as director, and shareholder meetings are not required. The trust company can be merged with other corporations and still administer the Keystone Bank Ltd. In short, for $15,000, plus annual fees of about $700 payable to the local government, you can run your own bank and put as much cash through the tills as you want.

This is not simply a laundryman's fantasy, it's a recurring reality.

There are scores of formation agents hawking banks throughout the Caribbean. One of them, Jerome Schneider of WFI Corporation in California, touted banks at seminars across the United States for years. His sales pitch hung on the undeniable fact that investors could "wield power and influence" with their own private offshore bank. For under $10,000, he provided clients with "a fully chartered private international bank in the Caribbean, plus a management subsidiary corporation in the Bahamas, plus connection with a professional Bahamas Management service."

Schneider roamed the Caribbean, looking for island authorities who would sell him banking charters in bulk. It's estimated that in seventeen years he bought and sold nearly a thousand of them. Once he sold a bank to a client, that was the end of his involvement. WFI did not manage assets or perform any administrative services for the companies it sold. So when it turned out that a woman in Houston, Texas, named Daisy Johnson Butler bought a company from Schneider called European Overseas Bank Ltd., chartered in Grenada, and used it to defraud sixty investors of $1 million, Schneider could quite innocently raise his arms and say it had nothing to do with him. In fact, he even claimed that when he first heard about Butler's misuse of the bank he acted promptly to get the authorities on Grenada to revoke the bank's registration.

A short hop from St. Kitts is the tiny British dependency of Montserrat. When the locals heard about the booming market for banking licenses, they jumped on the bandwagon and were soon invaded by an army of laundrymen with money to wash. At one point, the island, which has a population of ten thousand, boasted 350 chartered banks. Some had familiar-sounding names: Prudential Bank and Trust, Deutsche Bank (Suisse), Chase Overseas, Fidelity Development, and Manufacturers Overseas. There was even one called World Bank Ltd. They were never anything more than a brass plaque in a registered office — except in the case of the Zurich Overseas Bank. According to an indictment by the Justice Department against several Detroit loan brokers who bought Zurich Overseas from WFI, this one actually had an office — a table at the Chez Nous bar in Plymouth.

Montserrat banking was good enough for Panamanian laundrymen, who bought banks there to wash funds for the drug cartels and their former president, Manuel Noriega. It was good enough for Israeli Mossad agents, who used their bank there to launder money in a weapons deal with Colombian drug barons in the mid-1980s. It was also, presumably, good enough for Robert Graven, alias Brother Eduardo of the Circles of Light Church. Working out of Montserrat, with the stated mission of feeding starving children around the world, he convinced thirty thousand Americans to send a total of $3 million to the island's First American Bank. The FBI, working alongside British police, eventually established that Brother Eduardo's true mission on Montserrat was to fill Graven's own bank, and he has since been convicted of fraud in Philadelphia.

Such is the demand for these banks that it has created a cottage industry of Montserrat bank wholesalers. Recently, the situation got so out of control that Britain was forced into taking the unprecedented step of amending Montserrat's constitution. Responsibility for the financial industry was taken away from local politicians and placed under the authority of Her Majesty's appointed governor. And the first thing he did was revoke 311 banking licenses.

The laundrymen were forced to move on. But they never have to go very far. The Caribbean isn't that big.

The British Virgin Islands are thirty-six dots of land with names like Tortola, Virgin Gorda, Anegada, and Jost Van Dyke, poking up out of blue waters northeast of Puerto Rico and west of the Leewards. The year-round population of just twelve thousand is culturally linked to Great Britain but constitutionally independent. More importantly, it is very dependent on its neighbor to the south, the U.S. Virgin Islands. So much so that U.S. dollars are the official currency.

The weather is perfect and English is spoken. So when a young Irish accountant named Shaun Murphy heard about the BVI, and realized that paradise offered untold possibilities for a struggling laundryman, he opened a small practice there.

A gentle man with a soft accent, Murphy started by forming companies for his clients in the BVI, using a company to open an account at a U.K. bank on the Isle of Man and depositing cash there. He'd then form a second company, open an account for it at a Swiss bank in Panama, and wire transfer the money out of Man. Next would come a third company, with an account at a U.K. bank back in the BVI. From there, he could easily wire money on to his client anywhere in the world.

It was as good a method as any. Except after a while, Murphy started thinking it wasn't complicated enough. He decided he could provide his clients with a better service, with as many cutoff points as possible to make their money virtually untraceable. He hung a huge map of the world on the wall behind his desk and sat in his swivel chair for hours staring at it, picking out all sorts of strange places to open accounts. For one client, he formed forty different companies and opened ninety different bank accounts in forty different places around the world. This same client once dropped a Samsonite suitcase with $2.3 million stuffed inside to him from a passing airplane. It took a local bank two days just to count it.

The more complicated Murphy could make these transactions, the better it suited him. Even his own company, Offshore Formation, wasn't easily traceable to him. It was owned by two other companies: Romulus, which he secretly owned, and Remus, which was secretly owned by his friend Cyril Romney, who happened to be the prime minister of the BVI.

Growing ever more sophisticated as a laundryman and better connected in the underworld, Murphy soon had clients such as Ben Kramer, who together with his father, Jack, were high-profile powerboat builders in North Miami. Ben Kramer was also a heavy-duty drug dealer.

A habitué of the Miami-to-Bimini powerboat race, Kramer had worked out a near-foolproof gimmick to bring drugs into the United States. He'd enter three boats in the race, one of which would invariably break down. The boat would sit dead in the water while the rest of the boats disappeared over the horizon, at which time a mother ship would come alongside and load the stricken boat with drugs. When that was done, Ben's rescue boat would show up and tow the racer back to Miami. Finely tuned powerboats break down all the time, so no one thought twice when one of Kramer's was winched out of the water, loaded onto a trailer, and carted away. Over a five-year period, Ben Kramer smuggled $200 million worth of cocaine into the United States with his boats.

Murphy set up two shell companies for the Kramers, both of which had such an air of legitimacy about them that Kramer could use them as official sponsors for his powerboat racing team. One was supposed to be a clothing firm. It had a London address on Saville Row, but otherwise didn't exist. The second, chartered in the Netherlands Antilles, was called Lamborghini. It was not a car company, although Murphy and Kramer never said so, especially if someone assumed it was. Drug money went into the companies, which financed the boats, which financed the drug running, which financed the companies. Somewhere along the line, Murphy also bought Kramer a car rental franchise in Florida, some real estate in Los Angeles, and a company in Liechtenstein called Cortrust. Kramer quickly filled Cortrust's accounts with drug money, which just as quickly came back to him, filtered through several other shell companies in the form of loans he used to build a brand-new marina and finance bigger boats.

Quite apart from their dealings with Murphy, the Kramers got mixed up in the investigation of the murder of Don Aranow, the man who built the famous Cigarette and Blue Thunder powerboats. And that was the beginning of the end of the story for the Kramers.

Murphy's walls came tumbling down because of the Brinks-Mat case. When the British police investigating the case stumbled onto him, he sang. They immediately realized he had serious clients in the United States, and after hearing what he had to say about Brinks-Mat they passed him on to the Americans. Murphy not only told the DEA everything he knew about the Kramers, but helped them get seventy separate indictments against other drug dealers and money launderers. The DEA came to like him so much they spent three years debriefing him. For his help, they paid him $200,000, gave him a brand-new identity, and sent him off to live somewhere in the Mediterranean.

The Caymans are a small string of islands northwest of Jamaica, a relaxed 90-minute luncheon flight from Miami. Once the hideout for Edward Teach, also known as Blackbeard the Pirate, they have come to be known over the past twenty years as one of the world's most preferred financial hideouts. Sometimes called "The Geneva of the Caribbean," the islands — consisting of Grand Cayman, Cayman Brac, and Little Cayman — are long on sand, sun, and confidentiality, while decidedly short on regulation and taxes.

Georgetown, the capital on Grand Cayman, boasts 550 banks — that's one for every fifty residents — with assets in excess of $400 billion. Most of the banks are brass plaques, simply booking centers where loans and deposits are recorded but where nothing more than paperwork changes hands. There are no tellers, no vaults, no free bathroom scales given as a gift for opening a holiday savings account. Fewer than 15 percent of the banks registered and operating in the Caymans ever see any cash.

Originally a dependency of Jamaica, the Caymans elected to take on British Crown Colony status in 1962, when Jamaica declared independence from Britain. Like Hong Kong, the Caymans run their own affairs. There is a British governor in residence, but in reality he does little more than cut ribbons at supermarket openings. The Bank of England has no say, nor any control, over banks in the Caymans.

In 1976, the legislature passed the Confidential Relationships Preservation Law, which, similar to what exists in Switzerland, made it a criminal act for anyone to reveal information about someone's banking or financial associations. Not surprisingly, most of the major American banks have offices there. In fact, a large percentage of the 25,000 Cayman companies and trusts registered on the island are beneficially owned by Americans. Whether or not these companies and the accounts they control ever get reported to the IRS, as required by U.S. law, is another matter. Almost certainly, most of them do not. After all, if a wealthy man wanted to pay taxes on his income, he wouldn't buy a shell company and hide his money in the Caymans. That's why Oliver North set up a dummy company there. That's also why Agha Hasan Abedi opened a BCCI office there, channeling money through the Caymans to buy his way illegally into First American.

Bilateral agreements exist between the United States and some island governments, the Caymans and the Bahamas included, that are supposed to allow American investigators a glimpse behind the curtains of financial stealth. The Mutual Legal Assistance Treaty, ratified in 1988, stipulates that if American authorities request information on specific drug cases and fraud, the Royal Cayman Islands Police will cooperate.

Two years after that, under pressure from the Americans, bankers in the Caymans drafted a code of conduct, requiring them to refuse any suspicious cash deposits in excess of $10,000. The idea was to put an end to the stream of men in shiny suits with gold chains and attaché cases filled with cash. But "suspicious cash deposits in excess of $10,000" doesn't necessarily exclude suspicious cash deposits under $10,000, or unsuspicious cash deposits of any amount. So the men with the shiny suits and gold chains changed clothes.

On paper, all of this is fine. In practice, the agreements and codes fall pitifully short of the mark. One obvious reason is that it's left to the Cayman police to decide whether or not the Americans should be granted cooperation. In cases of tax fraud, the answer is always no, because tax fraud is not a crime in the Caymans. Secondly, the good guys are up against a simple, undeniable fact: hiding assets is big business. Any offshore haven that opted to put an end to it would be committing economic suicide. It wouldn't solve the drug problem; it would simply drive the laundrymen to other offshore jurisdictions where the politicians are less holy.

One such island is St. Maartens in the Netherlands Antilles. There, importing large amounts of cash is easy, customs controls are for all intents and purposes nonexistent, and bankers can't be bothered to ask questions. One estimate has it that shell companies in the Netherlands Antilles control nearly 40 percent of all foreign-owned farmland in the United States.

Because of the direct link to Holland, it's a smooth wire transfer from St. Maartens to the Rotterdam account of a Panamanian-registered shipping company in Malta. It sends the funds to Singapore for deposit into the account of a Liechtenstein-registered insurance company on the Isle of Man, which transfers the money on to a Hong Kong–registered real estate company, working out of Monaco, with an account in Los Angeles. Timed right, the entire process can be managed in under an hour. To get at the money, the laundryman borrows it from himself. This is known in the trade as the "Dutch sandwich," or loan-back. He walks into a legitimately licensed financial institution and negotiates a mortgage, using the Hong Kong company as guarantor, which secures the transaction with the laundered funds in Los Angeles.

A practical variation on that theme involves a pair of property development companies currently operating with total impunity in the United States. One is in the Washington, D.C., area. The other is in south Florida. The offices are staffed by Americans who act as agents for a group of foreign companies in apparently legitimate business centers such as Liechtenstein or Luxembourg. They specialize in property loans to developers who might be having trouble getting large loans through more conventional sources. There is no reason to believe that the people working in D.C. or Florida have any idea the source of the funds they're lending are drug-related.

Their clients come to them with a speculative idea, such as the development of a shopping mall. They're looking for, say, a seven-year, $7-million loan. These outfits then arrange a $10-million loan, to be repaid in seven years. With the extra $3 million, the developers are required to buy a zero-coupon U.S. Treasury bond, which they immediately sign over to the property company. They are then directed to a bank, where they secure a letter of credit for a sum equivalent to the total interest payment on the $7 million, using the shopping mall as collateral. That letter of credit is also signed over to the property company. The developers get the money they need to build their shopping center, while the property company gets a $3 million bond, guaranteed payments of interest, and the deeds to the mall if the developers somehow default. At the end of seven years, the developers pay off the principal and own a mall, while the laundrymen have $10 million, plus interest, in sparkling clean money.

13

DOWN AND OUT IN SWITZERLAND

"The Swiss wash whiter."
— Souvenir T-shirt in Zurich

Lugano is an Italian town permanently trapped inside the Swiss canton of Ticino, preserved like a two-headed mouse in a jar of formaldehyde.

Sheltering on the banks of the large, quiet lake that bears its name, Lugano at first glance appears to be little more than an overgrown depot on the main line of the St. Gotthard railway. There are a few decent hotels. There are some good restaurants. But this is not Lausanne, a sophisticated watering hole. This is not Geneva or Zurich, a crossroads for international business. Nor does anyone ever mistake Lugano for Gstaad or St. Moritz; the beautiful people don't come here to play. The locals like to think of Lugano as the Rio de Janeiro of Switzerland and drone on about how a nearby mountain peak looks exactly like — well, okay, sort of like — Corcovado. But the beach below is hardly Copacabana. And anyway, the Swiss do not samba.

In the past, the main reason for stopping here was because Lugano was a terrific place to hide money. That supposedly changed a few years ago when the Swiss introduced new banking regulations to combat fraud, tax evasion, and, specifically, money laundering. Since then, Lugano is still a terrific place to hide money.

There's a thriving casino across the lake on the Italian side, with frequent ferry service back and forth. Especially during the summer months, it's not uncommon to find well-dressed men and women stepping off the morning's first boat at the Debarcadero Centrale to take their croissant-and-espresso breakfast at one of the cafés on the Piazza Manzoni, or further along the Riva Giocondo Albertolli, near the lush Parco Civico on the lake's shore. It's hardly a coincidence that many of the café tables empty out at about the same time the banks open.

According to London's *Financial Times*, 40 percent of all private assets worldwide are managed in Switzerland — a staggering amount of money. But then, at last count, there were 108 banks in Lugano, and three times that many throughout Ticino. There are more banks there than in the more populated, more accessible Canton of Geneva. In fact, Lugano boasts one of the highest banks-per-capita ratios in the world, more than twice that of Switzerland's acknowledged banking capital, Zurich.

While every bank in Lugano is regulated by Swiss banking laws and governed every bit as fastidiously as every other bank in the country, the easy access from Italy and the proximity of well-established casinos make banks here especially attractive for anyone seeking an especially "discreet" relationship. And because discretion is such a salient commodity, you learn quickly that you can't just walk into a bank and announce you want to hide money.

"I'd like to open a secret bank account," comes the request in a forthright tone. "*Un compte secret.*"

A woman at the first bank doesn't disguise her annoyance with such clumsiness. "We're not interested in any new business of that kind," she says.

The aspiration is repeated in a slightly less hearty voice at the second bank. "I'd like to open a secret bank account. *Un compte secret.*"

A woman there is hardly more congenial. "Do you mean a *compte anonyme*? May I suggest another bank that might be more receptive?"

She does.

It isn't.

"We are not taking on any new private banking business," a man at the third place explains to an increasingly unobtrusive inquirer. "Perhaps you might try somewhere else."

An official at the fourth stop, directly across the street, is even less affable, despite the ever-diminishing decibels. "There is no such thing here as a secret bank account. I'm terribly sorry to disappoint you. Secret Swiss bank accounts are only for the movies."

However, at the fifth bank, when a properly hushed desire is expressed to discuss "various benefits of private banking," the Special Affairs teller responds with a businesslike nod and directs her prospective client to a carpeted suite of offices behind a locked door. There, an impeccably tailored Gentleman introduces himself, wondering graciously if Signor would care to speak French, Italian, English, or German. Signor suggests English. The Gentleman nods and in a polished British accent, asks, "A coffee? Perhaps some tea?" After two pitch-black espressos arrive on a silver tray carried by a suitably attired waiter, the Gentleman closes his office door and asks how he may be of assistance.

Signor says he's interested in establishing "a discreet private banking relationship. Perhaps something along the lines of *un compte anonyme*."

"I must caution you," the Gentleman begins, "that this kind of facility has been much romanticized over the years. The so-called secret Swiss bank account is strictly for pulp fiction and the cinema."

"Now where," Signor probes, "do you suppose they got such a notion?"

He speculates, "Perhaps they've misinterpreted the banking rules in this country as they actually exist. What we do have to offer is a code that protects all bank accounts. Everything from your conventional current account to your child's savings account. It's a crime in Switzerland for anyone working in a bank, or anyone who has ever worked in a bank, to reveal any information whatsoever about an account. It is against the law even to say that a specific account exists."

"You mean you'd be breaking the law if you told me your wife kept her checking account in this branch?"

"That's correct."

But that's only half the story.

Swiss silence is by design, and in all but the rarest circumstances it is not merely 24-carat gold but inlaid with diamonds, rubies, and sapphires. Every account is protected, at times to an extreme degree.

Take the case where someone dies and his heirs attempt to discover if he's been stashing money in an account. All they will ever get out of any Swiss banker is a hollow stare and a slightly chilly reminder that banking codes prohibit disclosure of any information concerning any accounts. However, in this case there's more to it than a mere requirement to comply with the law. Banks zealously cloister their business behind strict banking codes because they're permitted to reap the bounty of accounts that have lain dormant for over twenty years. If you die and no one knows about your *compte anonyme,* the bank can claim your money. One estimate has it that at any given time there are tens of billions of dollars sitting unclaimed in Swiss banks.

So, technically, the Gentleman is right. What he hasn't endeavored to say is that in Switzerland not all accounts are protected equally, that some are considerably more equal than others.

Banks all over the world offer preferential facilities to customers willing to pay for the privilege. Private banking is standard product in today's financial services industry. Marketed as being extraexclusive, and therefore appropriately priced, it's even readily available in every major North American city, where banking secrecy is scarcely ironclad. However, when you speak about private banking in Switzerland, the accent really must be placed on the word *private.*

"In certain very particular cases, an account might be handled in a particularly special way," the Gentleman concedes.

"Like in the movies!"

"I wouldn't go quite that far. I'm afraid that the use of encoded midnight phone calls to unlock a *compte anonyme* is nothing but romantic legend. Also, please keep in mind that bank accounts throughout the world are identified with numbers. The notion that someone might be given information by ringing up to ask in a hoarse whisper about account number 12345 is ludicrous. I dare say that information is never given out by any bank anywhere in the world just because someone knows a number."

"Fair enough," Signor says. "But how about 'particular cases'? And 'in a particularly special way'?"

"By that I mean certain clients have certain banking needs for which we will provide."

"Such as hiding money."

"If that's what you're looking to do, you're probably in the wrong country. In Switzerland today there is a very precise code of conduct that requires us to exercise due diligence in knowing with whom we do business. These days we will only open accounts for people willing to disclose to us their identity and explain to our satisfaction the source of the funds they wish to deposit."

What he is trying to say, in essence, is that Swiss banking is not what it used to be.

Once upon a time, there were two distinctly different types of accounts, referred to by the printed forms used to open them. Form A, the standard product, included the name of the beneficial owner. Form B, the really good one, did not involve names and could be opened by an attorney or an accountant acting as an agent. Although the agent was required to state on the form that he knew the name of his client, he was not obligated to disclose that name to the bank. The beauty of Form B was that by using an attorney as your agent you could create a two-story wall of privacy. Superimposing Switzerland's banking codes over the secrecy afforded attorney-client privilege meant that no one could ever attach your name to the money in the bank. For really good measure, a Form B account opened in the name of an offshore holding company, which was then run by nominee directors, guaranteed that not even the Swiss attorney acting on your behalf knew your name. And if that offshore holding company was owned by other offshore holding companies run by nominee directors, beneficial ownership was virtually untraceable. The danger lay in the fact that you couldn't directly manage the account and had to trust your holdings to various agents. That said, the sort of person who bothered to construct such a complicated maze in order to hide his identity usually had the muscle to ensure that anyone having signature authority over the account was well aware of the risks involved with mismanagement.

But Form B accounts were abolished by law in July 1992.

"Come on," Signor urges, "I'm sure the laws of physics also apply to banking. Voids get filled. How do you open an account today without names attached?"

The Gentleman is naturally cautious. "Even if we used a system based on numbers, you must understand that someone in the bank will always know the name attached to those numbers. It comes down to how many, or how few, will ever be able to link your name with your account."

"How few is a few?"

"Perhaps three? Perhaps four? Only the bank's top executives. But it's reasonable to expect that someone must know whose money it is. How else could you get it when you need it? How else could we make certain it doesn't go to a person not authorized to use those funds? We need to protect our clients and ourselves from all eventualities."

Protecting themselves from all eventualities is the unwritten first rule of the banking business everywhere. Protecting their clients from all eventualities is what the Swiss have been doing for centuries.

Bankers there began offering secrecy to aristocrats for a fee during the French revolution. *Les comptes anonymes,* as we know them today, were invented by the gnomes at the end of the nineteenth century to attract fresh business from around the world. The idea was that if people wanted to hide money, whatever the reason — from tax evasion and fraud to politically unstable environments — the Swiss were willing to sell them that service. In 1934, secret banking was enshrined into Swiss law because a large number of wealthy Germans were willing to pay to protect their assets from the Nazis. When these cast-iron accounts were immortalized by a legion of thriller writers, Ian Fleming among them, legend outgrew reality.

A serious crack in the mask first appeared in 1977. The manager of the Credit Suisse branch in Chiasso, located on the border with Italy, had invested in excess of $500 million on behalf of a group of Italian clients. When the money disappeared with the investors, it was discovered that the local manager had been less than diligent. To repair the damage done to the national reputation, Swiss authorities called in the managers from all of the banks and together they wrote a code of conduct. The basis of the code is that responsibility must rest with the bank and its managers to know with whom they're dealing.

Because business is business and concealment is very good business, secrecy laws in one form or another exist in about fifty nations.

That's one-quarter of all the sovereign states on earth. But nowhere does it have the same cachet, the same claim to fame, as it does in Switzerland. Perhaps that's why it's no accident money laundering is something Swiss bankers and their clients know a great deal about.

In January 1992, four Hungarians wishing to wash $1.3 million in German marks arranged an appointment at the main offices of Credit Suisse on the Paradeplatz in Zurich. They were greeted in the huge, marbled lobby by two men who introduced themselves as officers of the bank. One took the suitcase to another room to count the money while the other invited the Hungarians to have coffee. When the first man did not come right back, the second excused himself, saying he wanted to see what the delay was. The four Hungarians are still staring into their coffee cups.

A week later, a Canadian businessman handed over the $2.5 million in Swiss francs he was trying to wash for another cup of Credit Suisse hospitality.

How the fraudsters were able to get into the bank and use the banking hall greatly concerned Credit Suisse, which, it must be pointed out, was not involved in any way. Still, their coffee is overpriced.

Although the Swiss are fast to pay lip service to the war against the laundrymen, they have been blatantly reluctant to kill the goose, preferring to say they are doing all they can to end money laundering while not actually doing much. Case in point: Two laws framed at the end of the 1980s aimed at putting an end to the influx of criminal funds into Swiss banks. The first made money laundering a crime and prescribed harsh penalties for related offenses, such as insider dealing, market manipulation, and tax fraud. Although it did not include tax evasion in a foreign country, the legislation did recognize as an offense the use of fraudulent documents to deny a foreign state its rightfully due taxes. The second law eliminated all of the 32,000 Form B accounts. Under pressure from various foreign governments, including the United States, the Swiss decreed that agents and representatives disclose to the banks the beneficial owners of those accounts. An attorney must now sign a sworn statement to the effect that his client is not abusing the Swiss banking laws and that the monies involved have not been derived from criminal activities. The new laws also stripped away a powerful buffer by specifying that any lawyer acting for a client in the capacity of an asset manager could not refuse to divulge information on this aspect of their relationship. In other words, that part of their business is no longer automatically protected by attorney-client privilege. These days, any client wishing to open an account, enter into a fiduciary transaction, rent a safe-deposit box, or make any type of cash transaction in excess of SFr 10,000 ($6,800) must be properly identified.

Furthermore, the Swiss Federal Banking Commission has provided banks with a set of ground rules. They warn bankers to be suspicious of any sudden activity in a long-dormant account, of cash being withdrawn immediately after it's deposited, of transactions that appear out of the ordinary for the specific client, and of customers who refuse to supply information. Bankers are also asked to be especially wary of any accounts opened with more than SFr 25,000 ($17,000) in cash. Counter staff are supposed to question anyone converting large amounts of cash into other currencies.

Some banks have proven more vigilant than others. A few even carry their obligations to excess, a trait peculiar to a people whose reputation, justifiably, derives from watches and chocolate and not their sense of humor. When the Compagnie de Banque et D'Investissement, now the Union Bancaire Privée, built new offices in Geneva, it petitioned the city council to change the name of its street because the directors thought the old name created the wrong image. The city council agreed. It's now the Place Camoletti. It used to be Rue de la Buanderie, Laundry Room Street.

In Switzerland today, unless you've got a false passport, you can no longer use a false name to open an account. It's easier and less dangerous to hop on a train to Austria, where banks don't much care who you are because they'll open accounts in any name. It was only in 1994 the Austrians finally bowed to foreign pressure and legislated against money laundering. Except, like so many other countries that reluctantly give in to international pressure, Austria only went halfway. They stopped short of putting an end to the *Sparbücher*, or anonymous savings books, of which there are more than twenty million in a country of fewer than eight million. The preferred method for tax evasion, a *Sparbuch* permits whoever owns it to be the owner of the money in the account. The name attached on it is nothing more than a password, which means you can call yourself anything from Bill Clinton to Popeye the Sailor Man. While these accounts are limited to a maximum of ten million Austrian schillings ($900,000), you're welcome to have one in the name of Snow White and seven others in the names of the dwarves. Add in all your other favorite Disney characters and you're getting up into serious numbers. The burden of proof is on the bank, but you can get around that by hiring a financial advisor to open the account for you. Manuel Noriega had a certain bias for Austrian banking, as did Imelda Marcos. The only limitation is that anyone using these accounts cannot deposit foreign currency. They're strictly for schillings. So arriving in Vienna with sacks of used $20 bills won't work.

But it does in Switzerland. Despite the new legislation, depositing mountains of used $20 bills is not a crime. All you have to do is convince the bank that the money is not the proceeds of crime. Where you might have a bit of problem is in the pronounced tendency of the Swiss, nowadays, to assist foreign states in certain, very specific types of criminal investigations. Provided that a foreign government can prove to the satisfaction of the exceptionally skeptical Swiss judicial authorities that funds in an account derive from fraud, including tax fraud but excluding tax evasion, and that criminal proceedings have already been initiated in that foreign state against the beneficial owner of those funds, the Swiss are willing to seize assets.

Along similar lines, the Swiss were the first nation to sign a treaty with the United States to expose drug-related wealth. If the DEA is on a witch hunt, the Swiss won't cooperate. But if the Justice Department can identify drug money held in a Swiss account and, again, can substantiate those claims in accordance with dreadfully strict guidelines, the Swiss will intervene.

A controversial matter, to say the least, cooperation with foreign governments has been vehemently opposed by most Swiss bankers, who emphasize that every breach of banking secrecy contributes to a loss of confidence in the Swiss banking system. As an example of what invariably happens, they point to the Marcos case. By forcing banks to reveal the existence of Ferdinand and Imelda's accounts, and then freezing the money in them, the government gave the impression that banking secrecy would no longer be adequately safeguarded. The immediate result was a rush of funds out of Switzerland and into Luxembourg, Liechtenstein, and the Caribbean.

No one has to remind Swiss lawmakers that if the people who were doing battle against the laundrymen had a magic wand, waved it, and tomorrow there was no more secret banking in Switzerland, tens of billions of dollars would flood across the border to Vaduz. Or be on the next plane to Grand Cayman. Abolishing secrecy wouldn't solve the money laundering problem, it would merely create unemployment. And in a country that has traditionally known very little unemployment, a country that takes its prosperity seriously, opening bank accounts to closer scrutiny is not a platform on which any politician looking at reelection would dare base a campaign.

On rare occasions, however, someone does break ranks. In 1995, Lugano's federal prosecutor, Carla Del Ponte, lashed out at the Swiss banking industry for doing so little to combat money laundering. "Experience shows that all important proceedings against money launderers in this country have depended on information from abroad."

She said the obligation imposed on Swiss banks to report suspicious customers was clearly not being met because banks were afraid of scaring off potential customers. She admitted that huge sums of dirty money were coming into Switzerland from Russia and other eastern European countries. And then she told a harrowing tale of trying to help bust some Mafia heroin dealers.

In October 1994, Del Ponte said, she received a formal request from Italian authorities to ask banks in Ticino to reveal any accounts they might be holding for sixty named Italian heroin traffickers. She was certain the banks would cooperate. Instead, they filed appeals against her and made formal complaints to the government.

Only when faced with bad publicity or when it doesn't cost them too much do the Swiss make an effort to be helpful. After Juergen Schneider, formerly Germany's largest property developer, filed for bankruptcy and was indicted on fraud charges, the Swiss agreed to freeze the $142 million he'd been saving at a bank in Geneva. On a request from the Haitians, the authorities in Bern identified and froze private accounts held by Baby Doc Duvalier. When the Americans asked that they look into Manuel Noriega's affairs, the Swiss were accommodating enough to padlock his funds. It was the same story when the new Romanian government inquired about Nicolai Ceausescu's assets, when the Indonesian government sought help identifying funds stashed there by President Sukarno, and when the Americans came up with proof that a huge amount of money had been deposited in Switzerland by an Ecuadorian drug cartel.

The first time American authorities asked the Swiss to freeze the $2.2 million the Russians purportedly paid former CIA agent Aldrich Ames, they declined. But when it became evident that the CIA wasn't going to ask politely a second time, someone in Bern decided it might be prudent to comply. The CIA knew too much about Swiss banking and could have caused them a great deal of embarrassment, so the Swiss froze three accounts.

The Swiss also played ball with the DEA when it went after Jorgé Hugo Reyes-Torres, head of a family drug cartel in Ecuador, who'd been producing cocaine since the early 1970s, most of it for distribution in the United States. About 1990, some of Reyes-Torres's family settled in the Denver area, apparently planning to import a ton of cocaine a year. The results of the DEA's two-year investigation were put before a federal grand jury in May 1992, resulting in drug violation charges against Reyes-Torres and other members of his family. The following month, police in Ecuador raided his home and arrested him. They found documents identifying overseas bank accounts. The Justice Department sent them to Switzerland and asked that the accounts be frozen. Because this wasn't a fishing expedition and the Americans fully complied with the letter of the law, the Swiss were more than pleased to oblige. The U.S. attorney in Denver then obtained a civil forfeiture judgment against the $11.5 million sitting in Switzerland. The Swiss turned it over, and the United States handed back to the Swiss $3.8 million as a thank-you for their help.

It's probably just a coincidence that shortly after cashing the check, the Swiss came through yet again.

For twenty years, Julio Cesar Nasser David — who liked to call himself King Nasser David — operated one of the largest, most successful drug trafficking rings in America. Together with his wife Sheila Miriam Arana de Nasser, and members of both their families, Nasser smuggled nearly thirty tons of cocaine and fifteen hundred tons of marijuana into the United States.

The earliest records of their dealings date to 1976, when they opened an account at the Royal Trust Bank in Miami with $20,000. Over the next fifteen months they made twenty cash deposits totaling $4.49 million. After establishing a financial base for themselves in Switzerland with a Red Cross company registered in Liechtenstein called the Solimar Foundation, they used cashier's checks to transfer their money from Royal Trust to the Union Bank of Switzerland (UBS) in Geneva. Next, they opened an account at Landmark First National Bank in Fort Lauderdale and moved millions through there to UBS. In one frantic two-month burst of activity, April to May 1980, the Nassers conducted 117 separate transactions, sometimes as many as eight in one day. They deposited $3.69 million into Landmark and, using cashier's checks made payable to scores of fictitious names, transferred $4.39 million out.

By 1985, the Nassers were washing money through accounts at two more banks in Florida, as well as banks in Bogotá, Beirut, Barcelona, and Panama City. Because cash transaction reporting was beginning to be enforced, they switched to negotiable instruments, opened a dealing account at Merrill Lynch in Miami, and transferred $5 million from Solimar in Switzerland to UBS Panama. They put some money into a condominium in Coconut Grove and some into boats, both for pleasure and for smuggling drugs. They also opened new accounts at UBS — one in Switzerland under the name of the Liechtenstein-registered Proventina Foundation, and another in Panama under the name of the Liechtenstein-registered Mirasol Stiftung. Money was deposited into both from their Merrill Lynch account in Miami.

Over the course of twenty years, they'd laundered $755 million through eighteen bank accounts in eight countries and hid behind ten companies and nearly a hundred fictitious names. But in early 1995, as a result of a ten-month investigation, the U.S. attorney in Miami indicted the Nassers for the seventh time. In April, the Swiss arrested Sheila Nasser. They also froze $150 million of the Nassers' money at

UBS, representing the largest single cash seizure of narcotics proceeds to date.

Faced with the happy prospect of netting a one-third share of $150 million, the Swiss now signed a mutual assistance treaty with the United States, opened a liaison office in Washington, and stocked it with a senior police officer.

"So," the Gentleman makes his point, "you can plainly see how, and I hope can appreciate why, we are not interested in harboring criminal funds."

"Most definitely," Signor says, nodding. "But that's not my case."

The Gentleman is too polite to disagree. "Of course not."

Signor puts on his most reassuring expression. "Let's say I'm looking to invest some capital quietly. You understand. Without wanting to involve myself in various . . . international hassles, let's call them."

For some odd reason, he immediately assumes that "international hassles" means tax avoidance. "If you don't pay your taxes in the United States, that's hardly a problem for the Swiss government to worry about. Although I'm certain that I don't need to remind you how some countries, the United States and Great Britain among them, have laws that make undeclared bank accounts illegal. But it goes without saying, those laws are not binding in Switzerland."

Not wanting to worry him with minor details, such as how "international hassles" could also mean an arrest warrant issued by the FBI, Signor settles on, "Just how would someone go about opening such an account? How would you propose to fill the void left by the Form B?"

"For the sort of private facility you're alluding to, I think it would be fair to say that sufficiently large sums are required."

"What would you say to . . ." Signor picks a figure off the top of his head . . . "two point five?"

Taking for granted that there are five zeros at the end of the numbers two point five, he wonders, "Swiss francs?"

With enormous confidence, Signor informs him, "Dollars."

"Hmmmm." He likes that. "Yes, it is definitely in the range of business we would be willing to consider."

Now, here comes the not-so-subtle hint. "There may be a certain amount of cash involved."

"Ah." His eyebrows raise. "I see." Long pause. "Cash can present certain hurdles."

Signor reacts matter-of-factly. "Oh . . . but they're not necessarily insurmountable hurdles."

The Gentleman thinks for a moment. "We are required to exercise due diligence. Now, I don't take that to mean that we must insult dozens of new clients simply to identify a villain who, when we refuse his business here, will merely take his business somewhere else. But cash is, I'm sorry to say, often inconvenient. And large amounts of cash are, frankly, not very desirable."

"I understand." Signor leans forward. "Yet Switzerland is one of the world's largest bank note trading centers. I read somewhere that a ton and a half of foreign currency arrives every day at the airport in Zurich. Surely a few extra bank notes aren't going to cause anyone a problem."

With two and a half million dollars being dangled as an opening deposit, and the prospect of more to come, he doesn't want to see his prospective client walk across the street. "If we could be completely satisfied . . . "

"You mean, if the cash was coming from say, various business ventures in the Middle East? Or, a rather lucky evening at the gaming tables across the lake?" Signor hides his grin. "Would that make things more . . . convenient?"

Possibly reminding himself that there are 107 other banks in town and almost certainly other bankers would gladly take Signor's deposit — he does not know that four have already shown Signor to the door — he proposes, "If we could somehow satisfy ourselves as to where the cash came from, I'm certain that we can come to an arrangement."

"And this can be done verbally?"

He gazes at Signor for a very long time. "We might require some written evidence, depending on the nature of the verbal statement. Invoices, perhaps. Or contracts. Letters of agreement. Paperwork is good. And discreet inquiries will then be made. But please allow me to assure you, whatever is discussed between us remains in the strictest confidence. We may ask questions. However, once we're satisfied with the origin of the money and the integrity of our client, we never repeat any of the answers."

How comforting, Signor thinks, that with little more than a passport, well-prepared answers to the obvious questions, a handful of faxes for backup, and a hefty pile of dough, almost anyone can avail themselves of the most famous laundromat in the world, despite the fact that some Swiss would have you believe such facilities no longer exist.

"The money in question . . ." Signor looks straight into the Gentleman's eyes . . . "is perfectly clean. It's not drug money."

The Gentleman stares back and finally smiles warmly. "Then it will be a pleasure to do business with you."

14

ELI PINKAS: A MYSTERY STORY

*col•lec•tor (ke-lek'-ter) n. A person employed to collect taxes,
duties, or other payments.*
— **The American Heritage Dictionary**

Just after dawn on Tuesday morning, June 10, 1980, the Lausanne
police received an emergency call from a hysterical maid at the Villa
Gentilhommière, the luxury estate of a local businessman named Eli
Pinkas. She kept babbling on about a dog being murdered, and intruders. Several cars were dispatched. Arriving at the large gates that
guarded the villa, the police found them unlocked, so they hurried
inside the grounds. There was a Jaguar coupe in the garage, and when
one of the officers touched the hood, he found it was hot. Not simply warm, he later wrote in his report, but hot. The car had obviously
been driven a long time during the night. The villa seemed otherwise
quiet.

Almost as soon as the officer in charge rang the bell at the front
door, the maid threw it open, insisted the dog had been murdered by
intruders, and brought the officers inside. They found a German
shepherd dead in the hallway at the bottom of the stairs. Later, the
police were able to determine that the cause of death had been
cyanide poisoning.

Fanning out, they made their way through the house to search
for intruders. One officer went upstairs. In the master bedroom he
found Pinkas's body. On the night stand next to the bed was a hand-

written note. In it, Pinkas asked that his friends forgive him. The police were later able to determine that here too the cause of death had been cyanide poisoning.

No intruders were found. There were no signs of a break-in. As far as the police were concerned, it was obvious that Pinkas had killed the dog, and then had taken his own life.

Normally, an autopsy confirmation of suicide would have closed the case. Except, sometime that very same morning — but definitely before the Lausanne police went to La Gentilhommière — the police in Cannes, France, received an anonymous phone call summoning them to a penthouse apartment at the Grand Hotel.

The front door of the apartment had a series of locks, but when the police got there, none of them were bolted. Nothing in the apartment led them to believe there had been intruders. In the master bedroom they found a woman's body. Later they were able to determine that the cause of death had been cyanide poisoning.

On the floor at the foot of the bed was a note ripped into small pieces. "Flo, m'amour, I give you some last advice because I love you. Open these two packages and swallow these four capsules, which work very quickly, so that you can join me." It went on to warn that if she stayed alive she would suffer great difficulties and dishonor. "I've tried for years to reestablish my financial situation, but without success." It was signed, "I love you always and until the last breath of my life, your Eli."

At first glance, the matching suicides of two lovers, 208 miles apart, had a Romeo and Juliet quality about it.

But first glances are often deceptive.

Eli Pinkas was a cultured man who spoke French, English, German, Italian, and Bulgarian. Of average build but with heavy features — he had extremely large hands and a very wide forehead — he always dressed conservatively. His thinning dark hair was turning white.

Born in 1920, Pinkas's family had settled in Lausanne in 1941, war refugees from Bulgaria. He earned a degree in chemistry from the local university and became a successful and respected businessman.

His home was aptly named "The Gentleman's Manor," and he spent a great deal of time there, much of it in his garden tending to his roses. Pinkas was a private person; some people thought him aloof. His personal annual income was in the range of $1.5 million, yet he showed very little outward sign of extravagance, except perhaps for his love of Jaguars. He had several.

His business life consisted of a multilayered series of interests, almost all stemming from his background as a chemist. Being a serious man, Pinkas was invited by other serious businessmen to serve on their corporate boards. One of the boards he sat on was that of the very conservative Banque Vaudoise de Crédit.

The company Pinkas ran was called Socsil, and his factory in Lausanne was a large, heavily guarded, fully mechanized plant operating in three distinct fields. It manufactured mechanical pumps, using a process Pinkas had patented. It performed the chemical testing of raw materials being used to make a certain soft drink, the name of which was kept secret. Pinkas, however, once confided in a few close friends that it was Coca Cola and that he was the only person outside the United States to possess the secret Coke formula. But the most important and by far biggest share of the business was the production of the highly explosive gas nitrous oxide, popularly known as laughing gas.

Complementing that side of his business, Pinkas had, many years before, invented a chemical process that rendered nitrous oxide inert. Understanding the potential of nonexplosive nitrous oxide, he designed a medical kit for use in battlefield hospitals and sold these kits to dozens of militaries around the world. Among his clients were the NATO armies. Because a military buildup somewhere in the world was clearly reflected in increased orders for his battlefield kit, Pinkas was privy, albeit as an incidental party, to certain classified military intelligence — not that classified information was something he was unaccustomed to. In his spare time he was a major in the Swiss Army Reserve.

Or maybe he wasn't.

In Switzerland, just about every male citizen has a commitment to the military that lasts for a good part of his life. That's why it was hardly surprising when friends spotted Eli Pinkas walking through the streets of Lausanne wearing his reserve officer's uniform. Nor did any of those friends ever doubt him when he boasted of being the Swiss Army's Reserve Chief of Gas Warfare. After all, he was a chemist with a thorough knowledge of gases.

The Swiss, who are not a nuclear power, have historically depended on gas warfare as a last line of defense. If attacked, their battle plan is to retreat into the mountains and fill the valleys with gas. They believe it will make the country just about impregnable, at least to an army advancing on foot.

So Major Eli Pinkas, Reserve Chief of Gas Warfare for the Swiss Army, seemed totally plausible. What's more, Lausanne is a small town where everyone knows everyone else, and if Pinkas hadn't been who he said he was, word would have gotten around very quickly.

These days, however, the Swiss Ministry of Defense says Pinkas never had anything to do with the Army Gas Warfare Department. In fact, they claim he wasn't even a reserve officer.

In addition to Socsil, Pinkas had his fingers in a few other pies. In the mid-1960s he bought a 283-acre tract of land outside Lausanne to develop it into a resort area. He had tried to enlist the help of an American consortium, but Swiss laws discourage foreign ownership of property, and as a result, the Americans shied away. Instead, he used the land as collateral for loans with the banks when he wanted to swing other deals. One of his more ingenious deals involved the scrap steel business.

While selling nitrous oxide to the U.S. Army, Pinkas stumbled — at least this is what he told friends — across the curious fact that where the Americans were concerned, there was a difference between gas bottles that were "full" and gas bottles that were "almost full." When he shipped the bottles to them, they were checked and certified full. But the valves on those huge steel cylinders often leaked, and not all of them were 100-percent full by the time the U.S. Army got around to using them. Through some eccentric accounting regulation, bottles that were not 100-percent full, Pinkas explained, were written off by the Americans as unusable and discarded as scrap steel. So, he started buying the scrapped bottles, repainting them, topping them up with gas — he said there was usually no more than 15 to 20 percent missing — and selling them back to the Americans for the full price.

Pinkas used to brag to friends that it was a truly wonderful business, and let some of them invest in it. He'd even show them their gas cylinders whenever they visited the factory. And he did send them regular dividend checks. Because those friends were making money with him, none of them bothered looking any deeper into it. Although an official report later claimed Socsil was only doing $4.2 million a year worldwide in nitrous oxide sales, Pinkas flaunted records that showed he was doing $27 million a year just with the Sanitary Division of the United States Army.

As a contractor to the United States Government, Pinkas was in a position to discount U.S. paper. It's a standard procedure. When a company invoices the government for, say, a million dollars, and the government acknowledges the debt, promising to pay in sixty to ninety days, a businessman can take the invoice to a bank and get $1 million right away, minus whatever commission he's negotiated with the bank for taking over the sixty- to ninety-day debt. Uncle Sam's signature on U.S. Army invoices meant that any bank in the world would welcome Pinkas and his U.S. paper.

Except that Pinkas didn't actually discount the paper. Instead, he borrowed against it. He put the invoices down as security for loans. It was a slightly quirky thing to do, but most of the bankers he dealt with figured he was just trying to save a little money, so they went along with it. They couldn't know that Pinkas never intended to give a bank the opportunity to collect on this paper. When bank officials wanted to see balance sheets for Socsil, Pinkas showed them balance sheets. When they wanted to see his personal accounts, he showed them his personal accounts. Everyone who asked for paperwork got paperwork. And in every case, the bank looking at his accounts was listed in those reports as Pinkas's only creditor.

So banks gave him money against that paper as collateral. By backing it up with his balance sheets and, wherever necessary, his personal guarantee, the bankers with whom he dealt conveniently forgot the most basic lesson of the lending business: always check with the originator of a collateral note.

Pinkas's borrowing against U.S. government paper has now been traced as far back as 1948. Astonishingly, not one bank — not even one American bank — ever bothered checking with the United States Army Sanitary Division.

Enter now the former Mrs. Pinkas. Her name was Florence. She was two years older than Pinkas and a hopeless alcoholic.

Before Florence and Eli were married in 1943, she appeared on the scene as a dark-haired lady from Argentina who spoke beautiful Spanish, and French with a heavy accent. After they were divorced in 1964, she left Lausanne to live in the south of France and only rarely came to Switzerland. They never had children, which some people felt accounted for the touch of melancholy that often surrounded her. Or maybe she loved him and didn't want to live apart. They divorced in 1964, but their affair continued on a regular weekend basis. Pinkas would tell anyone who asked that he was totally devoted to her. And the proof of it was that every Thursday night he flew to Nice, telling anyone who asked that he always spent the weekend with her.

It now turns out that she was not from Argentina. Instead, she was born near Lausanne — she still has family there — and met Pinkas when she was working as a barmaid in a local hangout. Why the masquerade about being from Argentina? No one seems to understand. The important thing is that everyone either believed it or was at least willing to play along.

In the scheme of world history, the first week of June 1980 probably doesn't mean much. It wasn't as remarkable as the first week of June 1900, when the Boxer Rebellion engulfed the southern provinces of China. Or the first week of June 1920, when the Treaty of Trianon redrew the map of Europe. Or even the first week of June 1960, when President Eisenhower sent 120 planes to Southeast Asia, marking

America's toe-testing of the waters that would become the war in Vietnam. However, it was the final week of Eli and Florence Pinkas's lives.

At the beginning of the week, a clerk in the Banque de Paris et des Pays-Bas in Geneva who was auditing a lending portfolio noticed that ink had rubbed off on his hands. Curious, he sorted back through the stack of paperwork on his desk until he found some smudged letterheads from the United States Army Sanitary Division. Imagining that the Americans ought to have had better printing facilities, he studied the letters more closely, thought to himself that ink on U.S. government forms wasn't supposed to rub off, and sent a memo to his superior to report the matter. All his superior could think to do was wire the bank's office in Washington, D.C., and have them inform the army's Sanitary Division that there was a minor problem with their letterhead. Accordingly, someone in the bank's office in Washington phoned the Pentagon and asked to speak with the U.S. Army's Sanitary Division.

The operator on the other end wanted to know, "What's a Sanitary Division?"

For the price of better ink, the world was about to cave in on Eli Pinkas.

A telex went back from Washington to Geneva. The smudged paperwork was sent to a senior officer at the bank who inspected it, and then studied the rest of the file. He was inclined to phone Pinkas to ask him what this was all about, but just to be prudent, he decided first to show the entire dossier to his lawyers. They demanded he call the police.

Being so well connected, Pinkas must have learned what was happening because by the middle of that week he began paying back a number of small outstanding loans — a few thousand dollars here, a few thousand francs there. And in every case, he paid cash. He also wrote letters to at least six people, asking that they forgive him, although he never spelled out what for.

On Friday, June 6, the public prosecutor in Lausanne saw for the first time a document charging Eli Pinkas with fraud. He was absolutely stunned. The thought of someone as reputable as Pinkas being involved in such a crime was so worrying that he rang Pinkas to say, "I must see you."

Pinkas laughed, then agreed to meet with the man later the following week. After hanging up with the public prosecutor, Pinkas called two friends in the hierarchy of a local bank, asking them to meet him at his factory first thing Monday.

Almost as soon as they stepped into his office that morning, he informed them, "I'm being indicted."

They too were stunned.

Without going into detail, he admitted to "a few wrongdoings." "It's very little," he assured them, "but it's so embarrassing."

Back at their bank, the two decided they liked Pinkas enough to do something for him. So while one checked the records to establish the extent of Pinkas's borrowings there, the other approached the public prosecutor to see if their personal intervention might help Pinkas save face.

By Monday afternoon, everyone concerned was quickly coming to the conclusion that "a few wrongdoings" and "very little" was hardly the case.

Before dawn on Tuesday, Eli Pinkas was dead at La Gentilhommière, and Florence Pinkas was dead in Cannes.

The Swiss press announced the Pinkas affair with headlines labeling him a "Fraudster Bulgarian Jew." But he wasn't a Bulgarian. He'd taken Swiss citizenship and had carried a Swiss passport for nearly forty years. Nor was Pinkas still a Jew. He'd converted to Protestantism in the 1950s; whether for business reasons or because he really believed, no one knows. The point is, he did not openly acknowledge Judaism for at least the last twenty-five years of his life.

That he was a fraudster, however, is another matter.

When the police went to the Socsil offices after his death, they found that a large number of documents had been destroyed. They assumed Pinkas had gotten to them first. Yet from what remained, they were able to determine that he'd used United States Army Sanitary Division invoices, similar invoices from the German army, and a guarantee for $30 million from the Swiss bank UBS as collateral for loans that totaled a staggering $300 million.

When the police established that the bogus invoices were printed in Cannes, the French were called in. The printer who did the work for Pinkas later claimed he didn't know what he was printing. He said he didn't speak English; and besides, it wasn't any of his business what a client wanted printed on a form. All he'd say was that Pinkas paid for his work on time and in cash. In the end, the printer was the only person to go to jail in connection with the affair, sentenced to two years for not declaring that cash to the French tax authorities.

As investigators got deeper into his affairs, it became obvious to them that Pinkas had somehow managed to convince American banks to make wire transfers to Switzerland by order of the U.S. Army Sanitary Division. He needed them to do that in order to make everything look absolutely official. He needed to have payments coming in to Switzerland from the U.S. government. After all, if he was supposed to be doing business with the Army, he couldn't deposit money in Switzerland and simply ask his bankers to believe it was from the Army. But no one was ever able to figure out exactly how he managed that.

Over the course of the next two years, the Swiss tried to trace the money Pinkas brought into the system. Believing at first the sums involved were perhaps "as much as" $300 million, they located hundreds of companies around the world Pinkas was using to launder money, and were forced to revise their estimate. "As much as" $300 million was changed to "perhaps as high as" $800 million. Yet the grand total of liquid assets attributable to Eli Pinkas, once every book was examined, only came to $1.5 million.

At that point, the case was officially closed. It was as if the Swiss suddenly didn't want anyone to know exactly how much money was missing or where it might have gone.

Six week's after Pinkas's death, the *Washington Post* reported that Pinkas had effectively stolen $140 million. Just over $112 million of it came from eighteen banks around the world: eight in Switzerland, four in France, one in Britain, one in Israel, and four in the United States, including Citibank and First National of Minneapolis. The rest of whatever money Pinkas had, at least according to the *Washington Post,* came from his friends and business associates. Other newspapers have since suggested that on top of the $140 million there might be as much as $20 million more that's been written off by creditors who for legal or personal reasons cannot publicly admit to having been involved.

Within two months of Pinkas's death, the *Wall Street Journal* quoted someone inside the Swiss banking authority as saying that the $140 million originally estimated was being revised down to $108.7 million. What's more, the Swiss Federal Banking Commission seemed content to write off the scandal as a bit of temporary craziness. It reported that because Pinkas was so heavily in debt, he had to keep borrowing just to pay the interest. That created more debt, which in turn created the need for more borrowing. In other words, it was a Ponzi scheme. It noted that Pinkas was alright as long as interest rates were low. But when he had to borrow at 19 percent to pay off loans that had been made at 12 percent, that strangled him.

Except that "temporary craziness" does not answer the question, Where did the money go?

Finding someone in authority these days who'll speak about Pinkas isn't easy. Their first reaction is that it was a long time ago. They suggest you just forget it. If you persist, they tell you in a whisper — as if they're doing you a favor and finally letting you in on a genuine secret — that the money went to pay for his lifestyle. They tell you he lost it gambling. They insist there's nothing else to say.

The problem is that Pinkas clearly lived within his own income, and he was not a gambler. He was, however, an extraordinarily talented laundryman.

The plumbing of his sink involved three companies. First, there was Socsil. Next, there was an investment company he'd founded in 1970 called Vilro. And finally, there was a land development company, Villas La Roche, which owned the property outside Lausanne Pinkas had once hoped to develop with American partners. Like spokes on a wheel, they branched out to those hundreds of companies he'd scattered around the world. To create cash flow, he oversubscribed the three main holdings, selling each share three and four times. Because every share is numbered, he needed to keep his creditors from comparing notes, so he skillfully used the "He's got a big mouth" technique.

It worked like this. Pinkas would strike up a relationship with Monsieur A. They would be discussing a business possibility when, by chance, Monsieur B's name came up. Immediately Pinkas would say to Monsieur A, "Listen, B is a great guy and I really like him, but this deal has got to be just between us. You see, the problem is that B has a big mouth. He talks too much. If you mention our business to him, it will be all over Lausanne in an hour." Naturally, Monsieur A would then make a point of shying away from Monsieur B. However, when Pinkas brought Monsieur B into his confidence, which he invariably would, and offered him a piece of the deal, he'd tell Monsieur B the same story about Monsieur A. "He's got a big mouth."

As simple as it was, he played on a common human trait: most people don't want other people to know the details of their business. It wasn't until long after his death that all sorts of people who otherwise knew each other's business, or at least thought they did, started comparing notes and realized that Pinkas had successfully kept them apart.

They also started to understand Pinkas's apparent aloofness. Some of his friends noted that he was a man with extraordinary control, a man who didn't seem to have a temper, and who never seemed to get into an argument with anyone. They thought it was just his nature. Now, they admit, considering the glass house in which he lived, it's obvious why he never threw stones.

Spinning money through the three main companies, sending it out to the others, then bringing more in when he needed to, Pinkas made the three main assets seem that much more liquid. And as capital built up from his borrowing schemes, he moved that money out.

But to where? All of those companies on the outer rim of the wheel were empty shells.

Sometime about 1975 there was a terrible accident at the Socsil factory. At six in the morning, while doing some sort of experiment with a gas that couldn't explode, the laboratory's chief engineer was killed when it did. There was an official investigation and the coroner's report settled on misadventure. No one thought again about that conclusion until Pinkas died. Then some people began to wonder if perhaps the chief engineer had stumbled onto something at the factory and had been eliminated.

Although some dark conspiracy remains nothing more than conjecture, with hindsight, it's plausible. Consider this: some months before his death, Pinkas added a clause to his will specifically to provide for his own funeral. He wanted a Valkyrie-like affair, with his ashes sprinkled across Lake Geneva. Perhaps it was just a coincidence he wrote the provision when he did. Or perhaps it wasn't. And what about the woman he loved so much he asked her to die with him? Could he possibly have forgotten to provide for her? He was by anyone's accounting a wealthy man. The apartment in Cannes was filled with antiques, paintings, and Oriental rugs. Florence had jewels. She also had 470 pairs of shoes in her closet. Yet she was buried in a commoner's grave because there wasn't enough money to pay for a funeral.

Did Florence take her own life? When the police got to Pinkas's home on the morning of his death, the hood of his car was hot. Could he have driven to Cannes the night before and killed her, trying to make it look like suicide? Could he have murdered her and then raced back to Lausanne and taken his own life?

Or maybe he drove somewhere else to meet someone else. Maybe he didn't take his own life. The note next to Florence's body looked as if it had been written by Pinkas, but it was never checked by experts. Why was it ripped up? Perhaps he failed to provide for her funeral because he didn't know she'd be needing one. The door of Florence's apartment had so many locks that friends who visited her joked that it looked like a fortress. Pinkas had keys to her apartment. So why, when the police arrived, were all of those bolts unlocked? Could she have let someone in who didn't have any keys to lock up on the way out?

Pinkas was a very proud man, and would have been incapable of suffering the indignity of a public trial or coping with a jail sentence. For those people who knew him well, suicide seems logical — a fast and simple way out of the problem. Negotiating a discreet settlement would have been equally logical, at least if he still had any of the money. There's nothing a jilted banker wants to see more than his money returned. In Switzerland especially, bankers instinctively avoid the sort of adverse publicity that would have certainly followed the arrest and trial of a man like Eli Pinkas. And he would have understood that.

The most logical reason why he didn't try to return the money is that he didn't have it. The money didn't go to any visible private causes, but is it possible it went to a public cause? Could there have been a circuit somewhere in Pinkas's brain labeled "fanatic"?

Consider this: in that Pinkas had access to certain military information, it was not surprising that the Swiss authorities found classified military documents stored in his factory office safe. He had been involved in global conflicts: the Cold War with the superpowers, the Gulf war with Iran and Iraq, heightened tensions throughout the Middle East, and brush fire wars throughout the rest of the world. Perhaps also there were people on either side of the fence — or someone sitting in the middle of that fence — who wanted to know whatever he knew.

The most obvious contact he might have had was Bulgaria. After all, he was twenty-one when he came to Switzerland from there, old enough to have befriended all sorts of people. The possibility exists that he was selling them information. If nothing else, doing so would be a source of cash in times of financial difficulties. But that would have brought money in, not made $300 to $800 million disappear. He could have been buying something from the Bulgarians, but they didn't have much to sell, except perhaps drugs, and Pinkas wasn't a drug trafficker. The Bulgarians, however, did have access to Russian weaponry, and consequently access to certain Russian nuclear secrets. But if he was dealing with the Bulgarians, whatever he was buying wasn't coming back to Switzerland.

Now the plot thickens.

Every Thursday evening, Eli Pinkas drove to Geneva Airport for the short flight to Nice, France. He returned to Switzerland on Monday morning. He always said he was going to Cannes to spend the weekend with Florence.

Except he didn't.

The reason he flew to Nice on Thursday nights, instead of Friday evening like so many people who regularly spent weekends in the south of France, was so that he could change flights there on Thursday nights and not on Friday nights.

El Al doesn't fly on Fridays after sundown.

The inconvenience of spending a few hours waiting in the tiny airport at Nice for the late-night flight to Tel Aviv was outweighed by the benefit that no one in Switzerland knew where he was going, and no one in France cared. On those very limited occasions when he bumped into someone he knew in Nice airport, Pinkas quietly confessed that he kept an apartment in Israel into which he had installed a lady friend. It seemed plausible enough.

Israeli law requires that foreigners owning property there, even if only a weekend residence, register it. Since Pinkas's death, the Israelis have categorically denied knowing anything about him and claim to have no record of his supposed apartment, nor any information about his supposed lady friend. Nor does Israeli immigration admit to knowledge of his frequent visits.

Now consider this: it is known that the Israelis were only able to fully develop and maintain their nuclear capability because of help from several sources. The United States was one. But Washington didn't foot the entire bill and couldn't be depended on for unhindered support. So the Israelis raised some money on their own, selling high-tech military equipment to low-tech nations, such as Iran, South Africa, and Chile. They raised the rest with "collectors."

Since independence in 1948, Israel has actively courted prominent people around the world who address themselves to selected sources of wealth in order to make their resources available when a need arises. There is nothing like an organized appeal by conscientious Jewish organizations that throw huge dinners, or doorstep charities that plant trees in Israel.

They do their work very quietly and very discreetly.

For example, in 1960 the Israelis put together their so-called "Group of 30" — an ad hoc brotherhood of two and a half dozen American millionaires quietly united by a common cause. The $40 million they donated helped pay for Israel's first nuclear reactor and the neighboring plutonium separation plant.

Eli Pinkas never spoke about Israel. He wasn't even a Jew any more. Yet he kept a residence there. Except the Israelis insist he didn't exist. And he was a man who knew how to launder money, how to make the paper trail disappear to obscure its source, or even better, how to obscure its destination. The Israelis built their bomb with other people's money. Did they spend any of it inside the Iron Curtain, buying secrets, or expertise, or designs, or perhaps even weapons-grade plutonium the Bulgarians might have stolen from the Russians?

The Israelis don't talk about their nuclear weapons program any more than they talk about their collectors.

$300 to $800 million later, why should they?

15

THE COKE CONNECTION

*"Drug money freely mingles with the life force of the world economy,
like a virus in the bloodstream."*
— *Time* magazine

The link between dirty money and drugs is absolute and indisputable.

The bulk of dirty money spinning around the world comes from the illicit drugs trade, and the whopping success of international drug traffickers is a direct consequence of their ability to launder their profits.

In any business, a certain percentage of turnover must be recycled into the costs of production and distribution. But where drugs are concerned, it's a small percentage because the wholesale markup ranges between 500 and 1,000 percent.

Drug traffickers don't count their money, they weigh it.

Washed, invested in legitimate businesses, then reinvested in criminal activity, drug money moves with the momentum and force of a cyclone. The local economies of small, dusty towns such as Atoka, Oklahoma, and Roma, Texas, were literally broken when cash-bearing Mexicans arrived to buy property. In countries like Bolivia, Peru, Ecuador, and Colombia, drugs and money laundering have bred violence and corruption, and become such a cancer they have subverted both the political and the judicial systems.

The narco-economy has made drug traffickers the most influential special-interest group in the world.

The money generated and controlled by traffickers has reached such monstrous proportions that dozens of Third World countries could not possibly underwrite their own existence were it not for drug money. It has become an unofficial form of U.S. foreign aid. Without an income from drug trafficking, Colombia, Bolivia, Ecuador, and Peru could not remain afloat. Even an oil-producing nation such as Venezuela might not survive without it.

In early 1990, the United States offered to pay Latin American countries $1.5 billion over a five-year period for crop-substitution programs. Colombia, Bolivia, and Peru rejected the gift as inadequate. The Bolivian government said it alone would need half that to make such a scheme work. The Peruvians stated that even if they got the entire $1.5 billion, they still couldn't guarantee success. Yet, even if America paid it, and even if Bolivia and Peru did destroy all the coca and put an end to all of the trafficking taking place inside their borders, the impact on the world market would be negligible. The demand would be met instantly by any of a dozen other drug-producing nations.

The sums involved are way beyond anything easily comprehensible. A few years ago, the late Colombian cocaine cartel boss Pablo Escobar had to write off $40 million in cash because it had literally rotted in a California basement. He wasn't able to get it into the washing cycle fast enough. He was already laundering so much that the machinery overheated and the system blew a fuse. When he was caught the first time, and word spread that he might be extradited to the United States, Escobar offered to barter for his freedom by personally paying off Colombia's national debt.

The most massive effort ever mounted against drugs coming into America began in secrecy in mid-1992. For twelve months, and at a cost of $1.1 billion, Customs and the Coast Guard joined forces to construct an electronic net rigged from the southern tip of Florida to the southeastern tip of Texas. They were backed up by the Navy, which kept fully armed guided missile cruisers on constant patrol in the Gulf of Mexico and the Caribbean to provide early warning detection. Anything and everything that moved across that invisible barrier, whether by air or water, was identified. If it was deemed suspicious, it was stopped and inspected. The U.S. government was determined to slam shut the door through which the bulk of drugs entered the country.

One year and $1.1 billion later, a classified National Security Council document proclaimed that there had not been any detectable difference whatsoever in the amount of drugs coming into the United States.

Attorney General Janet Reno reluctantly had to admit, "Interdiction, which has been very costly, does not work. I've not seen anything since I've been in office which would indicate to me that it's been a cost-effective effort."

With more drugs on the streets than ever before, and more money inexorably linked to them, it's little wonder so many policemen feel they're fighting a losing battle. How do you convince a 14-year-old kid in Harlem that if he goes to school, he'll learn a trade, and someday earn $10 an hour, when for the past two years he's been selling crack and pulling down $750 a day?

Dependency lies at the heart of the problem. Not only the physical dependency that creates demand — though it's true that if people didn't want to get stoned, or need to get stoned, there wouldn't be a market for drugs — but the economic dependency that comes from supplying that demand. Blaming drug addicts for the problem ignores the realities of Third World economics: to survive you must export; to export you must produce; there is more money to be made producing opium poppies and the coca bush than in producing oranges, cotton, bananas, or coffee.

Take the example of sugar cane. It is harvested, refined, packaged, shipped, marketed, and finally retailed in supermarkets for, say, 60 cents a pound. Then look at heroin. It goes through much the same process — harvesting, refining, packaging, shipping, marketing, and retailing — except that there's no supermarket overhead calculated into the price. And heroin can sell for $20,000 a pound. Given a choice, why would anyone in their right mind want to be in the sugar cane business?

What's more, narco-dollars are exogenous and offer a quick fix to the local standard of living. The money generated through the sale of drugs in North America and Europe comes back into the local economy as construction projects or luxury goods. Standards of living rise sharply. Of course, prices eventually catch up and drug money destabilizes the economy, creating inflation and making non-drug exports implausibly expensive. Nevertheless, many people in the Third World can't see how putting an end to drug trafficking is in their interest. They've never had it better.

Trying to convince them otherwise is pointless. Yet the West is filled with well-meaning souls who try, even though they don't have the slightest clue what life is like on the rest of the planet. Some years ago, do-gooders hoped to promote a crop substitution plan along the Afghan borders, where opium poppy is the main cash crop. They wanted to pay local farmers to grow orchids. Not only were the Afghans against the plan for economic reasons, but orchids couldn't grow there. Even if orchids could grow on the moon, a peasant doesn't need a degree from the Harvard Business School to know that if he sows opium poppy to satisfy a booming market he'll feed his family, and if he plants sorghum or sugar or tobacco leaf or orchids, they'll starve.

Legitimate commodity prices have plummeted in the past twenty years, at a time when Third World debt has skyrocketed. There might once have been a sensible argument for programs designed to replace Third World drug crops with maize, alfalfa, or tomatoes — that is, as long as there was a flourishing world market for maize, alfalfa, and tomatoes. But those days are over. Preaching to some Bolivian, or his compatriot in Colombia, or his cousin in Peru, about the joys of the simple life in the beetroot trade is an exercise in futility, as illogical as selling that New York City street kid on the benefits of going to plumbing school.

Some of the roots of economic dependency lie in the aggressive lending policies of American and European banks during the 1970s and 1980s. Defaults on those loans to developing countries almost derailed the Western banking system. As the cocaine industry is the major employer in Bolivia, Colombia, and Peru, it's hardly surprising that the proceeds of drug trafficking are showing up as loan repayments from Latin America. Those funds, now washed, are the same funds that have buoyed up the liquidity of Western banks. How ironic that drug money should now stretch from the valleys of Peru to hushed boardrooms overlooking the East River.

Coca production in Peru has increased seven- and eightfold over the past five years, and assets from the drug trade, at least those finding their way into nations belonging to the Bank for International Settlements, have grown from $350 billion to $500 billion. One half of that is said to belong to the major drug cartels. A report to the leaders of the seven largest industrial nations revealed that 50 to 70 percent of the proceeds from drug trafficking around the world gets laundered through the Western banking system. Drug traffickers operating in America and Europe alone are estimated to be washing more than $100 billion a year, a sum that exceeds the gross national product of 90 percent of the countries currently represented in the United Nations.

Official figures must always be taken with a grain of salt because it is standard operating procedure for government agencies throughout the world to exaggerate a threat in order to keep a straight face when asking for a budget increase. But as the global assets from the drug trade continue to rise, two facts undeniably stand out.

First, and most shockingly, more money is spent today worldwide on illicit drugs than on food.

And second, random forensic testing in the United States revealed that practically every bill in circulation throughout the entire country bears microscopic traces of cocaine. In other words, practically every bill in circulation has at some point been used in a drug deal.

The Medellín and Cali drug cartels used to be referred to as South America's only successful multinational enterprises. But then, they were in a business for which the production-to-profit ratio is staggeringly high. Approximately 20 percent of the wholesale price goes toward cultivation, bribes, smuggling, handling, and write-offs for drugs that are confiscated or stolen along the way. The rest, an astonishing 80 percent, is pure profit. If you accept the estimate that $200 billion worth of narcotics comes into the United States alone, roughly equivalent to one-third of all U.S. imports, then the lion's share of $160 billion filters back to the drug barons, putting them at the top of the list of the world's wealthiest people. Three Colombians were purported to be among the five richest men in the world, surpassed only by the Sultan of Brunei and King Fahd of Saudi Arabia. Even the cartels' lieutenants were once worth more than the Queen of England.

Only 10 percent of the world's cocaine is actually grown in Colombia. The cartels purchase most of their product from Peru and Bolivia. They then buy their processing chemicals in Germany, Brazil, and, ironically, the United States. Approximately 10 percent of Colombia's work force is somehow tied to the narcotics trade. Pablo Escobar Gaviria, founder of the Medellín drug cartel, was for a while the nation's largest and most important employer. Throughout the 1980s, he personally controlled 80 percent of the cocaine coming into the United States.

The city of Medellín, capital of Antioquia Province in west central Colombia, is located 155 miles from Bogotá. Settled in 1675, Medellin sits in a mountain valley five thousand feet above sea level, is the country's second-largest city — with a population of 1.6 million — and is its principal industrial center. Local manufacturers produce steel, textiles, rubber, electrical goods, and tobacco. It also used to be the most dangerous city in the Western hemisphere. Crimes in Medellín were rarely investigated because the police were intimidated. Even the DEA, which once had an office there, left town because they wanted to keep their operatives alive.

Escobar was plump, stood five feet six, had curly black hair, and occasionally sported a black mustache. Hardly menacing in appearance, he was a ruthless, cold-blooded murderer who'd spent years building a Robin Hood image. He told people he'd grown up in abject poverty, but it wasn't true. He was born in Rionegro in December 1949, and raised in Envigado, a working-class suburb of Medellín. His mother was a schoolteacher. His father was a fairly successful farmer.

Escobar's first job after high school was as an apprentice to a minor-league smuggler in small electronic appliances stolen from warehouses along the Panama Canal. He worked his way up into heavier crimes, but didn't make any real money until the early 1970s, when he orchestrated the kidnapping of a local industrialist. From there he drifted into the drug business. Arrested and convicted in September 1974 for trafficking ninety pounds of cocaine, he bribed enough people to be released after three months and have the charges against him dropped. Over the next five years, he continued to be arrested for drug dealing and continued to be let off. At first it was the evidence that disappeared. Then it was the witnesses, the arresting officers, and the judges.

When Carlos Mauro Hoyos, Colombia's attorney general, advocated extraditing drug traffickers to the United States, he was machine gunned in the center of Medellín by three carloads of Escobar's soldiers. In 1989, Escobar blew up an Avianca airliner, taking 107 lives. He was implicated in the murder of a Supreme Court judge and almost two dozen lower-court judges. He orchestrated a 1992 bombing campaign against government officials and rival gangs in Medellín, setting off three hundred bombs that killed as many people. At the beginning of 1993, his men went on a rampage and murdered 178 local policemen.

His conquest of the world of major-league drug dealing began with the help of one old friend and one new cohort.

Jorge Luis Ochoa Vasquez was Escobar's childhood companion. Along with brothers Juan and Fabio, Ochoa had pioneered a smuggling route into the United States while managing an import-export company called Sea-8 Trading in Miami. Sent there to take charge of a cocaine ring set up by his uncle, by 1978 Ochoa was independently bringing 225 pounds of drugs into Florida every week. The DEA got wise to him and sprung a trap, but he escaped literally within inches of his life, and hurried home to Colombia. His younger brother Fabio took over the Miami interests.

Back in Medellín, Jorge manifested his own ambitions. He ordered his uncle's murder and stepped in as head of the family business. For Escobar, an association with Ochoa was a natural way to expand both of their businesses. Until this point, the two were still small-time operators. That changed when Escobar and Ochoa befriended Carlos Enrique Lehder Rivas.

Born in Quinido Province, 180 miles south of Medellín, and the same age as Escobar and Ochoa, Lehder had moved with his mother to the United States when he was 15. Ten years later, he was sitting in a federal penitentiary for trafficking marijuana. His cell mate was a convicted dealer from Massachusetts named George Jung, and it was Jung who taught him the finer points of the drug business. Released in 1976, Lehder was deported to Colombia. He settled in Medellín, opened a car dealership, and contacted Jung, who was already out. As Jung's parole conditions prevented him from getting a passport, he sent his partner Frank Shea to Medellín. The result was a deal whereby Lehder agreed to supply cocaine to Jung and Shea, who would then distribute it through Jung's old marijuana network. To get product, Lehder turned to Escobar and Ochoa.

And the Medellín cartel was open for business.

Theorizing that the way to conquer the lucrative North American and European markets was to bombard them nonstop with drugs, Escobar accepted that a small percentage of his shipments would be stopped. But he was confident a larger percentage would get through. As he was taking a big chunk of that larger percentage, he saw himself in a no-lose situation. To ensure he stayed that way, he concocted an image. He rode around in a car once owned by Al Capone and opened the doors to his ranch in Puerto Triunfo, situated along the Magdalena River, allowing the public in to see "Pablo's Zoo" — a couple of giraffes, some camels, and a kangaroo. Mounted on the gates was a light airplane he bragged was the one he used to smuggle his first shipment of coke into the United States.

Setting off on a mission of benevolence, Escobar tried to straddle drug trafficking with right-wing populist politics. For every planeload of merchandise he sold, he offered a two-kilo kickback to feed, clothe, and house Medellín's poor. He supported local football teams and built hundreds of homes. In 1982, the people of Medellín elected him an alternate member of Colombia's House of Representatives.

After being accused of murdering the minister of justice in June 1984, Jorge Ochoa fled to Madrid, where he and his family lived on a false passport in a huge suburban villa. He bought a fleet of cars, invested in land for development, and paid for his luxurious lifestyle with money he'd already laundered in Europe. But within five months the Spanish police had found him.

An arrest warrant had already been issued against Ochoa in the United States on narcotics charges, so an official request was made for his extradition. For the next twenty months, Ochoa and his very expensive lawyers in Madrid fought that request. At one point, when it seemed as if the legal maneuvering might drag on forever, the DEA offered him a secret deal. If he would testify that Nicaragua's Sandinista government countenanced drug trafficking, the extradition request would be rejected by the Spanish foreign office. Ochoa's response was that he didn't know anything about that particular connection. Of course, he was lying, and the Americans knew it. They had plenty of evidence that Ochoa had personally negotiated with a high-level Sandinista official to build a cocaine processing lab in Nicaragua. Washington renewed its call for Ochoa's deportation. But the Spanish courts learned of the DEA's offer and, incensed that the Americans only wanted to use him to discredit the Sandinistas, denied the request. Ochoa was deported to Colombia in July 1986 and held in jail for six weeks.

Knowing the fate that awaited them in the States, Ochoa's friends in the cartel now threatened to eliminate political leaders one by one if he was handed over to the Americans. The government refused to bow to threats and pledged to prosecute Ochoa. Instead, he was "mistakenly" released. On the run for the next five years, Ochoa was captured again in 1991. By this time, he'd had enough. While awaiting trial, he negotiated a nine-year jail sentence, agreed to surrender some of his property, and paid a $9,500 fine — probably less than a day's interest on his laundered wealth.

Carlos Lehder fared considerably less well.

The man who prophetically described cocaine as "the Third World's atomic bomb" was captured after a shoot-out with Colombian government troops at his jungle mansion in 1987 and extradited. His trial in Florida was billed as one of the most important prosecutions in the history of American law enforcement. Dubbed by the press as the embodiment of a narco-terrorist, the tabloids called him *el loquito Carlos* — crazy Charlie. The media covered every facet of his life, real and imagined, giving particular play to the fact that he'd founded his own political party, the anti-Semitic, neo-Nazi Latin National Movement, which had some minor successes in local Colombian elections. Like Escobar, Lehder had also endowed low-cost housing for slum dwellers.

The prosecution claimed that in 1978 Lehder purchased the tiny island of Norman's Cay in the Bahamas, rebuilt the airstrip there, and used it to transship cocaine from Colombia to America. His former pilot testified that they'd fly drugs into Ft. Lauderdale's Executive Airport, off-load them without any interference from U.S. Customs, take on suitcases filled with cash — again, no one asked questions — and head straight back to Norman's Cay for the next load. Another witness described how Fidel Castro had introduced Lehder to Robert Vesco and how Vesco had taught Lehder the business of money laundering.

Lehder's defense hoped to make the jury believe that a 39-year-old coke addict — who had a yacht and nineteen cars, bragged about his endless supply of women, and who kept a naked, helmeted statue of John Lennon in his private discotheque — was an otherwise innocent businessman who had wanted to build a resort on Norman's Cay but backed off when he found it infested with drug traffickers. He was convicted and sentenced to life imprisonment plus 135 years.

Next came Escobar's surrender.

The Colombian government wanted him so badly it was willing to take him any way he'd agree to be taken. Early in the summer of 1991, he said he'd surrender to protective custody while waiting to stand trial for murder and drug trafficking, but only on two conditions: Bogotá had to guarantee that he wouldn't be extradited to the United States; and he had to be held in a prison designed expressly for him.

The government accepted his terms. They denied the American request for extradition and built the Envigado jail to his specifications in the hills overlooking Medellín. Hacienda style, it came complete with a swimming pool, tennis court, sauna, telephones, and fax machines. He was even permitted to bring his own plastic surgeon into the compound and have his face lifted. He was ensconced along with fifty of his own armed guards at a cost of half a million dollars a year, which included the security system that not only kept Escobar in, but kept possible assassins out.

A year later, his trial slated to begin, Escobar was informed he would be transferred to an ordinary cell. He refused. Negotiators came to see him and a hostage situation developed. The army arrived and in the confusion he escaped. A dramatic military and police manhunt searched fifteen thousand homes for him, to no avail. The State Department now considered Escobar so dangerous it put a $2-million price on his head. Coupled with the $1.4 million the Colombian government had already tagged on him, Escobar became the world's most wanted man.

After seventeen months in hiding, he died the way he'd lived — violently.

On December 2, 1993, the day after Escobar's 44th birthday, the Bloque de Bosqueda, the elite CIA-trained and DEA-funded "search unit" of the Colombian security police, located him in a residential neighborhood on the edges of Medellín. He was talking on the phone to his 16-year-old son. They burst in on him and showed no mercy. In a hail of bullets they promptly and efficiently gunned him down.

Escobar's ego was such that he might have liked to be remembered as the businessman who'd once cornered America's cocaine market. He'd crowed when he found his name on both the *Forbes* and *Fortune* lists of the world's richest men. His personal wealth was put at over $3 billion, prompting William Bennett, "drug czar" to the Bush administration, to remark, "He was richer than Ross Perot and more powerful than Genghis Khan. They said he was invincible."

Escobar thought so, too. Yet he wasn't invincible, any more than he was Robin Hood. Wanted internationally for drug trafficking, kidnapping, and murder, his legacy is that of a man who ridiculed the Colombian justice system, killed his enemies, slaughtered innocent people, threw his country into a long and debilitating political crisis, and wreaked havoc throughout the rest of the world, destroying untold numbers of lives with the drugs he sold.

But when they killed him, nothing changed.

Cali is in the heart of Colombia's agricultural region.

A city predating Medellín by a century, although with a slightly smaller population, it lies in the western part of the country, in the

Cauca Valley, not far from where the Cali River runs into the Pacific Ocean. It is a major distribution point for coffee, livestock, minerals, textiles, chemicals, tobacco, and paper products.

The drug traffickers operating out of Cali were never really a cartel, at least not in the same sense that the group from Medellín had been. Ostensibly formed by Gilberto Rodriguez Orejuela, a onetime pharmacy clerk known as "The Chess Player," it evolved along the lines of a consortium, more like a loose confederation of traffickers. Orejuela's partner was his attorney brother, Miguel Rodriguez Orejuela, sometimes called "Patricio," sometimes called "Manolo," but most often called "El Senor" because he ran the day-to-day affairs of the various "cells" they'd planted around the world.

The number three man was the very violent José Santacruz Londono. Nicknamed "Don Chepe," he preferred the more macho handle "007." Before joining up with the Rodriguezes, Santacruz had earned a reputation in the business shipping cocaine from Guatemala to Miami hidden in crates of frozen vegetables. His expertise in smuggling completed the cartel's inner circle.

Where Pablo Escobar and his cronies might have been the most famous traffickers in Colombia, the Cali bunch were without doubt the most dangerous. For a time their record for gratuitous violence actually surpassed Escobar's. Then they got smart and started spending their money on bribes. Once they changed tack, U.S. officials privately dubbed them the most sophisticated criminal organization in the world.

Gilberto was born in a working-class neighborhood of Cali in 1939. He got into drugs in the early 1970s, smuggling cocaine into New York, then expanding to Los Angeles and Miami. He and Miguel first came to prominence in November 1975, when police at Cali's airport discovered fourteen hundred pounds of coke hidden in a small plane that had just landed. The pilot and co-pilot were arrested. That weekend, forty people were murdered. A few years later, intelligence operatives working for Escobar got word that Jorge Ochoa's near-arrest in Miami had come as the result of a tip-off to the Americans from the Cali cartel. A wave of violence followed. The Rodriguezes and their camp immediately sought revenge. Cartel blood even spilled onto the streets of New York, as Medellín generals tried to force Cali dealers out of business.

The first of several American charges was lodged against Gilberto in 1978 for drug trafficking, conspiracy, and money laundering. Six years later, the Colombians turned down a formal request for Gilberto's extradition. In 1985, he and Miguel were arrested in Madrid. To dodge prosecution in the States, where life sentences were almost assured, they bribed their way through negotiations with Colombian authorities and were flown home. A Cali judge found them not guilty because of lack of evidence. The Colombian Supreme Court overturned the ruling, but by then the brothers had disappeared.

The not-guilty ruling led Pablo Escobar to believe that the Rodriguez brothers had struck a deal with the government. More deaths followed on both sides. At one point, Colombia's two cartel cities were averaging ten to fifteen murders a day. That's when Gilberto funded the vigilante group PEPES, People Persecuted by Pablo Escobar, which vindictively and stubbornly aided the authorities in the hunt for his chief rival.

In return, Colombian prosecutors adopted a more live-and-let-live attitude toward the Cali faction, rationalizing their stance by arguing that the Rodriguezes were not terrorists in they way Escobar had been. In fact, the Rodriguezes had supplied the critical information on Escobar's whereabouts that had led the Bloque de Bosqueda to him. They had already taken away a giant share of Escobar's business while he was alive; his death merely handed them the rest of it. At the height of their reign, the Cali cartel's annual profits were estimated at $7 billion, more than three times those of General Motors.

Long before Escobar's death, the Rodriguezes and Santacruz had begun to distance themselves from the retail business. They'd lost interest in smuggling drugs, tired of always having to worry about staying one step ahead of Customs and the DEA. They were more interested in developing a wholesale side to their business. Because anybody with collateral in Colombia can become a drug dealer, the Rodriguezes subcontracted, inspiring the development of minicartels. They continued to buy directly from the producers, but now sold the drugs to smaller groups in exchange for payment up front, franchising the transport, marketing, sales, and money laundering responsibilities. If cargoes were intercepted, it wasn't the Rodriguezes' product. If cash was confiscated, it wasn't the Rodriguezes' money. The deck was stacked in their favor. They couldn't lose. And yet, three hundred minicartels rushed into business with them.

Further diversifying, the Rodriguezes also began wholesaling to the Mexicans, unsuspectingly nominating their heir apparent.

Now the Feds were faced with a new problem. They'd seize a ton of cocaine knowing that the drugs originated with the Rodriguezes, but the seizure did no damage because the Rodriguezes used a broker. The minicartel guy might have had to give up his ranches and other property to pay for the lost drugs, but the Rodriguezes were still alive and living well in Cali.

By this point, they'd invested billions in real estate, purchased several banks, and owned the national drug store chain Drogas La Rebaja. They also bought the Cali soccer team America, and poured so much money into soccer, paying for the best players in Latin America, they inadvertently capsized the entire league because none of the other teams could compete.

At least as wealthy as Escobar ever was, the Rodriguezes proved themselves considerably more resourceful. To keep the CIA from intercepting their phone and fax communications, Gilberto almost got away with buying his own satellite. They were also better educated and spent far more on pragmatic matters, such as buying friends in high places. Among them was Gustavo Enrique Pastrana Gomez, an attaché at the Colombian Embassy in Uruguay. Arrested at the end of 1993, as the result of a DEA sting operation in Miami, Pastrana had been washing Rodriguez money through the purchase of polo ponies and automatic car washes in Argentina. The cousin of a nationally prominent Colombian politician, he bragged to an American undercover agent that he could launder $2 million a week through his network of banking contacts in Montevideo.

They spent money lobbying successfully for a constitutional ban on extraditing traffickers to the United States. They spent money lobbying, again successfully, for a law that allowed traffickers to turn themselves in, to exchange guilty pleas for light sentences, to be exonerated of more serious charges, and to be put in prisons where they could have private phones and fax machines. They built police stations in poor neighborhoods to help reduce street crime, and paid off the judiciary.

One of their judges in Bogotá released three Cali laundrymen, ruling that there were no charges to answer because the prosecutor never showed up. For some reason he'd been told to appear in one courtroom after the cartel's lawyers had moved the case to another.

A second judge, this one in Cali, ordered the release of a trafficker who'd been caught red-handed. It created such outrage that an appeal was rushed into the Supreme Court, which promptly overthrew the acquittal. But no one ever bothered rearresting the man.

A third judge even smuggled drugs for them. Esperanza Rodriguez-Arevalo was arrested in Miami when she flew in with a couple of pounds of uncut heroin in her luggage. The cartel had convinced her she could net upward of $250,000 wholesaling the drugs, which was more than she could expect to earn on the bench in her entire lifetime.

By 1990, the Cali cartel was moving $50 million monthly out of New York. Computer logs impounded after a nineteen-month covert operation led to the arrest of their top guy there, Ramiro Herrera, whose brother Pacho worked for the Rodriguezes. In addition to apprehending thirty-seven other cartel soldiers stationed in the States, the police grabbed 1.3 tons of cocaine and confiscated $16 million in cash. But it turned out to be little more than a hiccup on the cartel's ledgers. The Cali mob had dethroned Escobar's group as the world's dominant cocaine supplier.

Five years later, just as the Colombian government had finally gotten around to outlawing money laundering, the police finally caught up with Gilberto. On June 9, 1995, they raided a house in one of Cali's residential neighborhoods, arrested four people, and discovered the 56-year-old Rodriguez hiding behind a false wall. The cops announced they'd been working on an anonymous tip. In reality, Gilberto had been beaten by DEA surveillance and intelligence.

His capture signaled the beginning of the end for the cartel. The likelihood that Gilberto would barter a lighter sentence for their neck in the noose plainly worried some of his cronies. Within days, Henry "The Scorpion" Loaiza Ceballos, the cartel's military leader, turned himself in at an army base in Bogotá. One of the cartel's most hard-line members, he stands accused of the chain-saw slaughter of 107 peasants in southwestern Colombia who'd refused to cooperate with the cartel. A week later, Victor "The Chemist" Patino Fomeque, a former policeman and head of the cartel's naval smuggling operation, came out of hiding. He'd once commanded a mini-fleet of ships, including three submarines, which the cartel used to smuggle drugs into the United States.

With the walls unexpectedly crumbling around them, other members followed suit. Julio Fabio Urdinola and Jonier Ospina Montoya, men whose names were not widely known outside Colombia but who were already the object of international arrest warrants, negotiated surrenders.

Less than a month after Gilberto was taken, the police scored another major victory by capturing Santacruz. The search for him had intensified around Cali. Instead, he was spotted almost by accident at a restaurant in Bogotá. The police were called, and without any fanfare he was taken into custody. One newspaper later reported that before he left with the police he insisted on paying for his dinner.

An engineer by trade, the 52-year-old Santacruz had been on the DEA's most wanted list since 1980. One of the aliases he'd used was Victor Crespo, but in 1981 the DEA, which had a warrant out on Crespo, hadn't yet associated the two. On a tip that Crespo was coming to New York, agents stopped a fellow who'd gotten off a flight from Latin America. They checked his passport and because the name in it wasn't Crespo, they allowed the man who was called Jose Santacruz Londono to go about his business.

In 1990, two laundrymen working for Santacruz were arrested in Luxembourg. One of them, José Franklin Jurado Rodriguez, was a professional money manager with a degree from Harvard. He and his partner Edgar Alberto Garcia Montilla spent four years in jail in Luxembourg fighting extradition, but lost and were sent to the

United States to stand trial. According to them, Santacruz's money laundering cycle began in Panama, where cash was deposited in banks owned by members of the Cali cartel. From there, it was wired to banks around the world before being sent back to Colombian companies owned by Santacruz, his family, and his friends.

At one point considered the most dangerous man in Latin America, Santacruz was also thought to be the wealthiest of the Cali bunch. Legend has it that he was once refused admittance to an exclusive club in Cali, so he built a replica of it. His assets included thousands of apartments in Colombia. Along with the extradition of Jurado and Garcia, $30 million belonging to Santacruz was frozen. But anywhere from three to fifteen times as much could still be hiding in European banks. Besides drug trafficking and money laundering, Santacruz also stands accused of ordering the 1992 murder in New York of Cuban-born journalist Manuel de Dios Unanue, who'd been writing about him.

Once Santacruz was behind bars, Phanor Arizabaleta Arzayuz surrendered. A former cattle rancher, Arizabaleta was responsible for purchasing the chemicals the cartel used to process cocaine. A warrant had been issued against him for the murder of a police chief. That left only Helmer "Pacho" Herrera Buitrago, a 43-year-old smuggler from a long family of smugglers who headed up the cartel's military wing. And Miguel Rodriguez, who was now carrying a $2.5-million bounty on his head. Then Santacruz escaped by bribing his guards. But on the run, all three lived within diminishing circles and there was no doubt their days were numbered. Seven weeks later, Santacruz was killed by police in a shoot-out in Medellín, a mile or so, ironically, from where Pablo Escobar was killed.

The Colombian government had halfheartedly moved against both cartels in 1992 by levying a 10-percent tax on any cash imported into the country and deposited locally. Banks were also permitted to increase their fees for handling cash by about one-third. In response, the cartels took a leisurely sidestep, went north, and turned Venezuela into their newest amusement park. Within eighteen months, 75 percent of all Colombian cocaine was being exported through

Venezuela, and banks there held $14 billion for the drug dealers. More money was now being washed through Venezuela than the country earned in oil revenues. Nearly half a billion dollars has arrived in the past three years — most of it from the United States — in the form of cash, cashiers' checks, and bank transfers.

The long and rugged border that Colombia shares with Venezuela is a smuggler's utopia. From mountains in the north and flatlands and jungles in the south, the boundary is just about impossible to patrol. Cash and drugs move freely. What's more, Venezuela and Colombia are active trading partners, and banks from one country have branches in the other. Communications between the two are also good, making wire transfers easy. Venezuela has relatively sophisticated financial markets, and currency brokers there have boomed. So has the Caracas stock exchange, which quickly found itself transformed by narco-economics into an oversized sink. Likewise, banks have done a flourishing business in short-term treasury bills. Until recently there were no prescribed penalties in either country for failing to report large cash transactions, even if banks and brokers had good reason to suspect the money was derived from drug trafficking. The laws in Venezuela have since been amended. But the *laissez faire* attitude that continues to characterize sections of its financial community remains prevalent throughout Latin America.

Argentina is another example of a country ready and willing to pick up any slack. Once considered too far off the beaten path, it has attracted drug traffickers looking to use the country's newly won economic stability to wash money. Access in and out, for both product and funds, is easy, and the border with Bolivia presents few difficulties for smugglers. In addition, the markets of Buenos Aires present almost unlimited opportunities for turning cash into investments. Under the old regime, wealthy Argentines kept their money hidden overseas. Now they're bringing much of it back. That influx, coupled with foreign investments and the privatization of state-owned enterprises, means that whatever drug money gets shuffled into the deck is virtually impossible to spot. Furthermore, Argentina's cultural ties to Europe — notably Spain, because of its shared language, and Italy, because nearly half of all Argentines are of Italian extraction — make for unencumbered access to European markets, money, and criminal expertise.

Brazil has become a staging area for drugs on their way to Europe, and the economies of Recife and Sao Paulo, as well as the drug problems of Rio, are testimony to that. Paraguay is buoyant with foreign exchange: $66 billion moved through the markets in 1994, eight times the country's gross domestic product. It has also become an alternative smuggling route, used as an end run to get drugs from Colombia the long way around and into the United States. Peru is the world's largest producer of coca, and a working agreement that binds drug barons to local Maoist guerrillas has made the cocaine trade there bigger than ever. Ten percent of the entire population, more than two million people, are regular coca chewers. The most important producing region is the Upper Huallaga Valley, where today there are as many banks doing business in dollars as there are in many small American cities. On any given day along Ocona Street, the heart of Lima's informal foreign exchange market, $3 to $5 million in cash changes hands.

Across the border in Bolivia, the market in coca and coca paste constitutes over three-quarters of that nation's source of dollars. And for many years Bolivian drug baron Jorge Roca Suarez was Pablo Escobar's primary source of cocaine paste. Roca directed his worldwide operations from a nineteen-room mansion in San Marino, California. Escobar converted his paste into powder, smuggled it into the United States, sold it, and used part of the revenue to pay Roca. Supplying a ton of paste a week over a couple of years, Roca earned $50 million. In the beginning he shipped the money back to Bolivia using couriers. Later, his sister and his housekeeper found they could get cash to Bolivia by hiding it inside appliances, stuffing as much as $200,000 in a stereo speaker, $400,000 in a vacuum cleaner, and $2 million in a freezer. Arrested and convicted of conspiracy to manufacture cocaine, conspiracy to export currency, conspiracy to evade taxes, tax evasion, and money laundering, Roca was sentenced to thirty-five years. But Roca is not the problem, he's a symptom.

Under Bolivian law, it is perfectly legal to grow coca. The Bolivians chew it, smoke it, and use it in cooking — and they've done so since before the Incas. Although it has banned coca derivatives, the government permits coca to be grown, to keep the tradition alive, in the Yunga region of La Paz. To keep the tradition under control, it has set about trying to destroy coca bushes everywhere else in the country using herbicide spraying. However, the spraying renders large areas of the country's farmland barren. The CIA has been providing satellite intelligence, but there are limitations. Coca bushes only show up when they cover very large areas. Small plantations can't always be spotted. So for every big farm the government puts out of business, half a dozen smaller ones take its place. The Bolivians have also tried to locate and destroy the thousands of chemical labs scattered around the country, labs where the leaf is converted into cocaine.

Needles in haystacks are easier to find.

In confusion there is profit, and with the virtual demise of the Cali and Medellín cartels, there were a lot of profits to go around. The three hundred minicartels that had been doing business with Rodriguez brothers have vied for their shot at stardom. But they've found themselves up against one wounded politician and some very nasty people in Mexico.

President Ernesto Samper rode into office in August 1994 on a law-and-order platform, promising to do something about the drug cartels, despite allegations that the Rodriguezes had helped finance his campaign. Samper called the allegations campaign smears. Just two days after Samper took office, a weekly news magazine revealed that the brothers had been taped discussing the $3.7-million bribe. Samper denied taking any money from them and claimed to know nothing about it. But the next thing he did was reaffirm that Colombia would not extradite drug traffickers to the United States, that Colombians would have to be tried in Colombia.

He followed that with a call to the Rodriguez family. A Colombian army unit assigned to the war against the drug traffickers had received a tip-off that Miguel Rodriguez planned to attend his daughter's communion party at a Cali hotel, so they raided it. When they came up empty-handed, Samper personally apologized to the

Rodriguezes for having disrupted the celebrations and ordered Colombia's defense minister to stop further "arbitrary operations."

Clinton administration officials were understandably concerned. They were not only worried about the growing acreage of coca plantations in Colombia and the generous sentence reductions the government was granting to confessed drug traffickers, they were upset with Samper. A secret memorandum was sent from the State Department to Colombia's foreign minister. Because it was so highly critical, the foreign minister took the unprecedented step of publicly rebuking the State Department for the communiqué, although the details of the letter were not released. Samper also fought back with sound bites, vowing to prevent the United States from turning Colombia into "a kind of Vietnam in the fight against drugs." He added, "It is unacceptable that some consumer countries come here and wage a war that they haven't been able to win inside their own borders."

The Colombians did seize two Boeing 727s being used by the cartel for transporting drugs. But one estimate has put their aviation fleet at forty long-range passenger jets, some of which could carry nearly $2 billion worth of cocaine. Two planes out of forty isn't a very good percentage, so Clinton threatened Samper that if he didn't act more decisively, Colombia risked losing a portion of its $40-million aid program unrelated to counternarcotics efforts, as well as certain trade benefits and future membership in the North American Free Trade Agreement. A pair of U.S. senators upped the stakes further by threatening punitive legislation. Two Republicans on the Foreign Relations Committee, Jesse Helms of North Carolina and Connie Mack of Florida, proposed to shut down U.S.-Colombia relations within a year unless Samper implemented a series of very ambitious antinarcotics programs. Although the committee softened the measure, making the provisions discretionary rather than mandatory, things began to happen.

Gilberto Rodriguez was captured, for one thing.

Around the same time, Santiago Medina, Samper's campaign treasurer, was also arrested. Medina testified that Samper's campaign manager had known all about the Cali cartel's $3.7-million gift, having himself laundered most of the money in American banks. There must have been sneers on the faces of jailed cartel bosses when they heard that Samper's own campaign manager had been arrested. After all, Defense Minister Fernando Botero was the very man who'd organized their capture.

If the Cali cartel had indeed contributed to Samper's campaign, it didn't seem as if they had any markers left to call in. Fighting for his political survival, Samper fired fifty-one senior police officials in Cali after their names were discovered on a cartel payroll. He suspended eight senators from his own party, all of whom had been accused of having ties to the cartels, then froze bank accounts owned by three Rodriguez businesses: two drug store chains and a medical laboratory.

To remind Samper that America took this seriously, President Clinton ordered any U.S. assets belonging to thirty-three companies owned by the Cali cartel to be frozen, and forbade American companies from doing business with them. He also froze the assets of forty-seven American citizens identified as shareholders in those companies, as well as the Botero bank accounts in the States. Customs then announced they were investigating 105 American companies that had accepted money from the Cali cartel for electronics, auto parts, and other goods shipped to Colombia. A separate investigation was launched into small costume jewelry exporters in midtown Manhattan suspected of accepting Cali cash.

Samper tenaciously clung to power, his reign permanently tarnished.

Meanwhile, Mexican drug traffickers were trying to do to the minicartels what the Rodriguez brothers had done to Pablo Escobar.

The game is not over.

In many ways, it's like putting out brush fires. As soon as you put one out, another starts. And just because the Rodriguezes and their pals might be spending the rest of their lives in jail doesn't mean they're necessarily out of business. There are people in America who run some pretty significant criminal organizations from jail, and it's fair to assume that if it's possible in the States, it's probable in Colombia. Yet even if the Rodriguez boys decide someday they have grown too old for the game and hang up their spikes, there's a long list of people waiting for their turn at the plate. Many of them are as good as the Rodriguezes, know the business as well, and have learned from the Rodriguezes' mistakes.

No, the game is not over. Or even about to end.

In 1990, opium poppies were planted in the Andes mountains. Five years later, Colombia was the world's fourth biggest producer of heroin.

In 1994, the DEA targeted the Cali cartel, seized over $100 million in cash and property, and arrested 116 people. It changed the course of the river a little, but only a little; it didn't dam it up.

Carlos Lehder's arrest was once hailed as a major victory in the war on drugs, and yet the drugs continue to flow.

When Pablo Escobar was shot, the good guys boasted that the worst of the bad guys was permanently put out of business, and yet the drugs continue to flow.

Now they've busted the Cali gang.

And still the drugs continue to flow.

16

THE STINGS

*"Eventually you get to the point where you have to ask yourself,
are you part of the solution or are you now a part of the problem?"*
— **Special Agent Tom Cash, former head of the DEA's Miami office**

March 1986. They knew they could trust him. He was an Argentinean living in Uruguay, a precious metals dealer who did business with the jewelry trade in Los Angeles, a respectable enough figure on the surface, with a good reputation and all the proper contacts. And he was greedy. So the Colombians approached Raul Vivas with a straightforward deal. They wanted him to become their laundryman. They offered him a flat 5 percent off the top of everything he washed, and because they were throwing around figures like $500 million a year, Vivas didn't have to think about it for very long. Five percent of $500 million was more money than he'd ever dreamed of. He said, "Okay, cut me in." And they did.

Believing the simplest way is often the best, Vivas created a pair of front companies in Montevideo: Letra SA would deal in gold; Cambio Italia SA was to be a currency exchange business. Once they were in place, Vivas flew to Los Angeles, where he opened an office in the West Coast Jewelry Center, 610 South Broadway, overlooking Pershing Square in the heart of the city's diamond district.

Whatever money the Colombians collected from coke and crack deals around the United States was funneled through a front company in New York's jewelry district, transported by courier to Los Angeles, and delivered to 610 South Broadway. There it was counted and bundled. Vivas then used that money to buy gold in all of its various forms — scrap, bars, and shot — paying over the odds to dealers willing to handle substantial cash purchases. Once he had the gold, he melted it down and mixed it with silver to give it the look, feel, and weight of South American gold, which is traditionally of poorer quality than American gold. From Montevideo Letra shipped lead-plated bars to California, invoicing the consignment as South American gold. When they arrived, the lead-plated bars were destroyed. Raul's gold — complete with this apparently authentic documentation — was then sent to New York to be sold on the open market. The money from those sales would be wired to Cambio Italia. That company would pay Letra, and Letra would pay the Colombians.

For a while, it worked like a charm.

October 1987. Eduardo Martinez Romero was a sleazebag, a very rich sleazebag who lived on a huge, heavily fortified ranch outside Medellín. Like all of his very rich, sleazy friends, protection was one of Eduardo's biggest expenses.

Then in his mid-thirties and sturdily built, with a round, boyish face, dark hair, dark eyebrows, and a kid's mustache — that kind of thin stubble that makes a guy look as if he's only just started to shave — he didn't usually tell people much about himself. But when he felt like he wanted to, or felt as if he had to, he'd say he was an international economist, one of those globe-trotting businessmen who make money with money. Sometimes he even bragged about having an advanced degree in marketing. Not that he handed out business cards. But if he had been one of those glad-handing guys you sometimes get stuck next to on a plane — the ones who say, call me next time you're in town and we'll do lunch — his business card would have read, "Chief Financial Consultant to the Medellín Cocaine Cartel."

Knowing who Martinez was, a small-time Colombian drug trafficker came to see him. The two men sat down, face to face, and Small Time made his pitch. He said he represented some guys in the States who had a laundry and were looking for customers. Eduardo shrugged. "We don't have any wash to be done." Small Time insisted. "There's always wash to be done." Eduardo told him, "You're too late," and then bragged that he was already using the most efficient sink in America. Eduardo said it was so good he moved $12 million through there in just the past thirty days. He said it was like owning a gold mine.

In Spanish the word for mine is *la mina*.

Undeterred, Small Time argued that it was unwise for the cartel to put all of its eggs in one basket. That must have hit a nerve with Eduardo because Small Time was taken into another room, where he was introduced to Pablo Escobar.

He went through his spiel again. Escobar listened. Small Time figured he had a sale. But then one of Escobar's people jumped up and yelled he smelled a rat. He accused Small Time of being an undercover agent for the Americans. Instantly, the mood in the room turned sour. Facing death, Small Time bravely stuck to his story. The cartel members argued among themselves, debating Small Time's fate. And when the verdict came, Escobar let him live.

So Small Time and the guys he represented in the States went into business with the Medellín cartel. By January 1988 their joint venture had washed $12 million. But all wasn't well. The laundry wasn't living up to Small Time's promises. The washing cycle was taking too long and the boys in Colombia weren't known for their patience. Eduardo started complaining that La Mina did it faster. Small Time kept making excuses.

Then came a near-fatal hiccup. A courier with $1 million in the trunk of his car was stopped for speeding by a Los Angeles policeman. The cops seized the money. Eduardo was furious. He demanded that Small Time come up with a suitable explanation. When it wasn't forthcoming, Eduardo demanded a meeting with Small Time's boss.

The man who was running the laundromat called himself Jimmy Brown. A stocky, middle-aged New Yorker transplanted to Atlanta, Brown was an accountant turned businessman who claimed to have all the right Mafia connections. Except Jimmy didn't live in Atlanta any more. In real life he was John Featherly, and he'd been group supervisor of the DEA office in Atlanta. But between the time he helped set up the laundry and the time of the proposed meeting with Eduardo, he'd been transferred to Washington. He couldn't get away to make the meeting, so in his place went a man who was to be Jimmy Brown's assistant. A good-looking 30-year-old Cuban-born, Miami-raised hustler, he called himself Alex Carrera.

The deal was that Martinez and Carrera had to meet in neutral territory. Martinez wasn't stupid enough to come to the States, and going to Colombia was out of the question for Carrera because he couldn't afford to bump into someone who might recognize him as DEA Special Agent Cesar Diaz. The compromise was to hold the meeting at the Marriott Caesar Park Hotel in Panama City.

On Sunday night, January 17, 1988, Carrera and Martinez met. The Colombian told his laundryman he wasn't pleased with the way things were going, that the operation was too slow, that La Mina was much faster. Carrera answered that they were doing the best they could. Keeping the mood amicable, they had a few drinks downstairs in the bar and agreed to meet the next day at the main offices of the Banco de Occidente.

When Martinez walked in to the bank the following day he acted as if he owned it. He strutted around, playing the star, flaunting his power and crowing with enjoyment as the employees showed their reverence. But this time, when he and Carrera sat down to talk, Martinez took a more aggressive stance. He demanded Carrera provide an explanation for the lost million dollars and said, point blank, that the money had to be paid back. When Carrera suggested the cartel had already written it off, Martinez objected. "That's not how we do business." Then he asked Carrera to tell him how the Atlanta laundromat worked.

Carrera did his best to sidestep the question. Avoiding details, he explained that Jimmy Brown had set up a series of front companies through which he deposited money because the companies had exemptions from the cash transaction reporting rules. Martinez pressed for more information, forcing Carrera to confess that he didn't know much more about Brown's operation.

Martinez then embarked on a long explanation about how La Mina worked. He said they had gold shops set up all over the States and that it only took two to three days from the time La Mina got the money before it was wired back to Panama. He emphasized to Carrera, "Two to three days, when you take two to three weeks." There wasn't much Carrera could say. The meeting ended when Martinez announced that until he got some answers, until he met with Jimmy Brown, he wouldn't be putting any more money into their system.

January 1988. Raul Vivas had a serious problem. There was so much cash being fed into La Mina that the gold brokers he'd been using couldn't handle it all. He needed to expand. So he brought a few more people into the game. One of them was a 47-year-old Syrian named Wanis Koyomejian — Joe to his friends — who'd moved to the States in 1980. Joe owned a company called Ropex and worked out of a pair of fancy suites on the ninth floor of the International Jewelry Center. Raul also brought in the Andonian brothers — Nazareth and Vahe — who ran a brokerage on the third floor of one of the buildings at 220 West 5th Street. Beirut-born, they'd moved to the United States about the same time as Koyomejian.

Raul figured these three would be able to take up the slack on the additional cash pouring into New York. He also needed someone to handle all of the extra gold now pouring into the LA office. He farmed out some of that work to a couple of friends who'd set up in Miami. Before long, Raul needed to expand yet again. Now he brought in friends in New York and Houston. And he still couldn't keep up.

To say the least, La Mina was flourishing.

About the same time, a middle-aged woman in San Francisco was starting her new job in the investigations department of the Wells Fargo Banking Corporation. Her first assignment was the less-than-glamorous task of monitoring currency deposits. She sat in her office mechanically going through page after tedious page of computer printouts. But the tedium was broken when she got a call from a loan officer at the bank's Monterey Park branch, who wanted to know about a gold broker called Andonian Brothers, which in under three months had deposited nearly $25 million in cash. The woman duly gathered all of the documentation the bank had on the Andonian's accounts and put together a dossier of printouts that clearly showed cash deposits of almost $1 million a day. This struck her as highly suspect. Even in businesses that generated huge amounts of cash, a check or two usually gets mixed into the receipts. But this one didn't show any checks at all. She also couldn't understand why the company banked so far away when it would have been more convenient, and considerably safer, to deposit cash at a closer branch. So she did what she was supposed to do and took her concerns to her superiors. But none of them wanted to believe that Andonian Brothers was anything other than a legitimate business.

Persistent, she went off in search of someone who would agree that the Andonian's accounts were suspicious. And right up the ladder all she seemed to get were excuses. So they deal in cash, so what? She wound up making one last pitch to a senior manager who, almost as a concession, told her, okay, if you are truly convinced something is wrong, go ahead and call the cops. She wondered, the FBI, the IRS, or the DEA? He said, try all three, because he didn't think any of them would take her case.

March 1988. Eduardo Martinez met Jimmy Brown for the first time, and Alex Carrera for the second time, in Aruba, in a $500-a-night suite at the Golden Tulip Hotel that was bugged for sound and videotape.

Martinez still wanted his million dollars returned. Brown kept promising he would do his best to recover the money. Martinez kept boasting about La Mina's success. He said that since meeting Carrera in Panama City, he'd washed $28 million through La Mina. Brown kept pitching his own laundromat, saying that things had improved, that he could give Martinez the service he wanted. But Martinez was driving a hard bargain, and the later the hour got, the more he decided La Mina was a better system. Brown knew he was losing a sale. Martinez suggested that if Brown and Carrera really wanted any more money from him, they'd have to wash it in two days and take a 1-percent cut in commission, from seven to six. Brown objected, but Martinez made him understand that these conditions weren't negotiable. Brown promised to do what he could.

Martinez didn't know he was being set up.

And Featherly and Diaz didn't know that Martinez had no intention of sending them any more money.

September 1988. A shipping clerk from the Loomis Armored Car Company in Los Angeles was checking a cargo that had just come in on a United Parcel Service plane from New York. It was a routine job matching cartons, boxes, and packages against the manifest, checking waybill numbers, and making certain everything that should be there was there. Then he noticed that one box had accidentally ripped open.

According to the waybill, the shipment was supposed to contain scrap gold sent by a jeweler in New York to a gold dealer called Ropex. That didn't impress him because Loomis dealt with high-value shipments all the time. What struck him was that for such a valuable cargo the box had been pretty badly packed. He bent down to inspect the damage. That's when he noticed what was inside — neatly bundled stacks of cash.

Because the bill of lading said it was supposed to contain gold, he reported the package to his boss. A Loomis manager phoned Ropex to ask why the paperwork accompanying the shipment said one thing when the shipment contained something else. Joe Koyomejian answered that there had been a mix-up. He assured the man at Loomis that it was not a problem. He said, a guy I know in New York, a jeweler I do business with, is sending it to me because I can find better short-term interest rates in Los Angeles.

The fellow at Loomis agreed that mix-ups happened, and delivered the shipment to Ropex, as he was obliged to do. But in the age of electronic transfers, Koyomejian's excuse made no sense to him, so he took it upon himself to call the FBI.

December 1988. The Feds installed hidden video cameras in buildings all over the Los Angeles jewelry district and at specific locations in New York. They put wire taps on phones. They shadowed people in Los Angeles, New York, Florida, and Houston. They draped the neighborhood around Pershing Square with undercover agents disguised as maintenance men, garbage collectors, delivery boys, gold brokers, jewelers, and even homeless people. They recorded hundreds of hours of audio and video, and dug thousands of documents out of office garbage cans. They collected invoices that revealed the names and addresses of contacts in Canada, Mexico, and Great Britain. They found paperwork naming friendly bullion dealers. They gathered together documents outlining all sorts of transactions. They got canceled checks from which they were able to identify bank accounts.

They code named their La Mina investigation Polar Cap. And Polar Cap soon became the biggest surveillance operation in the history of American law enforcement.

February 1989. The task force assigned to shut down La Mina consisted of agents from the FBI, Customs, DEA, IRS, the Bureau of Alcohol, Tobacco and Firearms, as well as the U.S. Immigration and Naturalization Service. It was placed under the direct supervision of a senior, experienced assistant U.S. attorney. Once he was convinced he'd seen enough — which included evidence of 1,035 accounts located in 179 different banks in Central, South, and North America, and throughout most of Europe — he ordered the task force to arrest everyone.

Less than twenty-four hours after La Mina was shut down, Eduardo Martinez was on the phone with Alex Carrera. By then it had been nearly thirteen months since the Atlanta laundromat had seen any of Martinez's money. Now, without explaining why, he told Carrera he wanted to go back into business with Jimmy Brown.

They welcomed him with open arms. So Martinez sent $4.3 million, which went into the washing cycle but didn't come out. A week later, Martinez was on the phone asking about his money. It was the same week a U.S. federal grand jury returned a sealed indictment against him on charges of drug trafficking and money laundering. Carrera reassured Martinez the money was safe, then promised to deliver $5 million to him. A meeting was hastily arranged at the Marriott in Panama City.

To enforce a U.S. warrant there, the DEA needed one to be

issued by the Panamanian Defense Forces, Noriega's police department. There was no getting around that. Nor was there any way around the fact that the PDF couldn't be trusted. The contact was PDF Captain Luis Quiel, who was himself later arrested and extradited to Florida, where he pleaded guilty in a drug-money laundering case. The DEA agent in charge in Panama City met with Quiel at eight o'clock on Wednesday morning, March 29, 1989. Carrera's meeting with Martinez was set for nine. Typically inefficient, Quiel took too long, and when Carrera finally got to the Marriott, he was fifteen minutes late.

He was carrying a briefcase that was obviously too small to contain $5 million. And obviously too light. Had it been stuffed with $100 bills, it would have weighed over a hundred pounds. Had Martinez seen it, he might have realized what was happening. But Martinez wasn't at the hotel. Instead, there was a message waiting for Carrera with a number to phone. When Carrera got Martinez on the line, he was told to bring the money to the Banco Ganadero. Having seen Martinez's performance at the Banco de Occidente, Carrera worried that someone might spot the PDF's presence nearby and tip off Martinez. But if he and the DEA were going to get Martinez, Carrera didn't have much choice, so he carried the briefcase there and waited.

By eleven o'clock, Martinez still hadn't appeared.

Now the DEA had another problem. Attorney General Dick Thornburgh, together with FBI director William Sessions, DEA administrator Jack Lawn, and Assistant Secretary of the Treasury Sal Martoche, was holding a press conference, carried live on CNN around the world, to announce the success of Operation Polar Cap. Thornburgh revealed that three thousand pounds of cocaine had been seized, along with $45 million in cash and other assets. But most importantly, he said, there had been 127 indictments and almost as many arrests, with more arrests pending. Then he explained how Jimmy Brown's laundry worked.

When Lawn made his statement, he actually quoted some of the things Martinez had told Featherly and Diaz, albeit without mentioning names. But Martinez would know instantly whom Lawn was talking about, and if Martinez was watching television, Carrera's life was in very serious danger.

The decision was made to get Diaz out of Panama right away, and leave the search for Martinez to the PDF.

So Diaz came home and Martinez disappeared.

Polar Cap was nonetheless a major success, raising the stakes for the cartels, forcing them to find new ways to wash their money and to pay more for the service. The agents who'd failed to bring Martinez to justice consoled themselves with the knowledge that getting him to the States had always been a long shot.

Then in August, out of the blue, the Colombians announced they'd found Martinez hiding out in a small coastal town and had arrested him. Although the Colombians didn't easily extradite their own citizens, in this case they were willing to consider selling Martinez down the river.

Earlier that summer, President Virgilio Barco made noises about how Colombia needed American help to fight the drug barons. The Bush administration threw together a $65-million aid package. Purely by coincidence, three weeks after Martinez was captured, Barco handed him over to the DEA.

Eduardo Martinez was sentenced to six and a half years in prison. In 1992, he agreed to testify against Manuel Noriega and became part of the U.S. federal witness protection program. After serving just over four years, Martinez was released in November 1993, and placed on five years' probation. He quickly fled the country, violating his parole, and returned to Colombia, where he lives today as a free man.

It took a while after landing Martinez before life returned to normal for DEA Special Agent Albert "Skip" Latson and Assistant U.S. Attorney (AUSA) Wilmer "Buddy" Parker III. Both of them had been at the heart of the case since the beginning. Neither of them had ever grabbed such a prize before. But then, no one else in the business had either.

Originally from Georgia, Latson grew up in Houston and spent four years with Customs in Texas before transferring to the DEA. Parker, whose office is just down the hall from Latson's, is a 6-foot 2-inch college football player from Alabama, the kind of AUSA action guys like Latson know they can count on.

Because sting operations are manpower intensive and can take a long time, Latson, Parker, and the rest of the group making up what is now called the Southeast Region Organized Crime Drug Enforcement Task Force have completed only three or four, including Polar Cap. However, that's more than many other task forces. Atlanta, which is where the task force is headquartered, turns out to be a good place to run stings because it doesn't have as much street drug activity as the nation's largest cities, such as New York, for instance, where a huge immigrant Colombian population in Queens offers plenty of places for traffickers to hide.

Still high on the Martinez capture, Latson, Parker, and the others set up again. This time the target was the Cali cartel. The original idea was to run something simple. They'd turned a financial expert in Colombia into a confidential informant, and through him put out the word that there were some guys in the States who could wash money. Gradually the Colombians bought in. Latson and Parker organized cash pickups in New York, Houston, Miami, and Los Angeles, got the money into the banking system, and wire-transferred it out. From that they were able to identify some dealers, some laundrymen, and a few of their contacts. That information was passed along to DEA offices in those cities where independent investigations were started and arrests made.

Atlanta's brief was to launder as little as possible for the biggest possible return. The more they did it, the more the traffickers wanted to put into the washing cycle. Latson and Parker began to think that if they could get inside a complex laundry cycle, they could identify source accounts and would know where the traffickers assets were when it came time for the DEA to seize them.

And the best way to do that was to go into the banking business.

The idea was to buy a private Class B bank outside the United States, preferably in an English-speaking territory. This would not be the sort of bank that serves the public. There would be no tellers.

There would be no cash machines. There might not even be any customers. It would be a few pieces of paper that permit the owner of the paperwork to conduct banking business.

Not only had this never been done before, but when Latson and Parker started looking into it, they weren't sure they could do it. Only the attorney general could give federal agents permission essentially to violate all sorts of U.S. statutes and run a major sink for international drug traffickers. They got over that hurdle when in late 1992 William Barr approved the sting. They then let the British in on their plan for two reasons: first, the likeliest place to run it would be a British dependent island in the Caribbean, which would require approval from London; and second, the British had a long expertise in Caribbean banking, and if the guys in Atlanta were going to own one, they'd have to know how it worked.

Next, they needed to buy a bank.

The DEA put out feelers to a contact in the British West Indies. He warned them that Class B banks weren't as easy to come by as they'd once been, and that if they tried to purchase one off the shelf, there would be a two-year waiting list. Latson and Parker didn't want to sit around that long. They also realized that if they pulled strings to jump the line, they'd raise suspicions. The next best thing was to buy one already licensed. That same contact introduced them to a man in California who'd bought a bank and hadn't yet gotten around to using it. The official version of the story has it that he was a legitimate businessman, who, when Latson and Parker approached him, was more than happy to help. Unofficially, Latson and Parker put together a file on the fellow and made him an offer he couldn't refuse.

The bank was in Anguilla. One of the Leeward Islands discovered by Christopher Columbus in 1493, today it is a self-governing British crown colony whose thirty-five square miles of sand are covered with hotels, restaurants, and banks. For security reasons, the only person on the island allowed into the DEA's secret was the British governor general.

This initial phase took a year.

Once the DEA paid the activation fees for the bank, they were technically in business. But it took another year to set up everything so that it looked like a legitimate bank. They needed an office. They needed properly trained personnel. They needed brochures. They needed stationery. The Colombians have a problem dealing with any U.S. entity because they are paranoid about American law enforcement, so the bank had to be appropriately packaged. Right from the beginning, it had to act like a Caribbean bank. That meant paying attention to very minor details. For example, any bank operating in a British territory would use A4-size paper, which is 8" x 11½", and not American-size stationery, which is 8½" x 11". A little mistake like that could bring down the entire operation.

The DEA also had to build identities for their agents who would play the bankers. That was vitally important, and took a lot of time. The cartel employed lawyers and private detectives to do background checks on everyone with whom they did business. Knowing that, the DEA gave their men false names, false families, false home addresses — in one case they actually moved an agent into a house put in his new name — and more than enough references to pass muster.

The bank itself was never anything more than some desks, a computer, a fax machine, and a call forwarding system to an office in Puerto Rico, so that the Anguilla office didn't have to be manned all of the time. It was, however, backed up by a dozen front companies and more than fifty corporate accounts in other banks to provide clients with foreign-exchange facilities, cashier's checks, and wire transfers. From experience, Latson and Parker knew that once a trafficker decided he was dealing with real people, as opposed to cops, he would ask three questions: How fast can you wash my money? How can I be certain you will deliver it to me? What it will cost? If they could answer those questions to his satisfaction, he'd sign on. So they took as much time as they needed to get those answers right.

The sting was code named Operation Dinero. The bank opened its doors in July 1994 and shut them six months later. It had exactly seven customers, and none of them were legitimate. Alex Moussa, Harold Azcarate, Mike Perez, and Cristobal Tobon were cartel money brokers. Luis Eduardo Velez-Arias washed funds for his uncle, a senior cartel member named Humberto Arias. Marta Torres was a Colombian architect who occasionally used her studio to launder drug profits for friends such as Pacho Herrera, the smuggler who ran the Cali cartel's military wing and the last of the main board members to be captured.

Although business for the bank started slowly, ten weeks into the scam it had already washed $8 million. Then things really started jumping. During the first two weeks of December 1994, Perez used the bank to launder eight cash deposits totaling $2,895,468. Most of it came from drug sales in Chicago. In addition to cash, the seven clients washed checks through the bank, all of them drawn on banks in Mexico. On September 15, for example, Moussa delivered thirty Mexican checks to the bank totaling $1,484,160. Eleven days later, he was back with forty-four Mexican checks, this time totaling $1,872,488. At that point, he told his new bankers that he had $28 million in the States he needed to wash. In fact, he and the others seemed so pleased with their bankers they said they hoped to wash as much as $500 million through Anguilla. They also wanted to know if the bank could issue loans backed by deposits so that they could purchase ships.

With each deposit and each wire transfer, the Atlanta task force collected the names of players and evidence against them, then farmed out specific investigations to DEA offices in the field. The only proviso was that the field office had to build a wall between their enforcement activity and the undercover operation. In other words, any spin-off from the Anguilla sting needed to be developed using independent probable cause so as not to tip off the Colombians that the evidence was coming from the bank. At one point, the investigation uncovered two major Italian connections: Pasquale Locatelli and Roberto Severa.

Locatelli, a fugitive who'd escaped by helicopter from a French prison in which he was serving twenty years for drug distribution, had operations throughout Europe and in Canada. He specialized in transporting cocaine from Colombia to France, Romania, Croatia, Spain, Greece, and Canada. As a direct result of Operation Dinero, one of his ships was intercepted by NATO while trying to evade the UN arms embargo of Croatia, and was found to be carrying containers with small arms and ammunition.

Severa, a crime boss trafficking drugs in Rome, was found to be washing money through supermarkets and parking lots. His network extended to New York, Canada, and Colombia.

Expenses for the scam were taken out of the profits earned by the bank. They were, after all, charging their seven clients handsome fees. The entire operation paid for itself. It even turned a profit.

It also uncovered a few unusual assets. On Wednesday, December 14, Marta Torres arrived at Miami International Airport from Cali, Colombia, carrying three paintings: Pablo Picasso's "Head of a Beggar," Peter Paul Rubens's "St. Paul," and a Joshua Reynolds portrait of a man. They were valued collectively at about $20 million. She was met at the airport by one of her bankers and a woman Torres believed to be the art dealer who'd arranged to sell the paintings. A private jet was waiting to take them to the man supposed to be buying the paintings. During the flight, Torres explained that the money from the sale of the Rubens and the Reynolds was to go into Tobon's account, whereas the Picasso money was to be deposited into Moussa's account. She also said that Moussa had $3 million in drug money and eleven hundred pounds of cocaine in the Atlanta area, hidden in three trucks. As soon as the plane landed in Atlanta, Torres was arrested by Latson, and the paintings were seized.

After six months, word came to shut down Operation Dinero. They'd washed $52 million — through 92 cash transactions and 291 noncash transactions — and could have washed ten times as much had the powers-that-be not decided the bank had become part of the problem. Anyway, the object of the exercise was not to perform a service but to send people to jail. They made twenty-nine arrests in Miami, sixteen in Los Angeles, and thirteen in Houston. Thirty more arrests took place simultaneously in France, Italy, Spain, and Canada. In addition to the paintings, they seized $4.3 million in cash and a large quantity of cocaine in Los Angeles, New York, and Canada.

These days, neither Latson nor Parker cares to say if the Operation Dinero bank is a one-shot deal. It marked the first time the government bought a financial institution for the sole purpose of targeting laundrymen. The hint is, it won't be the last. They know it's tough to fool traffickers with the same scam twice. But at least for a while, the laundrymen will have to take the time to ask themselves whether they're dealing with a real bank or the DEA.

17

THE OLD THREAT

"If you fight the Mafia alone, you will lose."
— Assassinated anti-Mafia crusader Giovanni Falcone

The Yakuza, Japan's equivalent of the Italian Mafia, is said to consist of at least 165,000 members and to have an annual turnover approaching $70 billion.

A centuries-old traditional alliance made up of thousands of warrior clans, whose members identify themselves with multicolored tattoos, one of its more effective tactics has been company extortion. The Yakuza approach publicly held corporations and threaten that unless the company comes up with protection money, they'll disrupt the shareholders' next annual general meeting. This type of harassment had become so widespread that a few years ago Japanese corporations finally conspired against the Yakuza by holding their AGMs on the same day and at the same time.

They are also into dealing drugs, and seem to have cornered the "ice" market in Hawaii — "ice" being crystal methamphetamine, a staple of drug users in the islands — where cultural affinities make their dealing easy. At least fifty major properties in Hawaii are said to be owned by Japanese criminals. The FBI scored a big win there in 1992 when they lured Mitsuo Yoshimura out of Tokyo and into a Honolulu resort hotel. He thought he was there to finalize a $5-million "ice" deal. Arrested on U.S. soil, the 43-year-old boss of the Kyokushin-kai faction became the first, and to date only, Yakuza leader to be convicted in the United States.

But according to a former Yakuza member who testified before a Senate investigations panel, Hawaii is not their only area of interest in America. Hundreds of millions of dollars of Yakuza money has been poured into hotels and golf courses around the country. Many of the private Japanese gambling clubs that dot midtown Manhattan are also believed to be backed by Yakuza groups.

When they first went international, they relied almost entirely on banks to launder their money. At the beginning of the 1970s, however, the Yakuza discovered stockbroking. With the help of Malaysian Chinese gangs, they opened brokerages in Malaysia and Singapore. As their business grew, they moved quickly into Hong Kong, Australia, New Zealand, Indonesia, and the Philippines. It is alleged they've now opened shop in the United States. Cash is funneled in one end, and shares in legitimate companies that pay legitimate dividends come out the other. When one Yakuza stock market ring was shut down by the authorities in Malaysia, without charges ever being lodged against anyone, the same gang reappeared in London.

Most of the time they launder their money using tried-and-true methods. For example, they wash hundreds of millions of dollars annually through Tokyo real estate, buying and selling the same buildings to themselves. This artificially runs up prices. The Yakuza then back loans on those buildings with U.S. treasury bonds bought in the freewheeling, unregulated Hong Kong market.

Occasionally, though, they display real flair and venture into something new. In mid-1985, having generated enormous amounts of cash through its drug-dealing networks, one Yakuza syndicate turned its attention to the thriving trade in French designer luxury goods.

The first hurdle was getting their cash to Paris. Some of it was wired in, using Asian banks that routed it via Luxembourg, Switzerland, and the Channel Islands. The rest was smuggled in by couriers looking like well-dressed Japanese businessmen — unlikely candidates to have their attaché cases searched by French customs. Next, the ring leaders rented an apartment near the Madeleine in central Paris, took out classified ads in Asian-language newspapers, and recruited some three hundred Chinese, Vietnamese, and Japanese "customers." Every morning, each customer reported to the apartment, was given a bankroll of 500-franc notes, and was directed to shops —

primarily Vuitton and Hermes, but also Chanel and Lancel — where they bought handbags and scarves by the dozens. Every afternoon, the purchases were deposited at the apartment and packed for shipment. Having bribed a French customs official, the gang exported the goods with forged documents back to Japan, where they were wholesaled by a Yakuza shell company.

The operation was in business for six years before anyone became even slightly suspicious of it. Employees at Vuitton began to feel suspicious about the increasing numbers of shabbily dressed Asian clients, all of whom paid for expensive purchases with brand-new, crisp, 500-franc notes. The management at Vuitton tipped off the police, who soon discovered that although these goods were being shipped out of France and were therefore exempt from value-added tax, no one had ever bothered to apply for a VAT rebate. Subsequently, the police themselves began noticing long lines of shabbily dressed Asians waiting to get into an apartment near the Madeleine. All of them were carrying shopping bags filled with French designer goods.

The authorities started making arrests in the spring of 1992, and quickly pulled in nearly a hundred people. The stores themselves were not implicated. When the French police raided the apartment, they found $450,000 in cash and nearly $1.3 million in goods, including twenty-five hundred Vuitton and Hermes products waiting for shipment to Japan. They also found bank statements detailing $2.7 million in local accounts. No one knows exactly how much the syndicate had laundered since 1985, but French Customs were able to determine that in 1991 alone the gang managed to wash $73 million.

The Triads are the most notorious of the Chinese mobs — a blood brotherhood that materialized in the seventeenth century to overthrow the Ching Dynasty. When their rebellion ultimately failed two centuries later, many of their members fled to Hong Kong, Indochina, and North America.

Independent units linked by an oath of fraternity, the Triads do everything from drug trafficking and money laundering to business extortion and burglary. They are the primary force within Southeast

Asia's Golden Triangle. Spanning the mountains and valleys that cut across the borders of Laos, Thailand, and Myanmar — which used to be called Burma — the region produces anywhere from 60 to 120 tons of heroin annually. A kilo of this Triad-distributed drug whole-sales between $400,000 and $600,000. Cut to 6-percent purity, the street value can easily reach $10 million.

Triad is unquestionably the most powerful force in the world's heroin trade, and its share of the marketplace is growing. In 1997, Great Britain is scheduled to end 150 years of colonial rule by re-turning Hong Kong to the People's Republic of China. Uncertain as to what type of economic system will materialize in the new Hong Kong, and in genuine fear of an oppressive Communist regime, many of the capitalist-inclined crime lords have been seeking greener pastures, naturally favoring cities with indigenous Chinese popula-tions. Police in Hong Kong have identified fifty-seven active Triad organizations, which have offshoots in Taiwan, the Philippines, Viet-nam, and Australia.

But their real future lies in North America.

In late 1992, the *Toronto Globe and Mail* reported that seventeen senior Triad leaders had applied to emigrate to Canada. All of them were barred, as were an additional fourteen who applied in the first months of 1993. The seriousness of the threat was documented in a classified report of the Royal Canadian Mounted Police, which described the Triads as "heavily involved" in drug trafficking, gambling, extortion, smuggling, counterfeiting, armed robbery, and money laundering.

Similarly, a top-secret evaluation by a combined task force of Australian law enforcement agencies, including the National Crime Authority, the Federal Police, Customs, and various state police agencies, revealed that 85 to 90 percent of all the heroin coming into the country was owned by Chinese groups directly linked to orga-nized crime in Hong Kong and China. These gangs were addition-ally associated with groups operating out of Vietnam, Lebanon, Italy, Turkey, Romania, and New Zealand, and with a network of motor-cycle gangs in Australia that act as the backbone of their marketing operation.

The report, never intended for publication, identified hundreds of Chinese criminals operating in the country, many of them influential members of their local communities. It warned that these people and their associates had built an underground Chinese banking system to launder drug money and abet widespread extortion rackets. The report concluded that Australia was ill prepared to deal with this threat, having failed completely to understand the nature of Chinese organized crime.

Today, Chinese gangs are securely established in San Francisco, Los Angeles, New York, Toronto, and Vancouver. They have long had a presence in London, and are now beginning to show up in places where they have no traditional ties, such as Germany. Police there recently raided ninety Chinese restaurants, questioned 653 people, arrested 102 of them, and seized twenty-four false passports, more than $1 million in cash, large amounts of cocaine and heroin, and several weapons. They also uncovered evidence of what the police described as "Mafia-type" money laundering schemes.

In certain respects, organized crime throughout the world is similar. When the end of the Cold War left terrorists with no source of income, they turned to drug trafficking and money laundering. Today, drugs are the principal means of financing terrorism. And except for their claim to be waging political wars, groups such as the Irish Republican Army, the Basques' ETA, and the PLO are just as skilled at law breaking as the Yakuza and the Triads.

Despite peace initiatives in Northern Ireland, the IRA continues to ride shotgun on shipments for international traffickers, deal drugs, run protection rackets, and rob banks and post offices on mainland Britain. They were once believed to be responsible for up to twenty-five hundred armed robberies a year. Cash-rich, they wash their money through pubs and drinking clubs, construction firms, taxi companies, and private security services. Once they've laundered it, they invest their money in such places as the London Stock Exchange. Evidence has surfaced that during the early 1980s the IRA had bought shares in a quoted British company said to have been worth £200 million, then used offshore brokers to take it over. They permitted most of the company to be run legitimately, but kept a corner of it to themselves to wash £30 million over an eight-year period.

Nearly $5 million a year is sent to the IRA from the United States through NORAID. Considering the large Irish population in Massachusetts, it's hardly surprising the Bank of Boston has been used as a sink for a cell of the Provisional IRA. In the early 1970s, an ad hoc coalition was formed between active members of that cell and local Mafia dons. Organized crime wanted marijuana, the Provo sympathizers became the importers. The middleman, Joe Murray, was a large, ill-tempered man who ran a towing company in nearby Charlestown. Trusted by his Italian benefactors and dedicated to the British defeat in Ulster, Murray smuggled tons of drugs into the Boston area on fishing boats. The cash he received for his efforts, laundered through the Bank of Boston, was spent on arms, which those same boats then transported to Northern Ireland.

That terrorists should align themselves with organized criminals is obvious because the terrorists wind up being sent to the same jails as organized criminals. Its only natural that they bide their time comparing notes. It's just as natural that when they get out, they join forces.

The South American cartels are a one-product industry. By contrast, the Mafia is a multinational conglomerate with a wide array of commercial interests, ranging from extortion and prostitution to arms dealing, protection, gambling, money laundering, and drugs — both heroin and cocaine. They bring to their businesses a great deal of expertise. Organized crime in Italy is said to control as much as 20 percent of all commercial activity, and has interests ranging from drugs and murder to jeans and real estate. A recent study credited them with controlling half the financial holding companies in the country, 20 percent of the construction industry, and about a quarter of the food distribution business. Despite substantial crackdowns, they continue to reach into every aspect of national life, wielding influence in every town throughout the country. In the major cities, such as Rome, Milan, and Naples, at least half the shops, bars, and restaurants pay protection money to them. In Sicily, especially in the capital city of Palermo, all of them do.

Like any soundly run multinational looking for opportunity, they have now teamed up with Russian organized crime gangs for joint ventures in Eastern Europe and the former Soviet Union. In the past they've teamed up with the Colombian cartels, helping them find an ingenious way to smuggle drugs by turning cocaine into cardboard. A Mafia chemist discovered that he could mix unrefined cocaine paste with cellulose to produce boxes. A legitimate business was set up with an Italian front company selling the cardboard to a Colombian front company. Ordinary goods were then packed in them and shipped back from Columbia to Naples, where the cardboard was dissolved in acid, producing unrefined cocaine paste.

They also taught the Colombians a thing or two about money laundering. The cartel opened Universe Gold Enterprise and Symar Joyeros Mayoristas in Panama while the Mafia formed Aurea International Trading and Eurocatene in Italy. Cocaine cash was smuggled out of the United States; washed through banks in Switzerland, Spain, and Mexico; and then sent to Italy, where Aurea and Eurocatene used it to buy gold bars. They shipped the gold to Universe and Symar, which sold it using false invoices to front companies in Cali. The gold was then sold on the open market, and the now-laundered proceeds were deposited against sales receipts.

Apparently the DEA suspected something like this might be going on as long ago as 1981, but their investigation into Symar's operations was halted. General Noriega personally put a stop to it. When a lead to Symar was found in 1994, the Italian police put the ring under surveillance. They spent three months watching Aurea and Eurocatene move a ton of gold a month to Panama, worth $35 million, before shutting them down and arresting eight people: five Italians, two Panamanians, and Gustavo Upegui Del Gado, a man described as the Cali cartel's gold expert. However, during 1994 the Mafia-Cali link is believed to have moved over fifteen tons of gold, which is such an enormous amount that for a while they accidentally depressed the world market price.

The Mafia also dabbles in government. Until recently, it was the single most consistent political force in Italy since 1945. Known inside the country as "La Piovra," the Octopus, today's Mafia is three tightly entwined groups. There is the traditional bunch out of Sicily, the Camorra in Naples, and the Ndrangheta from Calabria. In recent years, they've all had their problems.

Giovanni Falcone was a magistrate determined to put an end to the Mafia's 35-year post-war reign of terror. In 1990, he discovered the Cassa Rurale e Artigiana di Monreale, a bank based in a small town near Palermo, which had been laundering Mafia money for nearly twenty years. Given time, it became clear he would get into the bank and pry loose its secrets. That hit too close to home for certain people, among them Salvatore "Toto" Riina, the so-called "boss of bosses." Also known as "The Beast," Riina had been in semihiding since 1975, living with his wife and children in the hills around the village of Corleone — a name made synonymous with the Mafia thanks to Mario Puzo's novel *The Godfather*. It now seems obvious he could have been found had the authorities looked hard enough, because when they needed to find him, they did. Anyway, he worried that Falcone was smart enough to realize the bank was the start of a money trail that led straight back to politicians and judges in Riina's pocket. Those were the same politicians and judges who were so conveniently forgetting Riina's address. Falcone had to be stopped. In May 1992, he was. He was killed, along with his wife and three bodyguards, when their cars were blown up.

Stepping in to take Falcone's place was his colleague Paolo Borsellino. And so no one mistook Riina's displeasure, Borsellino was also murdered.

But Riina had seriously misjudged the nation's patience with his violence, and as their anger swelled, the authorities began taking action. Politicians on his payroll were unable to contain the police. Raids across the country captured more than four thousand people who were then charged with criminal activities. Soldiers were sent into Palermo to patrol the streets. The sledgehammer approach had knocked the Sicilians so far off course that nearly five hundred mobsters were suddenly willing to renounce their once-cherished code of silence and exchange information for leniency. One charmer named Mario Santo "Half-Nose" Di Matteo turned on Riina and named him as Falcone's killer. Special airborne units were sent out, and in 1993 they arrested Riina, along with forty others, at the home he'd lived in for twenty years.

At the same time, the magistrate who succeeded Falcone and Borsellino now went after the Cassa Rurale e Artigiana di Monreale, bringing to justice a leading Sicilian businessman and three bank executives. Just as Riina had feared, the money trail led to certain politicians, including the former premier, Giulio Andreotti.

As the influence of the Sicilians crumbled, the Camorra were faring only slightly better. A huge money laundering racket was smashed in Naples, leading to nineteen arrests and the names of contacts in thirteen other countries. Among those captured was 72-year-old Roger D'Onofrio, an American the Italian authorities believe is a former CIA agent. Born in Italy, D'Onofrio had spent most of his life in the States, returning home in 1993. During his years at the CIA, the Italians believe, he was a laundryman who set up and maintained secret bank accounts around the world — notably in Switzerland — which the agency used to pay operatives.

All this was followed by a joint Italian-Spanish operation and the arrest of a hundred Mafia suspects. They linked forces when the Spanish asked the Italians for permission to question D'Onofrio about his ties to the Vatican Bank and about money supposedly laundered by the archbishop of Barcelona, Cardinal Ricard Maria Carles. He is alleged to have overseen the washing of $65 million through the Institute of Religious Work, charges reminiscent of those made against the now-retired American Cardinal Paul Marcinkus.

Rushing in to fill the vacuum left by the Sicilians and the Camorra is the Ndrangheta, a collection of some 160 rural clans tied together by secret rituals that derive from a clandestine organization in rural Calabria at the end of the nineteenth century. Bandits by profession, many of the members drifted into extortion, kidnapping, and eventually drug trafficking after World War II. Due almost entirely to the exclusive attention the Italian police has paid to the Sicilians and the Camorra, the Ndrangheta can now boast a near monopoly on European heroin trafficking. Years ago they emigrated to other countries — in particular, Australia — where today they are estimated to number as many as fifteen thousand. More recently they have infiltrated parts of Germany, Belgium, and Austria, and have an especially strong presence in the south of France.

It was the Sicilian branch, of course, that set up the first American subsidiaries. They arrived in the United States steerage class, in the first quarter of this century, along with great waves of other

Italian immigrants looking to escape war and famine. Banded together by family, village, and a common dialect, the Sicilians worked their way through Prohibition and into racketeering, gambling, and infiltration of the labor unions. Their children went into the family business, but they had enough money to see that the third generation, Don Corleone's grandchildren, so to speak, got a good education. Pushed to achieve more than their parents, they became lawyers who could protect the family interests. Or they earned themselves MBAs and taught their elders how to transform cash into legitimate, tax-paying concerns.

Often referred to as the Cosa Nostra, at the very height of their influence, in the 1950s and the 1960s, when policing methods were much less effective than they are today, they numbered about seven thousand. Now more dispersed and considerably smaller, they nonetheless maintain well-entrenched pockets of influence. It is said that for at least forty years the families who run New York have been the single largest commercial landlords in the city.

It is also known that the Mafia is the largest heroin dealer in the United States. For five years, from 1979 to 1984, a Mafia clique franchised the distribution of heroin through a network of pizzerias that stretched across the industrial Northeast and into the Midwest. The original idea was to use the restaurants to distribute the drug — heroin to go — as well as to launder money by mixing narcotics receipts with pizza sales. But heroin soon became the main item on the menu, and there was simply too much money to fit into the tills. They needed to find other ways to wash their profits.

One fellow with a solution was fish broker Sal Amendolito. Years before, he'd been involved with a financial consultancy in Milan that illegally moved currency to Switzerland for wealthy Italians. When that dried up, he imported fish into Italy. After a while, he moved to the States and exported fish to Europe. In 1980, he was contacted by his former associate in Milan, Sal Miniati, who told Amendolito he was representing a Sicilian construction firm. Miniati's story was that they were building a large resort with American investors, all of whom happened to run pizzerias. He explained that they had a lot of cash that needed to get to Switzerland to pay for the shares in the investment, without attracting any attention.

Miniati said $9 million was waiting to be moved. For his services, Miniati offered his old friend $90,000.

Amendolito agreed and the first installment of $100,000 was delivered to him that July. To keep deposits below the $10,000 reporting limit, he opened accounts in a dozen banks. A few days later, he bought cashier's checks for the amount on deposit, subtracted his 1-percent commission, and consolidated the stash in new accounts opened in four different banks. From there the money was wired to Switzerland, where Miniati took over.

This laundry service was rudimentary, to say the least, leaving a paper trail wide enough for a child to follow. But Amendolito felt it would work fine as long as the payments stayed relatively small and he could manage it a few more times with $100,000 amounts. Toward the end of July, however, Amendolito was handed $550,000 in small bills. Now he had a problem. It was too much money for his established banking network.

Through a contact at the Swiss investment house Finagest, he was told that Conti Commodity Services in the World Trade Center could accommodate him. However, when he arrived at Conti's offices carrying four small suitcases packed with cash, they said they didn't have the facilities for that much and referred him to the Chase Manhattan Bank downstairs. An officer there repeated Conti's excuse and suggested Amendolita find a bigger branch. He wound up leaving the money at Chase headquarters a few blocks away, where it was credited to a Finagest account held at Credit Suisse in Lugano.

Realizing his method had been too haphazard, Amendolita went in search of a better way to wash large quantities of cash. He settled on smuggling it out of the country and depositing it in the Bahamas. Before long, as the amounts increased with each transaction, Amendolito had worked out a deal with Miniati that some of the money would be taken by couriers directly from New York to Switzerland.

Miniati now mentioned that some people in Sicily were interested in using his services. Amendolito demanded a larger percentage and settled at 4 percent. To handle their business, he opened an office on Madison Avenue, installed a cash-counting machine, and added a bank in Bermuda to his list for cash deposits. But Amendolito had the nasty little habit of sticking his fingers into the cookie jar. When one of his new friends in Sicily discovered he was helping himself to a few extra pennies on each deal, the man wasn't especially pleased, and politely suggested it might be healthier if Amendolito paid him back. Instead, Amendolito vanished.

The mob replaced Amendolito with an Italian banker, Antonio Cavalleri, who managed a Credit Suisse office in the alpine village of Bellinzona. Cavalleri was instrumental in creating a company called Traex, which supposedly dealt in property and raw materials. In reality it didn't do anything except wash pizza-connection money. With the help of a Swissair employee, $10 million was flown out of New York for deposit into the Traex account at Cavalleri's branch. As far as the mob knew, no one was yet on to them.

However, early in 1979, just as the pizza connection was really getting started, Italian customs stumbled across a suitcase at Palermo Airport containing $497,000. Their investigation led to the discovery of five working heroin laboratories in Sicily. The FBI heard about it and wanted to know more. Thanks to information the Italians were willing to share with them, the FBI identified Amendolito, followed some of his transactions, and located his office on Madison Avenue. From there it was easy to get phone records, and from them their interest broadened to a wider group of players.

Ironically, it was the as-yet-unsuspected Swissair employee who first started getting cold feet about all this smuggling. The mob replaced him with Franco Della Torre, a laundryman who'd worked for them in Switzerland. Della Torre came to New York as a certified representative of Traex, opened an account with stockbrokers Merrill Lynch, and during the first four months of 1982 washed $5 million there. Toward the end of April, he opened a Traex account with EF Hutton and by making eleven cash deposits in under ten weeks washed $7.4 million.

Worrying that the amounts could attract attention, Della Torre opened a second EF Hutton account, this one in the name of Acacias Development Company. Over the following ten weeks, he laundered a further $8.2 million through Hutton. But his concerns were well founded. Like Amendolito, he was leaving a broad paper trail. Merrill Lynch and Hutton both kept records of all these transactions.

In 1983, Amendolito resurfaced, arrested for fraud in New Orleans. By this time, the FBI were already on to Della Torre. So a joint task force was formed to work out of the office of Rudolph Giuliani, then a brash young U.S. attorney for the Southern District of New York. He attacked from two sides, going after the drug dealers and, separately, going after the laundrymen. Because none of his targets had developed very good money laundering skills, the second trail proved easier to follow. Agents from the FBI, Customs, the DEA, the IRS, and the Bureau of Alcohol, Tobacco and Firearms put a case together that brought grand jury indictments against thirty-nine members of the ring for their participation in drug trafficking and money laundering. Sal Amendolito became a government witness, testified against the others, and was never charged.

Because some of the culprits were hiding in Italy, including Della Torre, only twenty-two actually stood trial in New York. After seventeen months of hearings, 55,000 FBI wire taps — most of them in Italian — and the murder of one suspect, the twenty-one defendants were found guilty. The judge sentenced the five Mafia ring leaders to terms of twenty to forty-five years. He also ordered four defendants to pay $2.5 million to help fund treatments for heroin addicts.

The group had smuggled 750 kilos of heroin into the States, with an estimated street value of $1.6 billion. Some major financial institutions had also been embarrassed; namely, Merrill Lynch, EF Hutton, and Chemical Bank in New York, Handelsbank in Zurich, and, especially, Credit Suisse in Bellinzona. One of the accounts at Credit Suisse was secretly called "Wall Street 651." The owner was Oliviero Tognoli, a well-known industrialist to whom the Mafia chieftains secretly turned for financial advice. Nearly $20 million passed through his account.

Some powerful men were locked away for a long time, and the case was widely publicized as a major victory for the good guys. With hindsight, it was something more. The bad guys washed over $50 million. But for the first time in a major drugs case, the Feds were able to follow the money. Both sides now realized that the rules of engagement had changed.

Suddenly, the stakes were higher than ever.

*   *   *

Italian mobsters have had a presence in Latin America for many years, notably through the maritally linked Cuntrera and Caruana clans, which have overseen their heroin empire from a once-secure base in Venezuela. Little by little, though, the authorities have been able to chip away at their sovereignty. In 1985, British and Canadian police seized a $300-million shipment of heroin sent from London to Montreal, and convicted one of the Caruanas for it. Two years later, they put a dent in the families' budgets by grabbing a gigantic hashish cargo in Newfoundland. Another relative went down for that one. The following year, the Venezuelans arrested more kinfolk for conspiring to traffic cocaine. That particular bust was significant because until then the authorities had suspected, but could never prove, that the two families had ties to the Colombians. Now they understood that there was no way the families could have operated next door to the cartels without their permission.

A major break came that same year when John Galatolo, a south Florida businessman, was convicted of smuggling cocaine. He told the DEA he'd personally brokered a recent deal for the Mafia involving six hundred kilos of coke from the Cali cartel. According to Galatolo, that deal firmly established the Mafia's cocaine franchise for Italy.

Originally, the Colombians had restricted the Mafia to their home base, hoping to distribute their own powder throughout the rest of Europe. But Europe is a long way from Latin America, and although the Cali mob could function easily in Spain — after all, they spoke the language and often hid out there — northern Europe proved to be a more difficult market. Transactions started going wrong and shipments were seized. It finally came to a head in February 1990 when the Dutch police found three tons of cocaine hidden inside a consignment of fruit juice.

Pragmatists that they are, the Colombians acknowledged defeat. They needed the Mafia's established distribution networks throughout Europe and turned to the experts. Together they set up front companies to handle the drugs and bank accounts to wash the money. Stopping them would take an international cooperation that was, until that point, unprecedented.

The first hint that such an exploit might be possible came in April 1992, when the FBI arrested fourteen people in Florida for trafficking and money laundering. The bust was just one of several that month. What made it unique was that the evidence linked these people to the cartels in Colombia and a Calabrian Mafia cell in Toronto.

Five months later, on September 28, police from eight nations — America, Great Britain, Canada, Colombia, Costa Rica, Spain, Holland, and the Cayman Islands — launched what can only be described as an all-out nuclear attack against the Mafia-cartel connection. Code-named Green Ice, it represented the first time an international task force had been formed specifically to take on the laundrymen.

Undercover agents posed as money launderers, starting first in San Diego in 1989, then slowly building up contacts in Texas, Florida, Illinois, and New York. They ran a chain of leather goods stores, which were subsidiaries of Trans Americas Ventures Associates — a DEA front company that imported merchandise from Colombia. Each ton of imported leather was listed as twenty tons, creating enough false invoices to wash drug profits back to the cartel's banks in Colombia and Panama.

Before long, the Cali bunch became so happy with the way Trans Americas ran their sink that they asked them to expand overseas, first into Canada and the Caribbean, then into Europe. The agents working the scam were only too pleased, as were the various foreign law enforcement agencies brought into the operation as the money laundering sting expanded.

After nearly three years of groundwork, in one momentous, simultaneous swoop on three continents, they arrested more than two hundred people worldwide, including one hundred and twelve in the States, three in Britain, four in Spain, and thirty-four in Italy. Among the people nabbed were seven primary targets, then believed to be the top-ranking financial managers of the Cali cartel. They got Rodrigo Carlos Polania, a former inspector of Colombia's national bank, and José "Tony the Pope" Duran, described by the Italian police as the world's most important cocaine distributor. A subsequent request by Interpol for fingerprint files on him revealed dossiers in twenty countries, in which he'd used twenty names. He'd introduced Pedro Felipe Villaquiran, his chief European representative, to Mafia bosses in Rome and had met with Bettein Martens, a major Dutch money launderer. They too were arrested.

When the trap was snapped shut, fifteen money laundering front companies were raided and $54 million in cash was seized, along with three-quarters of a ton of cocaine. These companies included a pan-European animal protection society and a Sicilian wine exporter, as well as one in Mantua, Italy, run by an 80-year-old woman with no business experience, who had laundered tens of millions of dollars for her nephew.

Thousands of files were confiscated on both sides of the Atlantic. One truly outstanding prize was a wealth of computerized records found in an office belonging to the Rodriguez brothers, detailing the cartel's worldwide money laundering. Other documents pointed to several Mafia-cartel joint ventures, including drug trafficking along the French Riviera and money laundering in Germany.

After Green Ice, and largely as a result of it, the Central Operational Service of the Italian police and the Internal Security Service of the Interior Ministry arrested Giuseppe Madonia, the Mafia's number two man in Sicily; Carmine Alfieri, a *capo* in the Camorra; three Sicilian brothers, who'd come to be called the Mafia's private bankers; Antonio Sarnataro, who was the Camorra's chief laundryman; and, in May 1993, Michele "The Crazy One" Zaza, the alleged leader of the gang. Ten more Camorra members were arrested with Zaza on the French Riviera, where a Camorra money laundering network had invested $1.3 billion in hotels, stores, and small industry. Another forty suspects, all tied to Alfieri, Sarnataro, and Zaza, were taken into custody in Italy, Belgium, and Germany.

When the initial success of Green Ice was reported in the press, the then U.S. deputy attorney general, George Terwilliger, declared the operation "a stake through the heart of the illegal drug business."

In Colombia, a senior Cali cartel member more realistically labeled it "a disruption."

18

THE NEW THREAT

"Today's criminals make the Capone crowd and the old Mafia look like small-time crooks."
— Former secretary of state George Shultz

For anyone confident enough to entrust cash to the evolving nations of Africa, the Dark Continent offers a legion of possibilities. There, hard currency is king. And unlike many other fragile economies, for example, those in Eastern Europe, the Africans have known the potency of cash for decades.

The Kenyan government determined in late 1994 that anyone could export up to U.S. $500,000 without official approval. As a result, shell companies run from overseas now wash money in Nairobi before wiring it on to India and Switzerland. Despite pleas from the central bank for vigilance, many banks in Kenya ask no questions, and are reporting bumper profits.

Post-apartheid South Africa has also been invaded by traffickers and laundrymen who use the country as a staging area to transship drugs into Europe and North America. The Nigerians were the first to take advantage of the smuggling infrastructure developed by arms dealers and ivory poachers after the United States banned direct flights from Nigeria. They bring cocaine and heroin into South Africa through small, chaotic ports, then ship the drugs to New York on commercial flights out of Johannesburg and Cape Town — a considerably less risky run than sending those drugs directly from Colombia or Thailand.

Since Nelson Mandela's election in April 1994, South Africa has made a concerted effort to lure foreign investment. The well-developed, modern financial services industry not only offers a way for legitimate businesses to invest in Africa, it is accessible to laundrymen. A massive amount of cash flows through the banking system; controls are clearly inadequate. With as many as seventy known drug syndicates operating internationally out of South Africa, it has become the most violent country on earth. There are reportedly fifty murders a day.

Then there is Francophone Africa. According to a confidential report from the French Ministry of Foreign Affairs, tremendous sums of drug money are being washed through hotels in Senegal and the Ivory Coast, casinos in Gabon and Cameroon, fisheries in Guinea, and the vanilla trade in Madagascar. The French police have also found drug links to African horse racing and state-run lotteries. Heroin from southeast Asia is routed through Africa on its way to the United States.

But nowhere in Africa has money laundering and drug trafficking become such an enthusiastic national affair as in Nigeria.

Once awash in oil, today Nigeria is the center of the continent's drug trade. A 25-ounce unit of heroin can be imported from Southeast Asia for under $6,000, and resold to distributors in Lagos for $120,000. Organized crime is so blatant that Nigeria is the first and only African country to have been "decertified" by the United States, marking Washington's absolute dissatisfaction with the military ruler, General Sani Abacha. The depth and complexity of Nigerian involvement in drug trafficking is staggering. American undercover agents working in Brazil have uncovered an organization managed by Russians that relies entirely on Nigerians to move Colombian cocaine through West Africa before smuggling it into the United States.

The State Department has accused Nigeria of harboring some of the most sophisticated and finely tuned transshipment, money-moving, and document-forging organizations in the world. Furthermore, they calculate that as much as 40 percent of the heroin coming into the United States is brought in by Nigerians. These are not random mules or freelancers, but professional gangs who enjoy the protection of government officials. It's no coincidence that thousands of Nigerian drug couriers are in prisons around the world, making up the largest single national grouping. But the drug barons operating out of Lagos are virtually never caught.

The Nigerians vehemently deny that the problem is as grim as Washington contends, blaming such allegations on "wicked reporting." They brag that they had recently arrested a Nigerian man at Lagos airport when he tried to leave the country with $800 million in cash.

It takes a lot of wicked reporting to match eight tons of $100 bills!

In a country for which international fraud is the most expedient source of foreign income, organized criminals have built highly lucrative scams around dirty money.

An official-looking letter, usually with a return address in the United States or Europe, is sent to a prominent gentleman's home, never his office, with the promise of a huge commission for his help. It's signed by someone pretending to be an attorney or with some vague title, such as a Nigerian royal, who says he is affiliated with a company with an oddly familiar name, such as "Shell BP." He writes that he is acting on behalf of an official entity — Nigeria's national oil company is a favorite — because a particular problem has arisen with blocked funds. A large sum due the company is being held in a Swiss account and, as the result of some muddled legal complication, the money cannot be released directly to the company. The letter goes on, "We are anxiously looking forward to securing a foreign partner who can offer us the benefit of having some money remitted into any company's or personal buoyant account. This money runs in the millions of U.S. dollars."

If the prominent gentleman will allow the money to pass through his bank account — in other words, launder it — he will be paid handsomely for the service. A third party will wire the money due — for example, $10 million — into his account without the prominent gentleman assuming any liability. All he has to do is wait for the money to clear, then forward $7 million to the agent. The prominent gentleman is welcome to keep the $3 million difference as his share.

Reassuring the prominent gentleman he's not being asked to do anything illegal, simply to step into the middle of a legitimate commercial transaction, the agent offers to show him references and all of the necessary background paperwork. However, as there is a fast-approaching deadline on which this money must be paid, the agent suggests that to save time the prominent gentleman furnish him with his banking details, plus his personal authorization for the transfer, written on his own letterhead and signed by him. Needless to say, once the prominent gentleman supplies the agent with the information, that's the last he ever hears of the deal. The letterhead, signature, and banking details are used by Nigeria forgers to create a second letter, this one ordering the prominent gentleman's bank to wire out the balance of his account.

Nigerian conmen have also created all sorts of variations on the "advance-fee fraud." In one, they bait their wealthy target with letters and contracts from companies and banks, indicating why and how the money must be paid into the account of a disinterested person. Tempted by a huge commission, the prominent gentleman agrees to get involved. But this time, at the very last minute, there's an awkward holdup. The prominent gentleman is bombarded with telexes, faxes, and phone calls from very embarrassed bankers and very embarrassed lawyers, explaining that the party due those funds is insisting the money be simultaneously transferred. A conference call is hastily arranged to ensure that as the prominent gentleman authorizes his bank to wire out $7 million, lawyers representing the party paying the money will authorize their bank to transfer in $10 million. As soon as the prominent gentleman instructs his bank to send the $7 million, the conference call goes dead.

The Nigerians honed their criminal skills in the heady days of oil affluence, when greed reigned supreme. The Russians developed theirs in the bleak days of Communist oppression, when crime was franchised by the state and synonymous with survival.

The Soviet Union's command economy never really worked, but the black market always did. So, when the Kremlin's walls came tumbling down, organized gangs — who once ran the parallel economy — moved swiftly to replace the illusions of free-market capitalism with the realities of drugs, prostitution, fraud, murder, extortion, loan sharking, smuggling, the sale of nuclear materials, and money laundering.

Today, crime is the most exportable sector of the former Soviet Union.

As reported crimes increase at 30 to 50 percent a year, Mafia-style groups murder bankers who refuse to cooperate. They run protection rackets, extracting money from Westerners who think they can waltz into the former Soviet Union and make a killing. And they contract to have new and late-model cars stolen in Germany — tens of thousands of them annually — then driven back to Russia and sold for hard currency.

Through Cold War contacts developed around Eastern Europe, Russian gangs have had no trouble infiltrating Poland, Hungary, and the Czech Republic. But it was East Germany that turned out to be their gold mine. With unification came their foothold in the West; there are now more than three hundred variously Russian organized crime gangs operating in Germany — professional criminals who deal in anything and everything, including nuclear materials, which they flog to the highest bidders in the Third World.

From their German base, the Russians have established a presence in Britain. And that presence has become so worrisome that British police now revise their threat assessment every three months. In addition to using the City of London to launder their money, Russian crime syndicates, current thinking has it, will become the United Kingdom's major supplier of drugs and illegal weapons before the end of this decade.

The French have also seen the Russians coming. In Paris and along the Riviera, shops selling luxury goods display signs in Russian, reminiscent of the 1970s, when the petrodollar-rich Saudis were the invading force and the signs were in Arabic. But the money the French are seeing is not rubles from Moscow; it's dollars from New York. Like everyone else, the Russians have grasped the concept that jurisdiction stops at the border, and that the more borders they can put between the source of their cash and the place they spend it, the more difficult it will be for anyone to detect it.

Not that everyone bothers. When a group of Russians recently arrived in Luxembourg with bundles of cash, suspicious bankers explained to their prospective clients that due to international pressure they could not accept dirty money. So the Russians produced sworn affidavits from someone in the Ministry of Finance to prove that this money was clean. Forged papers were all the bankers needed to protect themselves, and they accepted the cash.

Until recently, it was thought that Russian mobs were operating independently of the more established international syndicates. That view has begun to change. A gang of Russian émigrés was indicted in New Jersey along with seven members of the Gambino crime family in May 1993 after police broke up a fuel-tax racket.

The scam they ran is known as a daisy chain. False invoices are moved through front companies to create the appearance that heating oil, for example, is being sold to various wholesalers. One of the shells — known as the "burn" company — shows the purchase of tax-free oil and the sale of tax-paid oil to the next shell on the chain. The burn company is liable to the government for the tax — which, of course was never paid — and when the government comes looking for its money, the burn company is impossible to find.

It's a standard pattern. Paper trails are made too complex to follow, and companies disappear. Even if some extra-savvy IRS inspector manages to wend his or her way through purchase orders, provisional invoices, final invoices, brokerage letters, wire-payment instructions, third-party payment letters, tax-exempt certificates, and twenty-eight shells, all that's likely to be found at the end of the chain is the burn company, which will turn out to be nothing more than a post-office box.

The New Jersey–based Russians laundered more than $66 million through banks in Aruba, the British Virgin Islands, Switzerland, and Greece. Included in the 101-count indictment against them were charges of racketeering, extortion, mail, wire fraud, state and federal tax evasion, and, of course, money laundering. But the most interesting aspect of the case centered on $6.7 million these Russians paid to the Gambino family to allow them to operate. This "mob tax" was the first indication that working agreements now exist between the Russians and the Mafia.

Although Justice Department officials couldn't link these

Russians directly to organized crime groups in Moscow, they have since made a connection between them and Brooklyn's Russian immigrant community. It happened when a ton of cocaine was confiscated near St. Petersburg. The biggest drug bust to date in Russia, it involved a ton of white powder hidden in cans marked "meat and potatoes" trucked in from Finland. With information supplied by the Russian Interior Ministry police, the FBI was able to establish that the cocaine had been owned by the Colombians, who were using Russia as a back door to Europe. By following the money trail, they were able to ascertain that the middlemen who'd brokered the deal were living in New York.

Finding that much cocaine in St. Petersburg came as a shock because the Russian cocaine market is still in its infancy, though no one in American law enforcement ever doubted that Russian gangs would one day spot the enormous possibilities on offer in the drug trade. But it was no less surprising to learn that Russians, who'd emigrated to the States in the late 1980s, had already made contact with the cartels by the early 1990s.

Even before anyone understood the significance of Colombian laundryman Franklin Jurado's arrest in 1991, while on his way to Moscow, it was difficult for Western authorities to come to terms with the breakdown in law and order in the former Soviet republics. No one in the States could even guess that Jurado had been introduced to the Russians by émigrés in America. Instead, the Justice Department had focused on the readily available raw materials that were putting the Russians into the narcotics trade. Their need for hard currency, combined with the large pool of well-trained chemists who found themselves out of work as the economy made the transition from controlled to market-oriented, and the opening of Russia's borders, all combined to make for ideal conditions.

No one in the States had yet imagined that Russia was destined to become a jungle in the snow, that it would perhaps be impossible to stop Russia from becoming another Colombia. Like Colombia, contempt for the law and random violence are rampant. Like Colombia, their prime target is the world's most important consumer market. And like Colombians, the Russians have well-established émigré communities in several major cities.

According to Alexei Belov, deputy head of the Russian Interior Ministry's criminal investigation department, there are now two dozen Russian organized crime groups operating in the States. Specializing in drugs and money laundering, they can be found in Boston, Philadelphia, San Francisco, Los Angeles, Miami, and Chicago.

But mostly they are in New York — especially Brooklyn's Brighton Beach, the heart of a 200,000-strong Russian community. There have always been Russian shops and Russian cafés, Russian restaurants, and Russian newspapers in the boardwalk neighborhood east of Coney Island. Until the late 1980s, Brighton Beach was just another ethnic neighborhood, similar in many ways to Little Italy in lower Manhattan. There were blood ties that stretched back to the old country, and, because of Russian emigration, to Israel. There was crime, but the mobs in Brooklyn were second string.

It all began to change with the fall of Communism. The exodus from Russia grew from a trickle to a flood. They headed to Europe, to Israel, and in large measure to the States, settling where Russians had traditionally settled — neighborhoods such as Brighton Beach. Like all immigrants who have come to America, they soon learned that the streets were paved with gold only for a few. The rest had to fight to earn a living, and many of them — uprooted from their culture, deprived of their language, and confused by their environment — could barely scrape by. Scientists drove taxis. Physicians waited on tables. Engineers carried baggage in hotels. Desperately seeking the American dream, many Russians were willing to do whatever they had to.

Toward the end of 1991, thirty Russian major-league gangsters met in a country house outside Moscow to divide up the world. They sensed that lawlessness would prevail throughout the Russian Republics and saw opportunity. They too wanted a slice of the American dream, especially dollars, and the center of their world became Brighton Beach. It was from there they intended to run their seventeen-city American drug network. They plotted to sell their drugs in America, launder their money in Israel, reinvest their capital in criminal activities in Europe — especially Germany and

Belgium — and use profits from those activities to put more drugs onto American streets. In their spare time, having become world-class experts under the Communists at cheating government, they reckoned to run their usual array of extortion, fraud, and fuel-tax scams.

The following year, Russian gangsters started arriving in Brooklyn and setting up business. Much of the Brighton Beach community was repelled by this new threat, but life in Russia had instilled in them a healthy mistrust of authority and they did not trust the police to protect them. The only people who stood in the way of this new wave were the old-guard mobsters, and although they resisted as best they could, they never stood a chance. Besides, others in the community were welcoming the arrival of men like Vyacheslav Ivankov.

Dubbed by the Communist press as "the father of Soviet extortion" and considered by the KGB one of the most dangerous men in the country, Ivankov was thrown into a Siberian jail in 1982 for fourteen years. But in 1991, someone let him out, and somehow he got a visa to emigrate to New York. He listed his occupation on the application as a film director. His reputation having preceded him, Ivankov had little trouble winning respect. He paid for some of it, and used muscle to extract the rest. He'd been sent by his partners in Moscow to organize America, and he was determined to do just that. For three years he ran Brighton Beach, rebuilding the criminal infrastructure there, establishing a new Russian authority in Brooklyn, and from Brooklyn expanding it to the rest of the country. The FBI finally caught up with him in mid-1995 and put him out of business. But they couldn't tear apart the base he'd built. And they hadn't yet figured out how to infiltrate this new enemy.

Ivankov might have been a professional gangster, but he'd probably seen too many movies. Anyway, the FBI was even more concerned with Ivankov's old enemies. Professionally trained and highly qualified former KGB agents have become Russia's most capable drug traffickers and laundrymen. The veterans of the state police network turned out to be model partners for organized criminals. They too are moving into Brooklyn, and they're bringing with them skills Ivankov never dreamed of, as well as a more global view of crime.

Here's where the Russians could make the Colombians look like amateurs.

The southern republics of the Commonwealth of Independent States are covered with gargantuan fields of wild marijuana. So are huge tracts of Russian Siberia, where the weed blankets several million acres, roughly the size of Connecticut. Those fields are just waiting to be harvested. Opium poppy also grows throughout the ex-Soviet republics. So far, it's being converted only into inexpensive opium-based compounds rather than being refined into heroin. Yet it is surely only a matter of time before heroin is produced on a grand scale throughout the region. The potential is especially frightening when you consider that 40 percent of the arable land in the former Soviet Union is ideally suited for growing heroin poppy.

Russian gangs, teamed up with former KGB operatives, are learning how to grow it, refine it, and ship it. They already know how to protect it. And now they have a base in Brooklyn from which they can distribute it. The Mafia won't like it, and neither will the Latin Americans, but this time they're not up against a few cowboys from Moscow; they're trying to stare down guys in black leather coats whose reputation for ruthlessness is well earned. The Mafia will be able to do little about the Russians, except perhaps decide that if they can't beat them they might as well join them. And that's a very real possibility.

The FBI has learned through Italian police intelligence that two summits have already been held. One took place in Warsaw in March 1991, the other in Prague in October 1992. Both were hosted by Russian organized crime bosses. The guests of honor were representatives from the Sicilian, Neapolitan, and Calabrian crime organizations. The main topics of discussion were narcotics, the sale of nuclear material, and money laundering. Since then, links between the Russians and the Italians have become more evident. Sicilians have been discovered operating refineries that supply the Russians with product. High-tech printing presses in Naples are furnishing the Russians with quality counterfeit American money. Italian gangsters are investing heavily in Russia's recently privatized companies, and Russian gangs are laundering some of their money in high-yield Italian government tax-exempt bearer bonds.

Rightfully concerned, the FBI has opened a liaison office in Moscow. And in case anyone thinks the rest of the world isn't worried about these new alliances, the Danes are so scared they've invited the FBI to open an office in Copenhagen just to monitor Russian organized crime making inroads into Scandinavia.

No less alarming is the fact that since the fall of the Soviet Union, when the state owned the country's only bank, two thousand banks have sprung up, and 95 percent of them are believed to be owned by, or at least controlled by, Russian organized criminal groups. Russia might boast it has one of the lowest bank robbery rates in the world, but the contract-killing rate has soared, with more than five hundred victims a year, mostly legitimate bankers and prominent businessmen, as organized crime is trying to muscle in on legitimate money.

To put the size of the threat into some perspective, Swiss authorities now admit that between 1992 and 1995 at least $54 billion has been deposited in Swiss banks from Russia. And Belov insists he's not exaggerating when he says, "The Italian Mafia is like a kindergarten compared to our Russians."

Understandably, criminal organizations in the great melting pot have traditionally relied on the sanctuary of tight-knit ethnic communities. In that respect, North America's Asian gangs have been compared to the Italians during the infancy of the Cosa Nostra. What's more, the Asian gangs seem to have learned some lessons from the early days of the Mafia in America. The Italians eventually opened their doors to non-Italians. The Asians are remaining steadfastly xenophobic, becoming immediately suspicious of any non-Asian trying to infiltrate their ranks. Better organized than the Russians, the Asians are today considered by the FBI to be the major new threat.

Since the war in Vietnam, the Southeast Asian community in southern California has carved out a niche for itself in what was once a Chinese and Mexican stronghold. They deal in drugs, stolen cars, stolen computer chips, extortion, fraud, and money laundering.

San Diego, with the best weather in America — and more golf courses per capita than anywhere else in the country — has become their major trading center. San Diego has become the Vietnamese version of Brighton Beach.

A joint task force of federal and state authorities tried to take them down in 1993. Planting a Vietnamese American undercover agent took months. Once he was inside, it took several more months before he could get another non-Vietnamese American agent involved in the sting. The feds were after Dung Cong Ta, a 43-year-old methamphetamine dealer who sported a pony tail and a little mustache and called himself "Don Mexico." He had his fingers in several pies, including cars, computer chips, and money laundering. The man they sent to stalk him was Quan Pham, a young agent working for the State Department of Motor Vehicles. He was given the identity of a drug dealer named Sonny.

Hanging out in the neighborhood, Sonny got to know people, and slowly started looking for someone to do deals with. He was eventually introduced to Dung Ta through a mutual friend at a restaurant in April 1993. Surprisingly, Dung Ta turned out to be trusting. Almost as soon as he and Sonny sat down to talk, he agreed to sell some meth. Within a few weeks, Dung Ta even agreed to meet Sonny's boss, the owner of a marijuana plantation in Hawaii who called himself Kimo Pomeroy. In real life, Kimo was Spencer Ellis, an undercover agent with the California Bureau of Narcotics Enforcement who was then assigned to U.S. Customs.

Throughout that spring and into the summer, Dung Ta and Kimo continued to do drug deals. In parallel with the undercover operation, police started busting gang members dealing in cars and computer chips. By July, Kimo felt confident enough to up the stakes by asking Dung Ta for advice on laundering money. Dung Ta responded by introducing him to his laundryman, a local attorney named Phillip Schuman.

Five years younger than Dung Ta, Schuman was tall, with curly dark hair and a receding hair line. He'd once been a cop in the Skokie Illinois Police Department, but left police work to spend a few years as a broker in the Chicago area, then move to California, where he got two master's degrees and then his law degree. A man who always seemed to have a wild look in his eyes, he opened three offices in and around San Diego. And while many lawyers work out of more than one office, a sole practitioner working out of three was odd. How successful he was has never been clear, but his presence in the Vietnamese community, and some of the information the police were able to glean through wiretaps, led them to believe that one of his specialties was false insurance claims.

Dung Ta praised Schuman's abilities as a laundryman, telling Kimo that Schuman hid money in the California State Bar Trust Fund — his client's account. But Schuman wasn't the only money laundering contact Dung Ta had. He also introduced Kimo to Nilo Fernandez, a Filipino who suggested that Kimo set up a U.S. corporation with overseas operations. Cash from marijuana sales could be taken to the Philippines, where Fernandez would wash it, then send back to San Diego, first as capitalization for Kimo's company, then as profits. It was a basic scheme, for which Fernandez was charging 16 percent. Kimo agreed to the deal and asked Schuman to set up the company.

In September, Kimo gave Fernandez $50,000 in cash as a test run to see how well the laundry functioned. Someone working for Fernandez smuggled the money out of the United States and into the Philippines. Shortly thereafter, $42,000 was wired back to the San Diego bank account of the newly incorporated Quasi Star International. Over the course of four months, Kimo gave Fernandez a total of $335,000, all of it to be washed through the Philippines. $222,000 of it came back to Quasi, along with all of the appropriate paperwork, disguised as venture capital from an investor Fernandez decided to call "Aquino."

Schuman told Kimo that Fernandez was overcharging for his laundry facilities. He said that he and Dung Ta would be willing to handle Kimo's account for half as much. Kimo expressed interest. Schuman suggested that there were plenty of other places to wash money besides the Philippines; for instance, through gambling facilities. Or, Schuman proposed, he could set up a law office in Hawaii, supposedly to collect on insurance fraud claims, and put money through his client's account. Or he could wash Kimo's money through shell companies banking in the Caymans, the Cooks, and the Channel Islands. Kimo settled on the last option and gave Schuman $20,000 to fly to the Channel Islands to set up an account. At the end of January 1994, Kimo handed Dung Ta $108,000 in cash to be deposited on the island of Jersey.

On January 25, 1994, Dung Ta and his wife left San Diego for Minneapolis, where they were scheduled to change planes for London. Before boarding in San Diego, Dung Ta tried to check a gray Samsonite suitcase through to Jersey, but was told it couldn't be done and that he would have to clear customs in London. The suitcase was seized by U.S. Customs agents in Minneapolis, who then stopped Dung Ta and his wife. They were asked if they were carrying more than $10,000 in cash. Neither had filled out a customs declaration to say they were, and both lied. A search produced $3,300 on his person, $8,600 on hers, and $90,000 in the suitcase. Dung Ta maintained the money was paid to one of his businesses for damage done by the Los Angeles earthquake. His wife claimed her $8,600 was a gift from a friend whose name she couldn't remember, and her sister, whose address she didn't know.

As soon as Dung Ta was in custody, Schuman was arrested. Because he was an attorney, extra caution was taken during the search of his offices. A customs agent who had not worked on the case was brought in to go through Schuman's computer files. Under strict instructions not to have any conversations with other agents involved in the case and not to copy or seize any documents that did not pertain to this particular case, he first introduced a special program into each computer to assure that nothing would be erased and that no additional writing could be added to any file. Next, he searched the hard drives for specific words — Dung Ta, Quasi, Kimo, Sonny, and so on. Similar precautions were taken with computer equipment found at Schuman's home.

In the end, charges were filed against twenty-one people, including Schuman, Dung Ta, and Fernandez. A market in stolen computer chips was shut down, as was a stolen-car ring, the money laundering route through the Philippines, and a thriving methamphetamine dealership. Having learned how to win in Southeast Asia, the Vietnamese are becoming equally skillful at doing just that in southern California.

19

FACTORIES SOUTH, MAYTAG NORTH

*"The most efficient means of battling organized crime
is to act against money laundering."*
— Louis J. Freeh, director of the FBI

The Mexicans have picked up where the Colombians left off. Today, 50 to 70 percent of all cocaine smuggled into the United States comes through Mexico. The country is also the primary source of opium gum, the base product of heroin. At the same time, Mexico is America's largest supplier of marijuana.

With a 2,000-mile common border that is at best badly patrolled, at worst unpatrollable, it's easy to understand why Mexico has become the front door to the world's most important drug market. Mexican police forces are inefficient, bribery is rampant, a large part of the judiciary is totally crooked, and the government has proved otherwise helpless. Literally thousands of Justice Ministry officials and federal judicial police have been fired in the past few years for conspiring with drug traffickers. These days, around Washington, and especially at the DEA, the feeling is that the Mexicans are our worst allies in the war on drugs.

In tandem with their newfound trafficking successes, the Mexicans face the problem of washing their money. At first they settled for the obvious ways. Where the Colombians favored cashier's checks, the Mexicans showed a preference for traveler's checks because the government does not require that records of them be kept. Laundrymen used to brag of buying a thousand of them in $1,000 units, stuffing five hundred in their left pocket, five hundred in their right pocket, and crossing the border with $1 million. The money would then be wired from a *cambio* to banks in the Caribbean before being brought back to the States as part of a real estate deal, the way it was done by Ricardo Aguirre Villagomez through the American Express Bank International. Mexican laundrymen have also sometimes seized an opportunity to spend it all in Mexico. Following a 40-percent devaluation of the peso, they simply went on a buying spree, turning dirty dollars into pesos to buy cars, vacation homes, and yachts, which they then marketed through shell companies to Americans for clean dollars.

Still, they weren't prepared at first to handle such vast amounts of cash. The Colombians were a lot more savvy about wiring things around. They'd taken the time to develop the proper contacts. When the Mexicans moved in on the remains of the Cali cartel, they took the core business but didn't secure, or perhaps couldn't secure, the logistical support. So for the most part they still bulk-ship their money out of the country. They run around southern California and Texas with truckloads of cash, and often see it get taken away.

At least until a couple of years ago, they didn't have much difficulty putting their money into banks. That's changing now because of the volume involved and because of the pressure Washington is trying to bring to bear on Mexico City.

After baiting the Colombians with a phony leather-goods company that could conceal international money transfers, Operation Green Ice led to 192 arrests in the United States, Italy, Canada, England, Spain, and Costa Rica; the seizure of more than $50 million; and revelations as to well-developed links between Colombian and Italian crime gangs. The sequel, known as Green Ice II, was run out of San Diego and aimed at the currency exchange houses that litter the U.S.-Mexico border. Setting up a *cambio* in Coronado, California, the DEA managed to lure some Cali cartel representatives into washing their money there. When it came time to pull the plug, fifty people were arrested in five states, Colombia, and Canada. Seven tons of cocaine, sixteen pounds of heroin, various weapons, and $12.8 million were seized. An additional thirty people were named in the indictments, and warrants were issued. Among those caught in the net were Mexican nationals living in the United States, confirming the link between Mexican dealers and the Colombian cartels.

Evidence then surfaced of other joint ventures between Colombian and Mexican traffickers, such as cement companies, construction firms, and factories, all specifically designed to launder money in Mexico. Further evidence suggests that drug traffickers are the largest single group of investors on the Mexican stock exchange.

Although the border with Mexico has been pockmarked with currency-exchange houses for years, the surplus of cash has turned it into a plague. They are not required by Mexican law to keep thorough records or to identify customers making large cash transactions. But then, neither are Mexican banks. There are no effective controls on cash being brought into or transferred out of the country. What's more, Mexico's laws do not necessarily consider any profits from drug sales illegal, and the authorities cannot ordinarily confiscate drug-derived property. If they catch a dealer flying drugs in his plane, they can claim the plane as a prize. But if that dealer uses his drug money to buy a fancy hotel in Puerto Vallarta, he gets to keep the hotel, even if he's convicted of trafficking. The situation has gotten so desperate that some people believe the United States needed the North American Free Trade Agreement simply to repatriate the drug money heading south.

Mexicans ship drugs across the border any way they can. They use planes, boats, tractor-trailers; they use cars with hidden compartments; they use people sneaking through holes in chain fences. They come in colossal waves. When the Colombians owned the game, at least in the beginning, drug seizures from Mexico were measured in pounds. Today they are measured in tons. The Mexican attorney general's office recently estimated that traffickers are making roughly $30 billion a year. That's four times more than the combined annual income of the Cali and Medellín cartels at their height.

The "Colombianization" of Mexico is in full swing.

With the demise of Escobar and the Rodriguezes, at least three Mexican groups have gained international influence. The Tijuana cartel is run by Ramón and Benjamin Arellano Felix, brothers who are now suspected of having murdered Cardinal Juan Jesus Posadas Ocampo. A third brother, Francisco Rafael, was arrested in 1993 for drug trafficking and is already in prison. The Juarez cartel is divided into two factions. One is controlled by the Fonseca Carrillo family. At the head of it is 39-year-old Amado Carrillo Fuentes. Wanted for drug-related crimes in the United States, Fuentes operates with apparent immunity from his ranch across the border from El Paso, Texas, having only ever been charged in Mexico with a weapons misdemeanor. Nicknamed "Lord of the Skies," he is famous in drug circles for buying Boeing 727s to fly his cocaine into the States. The other faction is under the thumb of Rafael Aguilar, a former federal police commander.

The third was, until 1996, the most dangerous. It had been run by Juan Garcia Abrego, heir apparent to the Cali cartel. Based in Tamaulipas, he and members of his family controlled Mexico's Gulf Coast region. Standing six feet tall and weighing two hundred pounds, Abrego was born in La Paloma, Texas. His first lessons in the drug business involved floating bales of marijuana across the Rio Grande. He graduated with honors, becoming the first international drug dealer to make it onto the FBI's Ten Most Wanted list. Additions to the roster are usually announced in an FBI press release, but in December 1995, Attorney General Janet Reno showed her determination to put an end to Abrego's reign by personally announcing his inclusion. In an aside, she wondered why drug traffickers had not historically been considered worthy of the FBI's Ten Most Wanted.

Like Escobar and the Rodriguezes, Abrego had also been glamorized by the press. He is said to have fathered several children by different women — in keeping with a macho image — and is apparently so superstitious that he had witch doctors on permanent call to help protect him. Less glamorously, he was responsible for more than one hundred murders on both sides of the border. In fact, it was Abrego's massacre of six rivals in 1984 that made him Mexico's principal cocaine trafficker. Also, like the Colombians, he set up distribution units around America. The main ones were in San Antonio, Houston, and New York, but others have flourished all along the border, across the Gulf in Florida, and as far north as Milwaukee and Seattle.

Abrego was nicknamed "La Muneca" — the Doll — and there was $2 million on his head. Wanted in both the United States and Mexico for trafficking multi-ton quantities of cocaine, he'd been indicted in Houston in 1993 for drug trafficking and money laundering. His name had also been linked in Mexico to the killing of a commander of the Federal Security Department, the May 1991 massacre of several reporters who'd refused his bribes, and the 1994 murders of José Francisco Ruiz Massieu, secretary general of Mexico's ruling Institutional Revolutionary Party, and PRI presidential candidate Luis Colosio.

In January 1996, fifteen hand-picked agents from Mexico's National Institute for Combating Drugs surrounded Garcia's fortified ranch in the northern city of Monterey. Camouflaged as shrubs, they got so close that when they finally spotted him it only took a foot race to snare him. Within hours he was on a plane for Houston — deported without due process by the Mexicans because they considered him a United States citizen — to face a 26-count indictment for drug trafficking, money laundering, and murder.

The FBI called it a major victory. But the Mexican media put a damper on the celebrations by reporting that Garcia's lieutenant, 37-year-old Oscar Malherbe, had already seized command of the Gulf cartel. How effective he will be in keeping the vultures from Garcia's pickings remains to be seen. But then, it was only after Garcia had made it to the Ten Most Wanted list that the Mexican government seriously pursued him. Until then, Garcia was shelling out $50 million a month in bribes to keep the authorities off his back.

In Mexico, along with drug trafficking and money laundering, corruption is a fact of daily life.

It reaches to the highest levels. After José Francisco Ruiz Massieu was murdered, his own brother, Mario Ruiz Massieu, once the nation's chief drug prosecutor, was accused of covering up the plot to kill him. He was stopped at Newark Airport in 1995 on his way to Madrid for failing to declare the $40,000 in cash he was carrying. U.S. Customs has since located $9 million in one of his Texas bank accounts. Officials now suggest that some of that money came from Garcia, who kept the assistant attorney general on his payroll.

The plot thickens when you add to it Raul Salinas de Gortari, the brother of former president Carlos Salinas de Gortari, who was actually arrested for that murder. In June 1995 it was announced that the former president himself was being investigated on suspicion that he knew his brother Raul had masterminded the Ruiz Massieu assassination. Shortly thereafter, Raul's wife Paulina Castanon was arrested in Geneva. She'd apparently gone there to make an $840-million withdrawal from Raul's account. The Swiss froze that account and others they believed to have been owned by Raul under false names. The total is said to exceed $100 million. Mexican authorities also turned up an account apparently owned by Raul in London containing another $20 million. While all of this was going on, Carlos Salinas was on an extended vacation. Rumored at various times to be in sunny Cuba, he wound up spending six months in snowy Canada.

Perhaps skiing wasn't the reason why.

Described by U.S. Customs officials as "The Maytag of the money laundering industry," it's amazing how precisely Canada fits the off-shore gospel according to Lansky.

A firmly established democracy, Canada has a sound banking infrastructure, highly advanced communications, and easy access to the world's most important drug market. The U.S.-Canadian border, nearly five thousand miles long, is the longest undefended border in the world. Where there are checkpoints, American and Canadian citizens pass largely unhindered. The only thing that unequivocally stops at the border is U.S. federal jurisdiction.

Every now and then, when luck is on their side, Canadian Customs do catch someone trying to smuggle something. A few years ago they nabbed some Mexican laundrymen trying to cross the border at Surrey, British Colombia. Because these two were such a long way from home and didn't look like your average tourists, they were asked to open the trunk of their car. An especially alert officer happened to notice that the spare tire did not fit the car. He ripped it open and found $800,000.

But that's the exception.

A spare tire that does fit on a well-maintained car with New

York State license plates and skis lashed to the roof, driven by a well-dressed young American couple heading for northern Ontario late on a Friday afternoon, might attract someone's attention in July, but no one would think twice about it during the winter.

Before 1989, when money laundering finally became a criminal offense in Canada, hardly anyone thought twice about cash. The Mulroney government attempted to change that by introducing currency transaction reporting. But it's not mandatory. Banks voluntarily agree to ask depositors about cash. And because no one will prosecute them if they don't, they sometimes "forget." Combining the laxity built into all voluntary systems with a modern, internationally networked financial services industry, it's no surprise to discover that Canadian banks have for years maintained a major commercial presence in tax havens such as in the Caribbean.

Bruce "Peewee" Griffin, a convicted drug smuggler from Florida, had a well-established relationship with one of Canada's largest financial institutions: the Bank of Nova Scotia in the Bahamas. According to the FBI, between 1975 and 1981 Griffin laundered more than $100 million through the Scotiabank branch in Nassau, almost a quarter of it during one hectic four-month stretch in 1979. He kept several accounts there in the names of Bahamas-registered shell companies. To consolidate his holdings, he wired money to Scotiabank Cayman Islands and into an account it held for a Cayman-registered shell, Cobalt Ltd. From there, the money traveled through Scotiabank to New York, before being dispersed into several U.S. companies controlled by Griffin. When Griffin was finally indicted in 1983, along with a hundred associates, his assets included racing cars, racing boats, and a Texas horse ranch.

In those days, the Bank of Nova Scotia was famous for not asking questions about large cash deposits, and for ignoring normal banking practices. Among other things, it purposely kept minimal records in order to hide the identity of its depositors. What's more, some Scotiabank employees in the Caribbean actually received tips in the thousands of dollars from their clients for their help in washing drug money. In 1984, a U.S. federal court in Miami fined Scotiabank $1.8 million for refusing to turn over to a federal grand jury records they'd subpoenaed.

One of Griffin's associates was a Bahamian lawyer named Nigel Bowe. It was Bowe who introduced Griffin to Bahamian prime minister Lynden Oscar Pindling. Not coincidentally, the Bank of Nova Scotia was also where Mr. Pindling kept his money. Under investigation for allegedly receiving $100,000 in monthly drug bribes, Pindling owed much of his success to his old friend and mentor, Meyer Lansky.

Having the right friends can yield dividends. If you can get a politician, a lawyer, and a bank manager on your side, you can launder any amount with ease. But many laundrymen work wonders with only one of out three.

When a group of Canadians with plenty of money to wash stumbled across the ever-affable Aldo Tucci at the City and District Savings Bank in Dollard des Ormeaux, Quebec, they couldn't believe their luck. Tucci was so eager for their business he was willing to do just about anything. They invited him to administer six of their companies, and in the first year alone they put $13 million through his branch. To keep such clients happy, and to encourage more of their business, Tucci took it upon himself to make special arrangements for the group to deliver their cash-laden tote bags at the bank's back door. In fact, the gang and Tucci got along so well that when he was transferred to another branch in Montreal, they moved their accounts to his new office.

This same bunch got lucky again when they opened accounts at a rival bank. The manager there became concerned with the amounts of cash they were bringing into his branch — in just over a year they'd delivered $14 million, stuffed in suitcases and paper bags — and asked them to be kind enough to tie the money into $5,000 bundles. Naturally, they obliged.

And then there was Gary Henden, a Canadian lawyer who became a legend in his laundryman's lifetime by having a 15-year-old boy on a bicycle deliver parcels of cash to banks around Ontario. For some bizarre reason, a child carrying $250,000 in small bills didn't arouse the bank managers' suspicions. The Royal Canadian Mounted Police (RCMP) later claimed the banks should have questioned the teenager's deposits. The banks maintained it was none of their business.

Employed by Canadian drug traffickers, Henden set up a company called Antillean Management and opened foreign bank accounts in that name. He then created one called Rosegarden Construction. When he found property to buy, money would be wired from the Netherlands Antilles company to the M&M Currency Exchange in Canada, yet another Henden shell. From there it would go into Cencan Investments Ltd., also a Henden invention, which would loan it to Rosegarden. Cencan would issue a check that would be deposited by Henden, as the attorney acting for Rosegarden, into his client account. Henden then paid for the purchase, but registered the mortgage in favor of "Gary Henden, Attorney at Law, In Trust." Needless to say, those mortgages were never repaid.

Henden eventually admitted to having washed $12 million over a three-year period for a drug trafficking syndicate. The police feel a more accurate figure might be five times as high. Still, had they not been able to establish a direct link between Henden's assets and drug trafficking, they would never have broken through the screen he'd erected around attorney-client privilege.

It was much the same for the Vancouver attorney working on a flat percentage when he deposited $7.4 million in cash into his client account at a local branch of the now infamous BCCI between March 1985 and July 1987. He also turned C$3.1 million into U.S. dollars, walking into the bank with amounts ranging anywhere from $56,000 to $396,000 in his briefcase, presorted into piles of $20 and $50 notes. When the bank manager asked about the money, the man explained that he was a lawyer acting for a client and refused to say anything more about it. The bank manager reassured the lawyer he respected attorney-client privilege and that his business was welcome.

The Canadian-Caribbean connection made the front pages in September 1988 when sprinter Ben Johnson won his Olympic gold medal. He was accused of using steroids and later deprived of his medal. Johnson's pusher turned out to be George Jamie Astaphan, a doctor from St. Kitts with a license to practice medicine in Canada.

Politically well connected on the island, Astaphan became the object of separate drugs and money laundering investigations in both the United States and Canada. In late 1991 and early 1992, he delivered steroids to two men in Buffalo, New York, who claimed to be running a chain of weightlifting clubs. About the same time he was conspiring with undercover agents in Florida, where he tried to purchase a hundred pounds of cocaine. But the investigation into Astaphan's dealings goes far beyond those two incidents. One source puts Astaphan in the middle of a St. Kitts money laundering ring that uses casinos throughout the Caribbean to wash money, which is then sent through a company in Montreal before being reinvested in drugs. That investigation never got very far in St. Kitts, but apparently continues in Canada. Whether or not Astaphan himself is cooperating, no one will say. The answer is, probably not. He has very little incentive to do so, and his life wouldn't be worth much if he did.

He boarded a BWIA flight in Antigua bound for Toronto on January 8, 1994. The weather had supposedly closed the airport in Toronto — at least that's what the airline still claims — and the plane was forced to land at JFK in New York. Knowing that Astaphan was on board, FBI agents met the plane and arrested him. It's a moot point whether or not the FBI coerced BWIA into making a stop in New York. Had Astaphan made it to Toronto, the RCMP would have arrested him there.

Arraigned in Buffalo and tried in Tampa, he was not prosecuted for money laundering. However, he was convicted of possession of steroids and possession of cocaine, with intent to distribute both. He was sentenced to two years.

Instead of going after small fry like Astaphan, the Canadians take a more long-term view. In 1990, the RCMP in Montreal set up an exchange counter at the International Money Center. They were working on information that Canadian drug traffickers had washed $130 million in drug money through the Center. Having opened a major laundromat, the RCMP sat back and watched as three specific groups emerged. The first was run by Joseph Lagana, an attorney whose client was Vito Rizzuto, the suspected head of the Canadian-Italian Mafia. The second was run by Dominic Tozzi, who worked for a rival gang headed by Vincenzo di Maulo. The third was run by Samy Nicolucci, who not only shared an office with Tozzi but worked with several people in the Rizzuto mob.

Working alongside Lagana in this operation were a pair of attorneys from his office, Vincenzo Vecchio and Richard Judd. Two other men stand out: Norman Rosenblum, who dealt with logistics for the first group's drugs and had the ill fortune of being present when half a ton of cocaine was delivered over in the middle of the Caribbean to a ship manned by undercover RCMP and U.S. Customs agents; and David Rouleau, whose job it was to collect money from the group's primary drug distributors, a chapter of the Hell's Angels motorcycle gang. The groups brought bags of Canadian and U.S. dollars to the Center and deposited it there with the RCMP undercover agents for wire transfer to Venezuela, Florida, New York, Liechtenstein, Panama, and Switzerland.

As the investigation branched out, the RCMP called for help from America, Italy, Switzerland, France, and Panama. Together, they were able to follow money to the Italian-Panama gold connection. They were able to identify back-to-back loans made through Switzerland for the purchase of real estate in Canada. And they were able to locate more property in the south of France and Florida held by the suspects. After four years of laundering drug money for this group, and moving $73 million through the Center, the RCMP arrested forty-one people and froze over two hundred accounts in twenty-nine banking institutions. It was their biggest money laundering bust to date.

But that's about to change.

The United States has, in its infinite wisdom, decided that border crossings north and south take too long. So it has instituted a program called Line Release, which reduces regular cargo inspections of trucks crossing into and out of the country. Preapproved transport companies are granted totally free access and not subjected to spot checks. The Mexican drug barons no longer need to invest in 727s and superfast speedboats. All they have to do is throw trucks at the border and simply hire approved transporters who will unknowingly allow them to mix narcotics with legitimate cargo.

Forced to comply with a policy many inspectors know is giving the Mexicans a free hand, Customs came up with Hard Line, which is supposed to supplement spot checks at heavily trafficked border crossings with increased intelligence and sniffer dogs. But even with Hard Line, preapproved trucking companies still enjoy priorities. One of them, Hipodromo de Agua Caliente, is a horse van owned by a race track in Tijuana. They were given approval to transport racehorses across the border. Except that Agua Caliente track is out of business. And a few years ago the track's owner was investigated by U.S. Customs on money laundering suspicions.

All this was known when the truck was given Line Release approval. In the name of progress, the factories in the south are now linked by road with the laundromat in the north.

Call it the superhighway for smugglers.

It's an advantage the Colombians would have killed for.

It's a convenience that American and Canadian kids will end up dying for.

20

HANGING OUT THE WASH

"Money laundering is the crime of the '90s."
— **Business Week**

In the summer of 1969, Richard Nixon pledged to formulate a new national policy in the fight against drugs. He might even have elevated that fight to a full-blown war had it not been for America's ongoing "police action" in Southeast Asia.

Colombian cartel cocaine was just beginning its infiltration of American culture. Nixon, underestimating how complex the problem was, arrived at the conclusion that marijuana and cocaine were equally dangerous. Needing a culprit, he settled on Mexico. Accordingly, he stepped up surveillance of America's southern border and coerced the Mexican government into herbiciding marijuana fields. He succeeded in putting amateur, freelance smugglers out of business — kids who dealt homegrown marijuana — but left the field wide open for professionals, grown-ups flogging cocaine. Because coke is a powder, it's easier to smuggle than bales of marijuana, and is therefore less risky. It also earns higher profits. Nixon's new national policy did little more than create a huge competitive advantage for the deadlier drug.

By the time Jimmy Carter moved into the White House, things were getting out of hand. American cities were being transformed from wholesale marijuana markets into major cocaine trading centers. It was party time for street pushers, pimps, pilots, speedboat captains, and any federal agent who could be bought.

For the laundrymen, it was the Second Coming.

The television program "60 Minutes" was one of the first to show the depth of the problem and bring it into the nation's living rooms, exposing how otherwise respectable businessmen were jumping on this profit bandwagon. Carter reacted by approving an interagency task force called Operation Greenback. Customs officers and IRS agents identified and approached individuals who'd banked large amounts of cash. Their question was, "Where did you get the money?" If they answered that it was U.S.-generated income, the IRS would mention the words *tax evasion*. If they replied it was imported, Customs would suggest the word *smuggling*. If they didn't answer, or couldn't answer, without admitting it was drug money, they were immediately slapped with charges of drug trafficking, conspiracy, and money laundering. The success of Operation Greenback — 215 indictments, the seizure of $38.8 million in currency and $14.6 million in property, and $120 million in fines — formed the model for other multiagency joint ventures, including the creation in 1984 of organized crime drug enforcement task forces.

Ronald Reagan appointed George Bush to spearhead the nation's assault against drugs, but Bush, for all his good intentions, never had much of a stomach for severe financial prosecution. Within a year, he downgraded Operation Greenback from a large-scale interagency effort directed out of Washington to a small unit working out of the U.S. attorney's office in Miami.

One gauge of Bush's failure to grasp the problem was reflected in the cash surplus figures. The federal government monitors the total amount of currency in the banking system. A cash surplus means there is more money in a particular area than under normal banking conditions. When Bush deemphasized Operation Greenback, the cash surplus in Jacksonville and Miami shot up by $5.2 billion. Just as Nixon had targeted the Mexican border, Bush concentrated his forces in south Florida, and the moment he did, the laundrymen headed for healthier climates. In this case they went to southern California, where the cash surplus quickly topped $3 billion.

In spite of evidence to the contrary, Reagan somehow seemed convinced that money launderers didn't bother with cash anymore. He even went on record as saying that professional criminal financial managers did their banking electronically. As for the cash-filled garbage bags shown on the evening news with every drug bust? He shrugged. All entrepreneurs keep petty cash on hand.

While Reagan and Bush weren't looking, along came crack.

A crystallized form of cocaine, cheaper than heroin or coke, crack can be smoked like hashish. With the North American coke market saturated and prices falling, the cartels welcomed crack as a godsend. One ounce of cocaine could become three hundred to four hundred crack vials. By the mid-1980s, both of Colombia's main cartels were shipping crack by the ton.

The nickel and dime bags, $5 and $10 worth, widened the cartels' market by attracting middle-class white consumers who gave crack a certain social status. Because this business didn't require more than a few dollars start-up money, it also brought a new category of seller onto the street, black teenagers. There was a time when sports offered the main hope for any black kid who wanted to escape from the inner-city ghetto. If he could play baseball or football or, even better, could play great basketball, there were people who'd back him through high school and college. Only a tiny percentage of those kids ever got to the pros, but at least sports held out hope. And, in some cases, hope was enough.

Crack changed that.

When George Bush moved into the Oval Office, Customs and DEA officials tried to persuade him that a full-scale attempt to eradicate the production of illicit drugs around the world would be costly and futile. Government officials in some countries were openly cooperating with drug producers. A top-secret State Department document noted, for instance, that the narcotics trade in Laos had become such an integral part of the local economy that supporting it was "de facto government policy."

The president was also advised that Syria was directly involved in growing, refining, and trafficking drugs. The CIA repeatedly informed Bush that Damascus was earning up to $1 billion a year, about 20 percent of its national income, by subsidizing the opium and hashish industry in the Bekka Valley of Lebanon. The main market was then, and is still, the United States. Named as the main culprits by the CIA were Syrian president Hassad's brother, the defense minister, and the commander of Syrian military intelligence. But Bush needed the Syrians during Operation Desert Storm — and later to stay at the table during the peace talks — so at least in the short term it suited American foreign policy to turn a blind eye to Syrian international heroin trafficking.

Those who understood what the war on drugs was really all about urged Bush to put his resources into the battle being waged on the financial front. The president's response was a two-pronged attack: at home, he planned to wipe out street dealers by discouraging demand through education; overseas, he plotted sending U.S. troops into the mountains of Colombia, making a massive storm of arrests their top priority.

The massive storm turned out to be nothing more than a brief flurry. Between 1989 and 1991, twenty-six cartel members were captured and sent to the United States. For a while it appeared as if Bogotá was willing to appease Washington. Then the Colombians made extradition unconstitutional and Saddam Hussein invaded Kuwait. The president's attention turned back to foreign policy.

His Gulf War was still to be fought.

His drug war had already been lost.

Bill Clinton didn't have to inhale to understand something his immediate predecessors did not: 90 percent of all crime is financially motivated, and therefore the most effective way to fight criminals is to go after their money. And he put money laundering on the agenda at the celebrations for the fiftieth anniversary of the United Nations in 1995 by warning drug traffickers, terrorists, and the world's organized criminals, "Your dirty laundry is no longer welcome."

Congress has mandated a certification process requiring the president to assess foreign cooperation in counternarcotics efforts on a yearly basis. The State Department named eleven nations seen to be aiding and abetting the laundrymen. However, six of them — Bolivia, Colombia, Lebanon, Pakistan, Paraguay, and Peru — were considered vital enough to national interests to justify continued support from Washington. The remaining five are Afghanistan, Burma, Iran,

Nigeria, and Syria. An additional State Department roster, not publicly released, added to the usual suspects — Antigua, the Cayman Islands, Venezuela, Thailand, Austria, and Cyprus.

The certification process is like a report card on which the grades are pass, fail, and still thinking about it. Countries that care about passing have long since started doing something about money laundering, whereas countries that couldn't care less about failing get so much income from drug dealing that only the most severe economic sanctions could grab their attention. However, to make sanctions effective requires a global effort, and it is clear from the way recent embargoes have been violated in Iraq and Bosnia that most offending countries disregard most of the globe. It is equally clear that most of the globe doesn't care a hell of a lot about America's drug problem.

Had the list been compiled using the same criteria by another government, the United States would be cited as the world's biggest per-capita user of illegal drugs, and therefore wouldn't pass. That brings the argument straight back to the Third World's contention: "Before you tell us how to live, clean up your own streets."

Clinton plainly hoped to do just that by putting more policemen on the beat. But that fails to consider the fact that once drugs reach the streets, it's probably too late. What's more, arresting, convicting, and imprisoning traffickers does not always prevent them from running their cartels. And for every trafficker taken out of circulation, a dozen more are willing to take his place.

For the first time, money laundering statutes have been used to prosecute a trafficker for a drug deal conducted outside the United States. A Pakistani, Asif Ali Khan, was indicted in Louisiana in 1995 after purportedly smuggling ten tons of hashish between Australia and Pakistan. The Justice Department claimed jurisdiction because $300,000 worth of the $67-million deal was washed through the Pioneer Bank and Trust Company of Shreveport, Louisiana. By concentrating on the laundrymen, and by following the money trail and going after that money, the government continues to drive up a trafficker's cost of doing business. He's now paying anywhere between 6 and 25 percent to get his money collected, washed, and into his pocket. The added expenses are reflected in the street price, and there is a direct correlation between increased street prices and increased street crime.

From the middle of the last decade to the middle of this one, the war on drugs has cost more than $100 billion. It is fair to ask, what has America gotten for its money? The answer is, not a lot. Doing nothing may have created anarchy, but in that same ten-year period drug-related deaths have doubled and drug-related murders have tripled. $100 billion later, the problem has gotten so drastic that only drastic solutions can solve it.

Because the underground economy functions almost exclusively with dollars, one of the more radical proposals has been to render the traffickers' dollar mountains useless by changing the color of money. The United States is the only country in the world whose currency is both the same size and the same color in all denominations. America's paper money has always been green. Under the Reagan administration, a proposal floated around the Senate to end that same-color, same-size tradition. Supported by Treasury Secretary Donald Regan, the plan was to announce on a given Monday morning that within seven days green $20, $50, and $100 bills would no longer be considered legal tender. Instead, the government would be issuing newly designed bank notes — bigger, smaller, yellow, red, or blue. All anyone would have had to do was walk into a bank and exchange the old notes for the new notes. Any cash transaction over $1,000 would be recorded and the information passed on to the IRS and the DEA. For the average person, the switch wouldn't have been anything more than a minor nuisance. Even if someone always carried a few thousand dollars in his pocket, it would take only a few minutes. But it could cripple a drug dealer with several million in cash hidden under his mattress. Swapping thousands of old $20, $50, and $100 bills for the new money in such a short period, even using an army of smurfs, would be out of the question. And once the week was up, his cash mountain would be worthless.

The DEA then suggested that government print two types of currency. One would be legal tender exclusively inside the country, the other legal tender exclusively outside the country. The two would be interchangeable only at specially controlled financial institutions. At least in theory, that should put an end to dollar smuggling.

There have even been calls to do away with all paper money, to turn the American economy from a currency-based system into one that functions solely with checks and plastic. There might have to be some coins left in circulation, if for no other reason than to keep the vending-machine industry happy. Relegating folding money to the dustbins of history would deliver a blow to drug dealers. It would also be a positive step toward putting loan sharks, tax evaders, protection racketeers, and kidnappers out of business.

None of these plans has gotten very far. Legislators have written them off as unrealistic. They claim that such a stunt would be too disruptive and cause too much of an inconvenience for tens of millions of Americans. The truth is, tampering with the currency to knock out the laundrymen is not an issue that will win reelection votes.

Another idea, perhaps one less difficult to drive home to the electorate, would be to pass laws that distinguish the professional, international drug trafficker from people who deal in small amounts simply to support their own drug taking.

When someone buys three grams of coke and sells two to make the money that pays for one, technically that's dealing. And in some states, a few ounces can put you away for a very long time. But were drug addiction seen as an illness — the way alcoholism generally is — this sort of amateur dealing would rightfully be considered a symptom of that illness. The idea is not to decriminalize drug dealing, but to treat amateur dealing more humanely than many states currently do, while enacting legislating that makes global trafficking a capital offense.

Instituting that distinction could make a difference.

What men such as Escobar and the Rodriguez brothers fear most is extradition to the United States. But simply indicting them here and demanding other countries hand them over probably wouldn't put them out of business — even with the possibility of the death penalty hanging over their heads. However, by imposing severe economic sanctions on any country harboring traffickers; by sending special CIA/DEA/FBI commandos into the country to kidnap them and bring them back to the States; and by putting a couple of million dollars on their heads, it's a good bet some traffickers would give up drug dealing and concentrate full-time on mere survival.

Anyone who has any professional dealings whatsoever with these indicted traffickers would also be subject to charges of global trafficking and risk capital punishment. It would be like being an accomplice to murder.

To deal drugs, global traffickers have set up huge corporate structures — taking several pages out of the best management books — and have constructed multinational organizations. They deliberately separate the marketing and financial sides of their business, keeping them as far apart as possible, so that the drug dealers never know about money laundering, and the laundrymen — white collar professionals whose business it is to handle money — never see drugs.

By being tossed into the same boat with street dealers and smugglers, marketers, bankers, accountants, front-company workers, and lawyers — the laundrymen — would be forced to confront what they do, and their "plausible denial" would fall on deaf ears. Their only way out would be to plea bargain. In exchange for traffickers' assets, the names of other accomplices, and other invaluable information, they could trade the electric chair for a term of life imprisonment.

It is draconian, to say the least.

Although making global trafficking a capital offense might not put an end to America's drug problems, it would get the attention of America's laundrymen.

In 1989, the heads of state of the seven leading industrial nations, known as the G-7, officially recognized, for the first time, that money laundering was a runaway global crisis. They formed the Financial Action Task Force (FATF) to coordinate a multinational approach to dealing with the problem. Membership was promptly opened to countries outside the G-7 nations, and now includes the OECD countries, Hong Kong, Singapore, the Gulf Cooperation Council, and the European Commission. Every member has endorsed a blueprint consisting of forty measures intended to deal a lethal blow to the laundrymen. To date, not a single member has adopted the entire blueprint into law.

Since then, however, all sorts of special-interest groups have put money laundering at the top of their annual general meeting agenda. Their intentions are good, and the delegates' hearts are mostly in the right place. In 1995 alone, experts from forty nations met in France to recommend measures to halt money laundering in Russia and Eastern Europe; representatives from 140 governments met in Italy to formulate a strategy against the world's criminal organizations; delegates from 180 governments convened in Egypt to mount a global front against organized crime; American lawyers met in Washington to discuss their responsibilities vis-à-vis money laundering and attorney-client privilege; ministers from twenty-five nations met in Argentina, committing their administrations to fight money laundering; and six hundred international law enforcement professionals assembled in England to call for rolling back banking secrecy laws. But most of those money laundering conferences are little more than excuses for officials to enjoy "working visits" to good weather. Conclusions are published and then generally disregarded. Still, it must be said that conferences do bring together people who might not otherwise have met, and give them an opportunity to network. Between the banquets and the cocktail parties, experts from member states working in various fields — customs, drug enforcement, banking, and financial supervision — can exchange phone numbers. The bad guys know the other bad guys. If nothing else, the good guys are now getting to know the other good guys.

Even if every member of FATF complied fully with the organizations' forty directives, they still wouldn't work.

Money is at the root of the problem, and money is at the root of the solution. Wherever such huge sums are bandied about, common sense is often given a backseat ride.

Start with the genius who wrote the manual for administrative budgeting. Government accountants set annual budgets with two factors in mind: how much is needed next year, and how much was spent this year. If an agency was handed $10 billion last year and only spent $9 billion this year, it risks getting only $9 billion next year. So bureaucrats rush around in the final month of the fiscal year to make certain that all of their allocated money is used up. Then, to justify an increase for their next budget, they naturally inflate whatever threat it is they're battling. They may know that $250 billion a year is being laundered, but find an expert to swear the amount is actually $350 billion, and warn that if they don't get increased funding they'll never be able to do their job. When they get more than they previously got, they have to spend it all or they'll lose it the following year. Waste is factored into the equation and annually regenerates itself. So do egos. Like the company chairman who brags that he heads a $10-billion organization, in government, too, there's a tendency to confuse real importance with allocated revenue.

Nowhere is that more visible than in asset-sharing programs, which offer law enforcement agencies a portion of the bounty they confiscate. Competition is stiff for the right to claim a goal and not just an assist. Law enforcement agencies can pull together, but only up to a point, after which it's a free-for-all. Customs, the DEA, the FBI, and the IRS run operations together, and often with great success, but each agency fights for control of the task force because being chief pays better than being just another brave. Some agencies only go after cases that produce big cash rewards instead of pursuing more difficult and often more important cases for which the prize is nothing but moral satisfaction.

Human temptation also gets in the way.

Four federal agents in south Florida, three from the FBI and one from Customs, were caught by undercover officers in a sting operation in 1992 and charged with stealing a total of $200,000 from drug dealers. One of the four happened to have a girlfriend who managed a Great Western Savings Bank branch in suburban Miami, and she washed their cash. No sooner had that case broken when another Customs agent in Florida was arrested on charges of trafficking and money laundering in a separate case. He had been approached to help launder cash from the sale of counterfeit goods. The agent held down a second job at a financial investment firm, and had no trouble laundering his money there in his spare time.

The headlines are full of similar stories. Three sheriff's deputies

in Los Angeles were convicted in 1993 of stealing $750,000 in con-
fiscated drug money and laundering it through a gun store. That
same year, a Tampa police "Officer of the Year" pleaded guilty to five
federal drug-related charges. And Rene De La Cova, the DEA agent
who personally served Manuel Noriega with his arrest warrant, admitted stealing $700,000 while working on an unrelated money
laundering sting.

It's naive to expect there won't always be rotten apples. Fortu-
nately, the overwhelming majority of law enforcement officers involved with this sort of work do it because they sincerely believe it's
a job that needs to be done. And the sacrifices they're called upon to
make to accomplish that mission are most often made unselfishly,
honorably, and with justifiable pride.

It's taken a long time, but money laundering is finally being perceived
as both a crime and a symptom of other crimes. Accepting that the
best way to combat drug trafficking must be to use methods that de-
prive criminals of their profits, one logical conclusion is that the day
the drug problem is defeated, the money laundering problem will
also be defeated. Alongside comes the argument: if you really want to
conquer drug trafficking, you have to eradicate demand.

If the Ayatollah Khomeini couldn't keep drugs out of Iran, and
if Fidel Castro can't keep drugs out of Cuba, and if Saddam Hussein
can't keep drugs out of Iraq, how can anyone seriously expect dem-
ocratically elected leaders to keep drugs out of the West? A drug-free
America is a pipe dream.

One recent survey suggested that even if law enforcement agencies throughout North America and Europe increased their seizures
by 40 percent, the availability of drugs on the streets of their major
cities would be virtually unchanged. Traffickers view confiscation as
little more than a tax. Either they write off a cargo entirely, or, in
some places, especially around the Caribbean, simply buy it back for
a handful of cash.

What's more, there are literally dozens of nations whose government's revenue is smaller than the profits made by the drug cartels. Those nations are ripe for the picking. The traffickers move in

and turn the country into a laundryman's playground. Imagine trying to enforce justice and protect citizens in a country where organized crime is wealthier and better armed than the government.

Interviewed by *Time* magazine several years before his capture, Cali cartel boss Gilberto Rodriguez Orejuela wondered out loud, "Why are countries such as Germany free to export materials used to refine cocaine? Why do countries like Switzerland, Panama, and even the U.S. protect money whose origin is dubious?" The question clearly reflected his grasp of the narco-economy, which could not possibly survive if otherwise honest men and otherwise legitimate businesses were not prepared to facilitate the laundrymen.

The very groups that could turn the tide in the war against the laundrymen — bankers, attorneys, company-formation agents, and politicians — have the least incentive to. As long as otherwise honest businessmen have a thread on which to hang their belief that what they're doing is legitimate, they will continue doing it. They will ask, Am I supposed to be a policeman? They may acknowledge that drugs equals money equals drugs, but never in the context of their own money. They will insist, If I had to ask where my clients' money comes from every time I get a new client, I won't have any new clients. As long as they can plausibly deny that they are as guilty of drug trafficking as the dealers they serve, it will be business as usual.

And that business is usually death.

The North Vietnamese and the Vietcong used drugs as an effective weapon in the guerrilla war against the United States. The Mujahideen in Afghanistan took a page out of that book and made heroin easily available to the invading Soviets. They hooked the Red Army so badly that soldiers were exchanging their weapons for drugs. Mikhail Gorbachev pulled his soldiers out not because the Afghans had rocket launchers but because his army had been soundly defeated by hypodermic needles and white powder.

Legalization of drugs, or at the very least decriminalization of some of them, are widely touted as solutions. There is no disputing that both would help keep some kids out of jail, but there is no evidence whatsoever that either would keep drugs out of those kids.

In jurisdictions where they've eased prohibition, the experiment has failed repeatedly. It has created massive health problems, spread drug consumption across wider sections of the population, and fueled other crimes. In the Netherlands, for instance, decriminalized drugs feed a growing and terribly violent white-slave trade.

Legitimizing drugs also means legitimizing the traffickers and the money launderers. Turning the Treasury into a pusher so that it can tax drugs won't pay for the damage that drugs do, any more than it will put organized criminals out of business. Until someone finds a workable solution — and there are some people who have arrived at the tragic conclusion that the problem has now become unsolvable — the advantage remains clearly on the side of the laundrymen.

This is all the more the case as modern technology is about to render the fight against them futile. Rechargeable cash cards will allow criminals to bypass the banking system altogether and launder profits via the Internet. Computer chips weigh the same whether they carry $10 or $10 million and, unlike credit cards, there'll be no record of transactions. In its simplest form, digital cash already exists. Phone cards, for example, carry a certain amount of credit. Deductions are made from the chip with each call. The next step will be cards worth $100 worth of credit, which you'll use to buy gum, a ride on a subway, food in a restaurant, or a new baseball mitt. Instead of handing the salesperson a piece of plastic that sends the transaction to a central computer for billing later, or plastic that simultaneously debits your bank account and credits the sellers, you'll put your card into a machine and the proper sum will be moved off your computer chip and onto the seller's.

It will work the same way for drug deals.

Just around the corner are smart cards embedded with enough memory to hold all sorts of data. Once encrypted software has been developed to ensure privacy, you'll download money from the cards onto your home computer — turning your hard disk into your virtual bank account — access the Internet with your modem, and move assets from one jurisdiction to another instantaneously and invisibly. Mastercard and Visa are both developing smart card systems, although their version will deliberately generate an audit trail because that's their business. Other companies, however, including banks, are developing smart cards that won't leave an audit trail because digital currency technology will bring huge profits.

There is no doubt that all of this will change the way we spend our money and therefore change the way we live. Eventually, electronic money should replace cash. Consumer habits die hard, and there is always great resistance to great change, but once upon a time there were people who refused to believe that someday everyone would carry plastic.

Nor is there any doubt that cybercash risks might undermine both the world's banking system and the administration of justice. The problem is compounded by lawmakers who, like generals, are still fighting yesterday's battles. By definition, cyberspace transcends governments and national boundaries. Unless Congress comes to grips with it in time, those who stand to profit most from the future — and the obvious two are banks and organized criminals — will have long since found a way to make the system Congress-proof.

In the meantime, the bad guys can bide their time, find helpful banks, and buy crooked lawyers. They only need to find one country or one bank willing to do their laundry; it doesn't really matter if that country is halfway around the world, or if that bank is just across the border. As long as one country or one bank is willing to cheat on behalf of the laundrymen, there is nothing the others can do.

The good guys are hampered by a lack of personnel, limited by financial constraints, and denied the tools they need by legislatures that must balance judicial concerns with the free flow of honest business.

In other words, the good guys are seriously outgunned.

It's gotten to the point where U.S. law enforcement officers now admit that in money laundering cases, unless there's a minimum of $5 million involved, no agency in Washington can be bothered to open a file.

ACKNOWLEDGMENTS

This book began with John Hurley, who was until the end of 1992 customs attaché at the U.S. Embassy in London. First he fired my enthusiasm, then he proceeded to open countless doors for me, doors that quite clearly would never have opened without him. I shamelessly dropped his name at every turn because the response was always, "If you're a friend of John's, that's all right with me." I hope he and his wife Eileen know the extent of the esteem in which he is held by people who have worked with him, and the extent of the admiration with which they are both regarded by my wife and me.

I am also grateful to the many men and women who so kindly assisted me on this project: in the United States, at the Department of Justice, U.S. Customs, the Federal Bureau of Investigation (FBI), the Drug Enforcement Administration (DEA), the Criminal Investigation Division of the Internal Revenue Service (IRS), the office of the District Attorney for New York County, and the offices of the United States Attorneys in Boston, Newark, New York, Atlanta, Miami, Houston, San Diego, Los Angeles, San Francisco, and Seattle; in Great Britain, at HM Customs, the National Criminal Intelligence Service (NCIS), and the Metropolitan Police; in Canada, at the Office of the Solicitor General, the Royal Canadian Mounted Police (RCMP), and the Canadian High Commission in London; in Australia, at the Office of the Attorney General and the National Crimes

Authority (NCA); and throughout the rest of Europe, in various law enforcement and financial regulation authorities.

For their time, encouragement, and support, I would particularly like to thank Peter Nunez, former assistant secretary of the Treasury, Enforcement; Roger Urbanski, Armando Ramirez, and Bob Gerber of U.S. Customs; Fran Dyer of the Criminal Investigation Division of the IRS; United States attorneys Alan Bersin, Kendall Coffey, Faith Hochberg, Eric Holder, Gaynelle Griffin Jones, Donald Stern, Mary Jo White, and Joe Whitley; assistant United States attorneys Mark Bartlett, Cyndi Bashant, Joseph Guerra III, Linda McNamara, Wilmer Parker III, and Robert Stahl; and various staff members at the offices of the United States attorneys, including Susan Snook in Miami and Marvin Smilon in the Southern District of New York; Brian Bruh and Anna Fotias of the Financial Crimes Enforcement Network (FINCEN); Special Agent Albert "Skip" Latson of the DEA; Tom Cash, formerly of the DEA and now with the Kroll Agency; Dianne Carr of the American Bar Association; and attorneys Gerald Lefcourt and John Zwerling.

In Canada, SSgt. Yvon Gagnon and Sgt. Yvon Poirier, both of the RCMP. In Britain, Charles Hill, Graham Saltmarsh, Terry Burke, and Tim Wren at NCIS; Billy Miller and Tony Curtis of the Metropolitan Police; Tony Brightwell of Bishops International; Dr. Barry A. K. Rider, Executive Director, Centre for International Documentation on Organized and Economic Crime, Jesus College, Cambridge; Rowan Bosworth-Davies of Richards Butler; Bob Denmark, Graham White, and Trevor Taylor of the Royal Lancashire Constabulary; Lucy Lloyd and Henry Stewart Conference Studies for documentation on their money laundering conferences; Michael Hyland, head of Midland Group Security; John Drage of the Bank of England; Eric and Lynn Ellen of the International Maritime Bureau; and Michael Ashe, attorney at law.

In Switzerland, Ticino State Prosecutor Dick Marty and journalist Pascal Auschlain; in the Netherlands, Jan Van Doorn of the Dutch Centrale Recherche Informatiedienst (CRI); on the Isle of Man, Mark Solly; and in France, Rene Wack, chief of the Central Office for the Repression of Major Financial Crimes, and attorney-at-law Ron Sokol.

I also wish to thank some fifty bankers around the world, who gave me their time — many of them speaking frankly enough about specific practices and case studies to jeopardize their own positions. Research for a book like this often gets done on the understanding that certain sources, such as these bankers, never be identified. This means that there are some I cannot thank openly. As matter of fact there are several, not including the aforementioned bankers, to whom I owe a very special debt. Spread out around the world, doing whatever it is they do, they were an invaluable reservoir of information. Needless to say, a few weren't necessarily pleased I'd managed to locate them, and agreed to speak with me only on the clear understanding that I would not help anyone else find them. Others, who might have been easier to come across, spoke with me only after I agreed that no one would ever know who they were or what they'd said. Without wishing to make this sound overly dramatic, it's an easy condition to accept when you understand that my divulging any information about these sources could quite easily turn out to be hazardous to their health. I wholly respect their wishes. But I do have a touch of regret that I cannot thank them individually by name. After all, I am not just indebted to them for their confidences, I genuinely respect their trust.

Finally, many thanks to my old pal Gerald Chappell, attorney at law, for his consistently sound advice; Nick Webb at Simon & Schuster in London; Tim Bent at Arcade in New York; agent extraordinaire Mildred Marmur; and, of course, La Benayoun.

JR/New York, 1996

BIBLIOGRAPHY

BOOKS

Adams, J.: *The Financing of Terror;* New English Library, London, 1986.

Adams, James Ring, and Douglas Frantz: *A Full Service Bank: How BCCI Stole Billions Around the World;* Pocket Books, New York, 1992.

Alexander, Shana: *The Pizza Connection;* Weidenfeld, New York, 1988.

Allsop, Kenneth: *The Bootleggers;* Hutchinson, London, 1961.

Anderson, Annelise Graebner: *The Business of Organized Crime;* Hoover Institution Press, Stanford, 1979.

Balsamo, William, and George Carpozi, Jr.,: *Crime Incorporated;* W. H. Allen, London, 1988.

Beschloss, Michael: *Kennedy Versus Khrushchev: The Crisis Years 1960–1963;* HarperCollins, New York, 1991.

Black, David: *Triad Takeover;* Sidgwick & Jackson, London, 1991.

Booth, Martin: *The Triads;* Grafton Books, London, 1990.

Brashler, William: *The Don;* Harper & Row, New York, 1977.

Bresler, Fenton: *Trail of the Triads;* Weidenfeld, London, 1985.

Burdick, Thomas: *Blue Thunder;* Simon & Schuster, London, 1990.

Campbell, Duncan: *That Was Business, This Is Personal;* Secker & Warburg, London, 1990.

Charbonneau, Jean-Pierre: *The Canadian Connection;* Optimum, Ottawa, 1976.

Clark, T., and J. J. Tigue: *Dirty Money;* Millington Books, London, 1975.

Clifford, Clark: *Counsel to the President;* Random House, New York, 1991.

Clutterbuck, R.: *Terrorism, Drugs and Crime in Europe after 1992;* Routledge & Kegan Paul, London, 1990.

Colodny, Len, and Robert Gettlin: *Silent Coup: The Removal of Richard Nixon;* Gollancz, London, 1991.

Cummings, John, and Ernest Volkman: *Goombata;* Little, Brown, Boston, 1990.

Dean, John: *Blind Ambition;* Simon & Schuster, New York, 1976.

De Grazia, Jessica: *DEA: The War Against Drugs;* BBC Books, London, 1991.

Di Fonzo, Luigi: *St. Peter's Banker: Michele Sindona;* Franklin Watts, New York, 1983.

Dinges, John: *Our Man in Panama;* Random House, New York, 1990.

Eddy, Paul: *The Cocaine Wars;* Century Hutchinson, London, 1988.

Ehrenfeld, Rachel: *Evil Money;* HarperCollins, New York, 1992.

Ehrenfeld, Rachel: *Narco Terrorism;* Basic Books, New York, 1990.

Eisenberg, Dennis, with Uri Dann and Eli Landau: *Meyer Lansky;* Paddington, London, 1979.

Eppolito, Lou, and Bob Drury: *Mafia Cop;* Simon & Schuster, New York, 1992.

Faith, Nicholas: *Safety in Numbers: The Mysterious World of Swiss Banking;* Hamish Hamilton, London, 1984.

Frances, Diane: *Contrepreneurs;* Macmillan, Toronto, 1988.

Franklin, R.: *Profits of Deceit;* Heinemann, London, 1990.

Franzese, Michael, and Dary Matera: *Quitting the Mob;* HarperCollins, New York, 1992.

Freemantle, Brian: *The Fix;* Michael Joseph, London, 1985.

Gardner, Paul: *The Drug Smugglers;* Robert Hale, London, 1989.

Garrison, Jim: *A Heritage of Stone;* Putnam's Sons, New York, 1970.

Garrison, Jim: *On the Trail of the Assassins;* Penguin, London, 1992.

Gugliotta, Guy, and Jeff Leen: *Kings of Cocaine;* Simon & Schuster, New York, 1989.

Gurwin, Larry: *The Calvi Affair;* Macmillan, London, 1983.

Hess, Henner: *Mafia and Mafiosi;* Saxon Hall, New York, 1973.

Hogg, Andrew, Jim McDougal, and Robin Morgan: *Bullion;* Penguin, London, 1988.

Ianni, Francis, and Elizabeth Reuss-Ianni: *The Crime Society;* New American Library, New York, 1976.

Intriago, Charles A.: *International Money Laundering;* Eurostudy, London, 1991.

Jennings, Andrew, Paul Lashmar, and Vyv Simson: *Scotland Yard's Cocaine Connection;* Cape, London, 1990.

Kaplan, David: *Yakuza;* Queen Anne, London, 1987.

Karchmer, Cliff: *Illegal Money Laundering: A Strategy & Resource Guide for Law Enforcement Agencies;* Police Executive Resources, Washington, D.C., 1988.

Katcher, Leo: *The Big Bankroll;* Harper & Row, New York, 1959.

Kempe, Frederick: *Divorcing the Dictator: America's Bungled Affair with Noriega;* Putnam, New York, 1990.

Kobler, John: *Capone;* Michael Joseph, London, 1972.

Kochan, Nick, with Bob Whittington and Mark Potts: *Dirty Money: The Inside Story of the World's Sleaziest Bank;* National Press Books, Washington, D.C., 1992.

Koster, R. M., and G. S. Borbon: *In the Time of the Tyrants;* Secker & Warburg, London, 1990.

Kwitney, Jonathan: *The Crimes of Patriots;* Touchstone, New York, 1987.

Kwitney, Jonathan: *The Fountain Pen Conspiracy;* Knopf, New York, 1973.

Lacy, Robert: *Little Man;* Little, Brown, New York, 1991.

Lance, Burt: *The Truth of the Matter;* Summit, New York, 1991.

Lane, Mark: *Plausible Denial;* Plexus, London, 1992.

Lernoux, Penny: *In Banks We Trust;* Anchor Press, New York, 1984.

Loftus, John, and Emily McIntyre: *Valhallas Wake;* Atlantic Monthly Press, New York, 1989.

McAlary, Mark: *Crack War;* Robinson Publishing, London, 1990.

McCarl, Henry N.: *Economic Impact of the Underground Economy: A Bibliography on Money Laundering and Other Aspects of Off-the-Record Economic Transactions;* Vance Bibliographies, Monticello, Ill., 1989.

Marchetti, Victor, and John D. Marks: *The CIA and the Cult of Intelligence;* Dell, New York, *1980.*

Milgate, Brian: *The Cochin Connection;* Chatto & Windus, London, 1987.

Mills, James: *The Underground Empire;* Doubleday, Garden City, N.Y., 1986.

Mustain, Gene, and Jerry Capeci: *Mob Star: The Story of John Gotti;* Franklin Watts, New York, 1988.

Nash, Jay Robert: *Encyclopedia of World Crime;* Crime Books, New York, 1989.

Nash, Jay Robert: *Hustlers and Con Men;* Evans, New York, 1976.

Naylor, R. T.: *Hot Money and the Politics of Debt;* Unwin Hyman, London, 1987.

Naylor, R. T.: *Bankers, Bagmen and Bandits;* Black Rose, New York, 1990.

Nicholl, Charles: *The Fruit Palace;* Heineman, London, 1985.

Nown, Graham: *The English Godfather;* Ward Lock, London, 1987.

O'Brien, Joseph: *Boss of Bosses;* Simon & Schuster, New York, 1991.

Perisco, Joseph: *Casey;* Penguin, New York, 1990.

Poppa, Terrence E.: *Drug Lord;* Pharos Books, New York, 1990.

Posner, Gerald: *Warlords of Crime;* Queen Anne, London, 1989.

Possamai, Mario: *Money on the Run;* Penguin, Toronto, 1992.

Powers, Thomas: *The Man Who Kept the Secrets: Richard Helms and the CIA;* Pocket Books, New York, 1981.

Powis, Robert: *The Money Launderers;* Probus Publishing, Chicago, 1992.

Prados, John: *Keepers of the Keys: A History of the National Security Council from Truman to Bush;* Morrow, New York, 1991.

Prince, Carl, and Mollie Keller: *The US Customs Service: A Bicentennial History;* Department of the Treasury, Washington, D.C., 1989.

Reader's Digest: *The Greatest Cases of Interpol;* Reader's Digest Books, New York, 1982.

Roark, Garland: *The Coin of Contraband;* Doubleday, Garden City, N.Y., 1984.

Robinson, Jeffrey: *Minus Millionaires;* Grafton, London, 1988.

Scheim, David: *The Mafia Killed President Kennedy;* W. H. Allen, London, 1988.

Shannon, Elaine: *Desperadoes;* Viking, New York, 1988.

Short, Martin: *Crime Inc;* Thames Mandarin, London, 1991.

Short, Martin: *Lundy;* Grafton, London, 1992.

Sterling, Claire: *The Mafia;* Hamish Hamilton, London, 1990.

Stewart, James B.: *Den of Thieves;* Simon & Schuster, London, 1992.

Tanzi, Vito, ed.: *The Underground Economy in the United States and Abroad;* collected articles for the International Money Fund, Lexington Books, Lexington, Mass., 1982.

Truell, Peter, and Larry Gurwin: *BCCI;* Bloomsbury, London, 1992.

Tyler, Gus: *Organized Crime in America;* University of Michigan Press, Ann Arbor, Mich., 1962.

Villa, John K.: *Banking Crimes: Fraud, Money Laundering and Embezzlement;* Clark Boardman, New York, 1987.

Walter, Ingo: *Secret Money: The Shadowy World of Tax Evasion, Capital Flight and Fraud;* Unwin Hyman, London, 1989.

Woodward, Bob: *Veil: The Secret Wars of the CIA;* Simon & Schuster, New York, 1987.

Woodward, Bob, and Carl Bernstein: *All the President's Men;* Secker & Warburg, London, 1974.

Woodward, Bob, and Carl Bernstein: *The Final Days;* Avon Books, New York, 1976.

PERIODICALS

ABA Banking Journal:

Aug. 1995: "Son of CRF: Suspicious activity form proposed."

May 1994: "Treasury gets direct banker input on Bank Secrecy Act."

June 1993: "Dialup help for Bank Secrecy Act compliance."

Feb. 1993: "Money laundering law is (so far) mostly a blessing; new legislation could provide some significant relief to bankers, but the regs aren't written yet."

July 1992: "When money laundering law meets environment risks."

Jan. 1991: "Spotting and handling suspicious transactions."

Dec. 1990: "Treasury takes next step on wire transfers."

March 1990: "From the money laundering front."

March 1990: "Stop the smurfs."

Nov. 1989: "Bank secrecy revisited."

July 1985: "What you should know about money laundering law."

Accounting Today:

Jan. 3, 1994: "Quik Tax chief charged with fraud."

July 19, 1993: "SEC suspends Oregon CPA."

American Banker:

Nov. 22, 1995: "Money police face tough beat on Internet."

Aug. 3, 1995: "Tribal casinos face money-laundering regs."

July 19, 1995: "Technology best bet for avoiding risks of anti-laundering rules."

May 18, 1995: "Slimmer currency transaction report set."

April 20, 1995: "U.S. will lean on banks, nonbanks in battle against money laundering."

March 30, 1995: "Coming soon: 'Know your customer' rules to fight money laundering."

Feb. 16, 1995: "Fed aide says one-shot criminal referral form will ease red tape."

Jan. 19, 1995: "Laundering rules seen as too little, too late."

Dec. 15, 1994: "Citibank helps U.S. prosecution and ends up with a PR nightmare."

Dec. 8, 1994: "American Express Bank paying $14M to settle fraud charges."

Dec. 5, 1994: "Treasury extends laundering rules to casinos."

Dec. 1, 1994: "Treasury's crime unit undergoing a face-lift."

Nov. 3, 1994: "Treasury to step up war on money launderers."

Oct. 20, 1994: "Treasury eases banks' burden in fight against laundering."

Oct. 6, 1994: "U.S. denies a report it's probing brokerages for money laundering."

Sept. 21, 1994: "Bill would hamper laundering while slashing banks paperwork."

Sept. 8, 1994: "Program shows tricks of trade in laundering."

Sept. 1, 1994: "Justice division on laundering to be dissolved."

Aug. 29, 1994: "Crime act to be tough on card laundering, telemarketing fraud."

July 25, 1994: "Peter G. Djinis, Department of the Treasury, Director of office of financial enforcement."

June 30, 1994: "Laundering experts say banks shouldn't be afraid to close suspect accounts."

June 21, 1994: "Treasury aide chosen to lead money laundering task force."

May 5, 1994: "Money-laundering cop focuses on lawbreakers."

April 8, 1994: "GAO: Disclosure law scaring money launderers from banks."

March 17, 1994: "Wipeout of laundering unit opposed."

March 14, 1994: "Private sector advisory committee to study money laundering laws."

March 10, 1994: "IRS jumped gun in warnings about anti-laundering law."

March 1, 1994: "House subcommittee to vote on laundering bill."

Feb. 25, 1994: "Ex-director convicted in con scheme is sought."

Jan. 12, 1994: "Top court makes prosecution of currency cases tougher."

Jan. 6, 1994: "FBI forms unit to fight money laundering."

Dec. 22, 1993: "Indictment: head of tax service bilked banks."

Dec. 21, 1993: "A Swiss bank confesses to laundering drug money."

Dec. 8, 1993: "Eased cash-reports rule seen slashing red tape."

Nov. 18, 1993: "For Treasury's point man on money laundering, new responsibilities recall an early triumph."

Oct. 21, 1993: "Old-fashioned weapon urged for the fight against money laundering — common sense."

Oct. 19, 1993: "U.S. hopes to lighten compliance burden of money laundering laws."

Oct. 8, 1993: "Gonzalez money laundering bill reduces bank currency reports."

Sept. 30, 1993: "Form for reporting crimes simplified."

Sept. 23, 1993: "Treasury planning changes in money-laundering rules."

Sept. 16, 1993: "Bankers vie for a say in war on money laundering."

Sept. 2, 1993: "Treasury Dept. unveils rules on wire transfers."

Aug. 26, 1993: "He's the ABA's point man on money laundering."

Aug. 19, 1993: "Money laundering goes on with ease, U.S. aide says."

Aug. 12, 1993: "Fed, Treasury seek to standardize wire-transfer record keeping."

July 9, 1993: "How to avoid being stuck with a laundering bill."

July 9, 1993: "Treasury Department to give Texas police access to cash transaction records."

July 6, 1993: "Former thrift owner guilty of fraud."

June 11, 1993: "Price software might help detect laundering."

June 2, 1993: "Bankers wary of new rules on wire transfers."

May 26, 1993: "Agencies moving to ease rules on currency transaction reports."

April 29, 1993: "Banks get easy access to latest data on money laundering."

Feb. 17, 1993: "Cross-border banking faulted for laxness."

Jan. 22, 1993: "Norwest unit to pay $328,000 in money-laundering case."

Jan. 21, 1993: "Marine Midland says U.S. wrongfully seized cash."

Jan. 4, 1993: "Dallas developer indicted again on federal bank fraud charges."

American Metal Market:

Aug. 30, 1993: "Nigerians seek Mexican bank laundering."

April 19, 1993: "Former PGP staffer admits $7.8M fraud."

American Spectator:

June 1992: "The great ruble scam."

Sept. 1988: "Losing the drug war."

Atlantic:

Jan. 1986: "Coping with cocaine."

Baltimore Business Journal:

Feb. 10, 1995: "Muller moves to stop money launderers."

June 25, 1990: "Ruling links 1st National with CIA: suit names CIA as a codefendant."

Banker:

Aug. 1995: "Banks in a spin: Money laundering."

Nov. 1994: "The buck never stops."

April 1990: "What's in the suitcase?"

Bank Management:

April 1991: "Wire transfer proposal: Treasury considers banker concerns."

March 1991: "Money laundering experts team up, on and off the job."

Banker's Magazine:

March–April 1990: "Money laundering."

Banker's Monthly:

June 1988: "Panama's banks take it on the chin."

Barron's:

July 11, 1983: "Where hot money hides: Havens spring up all over the globe."

Boston Business Journal:

July 15, 1991: "Brockton Financial Services."

Boston College International and Comparative Law Review:

Winter 1991: "Bankers, guns, and money."

Boston Magazine:

July 1990: "Bad influence: The trial of Joe Balliro."

Bottomline:

March–April 1992: "The bank secrecy law demands delicate decision making."

Business:

June 1988: "Underworld hijacks underground banking."

Business Horizons:

Sept.–Oct. 1990: "The continuing expansion of RICO in business litigation."

Business Journal of New Jersey:

November 1990: "A crazy scheme?"

Business Journal Serving Charlotte and the Metropolitan Area:

April 13, 1992: "Lawyer's conviction chills legal community."

The Business Journal Serving Greater Sacramento:

June 4, 1990: "Local money launderer prison bound."

Business Journal Serving Phoenix & the Valley of the Sun:

March 11, 1991: "Agreement reached on legislation aimed at money laundering."

Business Week:

March 1, 1993: "Cleaning up corruption is clobbering Italy Inc."

April 13, 1992: "How did so many get away with so much for so long?"

April 6, 1992: "Germany's brash new import: Dirt money."

Dec. 16, 1991: "Zorro, Gorby and Howard the duck."

Oct. 7, 1991: "Could China become a least favored nation?"

Sept. 23, 1991: "Psst, wanna buy a bank? How about a few dozen?"

Aug. 26, 1991: "Can Noriega drag the CIA into the dock with him?"

July 22, 1991: "The long and winding road to BCCI's dead end."

May 20, 1991: "The days are numbered for secret accounts."

Aug. 27, 1990: "Centrust, the Saudi and the Luxembourg bank."

Aug. 27, 1990: "Insider trading: The intricate case of Ellis AG."

June 4, 1990: "Grabbing dirty money."

Feb. 19, 1990: "Gambling big to nail Noriega."

Jan. 22, 1990: "The Noriega 'treasure chest.'"

Oct. 2, 1989: "The drug war European style."

May 1, 1989: "He started at the top and worked his way down."

April 17, 1989: "Getting banks to just say 'no.'"

Oct. 24, 1988: "This bank may have been a laundry, too."

May 23, 1988: "The Oklahoma town that drug money bought."

April 18, 1988: "The Sicilian Mafia is still going strong."

Sept. 16, 1985: "Big brother wants to see your bank book."

Sept. 9, 1985: "The bank sting that's rocking Puerto Rico."

March 25, 1985: "Money laundering: The defense gets a star witness."

March 18, 1985: "Enlisting banks in the war on drugs"; "The long and growing list of hot money havens"; "In Colombia, dirty money passes through very clean hands"; "Money laundering: Who's involved, how it works, and where it's spreading."

March 11, 1985: "Two brokerages get tangled in the money laundering net."

March 4, 1985: "Bank of Boston."

Feb. 25, 1985: "An all out attack on banks that launder money."

Dec. 24, 1984: "How Deak & Co. got caught in its own tangled web."

Business Wire:

Oct. 3, 1995: "Federal grand jury returned fifteen count indictment."

July 17, 1995: "President of nationwide tax preparation service sentenced in one of the largest ever electronic filing cases."

May 1, 1995: "Yerardi pleads guilty to federal racketeering, loansharking, and money laundering."

Chain Drug Review:

July 18, 1994: "Monus trial ends in hung jury; tampering charged."

June 20, 1994: "Former Phar-Mor execs square off."

Feb. 15, 1993: "Monus faces 129-count indictment."

Columbia Journalism Review:

March–April 1993: "Dead right: The assassination of journalist Manuel de Dios Unanue."

Sept.–Oct. 1991: "Follow the drug money."

Commuter-Regional Airline News:

May 25, 1992: "L'Express owner gets prison term for money laundering."

Contemporary Crises:

March 1990: "The Chinese laundry."

Crain's Cleveland Business:

June 13, 1994: "Fired Eaton workers indicted."

Criminal Law Forum:

Spring 1991: "Money laundering,an investigory perspective"; "Convention on laundering."

Dallas Business Journal:

April 19, 1991: "Feds accused of misconduct in probe: Defendants in money laundering case claim agents hired prostitute."

Sept. 28, 1990: "Reese deals probed as suits mount."

May 7, 1990: "Law firms fight over allegations of misconduct."

Dealer Business:

April 1993: "Crackdown on drugs; though most auto dealerships don't realize it, they face a threat potentially much greater than lagging sales or declining profits."

Dispatch:

March 2, 1992: "Fact sheet: combating drug money-laundering."

Drug Store News:

Feb. 15, 1993: "Phar-Mor's Monus, Finn charged."

Economic Progress Report:

June 1990: "Action on money laundering."

Economist:

June 17, 1995: "One down, more to go."

June 25, 1994: "Money launderers on the line."

March 12, 1994: "Back to the future: Panama."

Aug. 1, 1992: "The Escobar escape."

May 9, 1992: "Cash at any price."

April 25, 1992: "Cleaning up the rupees."

April 4, 1992: "Calling earth, calling earth: the Noriega trial."

Feb. 22, 1992: "Cleaning up whose act?"

Aug. 3, 1991: "The opening-up of BCCI; send for Richard Hannay; some of it will prove false but enough of the BCCI-spies story looks true to give the intelligence agencies some tough questions to answer."

June 15, 1991: "Gilded cage: Pablo Escobar, head of Colombia's most important drug cartel, builds the prison where he will be held."

March 16, 1991: "Oh, my brass plate in the sun."

Dec. 1, 1990: "Bombs and blackmail."

Oct. 27, 1990: "Closing down the launderette."

July 7, 1990: "A clockwork future for Finanzplatz Schweiz?"

June 9, 1990: "Crime cracker."

June 2, 1990: "A president with guts, and a bullet-proof waistcoat."

May 5, 1990: "Flushing funny money into the open."

May 5, 1990: "The muzziest of wars."

Jan. 27, 1990: "How BCCI grew and grew."

Dec. 9, 1989: "Stormy weather: Banking licenses and politics of Montserrat."

Oct. 21, 1989: "Follow the money."

Oct. 21, 1989: "On the run."

Sept. 16, 1989: "Gun law: Colombia."

Sept. 9, 1989: "Real war: The Medellín cartel in Colombia."

Aug. 26, 1989: "Colombia's cocaine overdose."

July 8, 1989: "Clive of Havana: General Arnaldo Ochoa Sanchez convicted of drug trafficking."

June 24, 1989: "Limitless discretion: A survey of private banking; money talks, wealth whispers."

March 11, 1989: "Dirty laundry."

March 4, 1989: "Whitewash or crackdown?"

Dec. 17, 1988: "BCCI stands accused."

Dec. 17, 1988: "Love, honour, obey and resign."

Nov. 12, 1988: "Check your case, sir?"

Oct. 15, 1988: "Till drugs do us part."

Aug. 27, 1988: "Five tiny secrets of success."

Aug. 20, 1988: "Cleaning up dirty laundering."

Aug. 6, 1988: "Columbus's islands."

Feb. 28, 1987: "Taking crooks to the cleaners."

Editor & Publisher:

March 19, 1994: "Maxwell's money laundry."

EFT Report:

Oct. 26, 1994: "Averting money laundering, and federal investigations."

Esquire:

Oct. 1983: "Cocaine, how you can bank on it."

EuroBusiness:

Nov. 1994: "Squeaky clean."

Oct. 1993: "Baby Doc's big haul."

June 1990: "Cleaning up money launderers."

Euromoney:

July 1989: "Can the UBS colonels win the overseas battle?"

Dec. 1988: "Sailing into the grand harbour."

March 1987: "Laundering law leaps across borders."

Europe 2000:

March 1990: "Commission declares war on money laundering."

European Journal of International Affairs:

Winter 1989: "Drug money, hot money and debt."

Far Eastern Economic Review:

March 15, 1990: "Japan: Dope dealers delight."

FBI Law Enforcement Bulletin:

March 1993: "Forensic examination of money laundering records."

Federal Reserve Bulletin:

July 1993: "Statements to the Congress."

Financial Market Trends:

June 1994: "Financial action task force on money laundering: Annual report 1993–1994."

The Financial Post:

Nov. 12, 1994: "Too easy to wash money in Canada."

July 6, 1991: "Bank shut in global crackdown."

Financial Services Report:

August 29, 1990: "Money laundering deterrence costs banks millions of dollars, survey shows."

Financial World:

Feb. 1, 1994: "Dirty dollars."

May 15, 1990: "Dr. Shoals."

March 21, 1989: "The IRS: The gang that can't shoot straight."

Nov. 29, 1988: "The bank that knows too much."

March 18, 1986: "Secret money: The world of international financial secrecy."

Sept. 18, 1985: "The flip side of the coin."

Forbes:

Aug. 14, 1995: "Salad oil, $720."

June 7, 1993: "Closing in: Tracking down laundered money in a consumer fraud case."

April 26, 1993: "Cash capital: Los Angeles replaces Miami as city where most money laundering activity occurs."

July 23, 1990: "The Americas."

July 23, 1990: "Middle East."

Nov. 13, 1989: "The paradox of antidrug enforcement."

Oct. 30, 1989: "In the all out drug war, a low cost blow to the jugular."

May 29, 1989: "Scam capital of the world."

April 17, 1989: "The Bulgarian connection."

Dec. 26, 1988: "Drug smuggler's startup."

Nov. 14, 1988: "Too rich to ignore."

June 1, 1987: "The biggest drug bust."

April 6, 1987: "Stash accounting."

Oct. 6, 1986: "See no evil."

May 5, 1986: "T-man videos."

April 7, 1986: "New hub for an old web."

Sept. 23, 1985: "America's hottest export: Funny money stocks."

Sept. 9, 1985: "How the smart crooks use plastic."

Jan. 28, 1985: "Guilt by association."

Dec. 5, 1983: "Everybody's favorite laundryman."

Foreign Affairs:

July–August 1994: "The drug money maze."

Fortune:

July 25, 1994: "Ask Mr. Statistics."

Nov. 5, 1990: "The S&L felons."

June 20, 1988: "The drug trade."

March 2, 1987: "Turmoil time in the casino business."

April 1, 1985: "Money laundering: More shocks ahead"; "Editor's desk."

April 4, 1983: "The feds eye the herd: Merrill Lynch swears off cash."

George Washington Journal of International Law and Economics:

Issue 3, 1989: "Dollar diplomacy."

Governing:

Oct. 1990: "To catch the drug kingpins, follow the money."

Government Computer News:

> Sept. 20, 1993: "Project Gateway gives state cops access to financial data."

Insight:

> Oct. 2, 1995: "Federal protection system could double as spy scam."

> July 23, 1990: "Cleaning out money launderers."

> Aug. 21, 1989: "Drug money soils cleanest hands."

International Bank Accountant:

> Feb. 15, 1993: "New guidance for U.K. accountants strengthens government's curb on money laundering."

International Financial Law Review:

> March 1990: "Bank liability under the UN drug trafficking convention."

International Management:

> May 1991: "Anxiety in the Alps."

Jewelers Circular Keystone:

> Oct. 1991: "Feds nab money launderers."

> May 1991: "LU Kustom indicted in money-laundering case."

Journal of Accountancy:

> Aug. 1995: "IRS cracking down on reports of cash transactions over $10,000."

> Feb. 1992: "IRS says more businesses are complying with anti-money-laundering rules."

> March 1990: "The telltale signs of money laundering."

Journal of the American Medical Association:

> Feb. 16, 1994: "Gifts from industry: Laundering money or supporting education."

Kansas City Business Journal:

> March 26, 1993: "Insurance executive's lawyer sees indictment as vendetta."

> Aug. 2, 1991: "FBI eyes financing efforts for topless bar."

Sept. 25, 1989: "Ex-AMC exec indicted over embezzlement; money laundering, tax evasion also alleged."

Kyodo:

July 29, 1992: "Bankers group compiles manual to tackle money laundering."

Law Enforcement Bulletin:

April 1990: "Laundering drug money."

Life:

March 1990: "Our man in Panama: The creation of a thug."

Los Angeles Business Journal:

Oct. 3, 1994: "Marathon council disclosure draws mixed response."

June 3, 1991: "Cash pay going under the table erodes economy."

July 13, 1987: "Barry Minkow's favorable treatment in press exposes reporters' own vulnerability to fraud."

Maclean's:

April 10, 1995: "'I'm a hostage': One Canadian's legal nightmare in Peru."

Sept. 12, 1994: "Drug-busting dramas: police forces mount two spectacular raids."

Aug. 5, 1991: "A scandal in waiting."

Oct. 23, 1989: "The laundering game: Cleaning dirty money is crucial"; "Canada's crackdown: A new law has led to more seizures"; "Grabbing the drug bounty: The Miami tally is $150 million"; "Hiding the drug money: Criminals are using Canada to launder billions of dollars in drug profits."

Sept. 11, 1989: "Terror in the drug world."

Sept. 4, 1989: "The cocaine war: Washington and Bogotá battle the drug lords."

May 29, 1989: "Battling crime through the banks."

Oct. 31, 1988: "A dangerous trail: Police pursue profits from drug sales."

Nov. 2, 1987: "Cashin' in on ill-gotten gains."

Aug. 17, 1987: "The criminal element."

March 25, 1985: "Trailing laundered cash."

Feb. 11, 1985: "Questions behind locked doors."

April 4, 1983: "Offshore banking secrets."

MacWEEK:

March 29, 1993: "MacFriends duo to be sentenced."

Management Today:

May 1990: "The Mafia: The long reach of the international Sicilian Mafia."

Money:

Nov. 1989: "Life styles of the rich and heinous."

Mother Jones:

March–April 1994: "Kafka's banker: Bob Maxwell's nightmarish ride from banker to bartender."

Multichannel News:

Aug. 19, 1991: "Magness and Romrell tied to BCCI affiliate."

Nation:

Oct. 7, 1991: "The C.I.A. and the cocaine coup."

Feb. 4, 1991: "Tinker, tailor, banker, spy."

Nov. 19, 1990: "The looting decade: S&Ls, big banks and other triumphs of capitalism."

July 9, 1990: "Minority Report: CIA involvement."

March 26, 1990: "Drugs."

Nov. 13, 1989: "Get Noriega but don't touch the bankers."

Oct. 2, 1989: "Contradictions of cocaine capitalism."

Aug. 27, 1988: "Dealing with Noriega."

Feb. 20, 1988: "Our man in Panama."

Nov. 7, 1987: "The crimes of patriots: A true tale of dope, dirty money, and the CIA."

Sept. 5, 1987: "How the drug czar got away."

Aug. 29, 1987: "The Iran Contra connection: Secret teams and covert operations in the Reagan era."

Feb. 21, 1987: "Crazy Charlie — Carlos Lehder Rivas."

Sept. 6, 1986: "The offshore money: Swiss banks still sell secrecy."

Feb. 23, 1985: "Stop blaming the system."

Feb. 18, 1984: "The Miami connection."

Nation's Cities Weekly:

July 24, 1989: "Crime pays off for Torrance Calif."

National Review:

Sept. 11, 1995: "Gekko."

March 30, 1992: "BCCI and Senator Kerry revisited."

Dec. 16, 1991: "Godfather Fidel."

Oct. 7, 1991: "The real scandal: BCCI."

National Underwriter Property & Casualty-Risk & Benefits Management:

June 24, 1991: "La. regulator sent to prison; called amoral."

June 11, 1990: "Grand jury indicts La. commissioner in Champion case."

New Internationalist:

Oct. 1991: "How to make dirty money squeaky clean."

New Leader:

Sept. 18, 1989: "A country under siege: Fighting anarchy in Colombia."

New Republic:

Nov. 27, 1989: "The kingdom of cocaine: The shocking story of Colombia's habit."

Sept. 18, 1989: "A mess in the Andes: Columbia's government-by-cocaine."

June 12, 1989: "Dear Manny."

March 13, 1989: "Robbin' Hoods: How the big banks spell debt 'relief.'"

April 15, 1985: "Inside dope in El Salvador: Where did d'Aubuisson's pal come up with $6 million in cash?"

Newsweek:

Nov. 16, 1992: "A CIA-BNL link?"

Oct. 12, 1992: "The last martini."

Aug. 21, 1991: "The CIA and BCCI"; "The bank that prays together."

Aug. 5, 1991: "What did they know — and when?"

March 18, 1991: "The pain of a power broker."

April 10, 1989: "A drug crackdown in the Alps"; "A bungled deal with Panama."

March 27, 1989: "Scandal in Switzerland."

Feb. 22, 1988: "The dictator on the dock."

Sept. 23, 1985: "Hong Kong's funny money."

May 20, 1985: "E.F. Hutton: It's not over yet."

Feb. 25, 1985: "Banking by paper bag."

March 28, 1983: "Trying to shut down the money laundry"; "The grandma Mafia on trial."

New York:

Aug. 26, 1991: "A Noriega laundry."

Jan. 22, 1990: "The Panama connection."

Oct. 31, 1983: "Money laundering: How crooks recycle $80 billion a year in dirty money."

Jan. 23, 1978: "Ladies of the night clean up their act."

New York Times Magazine:

March 29, 1992: "Where the money washes up."

New York University Journal of International Law and Politics:

Summer 1984: "The use of offshore institutions to facilitate criminal activities in the United States."

Penthouse:

April 1984: "Blood money."

People:

Aug. 6, 1990: "A conspiracy of crowns."

June 19, 1989: "Masters of deception: A prominent Indiana family in exile is accused of running a drug ring."

Philadelphia Magazine:

July 1985: "The day they raided Shearson."

Pittsburgh Business Times:

Oct. 14, 1991: "Coastal Marketing owner pleads guilty to $2.2 million loan scam."

March 18, 1991: "Local businessmen indicted in alleged drug-money deals."

Playboy:

May 1990: "Just say nothing, Noriega; we created the monster we've now propped up on trial. Could be kind of awkward."

Nov. 1989: "Inside job: The looting of America's savings and loans."

Nov. 1987: "The crimes of patriots."

Progressive:

June 1992: "The banker who said no to the CIA."

Reader's Digest:

Sept. 1978: "The Swiss connection."

Real Estate Today:

Sept. 1993: "Don't be blind to the buyer's money source."

Regardie's Magazine:

April–May 1991: "What did Clark Clifford know, and when did he know it?"

March 1990: "R.I.P. DRG: The rise and fall of a real estate dynasty."

San Antonio Business Journal:

June 21, 1991: "Feds crack down on exchange houses."

San Diego Business Journal:

Oct. 8, 1990: "Silberman is fined for money laundering role."

Security Management:

May 1990: "When the walls come tumbling down."

Social Studies Review:

June 1991: "Big crime: The international drug trade."

South Florida Business Journal:

July 8, 1994: "Miamians convicted in loan scam."

State Legislatures:

Feb. 1994: "Texas cleans up money laundering."

Supermarket News:

Nov. 1, 1993: "Court papers detail Leonard scheme."

SwissBusiness:

May–June 1990: "Keeping to the code: Switzerland's bankers have set up their own good-conduct guidelines."

Jan.–Feb. 1990: "Tackling a tarnished image."

Sunday Correspondent Magazine:

July 1990: "The Florida sting."

Time:

June 19, 1995: "Kingpin checkmate."

Nov. 7, 1994: "Sweet, sweet surrender."

Oct. 12, 1992: "Follow the money."

April 20, 1992: "A worrisome brand of Japanese investor — Money laundering by the Japanese mob: The Yakuza."

March 23, 1992: "Drug money fears halt state bond sale."

Dec. 16, 1991: "All that glitters."

July 21, 1991: "The dirtiest bank of all."

July 1, 1991: "A day with the chess player."

March 4, 1991: "A capital scandal."

Dec. 3, 1990: "The fling of the high roller: Living a ghetto, the coke trade from poverty to riches and into prison"; "Meanwhile, in Latin America: With whole economies at stake, the drug war rages on."

Nov. 26, 1990: "Meanwhile, back in Panama: If the Noriega trial seems like a fiasco, consider the plight of his country one year after the U.S. invasion."

June 25, 1990: "Grapevine: France may legalize brothels to combat AIDS, drug money laundering."

Feb. 19, 1990: "Too soft on the laundry."

Jan. 29, 1990: "Kink in the drug pipeline."

Jan. 15, 1990: "Noriega on ice."

Dec. 18, 1989: "A torrent of dirty dollars."

Oct. 16, 1989: "Putting an ear to the wires."

Aug. 21, 1989: "Wringing out a money laundry."

April 24, 1989: "Crackdown on Swiss laundry."

Oct. 31, 1988: "Indicted, Patrick Swindall."

Oct. 24, 1988: "The cash cleaners."

Feb. 22, 1988: "Noriega's money machine: His former aides tell of corruption on a grand scale."

Feb. 8, 1988: "A briefcase for the general?"

Jan. 18, 1988: "Afoot in a field of men."

July 20, 1987: "ZZZZ best may be ZZZZ worst."

May 18, 1987: "Hooking some big fish."

July 7, 1986: "Washday blues: Scandal strikes Shearson."

Feb. 3, 1986: "Painful legacy: BankAmerica's bad days."

Dec. 2, 1985: "Fetal delusions: A shooting on Wall Street."

Oct. 28, 1985: "My, what a friendly customer."

Sept. 9, 1985: "Record fine for Crocker National Bank."

July 1, 1985: "Cleaning up the cash laundry."

March 25, 1985: "Crackdown on greenwashing: Lawmakers warn banks to quit helping criminals launder money."

March 11, 1985: "Boston's embattled bank."

Feb. 25, 1985: "Dirty cash and tarnished vaults: Two large U.S. banks struggle to recover from serious missteps."

Feb. 25, 1985: "Fighting the cocaine wars: Drug traffic spreads, and the U.S. finds itself mired in a violent, losing battle."

Feb. 18, 1985: "Carry on cash connection."

Nov. 12, 1984: "Dirty money in the spotlight: A proposal to get tough on banks that launder cash."

Travel Weekly:

June 4, 1992: "Helping the IRS."

May 28, 1992: "Money-laundering regulations redefine cash."

Dec. 17, 1990: "Large cash sales must be reported."

April 23, 1987: "Drug trafficking, money laundering, and the travel industry."

March 9, 1987: "Weak currencies and weak agencies recipe for riches in Nigerian scheme"; "Airline crackdown shows results against money-laundering scam."

UN Chronicle:

Sept. 1993: "World conferences on organized crime, money laundering to be hosted by Italy."

Underwriter Life & Health-Financial Services:

Aug. 21, 1995: "Execs of insolvent N.C. insurer convicted of fraud."

United States Banker:

Nov. 1989: "Snaring the smurfs."

U.S. Department of State Bulletin:

Sept. 1986: "Narcotics trafficking in Southwest Asia."

U.S. Department of State Dispatch:

Aug. 17, 1992: "Statement on Pablo Escobar Gaviria."

May 11, 1992: "Narcotics activities in Panama: Mutual legal assistance treaty needed." (R. Grant Smith address.)

March 2, 1992: "Fact sheet: Combating drug money-laundering."

March 2, 1992: "Progress in the international war against illicit drugs." (Melvyn Levitsky address.)

Sept. 10, 1990: "International narcotics control."

Sept. 3, 1990: "Narcotics: Threat to global security."

U.S. Distribution Journal:

Nov. 1989: "Cash business targeted for laundering probe."

U.S. News & World Report:

Oct. 19, 1992: "Cocaine kings and mafia dons — Crime in Italy and Colombia."

Dec. 23, 1991: "New target: The Cali cartel."

Aug. 26, 1991: "Washing the dirtiest money: Why drug lords don't need BCCI to launder cash."

Aug. 19, 1991: "How BCCI banked on global secrecy."

Aug. 5, 1991: "Was there a BCCI coverup? In Washington and London, fallout from the rogue bank is spreading."

Jan. 28, 1991: "Jorge Luis Ochoa Vasquez."

Dec. 31, 1990: "Easing back in the war on drugs?"

April 30, 1990: "The drug warriors' blues."

Jan. 29, 1990: "The godfathers of cocaine cry uncle."

Jan. 15, 1990: "The case against Noriega."

Dec. 18, 1989: "To each according to his greed?"

Aug. 21, 1989: "The drug money hunt."

April 10, 1989: "Hot money: City of angels, indeed."

Oct. 24, 1988: "Caught in the money laundry wringer."

July 4, 1988: "Psst — Swiss accounts are no secret."

May 30, 1988: "A kingpin falls."

April 11, 1988: "Inside America's biggest drug bust."

Feb. 15, 1988: "Tales of a pineapple pol."

Feb. 8, 1988: "How cocaine rules the law in Colombia."

Jan. 11, 1988: "The Honduras connection: Drugs and money."

Jan. 11, 1988: "A narco traficante's worst nightmare."

Feb. 16, 1987: "Caught — Cocaine's Mr. Big."

Dec. 8, 1986: "How White House built a 'black ops' fund."

June 2, 1986: "Why it's getting tougher to hide money."

March 31, 1986: "Europe's immigration battles: Slowdown of economies, ethnic discord set off backlash."

Feb. 3, 1986: "Busting the mob."

March 11, 1985: "Banks caught in fed's squeeze on mobsters."

Nov. 5, 1984: "Asian gangs stake out turf in U.S."

April 23, 1984: "Breaking up the pizza connection."

Aug. 1, 1983: "Computer cops: On the trail of runaway dollars."

Aug. 1, 1983: "Offshore tax havens lure Main Street money."

Variety:

May 15, 1985: "Casino industry united in opposition to laundering regs."

Vital Speeches:

July 15, 1990: "Money laundering: You make it, we'll take it." (Richard Thornburgh address.)

April 15, 1990: "Dirty business: Money laundering and the war on drugs." (Helen K. Sinclair address.)

Washington Business Journal:

June 25, 1990: "Suit says Maryland bank masked CIA transactions."

Washington Monthly:

June 1991: "Cliffhanging: How the consummate counsel came to need a lawyer."

Oct. 1987: "Hot money and the politics of debt."

Washingtonian:

Jan. 1992: "Dirty money."

Whole Earth Review:

Spring 1988: "The Iran Contra Connection."

Women's Wear Daily:

April 7, 1992: "Paris cops bust 100 laundering money in luxury shops."

World of Banking:

Sept.–Oct. 1990: "Money laundering: Problems and solutions for the banking industry."

World Press Review:

Nov. 1985: "Drugs and tax havens."

NEWSPAPERS

Specific newspaper sources are too many to list individually. Suffice it to say that articles consulted appeared in, among other places:

North America: *The Atlanta Constitution, The Boston Globe, The Chicago Daily News, The Chicago Tribune, The Christian Science Monitor, The Dallas Morning News, The Detroit News, The Los Angeles Times, The Miami Herald, The Montreal Gazette, The New York Times, The Toronto Globe and Mail, The Wall Street Journal,* and *The Washington Post.* The wires of the Associated Press.

United Kingdom: *The Financial Times, The Guardian, The Independent, The International Herald Tribune, The Mail, The Mail on Sunday, The Sunday Independent, The Sunday Telegraph, The Sunday Times, The Telegraph,* and *The Times.* The wires of Reuters and the Press Association.

Continental newspapers include leading dailies in France, Italy, Germany, and Switzerland, in addition to the wire services of Agence France Press.

MISCELLANEOUS SOURCES: REPORTS, PAPERS, TRANSCRIPTS

Ashe, Michael: *Money Laundering: Domestic Legal Issues;* paper delivered to the Conference on Money Laundering, Richards Butler, London, 1992.

Ashe, Michael: *Reflections on Civil Liability;* paper delivered to the Conference on Money Laundering, Henry Stewart Conference Studies, London, 1991.

The Bank of England: *Countering Money Laundering;* London, 1992.

The Bank of England: *Money Laundering: Guidance Notes for Banks and Building Societies;* London, 1990.

The Bank for International Settlements: *Statistics on Payment Systems in Eleven Developed Countries;* Basle, 1992.

The Basle Committee on Banking Regulations and Supervisory Practices: *Statement of Principles on Prevention of Criminal Use of the Banking System for the Purpose of Money Laundering;* Basle, 1988.

Bosworth-Davies, Rowan: *Money Laundering: Looking Towards the Future from a European Perspective;* private paper, London, 1992.

Bosworth-Davies, Rowan: *What Money Is It?;* paper delivered to the Conference on Money Laundering, Henry Stewart Conference Studies, London, 1991.

Brightwell, Tony: *The Laundering of Criminal Funds;* paper delivered to the Conference on Money Laundering, Richards Butler, London, 1992.

The British Commonwealth: *Extracts from the Commonwealth Heads of Government Meeting;* Kuala Lampur, 1989.

The British Commonwealth: *International Efforts to Combat Money Laundering;* Cambridge International Document Series, Vol. 4, Grotius Publishing, Cambridge, England, 1992.

The British Commonwealth: *Scheme Relating to Mutual Assistance in Criminal Matters Within the Commonwealth, Including Explanatory Commentary;* London, 1990.

Brooks, Christopher: *What the Police Are Doing: When and How to Contact Them;* paper delivered to the Conference on Money Laundering, Henry Stewart Conference Studies, London, 1991.

Cassidy, William: *Fei-Ch'ien — Flying Money — A Study of Chinese Underground Banking;* annotated text of an address before the Asian Organized Crime Conference, Ft. Lauderdale, 1990.

Clutterbuck, R.: *Terrorism;* Wrexton Paper Series, Wrexton College, Wrexton Abbey, England, 1990.

Conway, Robert: *The Techniques of Money Laundering: Who Does What;* paper delivered to the Conference on Money Laundering, Henry Stewart Conference Studies, London, 1991.

The Council of Europe: *Recommendations of the Committee of Ministers on Measures Against the Transfer and Safekeeping of Funds of Criminal Origin;* Strasbourg, 1980.

The European Economic Community: *The Convention on Laundering, Search, Seizure and Confiscation of the Proceeds from Crime;* Brussels, 1990.

The European Economic Community: *Payment Systems in EC Member States;* Committee of Governors of the Central Banks of the Member States of the European Economic Community, Brussels, 1992.

The European Economic Community: *Proposal for a Council Directive on Prevention and Use of the Financial System for the Purpose of Money Laundering;* Brussels, 1989.

The Federal Bureau of Investigation, Criminal Investigation Division: *Colombian Narcotics: Trafficking Organizations;* Washington, D.C., 1986.

The Federal Bureau of Investigation, Criminal Investigation Division: *The Cosa Nostra in Canada;* Washington, D.C., 1985.

The Financial Action Task Force: *Economic Declaration of the G-7;* Paris, 1990.

The Financial Action Task Force: *Notes from the Caribbean Drug Money Laundering Conference;* Aruba, 1990.

The Financial Action Task Force: *Report on Money Laundering;* Paris, 1990.

Gilmore, Dr. William C.: *International Responses to Money Laundering: A General Overview;* paper given at the Money Laundering Conference of the European Committee on Crime Problems, Strasbourg, 1992.

Haines, Peter: *How to Identify and Prevent Potential Money Laundering Schemes;* paper delivered to the Conference on Money Laundering, Henry Stewart Conference Studies, London, 1991.

The House of Commons, Treasury Committee: *Report on Banking Supervision and BCCI : International and National Regulation;* London, 1991.

Hurley, Peter: *Prevention and Staff Training;* paper delivered to the Conference on Money Laundering, Henry Stewart Conference Studies, London, 1991.

Hyland, Michael: *The British Bankers Approach;* paper delivered to the Conference on Money Laundering, Henry Stewart Conference Studies, London, 1991.

The National Crime Authority of Australia: *Taken to the Cleaners — Money Laundering in Australia;* Canberra, 1992.

The President's Commission on Organized Crime: *Cash Connection: The Interim Report on Organized Crime, Financial Institutions and Money Laundering;* Washington, D.C., 1984.

The President's Commission on Organized Crime: *The Impact: Organized Crime Today.*; Washington, D.C., 1986.

The President's Commission on Organized Crime: *A Report to the President and the Attorney General of the United States: America's Habit — Drug Abuse, Drug Trafficking and Organized Crime;* Washington, D.C., 1986.

Rider, Dr. Barry A. K.: *Fei Ch'ien Laundries: The Pursuit of Flying Money; The Journal of International Planning,* August, 1992.

Rider, Dr. Barry A. K.: *Techniques of Money Laundering;* paper delivered to the Conference on Money Laundering, Richards Butler, London, 1992.

Saltmarsh, Graham: *Understanding the U.K. Legislation;* paper delivered to the Conference on Money Laundering, Henry Stewart Conference Studies, London, 1991.

Solly, Mark W.: *Offshore Havens: The Role and Responsibility of Financia Institutions to Assist in the Prevention of Money Laundering;* Financial Supervision Commission, Isle of Man, 1989.

Stucki, Dr. H. U.: *Swiss Banking Secrecy Revisited;* private paper, Stucki & de Senarclens, Attorneys at Law, Zurich, September 9, 1992.

Tattersall, John: *Providing Assurance That All Is Well: What Role for the Internal and External Auditor;* paper delivered to the Conference on Money Laundering, Henry Stewart Conference Studies, London, 1991.

Tenth International Symposium on Economic Crime: *Hot, Dirty and Stolen Money: Identifying, Tracing and Restoring Flight Capital and the Proceeds of Crime;* collected papers, delivered July 12–18, 1992, Jesus College, Cambridge.

Tupman, William: *The Laundering of Terrorist Activities;* paper delivered to the Conference on Money Laundering, Richards Butler, London, 1992.

The United Nations: *Comprehensive Multidisciplinary Outline of Future Activities in Drug Abuse Control;* New York, 1987.

The United Nations: *Convention Against the Illicit Traffic in Narcotics, Drugs, and Psychotropic Substances;* New York, 1988.

The United Nations: *Political Declaration and Global Program of Action of the General Assembly;* New York, 1990.

The United States Attorney for the U.S. Southern Dictrict, Manhattan: *Chronology of Events.* (Prepared for the jury considering the case known as "The Pizza Connection.") New York, 1985.

The United States Court of Appeals for the Fourth District: *The United States of America versus Moffitt, Zwerling and Kemler* — Appeals, transcripts and briefs.

The United States Department of State: *Agreement with the Government of Venezuela Regarding Cooperation in the Prevention and Control of Money Laundering Arising from Illicit Trafficking in Narcotic Drugs and Psychotropic Substances;* Washington, D.C., 1990.

The United States Department of State: *Progress in the International War Against Illicit Drugs;* transcript of an address by Melvyn Levitsky, Assistant Secretary of State for International Narcotics Matters, Washington, D.C., March 2, 1992.

The United States Department of State, Bureau of International Narcotics Matters: *International Narcotics Control Strategy Reports;* Washington, D.C., 1988, 1989, 1990, 1991.

The United States Department of the Treasury, Financial Crimes Enforcement Network: *An Assessment of Narcotics Related Money Laundering;* Washington, D.C., 1992.

The United States House of Representatives, Hearings Before the Committee on Banking, Finance, and Urban Affairs: *Bank of Credit and Commerce International (BCCI) Investigation;* Washington, D.C., 1991, 1992.

The United States House of Representatives, Subcommittee on Financial Institutions, Supervision, Regulation, and Insurance of the Committee on Banking, Finance, and Urban Affairs: *Statement on Behalf of the American Bankers Association on Money Laundering Deterrence by Boris F. Melinkoff;* Washington, D.C., March 8, 1990.

The United States Senate, Foreign Relations Committee: *Testimony of the Deputy Secretary of the Treasury, the Honorable John E. Robson, on the Work of the G-7 Financial Action Task Force on Money Laundering;* Washington, D.C., April 27, 1990.

The United States Senate, Permanent Subcommittee on Investigations of the Committee on Government Operations. *Final Report of the McClellan Subcommittee: Organized Crime and Illicit Traffic in Narcotics;* Washington D.C., 1965.

The United States Senate, Hearings Before the Permanent Subcommittee on Investigations of the Committee on Governmental Affairs: *Drugs and Money Laundering in Panama;* Washington, D.C., 1988.

The United States Senate, Hearings Before the Subcommittee on Terrorism, Narcotics, and International Operations of the Committee on Foreign Relations: *The BCCI Affair;* Washington, D.C., 1991, 1992.

The United States Senate, Hearings Before the Subcommittee on Terrorism, Narcotics, and International Operations of the Committee on Foreign Relations: *Panama;* Washington, D.C., 1988.

The United States Senate, Hearings Before the Subcommittee on Consumer and Regulatory Affairs of the Committee on Banking, Housing, and Urban Affairs: *The Bank of Credit and Commerce International;* Washington, D.C., 1991.

The United States Senate, Report of the Subcommittee on Terrorism, Narcotics, and International Operations of the Committee on Foreign Relations: *The BCCI Affair;* Washington, D.C., 1992.

The World Ministerial Summit: *Declaration to Reduce Demand for Drugs and to Combat the Cocaine Threat;* London, 1990.

Wren, Tim: *Money Laundering Legislation;* paper delivered to the Conference on Money Laundering, Richards Butler, London, 1992.

INDEX